Linux Programming

White Papers

David A. Rusling ◆ Ori Pomerantz ◆ Sven Goldt

Sven van der Meer ◆ Scott Burkett ◆ Matt Welsh

Ivan Bowman ◆ Saheem Siddiqi ◆ Meyer C. Tanuan

CORIOLIS

President, CEO
Keith Weiskamp

Publisher
Steve Sayre

Acquisitions Editor
Stephanie Wall

Marketing Specialist
Tracy Schofield

Project Editor
Sharon Sanchez McCarson

Production Coordinator
Jon Gabriel

Cover Design
Jesse Dunn

Layout Design
April Nielsen

Linux Programming White Papers
This book is covered by the GNU Public License. Please see Appendix B for more information.

The Linux Kernel
© 1996-1998 David A. Rusling
This book is freely distributable; you may copy and redistribute it under certain conditions.
Please refer to the copyright and distribution statement.
Version 0.8-3
David A. Rusling

The Linux Kernel Module Programming Guide
© 1999 Ori Pomerantz

The Linux Programmer's Guide
© 1994, 1995 by Sven Goldt
Sven Goldt, Sachsendamm 47b, 10829 Berlin, Germany (goldt@math.tu-berlin.de)
Chapter 6 is © 1995 by Scott Burkett (scottb@IntNet.net)
Chapter 8 is © 1994, 1995 by Sven van der Meer (vdmeer@cs.tu-berlin.de)
Chapter 10 is © 1994, 1995 by Matt Welsh (mdw@cs.cornell.edu)
Special thanks go to John D. Harper (jharper@uiuc.edu) for proofreading this guide.
Permission to reproduce this document in whole or in part is subject to the following conditions:
• The copyright notice remains intact and is included.
• If you make money with it the authors want a share.
• The authors are not responsible for any harm that might arise by the use of it.

Limits Of Liability And Disclaimer Of Warranty
The author and publisher of this book have used their best efforts in preparing the book and the programs contained in it. These efforts include the development, research, and testing of the theories and programs to determine their effectiveness. The author and publisher make no warranty of any kind, expressed or implied, with regard to these programs or the documentation contained in this book.

The author and publisher shall not be liable in the event of incidental or consequential damages in connection with, or arising out of, the furnishing, performance, or use of the programs, associated instructions, and/or claims of productivity gains.

Trademarks
Trademarked names appear throughout this book. Rather than list the names and entities that own the trademarks or insert a trademark symbol with each mention of the trademarked name, the publisher states that it is using the names for editorial purposes only and to the benefit of the trademark owner, with no intention of infringing upon that trademark.

The Coriolis Group, LLC
14455 North Hayden Road
Suite 220
Scottsdale, Arizona 85260

480/483-0192
FAX 480/483-0193
http://www.coriolis.com

Library of Congress Cataloging-in-Publication Data
Rusling, David A. [et al]
    Linux programming white papers / by David A. Rusling
        p.   cm.
    ISBN 1-57610-473-7
    1. Linux   2. Operating systems (Computers).   I. Rusling, David A.
QA76.76.O63 L5487 1999
005.4'469—dc21   99-047031
                                                                    CIP

Printed in the United States of America
10 9 8 7 6 5 4 3 2 1

14455 North Hayden Road, Suite 220 • Scottsdale, Arizona 85260

Dear Reader:

CoriolisOpen™ Press was founded to create a very elite group of books: the ones you keep closest to your machine. Sure, everyone would like to have the Library of Congress at arm's reach, but in the real world, you have to choose the books you rely on every day *very* carefully.

To win a place for our books on that coveted shelf beside your PC, we guarantee several important qualities in every book we publish. These qualities are:

- *Technical accuracy*—It's no good if it doesn't work. Every CoriolisOpen™ Press book is reviewed by technical experts in the topic field, and is sent through several editing and proofreading passes in order to create the piece of work you now hold in your hands.

- *Innovative editorial design*—We've put years of research and refinement into the ways we present information in our books. Our books' editorial approach is uniquely designed to reflect the way people learn new technologies and search for solutions to technology problems.

- *Practical focus*—We put only pertinent information into our books and avoid any fluff. Every fact included between these two covers must serve the mission of the book as a whole.

- *Accessibility*—The information in a book is worthless unless you can find it quickly when you need it. We put a lot of effort into our indexes, and heavily cross-reference our chapters, to make it easy for you to move right to the information you need.

Here at The Coriolis Group we have been publishing and packaging books, technical journals, and training materials since 1989. We're programmers and authors ourselves, and we take an ongoing active role in defining what we publish and how we publish it. We have put a lot of thought into our books; please write to us at **ctp@coriolis.com** and let us know what you think. We hope that you're happy with the book in your hands, and that in the future, when you reach for software development and networking information, you'll turn to one of our books first.

Keith Weiskamp
President and CEO

Jeff Duntemann
VP and Editorial Director

Look For These Other Books From The Coriolis Group:

Contents At A Glance

Table Of Contents

Part II   The Linux Kernel Module Programming Guide
by Ori Pomerantz

Part III   The Linux Programmer's Guide
by Sven Goldt, Sven van der Meer, Scott Burkett, and Matt Welsh

Foreword

By Eric Raymond

Long-established folklore in the computing industry has it that programmers hate writing documentation. Not true, as it turns out—many programmers will cheerfully write documentation for the programs that they truly care about. No better illustration of this could be found than in the book you are about to read.

Linux is a labor of love for the people who develop it. Its astonishing success, taking it from zero visibility to a major contender in three years, demonstrates that love can be more powerful than gold for motivating high-quality creative work. But it takes gold to print books and press CDs, so the Linux world is evolving ways to cooperate with the market and build flourishing distribution industries around their OS. This book is also an illustration of that trend.

The Coriolis Group is exploring ways in which to cooperate with the Linux Documentation Project that will help Linux developers specialize in what they do best (coding and technical-reference documentation), while Coriolis supplies what it does best (editing, production, publication, and marketing). The result should be both nice profits for Coriolis and a better quality of online documentation for the Linux community. All LDP documentation will continue to be distributed under open-content licenses supporting free redistribution, and Coriolis's improvements will be donated back to the community.

Introduction

The *Linux Programming White Papers* is a printed edition of five online books (out of eight) hosted on the Linux Document Pages (LDP) Web site (**http://metalab.unc.edu/LDP/**). The Coriolis Group is exploring various ways to support Linux and the open source model of developing software. We felt that one way to accomplish this was to publish the LDP in two volumes; this one, and a second one to focus on administrative issues entitled *Linux Programming White Papers*. Please be sure to look at the LDP for additional Linux resources offered. As part of this introduction, you will find the LDP Manifesto. Please read it, as it will provide you with more information on the LDP.

By the grants outlined in the authors' copyrights for this material, we are able to publish it in paper form. This also means that the material contained in this book is freely redistributible as long as the copyright provisions put in place by the authors are upheld. Please refer to Appendix A for the Linux Documentation Project Copying License that clearly states what these copyright provisions are. In addition, please refer to Appendix B for the GNU Public License, the license in which Linux is covered under. If you have additional questions, please refer to the GNU Project website at **www.gnu.org**.

While reading this book you will notice that some material is a bit outdated and some examples may be missing. The reason for this is that in respecting the copyright provisions governing use of the LDP, we were not permitted to change the authors' material, even to correct errors and omissions; however, we did mark those places where we found missing or incorrect material. Be sure to refer to the online LDP for updated versions of the documentation in this book.

The Coriolis Group is always looking for ways to further support Linux. If you would like to share an idea with us here on how we can do this, please contact us directly at **ctp@coriolis.com**. We look forward to your comments.

The Coriolis Group

Linux Documentation Project "Manifesto"

Last Revision 21 September 1998, by Michael K. Johnson

This file describes the goals and current status of the Linux Documentation Project, including names of projects, volunteers, FTP sites, and so on.

Overview

The Linux Documentation Project is working on developing good, reliable docs for the Linux operating system. The overall goal of the LDP is to collaborate in taking care of all of the issues of Linux documentation, ranging from online docs (man pages, texinfo docs, and so on) to printed manuals covering topics such as installing, using, and running Linux. The LDP is essentially a loose team of volunteers with little central organization; anyone who is interested in helping is welcome to join in the effort. We feel that working together and agreeing on the direction and scope of Linux documentation is the best way to go, to reduce problems with conflicting efforts—two people writing two books on the same aspect of Linux wastes someone's time along the way.

The LDP is set out to produce the canonical set of Linux online and printed documentation. Because our docs will be freely available (like software licensed under the terms of the GNU GPL) and distributed on the net, we are able to easily update the documentation to stay on top of the many changes in the Linux world. If you are interested in publishing any of the LDP works, see the section "Publishing LDP Manuals," below.

Getting Involved

Send mail to **linux-howto@metalab.unc.edu**.

Of course, you'll also need to get in touch with the coordinator of whatever LDP projects you're interested in working on; see the next section.

Current Projects

For a list of current projects, see the LDP home page at **http://metalab.unc.edu/LDP/**. The best way to get involved with one of these projects is to pick up the current version of the manual and send revisions, editions, or suggestions to the coordinator. You probably want to coordinate with the author before sending revisions so that you know you are working together.

FTP Sites For LDP Works

LDP works can be found on **metalab.unc.edu** in the directory **/pub/Linux/docs**. LDP manuals are found in **/pub/Linux/docs/LDP**, HOWTOs and other documentation found in **/pub/ Linux/docs/HOWTO**.

Documentation Conventions

Here are the conventions that are currently used by LDP manuals. If you are interested in writing another manual using different conventions, please let us know of your plans first.

The *man pages*—the Unix standard for online manuals—are created with the Unix standard nroff man (or BSD mdoc) macros.

The *guides*—full books produced by the LDP—have historically been done in LaTeX, as their primary goal has been to be *printed* documentation. However, guide authors have been moving toward SGML with the DocBook DTD, because it allows them to create more different kinds of output, both printed and online. If you use LaTeX, we have a style file you can use to keep your printed look consistent with other LDP documents, and we suggest that you use it.

The *HOWTO* documents are all required to be in SGML format. Currently, they use the *linuxdoc* DTD, which is quite simple. There is a move afoot to switch to the DocBook DTD over time.

LDP documents must be freely redistributable without fees paid to the authors. It is not required that the text be modifiable, but it is encouraged. You can come up with your own license terms that satisfy this constraint, or you can use a previously prepared license. The LDP provides a boilerplate license that you can use, some people like to use the GPL, and others write their own.

The copyright for each manual should be in the name of the head writer or coordinator for the project. "The Linux Documentation Project'" isn't a formal entity and shouldn't be used to copyright the docs.

Copyright And License

Here is a "boilerplate" license you may apply to your work. It has not been reviewed by a lawyer; feel free to have your own lawyer review it (or your modification of it) for its applicability to your own desires. Remember that in order for your document to be part of the LDP, you must allow unlimited reproduction and distribution without fee.

This manual may be reproduced and distributed in whole or in part, without fee, subject to the following conditions:

♦ The copyright notice above and this permission notice must be preserved complete on all complete or partial copies.

♦ Any translation or derived work must be approved by the author in writing before distribution.

♦ If you distribute this work in part, instructions for obtaining the complete version of this manual must be included, and a means for obtaining a complete version provided.

♦ Small portions may be reproduced as illustrations for reviews or quotes in other works without this permission notice if proper citation is given.

Exceptions to these rules may be granted for academic purposes: Write to the author and ask. These restrictions are here to protect us as authors, not to restrict you as learners and educators.

All source code in this document is placed under the GNU General Public License, available via anonymous FTP from **ftp://prep.ai.mit.edu:/pub/gnu/COPYING**.

Publishing LDP Manuals

If you're a publishing company interested in distributing any of the LDP manuals, read on.

By the license requirements given previously, anyone is allowed to publish and distribute verbatim copies of the Linux Documentation Project manuals. You don't need our explicit permission for this. However, if you would like to distribute a translation or derivative work based on any of the LDP manuals, you may need to obtain permission from the author, in writing, before doing so, if the license requires that.

You may, of course, sell the LDP manuals for profit. We encourage you to do so. Keep in mind, however, that because the LDP manuals are freely distributable, anyone may photocopy or distribute printed copies free of charge, if they wish to do so.

We do not require to be paid royalties for any profit earned from selling LDP manuals. However, we would like to suggest that if you do sell LDP manuals for profit, that you either offer the author royalties, or donate a portion of your earnings to the author, the LDP as a whole, or to the Linux development community. You may also wish to send one or more free copies of the LDP manuals that you are distributing to the authors. Your show of support for the LDP and the Linux community will be very much appreciated.

We would like to be informed of any plans to publish or distribute LDP manuals, just so we know how they're becoming available. If you are publishing or planning to publish any LDP manuals, please send mail to **ldp-l@linux.org.au**. It's nice to know who's doing what.

We encourage Linux software distributors to distribute the LDP manuals (such as the Installation And Getting Started Guide) with their software. The LDP manuals are intended to be used as the "official" Linux documentation, and we are glad to see mail-order distributors bundling the LDP manuals with the software. As the LDP manuals mature, hopefully they will fulfill this goal more and more adequately.

Part I

The Linux Kernel

by David A. Rusling

This book is for Linux enthusiasts who want to know how the Linux kernel works. It is not an internals manual. Rather it describes the principles and mechanisms that Linux uses, how and why the Linux kernel works the way that it does.

Linux is a moving target; this book is based upon the current, stable, 2.0.33 sources as those are what most individuals and companies are now using.

This book is freely distributable, you may copy and redistribute it under certain conditions. Please refer to the copyright and distribution statement.

Version 0.8-3

David A Rusling (**david.rusling@arm.com**)

About The Author

I was born in 1957, a few weeks before Sputnik was launched, in the north of England. I first met Unix at university, where a lecturer used it as an example when teaching the notions of kernels, scheduling, and other operating systems goodies. I loved using the newly delivered PDP-11 for my final-year project. After graduating (in 1982 with a First Class Honours degree in Computer Science), I worked for Prime Computers (Primos) and then after a couple of years for Digital (VMS, Ultrix). At Digital I worked on many things, but for the last five years there, I worked for the semiconductor group on Alpha and StrongARM evaluation boards. In 1998, I moved to ARM where I have a small group of engineers writing low-level firmware and porting operating systems. My children (Esther and Stephen) describe me as a geek.

People often ask me about Linux at work and at home and I am only too happy to oblige. The more that I use Linux in both my professional and personal life the more that I become a Linux zealot. You may note that I use the term "zealot" and not "bigot"; I define a Linux zealot to be an enthusiast that recognizes that there are other operating systems but prefers not to use them. As my wife, Gill, who uses Windows 95, once remarked: "I never realized that we would have his and her operating systems." For me, as an engineer, Linux suits my needs perfectly. It is a superb, flexible, and adaptable engineering tool that I use at work and at home. Most freely available software easily builds on Linux, and I can often simply download prebuilt executable files or install them from a CD-ROM. What else could I use to learn to program in C++, Perl, or learn about Java for free?

David A. Rusling
3 Foxglove Close,
Wokingham,
Berkshire RG41 3NF,
United Kingdom

Acknowledgments

I must thank the many people who have been kind enough to take the time to email me with comments about this book. I have attempted to incorporated those comments in each new version that I have produced and I am more than happy to receive comments; however, please note my new email address.

A number of lecturers have written to me asking if they can use some or parts of this book in order to teach computing. My answer is an emphatic yes; this is one use of the book that I particularly wanted. Who knows, there may be another Linus Torvalds sitting in the class.

Special thanks must go to John Rigby and Michael Bauer who gave me full, detailed review notes of the whole book. Not an easy task. Alan Cox and Stephen Tweedie have patiently answered my questions—thanks. I used Larry Ewing's penguins to brighten up the chapters a bit. Finally, thank you to Greg Hankins for accepting this book into the Linux Documentation Project and onto their Web site.

Preface

Linux is a phenomenon of the Internet. Born out of the hobby project of a student, it has grown to become more popular than any other freely available operating system. To many, Linux is an enigma. How can something that is free be worthwhile? In a world dominated by a handful of large software corporations, how can something that has been written by a bunch of "hackers" [sic] hope to compete? How can software contributed to by many different people in many different countries around the world have a hope of being stable and effective? Yet stable and effective it is and compete it does. Many universities and research establishments use it for their everyday computing needs. People are running it on their home PCs, and I would wager that most companies are using it somewhere, even if they do not always realize that they do. Linux is used to browse the Web, host Web sites, write theses, send electronic mail, and, as always with computers, to play games. Linux is emphatically not a toy; it is a fully developed and professionally written operating system used by enthusiasts all over the world.

The roots of Linux can be traced back to the origins of Unix. In 1969, Ken Thompson of the Research Group at Bell Laboratories began experimenting on a multiuser, multitasking operating system, using an otherwise idle PDP-7. He was soon joined by Dennis Richie, and the two of them, along with other members of the Research Group, produced the early versions of Unix. Richie was strongly influenced by an earlier project, MULTICS, and the name Unix is itself a pun on the name MULTICS. Early versions were written in assembly code, but the third version was rewritten in a new programming language, C. C was designed and written by Richie expressly as a programming language for writing operating systems. This rewrite allowed Unix to move onto the more powerful PDP-11/45 and 11/70 computers then being produced by DIGITAL. The rest, as they say, is history. Unix moved out of the laboratory and into mainstream computing, and soon most major computer manufacturers were producing their own versions.

Linux was the solution to a simple need. The only software that Linus Torvalds, Linux's author and principle maintainer, was able to afford was Minix. Minix is a simple, Unix-like operating system widely used as a teaching aid. Linus was less than impressed with its features; his solution was to write his own software. He took Unix as his model, as that was an operating system that he was familiar with in his day-to-day student life. He started with an Intel 386-based PC and started to write. Progress was rapid and, excited by this, Linus offered his efforts to other students via the emerging worldwide computer networks, then mainly used by the academic community. Others saw the software and started contributing. Much of this new software was itself the solution to a problem that one of the contributors had. Before long, Linux had become an operating system. It is important to note that Linux contains no Unix code; it is a rewrite based on published POSIX standards. Linux is built with and uses a lot of the GNU (GNUs Not Unix) software produced by the Free Software Foundation in Cambridge, Massachusetts.

Most people use Linux as a simple tool, often just installing one of the many good CD-ROM-based distributions. A lot of Linux users use it to write applications or to run applications written by others. Many Linux users read the HOWTOs avidly and feel both the thrill of success when some part of the system has been correctly configured and the frustration of failure when it has not. A minority are bold enough to write device drivers and offer kernel patches to Linus Torvalds, the creator and maintainer of the Linux kernel. Linus accepts additions and modifications to the kernel sources from anyone, anywhere. This might sound like a recipe for anarchy, but Linus exercises strict quality control and merges all new code into the kernel himself. At any one time, though, there are only a handful of people contributing sources to the Linux kernel.

The majority of Linux users do not look at how the operating system works or how it fits together. This is a shame because looking at Linux is a very good way to learn more about how an operating system functions. Not only is it well written, but all the sources are freely available for you to look at. This is because although the authors retain the copyrights to their software, they allow the sources to be freely redistributable under the Free Software Foundation's GNU Public License. At first glance though, the sources can be confusing; you will see directories called `kernel`, `mm`, and `net`, but what do they contain and how does that code work? What is needed is a broader understanding of the overall structure and aims of Linux. This, in short, is the aim of this book: to promote a clear understanding of how Linux, the operating system, works. To provide a mind model that allows you to picture what is happening within the system as you copy a file from one place to another or read electronic mail. I well remember the excitement that I felt when I first realized just how an operating system actually worked. It is that excitement that I want to pass on to the readers of this book.

My involvement with Linux started late in 1994 when I visited Jim Paradis, who was working on a port of Linux to the Alpha AXP processor-based systems. I had worked for Digital Equipment Co. Limited since 1984, mostly in networks and communications, and in 1992 I started working for the newly formed Digital Semiconductor division. This division's goal was to enter fully into the merchant chip vendor market and sell chips, and in particular the Alpha AXP range of microprocessors, but also Alpha AXP system boards outside of Digital. When I first heard about Linux, I immediately saw an opportunity to have fun. Jim's enthusiasm was catching and I started to help on the port. As I worked on this, I began more and more to appreciate not only the operating system but also the community of engineers that produces it.

However, Alpha AXP is only one of the many hardware platforms that Linux runs on. Most Linux kernels are running on Intel processor-based systems, but a growing number of non-Intel Linux systems are becoming more commonly available. Amongst these are Alpha AXP, ARM, MIPS, Sparc, and PowerPC. I could have written this book using any one of those platforms, but my background and technical experiences with Linux are with Linux on the Alpha AXP and, to a lesser extent, on the ARM. This is why this book sometimes uses non-Intel hardware as an example to illustrate some key point. It must be noted that around 95 percent of the Linux kernel sources are common to all of the hardware platforms that it runs on. Likewise, around 95 percent of this book is about the machine-independent parts of the Linux kernel.

Reader Profile

This book does not make any assumptions about the knowledge or experience of the reader. I believe that interest in the subject matter will encourage a process of self-education where neccessary. That said, a degree of familiarity with computers, preferably the PC, will help the reader derive real benefit from the material, as will some knowledge of the C programming language.

Organization Of This Book

This book is *not* intended to be used as an internals manual for Linux. Instead it is an introduction to operating systems in general and to Linux in particular. The chapters each follow my rule of "working from the general to the particular." They first give an overview of the kernel subsystem that they are describing before launching into its gory details.

I have deliberately not described the kernel's algorithms, its methods of doing things, in terms of `routine_X()` calls `routine_Y()`, which increments the `foo` field of the `bar` data structure. You can read the code to find these things out. Whenever I need to understand a piece of code or describe it to someone else, I often start with drawing its data structures on the whiteboard. So, I have described many of the relevant kernel data structures and their interrelationships in a fair amount of detail.

Each chapter is fairly independent, like the Linux kernel subsystem that they each describe. Sometimes, though, there are linkages; for example, you cannot describe a process without understanding how virtual memory works.

The Hardware Basics chapter (Chapter 1) gives a brief introduction to the modern PC. An operating system has to work closely with the hardware system that acts as its foundations. The operating system needs certain services that can only be provided by the hardware. In order to fully understand the Linux operating system, you need to understand the basics of the underlying hardware.

The Software Basics chapter (Chapter 2) introduces basic software principles and looks at assembly and C programming languages. It looks at the tools that are used to build an operating system like Linux and it gives an overview of the aims and functions of an operating system.

The Memory Management chapter (Chapter 3) describes the way that Linux handles the physical and virtual memory in the system.

The Processes chapter (Chapter 4) describes what a process is and how the Linux kernel creates, manages, and deletes the processes in the system.

Processes communicate with each other and with the kernel to coordinate their activities. Linux supports a number of Interprocess Communication (IPC) mechanisms. Signals and pipes are two of them but Linux also supports the System V IPC mechanisms named after the Unix release in which they first appeared. These interprocess communications mechanisms are described in Chapter 5.

The Peripheral Component Interconnect (PCI) standard is now firmly established as the low cost, high performance data bus for PCs. The PCI chapter (Chapter 6) describes how the Linux kernel initializes and uses PCI buses and devices in the system.

The Interrupts And Interrupt Handling chapter (Chapter 7) looks at how the Linux kernel handles interrupts. While the kernel has generic mechanisms and interfaces for handling interrupts, some of the interrupt handling details are hardware and architecture specific.

One of Linux's strengths is its support for the many available hardware devices for the modern PC. The Device Drivers chapter (Chapter 8) describes how the Linux kernel controls the physical devices in the system.

The File System chapter (Chapter 9) describes how the Linux kernel maintains the files in the file systems that it supports. It describes the Virtual File System (VFS) and how the Linux kernel's real file systems are supported.

Networking and Linux are terms that are almost synonymous. In a very real sense, Linux is a product of the Internet or World Wide Web (WWW). Its developers and users use the Web to exchange information ideas and code, and Linux itself is often used to support the networking needs of organizations. Chapter 10 describes how Linux supports the network protocols known collectively as TCP/IP.

The Kernel Mechanisms chapter (Chapter 11) looks at some of the general tasks and mechanisms that the Linux kernel needs to supply so that other parts of the kernel work effectively together.

The Modules chapter (Chapter 12) describes how the Linux kernel can dynamically load functions, for example file systems, only when they are needed.

The Processors chapter (Chapter 13) gives a brief description of some of the processors that Linux has been ported to.

The Sources chapter (Chapter 14) describes where in the Linux kernel sources you should start looking for particular kernel functions.

Conventions Used In This Book

The following is a list of the typographical conventions used in this book.

sans serif font   Identifies commands or other text that is to be typed literally by the user

`type font`   Refers to data structures or fields within data structures

Throughout the text, there are references to pieces of code within the Linux kernel source tree (for example, the boxed margin note adjacent to this text). These are given in case you wish to look at the source code itself and all of the file references are relative to `/usr/src/linux`. Taking `foo/bar.c` as an example, the full file name would be `/usr/src/linux/foo/bar.c`. If you are running Linux (and you should), then looking at the code is a worthwhile experience and you can use this book as an aid to understanding the code and as a guide to its many data structures.

Trademarks

ARM is a trademark of ARM Holdings PLC.

Caldera, OpenLinux, and the "C" logo are trademarks of Caldera, Inc.

Caldera OpenDOS © 1997 Caldera, Inc.

DEC is a trademark of Digital Equipment Corporation.

DIGITAL is a trademark of Digital Equipment Corporation.

Linux is a trademark of Linus Torvalds.

Motif is a trademark of The Open System Foundation, Inc.

MS-DOS is a trademark of Microsoft Corporation.

Red Hat, glint, and the Red Hat logo are trademarks of Red Hat Software, Inc.

Unix is a registered trademark of X/Open.

XFree86 is a trademark of XFree86 Project, Inc.

X Window System is a trademark of the X Consortium and the Massachusetts Institute of Technology.

A HOWTO is just what it sounds like: a document describing how to do something. Many have been written for Linux and all are very useful.

Chapter 1

Hardware Basics

An operating system has to work closely with the hardware system that acts as its foundations. The operating system needs certain services that can only be provided by the hardware. In order to fully understand the Linux operating system, you need to understand the basics of the underlying hardware. This chapter gives a brief introduction to that hardware: the modern PC.

When *Popular Electronics* magazine for January 1975 was printed with an illustration of the Altair 8080 on its front cover, a revolution started. The Altair 8080, named after the destination of an early Star Trek episode, could be assembled by home electronics enthusiasts for a mere $397. With its Intel 8080 processor and 256 bytes of memory, but no screen or keyboard, it was puny by today's standards. Its inventor, Ed Roberts, coined the term "personal computer" to describe his new invention, but the term PC is now used to refer to almost any computer that you can pick up without needing help. By this definition, even some of the very powerful Alpha AXP systems are PCs.

Enthusiastic hackers saw the Altair's potential and started to write software and build hardware for it. To these early pioneers, it represented freedom: the freedom from huge batch processing mainframe systems run and guarded by an elite priesthood. Overnight fortunes were made by college dropouts fascinated by this new phenomenon, a computer that you could have at home on your kitchen table. A lot of hardware appeared, all different to some degree, and software hackers were happy to write software for these new machines. Paradoxically, it was IBM who firmly cast the mold of the modern PC, by announcing the IBM PC in 1981 and shipping it to customers early in 1982. With its Intel 8088 processor, 64K of memory (expandable to 256K), two floppy disks, and an 80-character by 25-lines Colour Graphics Adapter (CGA), it was not very powerful by today's standards, but it sold well. It was followed, in 1983, by the IBM PC-XT, which had the luxury of a 10MB hard drive. It was not long before IBM PC clones were being produced by a host of companies such as Compaq, and the architecture of the PC became a de facto standard. This de facto standard helped a multitude of hardware companies to compete together in a growing market, which, happily for consumers, kept prices low. Many of the system architectural features of these early PCs have carried over into the modern PC. For example, even the most powerful Intel Pentium Pro-based system starts running in the Intel 8086's addressing mode. When Linus Torvalds started writing what was to become Linux, he picked the most plentiful and reasonably priced hardware, an Intel 80386 PC.

Looking at a PC from the outside, the most obvious components are a system box, a keyboard, a mouse, and a video monitor. On the front of the system box are some buttons, a little display showing some numbers and a floppy drive. Most systems these days have a CD-ROM, and if you feel that you have to protect your data, then there will also be a tape drive for backups. These devices are collectively known as the peripherals.

Although the CPU is in overall control of the system, it is not the only intelligent device. All of the peripheral controllers, for example, the IDE controller, have some level of intelligence. Inside the PC (Figure 1.1) you will see a motherboard containing the CPU or microprocessor, the memory, and a number of slots for the ISA or PCI peripheral controllers. Some of the controllers, for example, the IDE disk controller, may be built directly onto the system board.

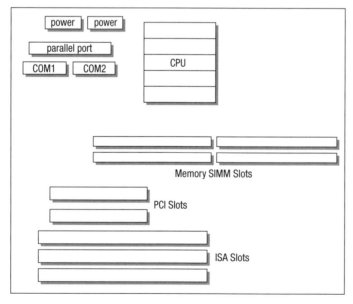

Figure 1.1
A typical PC motherboard.

1.1   The CPU

The *CPU*, or *microprocessor*, is the heart of any computer system. The microprocessor calculates, performs logical operations, and manages data flows by reading instructions from memory and then executing them. In the early days of computing, the functional components of the microprocessor were separate (and physically large) units. This is when the term *central processing unit* was coined. The modern microprocessor combines these components onto an integrated circuit etched onto a very small piece of silicon. The terms *CPU*, *microprocessor*, and *processor* are all used interchangeably in this book.

Microprocessors operate on binary data: that is, data composed of ones and zeros.

These ones and zeros correspond to electrical switches being either on or off. Just as 42 is a decimal number meaning "4 10s and 2 units," a binary number is a series of binary digits each one representing a power of 2. In this context, a power means the number of times that a number is multiplied by itself. 10 to the power 1 (10^1) is 10, 10 to the power 2 (10^2) is 10x10, 10^3 is 10x10x10 and so on. Binary 0001 is decimal 1, binary 0010 is decimal 2, binary 0011 is 3, binary 0100 is 4 and so on. So, 42 decimal is 101010 binary or (2 + 8 + 32 or 2^1 + 2^3 + 2^5). Rather than using binary to represent numbers in computer programs, another base, hexadecimal, is usually used.

In this base, each digital represents a power of 16. As decimal numbers only go from 0 to 9, the numbers 10 to 15 are represented as a single digit by the letters A, B, C, D, E, and F. For example, hexadecimal E is decimal 14 and hexadecimal 2A is decimal 42 ([two 16s] + 10). Using the C programming language notation (as I do throughout this book), hexadecimal numbers are prefaced by "0x"; hexadecimal 2A is written as 0x2A .

Microprocessors can perform arithmetic operations such as add, multiply, and divide and logical operations such as "is X greater than Y?"

The processor's execution is governed by an external clock. This clock, the *system clock*, generates regular clock pulses to the processor and, at each clock pulse, the processor does some work. For example, a processor could execute an instruction every clock pulse. A processor's speed is described in terms of the rate of the system clock ticks. A 100Mhz processor will receive 100 million clock ticks every second. It is misleading to describe the power of a CPU by its clock rate, as different processors perform different amounts of work per clock tick. However, all things being equal, a faster clock speed means a more powerful processor. The instructions executed by the processor are very simple; for example, "read the contents of memory at location X into register Y." *Registers* are the microprocessor's internal storage, used for storing data and performing operations on it. The operations performed may cause the processor to stop what it is doing and jump to another instruction somewhere else in memory. These tiny building blocks give the modern microprocessor almost limitless power as it can execute millions or even billions of instructions a second.

The instructions have to be fetched from memory as they are executed. Instructions may themselves reference data within memory and that data must be fetched from memory and saved there when appropriate.

The size, number and type of register within a microprocessor is entirely dependent on its type. An Intel 486 processor has a different register set to an Alpha AXP processor; for a start, the Intels are 32 bits wide and the Alpha AXPs are 64 bits wide. In general, though, any given processor will have a number of general purpose registers and a smaller number of dedicated registers. Most processors have the following special-purpose, dedicated registers:

♦ Program Counter (PC)—This register contains the address of the next instruction to be executed. The contents of the PC are automatically incremented each time an instruction is fetched.

♦ Stack Pointer (SP)—Processors have to have access to large amounts of external read/write *random access memory* (RAM), which facilitates temporary storage of data. The stack is a way of easily saving and restoring temporary values in external memory. Usually, processors have special instructions which allow you to push values onto the stack and to pop them off again later. The stack works on a last in first out (LIFO) basis. In other words, if you push two values, x and y, onto a stack and then pop a value off of the stack, then you will get back the value of y.

Some processor's stacks grow upwards toward the top of memory while others grow downwards toward the bottom, or *base*, of memory. Some processors support both types, for example ARM.

♦ Processor Status (PS)—Instructions may yield results; for example, "is the content of register X greater than the content of register Y?" will yield true or false as a result. The PS register holds this and other information about the current state of the processor. For example, most processors have at least two modes of operation, kernel (or supervisor) and user. The PS register would hold information identifying the current mode.

1.2   Memory

All systems have a memory hierarchy with memory at different speeds and sizes at different points in the hierarchy. The fastest memory is known as *cache memory* and is what it sounds like—memory that is used to temporarily hold, or cache, contents of the main memory. This sort of memory is very fast but expensive; therefore, most processors have a small amount of on-chip cache memory and more system-based (onboard) cache memory. Some processors have one cache to contain both instructions and data, but others have two: one for instructions and the other for data. The Alpha AXP processor has two internal memory caches: one for data (the D-Cache) and one for instructions (the I-Cache). The external cache (or B-Cache) mixes the two together. Finally, there is the *main memory* which, relative to the external cache memory, is very slow. Relative to the on-CPU cache, main memory is positively crawling.

The cache and main memories must be kept in step (coherent). In other words, if a word of main memory is held in one or more locations in cache, then the system must make sure that the contents of cache and memory are the same. The job of cache coherency is done partially by the hardware and partially by the operating system. This is also true for a number of major system tasks where the hardware and software must cooperate closely to achieve their aims.

1.3   Buses

The individual components of the system board are interconnected by multiple connection systems known as *buses*. The system bus is divided into three logical functions; the address bus, the data bus and the control bus. The address bus specifies the memory locations (addresses) for the data transfers. The data bus holds the data transferred. The data bus is bidirectional; it allows data to be read into the CPU and written from the CPU. The control bus contains various lines used to route timing and control signals throughout the system. Many flavours of bus exist; for example, ISA and PCI buses, are popular ways of connecting peripherals to the system.

1.4   Controllers And Peripherals

Peripherals are real devices, such as graphics cards or disks controlled by controller chips on the system board or on cards plugged into it. The IDE disks are controlled by the IDE controller chip and the SCSI disks by the SCSI disk controller chips and so on. These controllers are connected to the CPU and to each other by a variety of buses. Most systems built now use PCI and ISA buses to connect together the main system components. The controllers are processors like the CPU itself; they can be viewed as intelligent helpers to the CPU. The CPU is in overall control of the system.

All controllers are different, but they usually have registers which control them. Software running on the CPU must be able to read and write those controlling registers. One register might contain status describing an error. Another might be used for control purposes: changing the mode of the controller. Each controller on a bus can be individually addressed by the CPU; this is so that the software device driver can write to its registers and thus control it. The IDE ribbon is a good example, as it gives you the ability to access each drive on the bus separately. Another good example is the PCI bus, which allows each device (for example, a graphics card) to be accessed independently.

1.5   Address Spaces

The system bus connects the CPU with the main memory and is separate from the buses connecting the CPU with the system's hardware peripherals. Collectively, the memory space that the hardware peripherals exist in is known as *I/O space*. I/O space may itself be further subdivided, but we will not worry too much about that for the moment. The CPU can access both the system space memory and the I/O space memory, whereas the controllers themselves can only access system memory indirectly and then only with the help of the CPU. From the point of view of the device, say the floppy disk controller, it will see only the address space that its control registers are in (ISA), and not the system memory. Typically, a CPU will have separate instructions for accessing the memory and I/O space. For example, there might be an instruction that means "read a byte from I/O address 0x3f0 into register X." This is exactly how the CPU controls the system's hardware peripherals, by reading and writing to their registers in I/O space. Where in I/O space the common peripherals (IDE controller, serial port, floppy disk controller and so on) have their registers has been set by convention over the years as the PC architecture has developed. The I/O space address 0x3f0 just happens to be the address of one of the serial port's (COM1) control registers.

There are times when controllers need to read or write large amounts of data directly to or from system memory, for example, when user data is being written to the hard disk. In this case, direct memory access (DMA) controllers are used to allow hardware peripherals to directly access system memory but this access is under strict control and supervision of the CPU.

1.6 Timers

All operating systems need to know the time and so the modern PC includes a special peripheral called the *realtime clock* (RTC). This provides two things: a reliable time of day and an accurate timing interval. The RTC has its own battery, so that it continues to run even when the PC is not powered on; this is how your PC always "knows" the correct date and time. The interval timer allows the operating system to accurately schedule essential work.

Chapter 2
Software Basics

A program is a set of computer instructions that perform a particular task. That program can be written in *assembler*, a very low-level computer language, or in a high-level, machine-independent language, such as the C programming language. An *operating system* is a special program which allows the user to run applications such as spreadsheets and word processors. This chapter introduces basic programming principles and gives an overview of the aims and functions of an operating system.

2.1   Computer Languages

2.1.1   Assembly Languages

The instructions that a CPU fetches from memory and executes are not at all understandable to human beings. They are machine codes which tell the computer precisely what to do. The hexadecimal number 0x89E5 is an Intel 80486 instruction which copies the contents of the ESP register to the EBP register. One of the first software tools invented for the earliest computers was an assembler, a program which takes a human-readable source file and assembles it into machine code. Assembly languages explicitly handle registers and operations on data and they are specific to a particular microprocessor. The assembly language for an Intel X86 microprocessor is very different to the assembly language for an Alpha AXP microprocessor. The following Alpha AXP assembly code shows the sort of operations that a program can perform:

```
ldr r16, (r15)      ; Line 1
ldr r17, 4(r15)     ; Line 2
beq r16,r17,100     ; Line 3
```

```
    str r17, (r15)      ; Line 4
100:                    ; Line 5
```

The first statement (on line 1) loads register 16 from the address held in register 15. The next instruction loads register 17 from the next location in memory. Line 3 compares the contents of register 16 with that of register 17 and, if they are equal, branches to label 100. If the registers do not contain the same value then the program continues to line 4 where the contents of r17 are saved into memory. If the registers do contain the same value then no data needs to be saved. Assembly level programs are tedious and tricky to write and prone to errors. Very little of the Linux kernel is written in assembly language and those parts that are written only for efficiency and they are specific to particular microprocessors.

2.1.2   The C Programming Language And Compiler

Writing large programs in assembly language is a difficult and time-consuming task. It is prone to error and the resulting program is not portable, being tied to one particular processor family. It is far better to use a machine-independent language like C. C allows you to describe programs in terms of their logical algorithms and the data that they operate on. Special programs called *compilers* read the C program and translate it into assembly language, generating machine-specific code from it. A good compiler can generate assembly instructions that are very nearly as efficient as those written by a good assembly programmer. Most of the Linux kernel is written in the C language. The following C fragment:

```
if (x != y)
        x = y ;
```

performs exactly the same operations as the previous example assembly code. If the contents of the variable x are not the same as the contents of variable y then the contents of y will be copied to x. C code is organized into *routines*, each of which perform a task. Routines may return any value or data type supported by C. Large programs like the Linux kernel comprise many separate C source modules each with its own routines and data structures. These C source code modules group together logical functions such as file system handling code.

C supports many types of variables, a variable is a location in memory which can be referenced by a symbolic name. In the above C fragment x and y refer to locations in memory. The programmer does not care where in memory the variables are put, it is the linker (see below) that has to worry about that. Some variables contain different sorts of data, integer and floating point and others are pointers.

Pointers are variables that contain the address, the location in memory of other data. Consider a variable called *x*, it might live in memory at address 0x80010000. You could have a pointer, called *px*, which points at x. *px* might live at address 0x80010030. The value of *px* would be 0x80010000: the address of the variable *x*.

C allows you to bundle together related variables into data structures. For example,

```
struct {
        int i ;
        char b ;
} my_struct ;
```

is a data structure called my_struct which contains two elements: an integer (32 bits of data storage) called i and a character (8 bits of data) called b.

2.1.3 Linkers

Linkers are programs that link together several object modules and libraries to form a single, coherent, program. Object modules are the machine code output from an assembler or compiler and contain executable machine code and data together with information that allows the linker to combine the modules together to form a program. For example, one module might contain all of a program's database functions and another module its command line argument handling functions. Linkers fix up references between these object modules, where a routine or data structure referenced in one module actually exists in another module. The Linux kernel is a single, large program linked together from its many constituent object modules.

2.2 What Is An Operating System?

Without software, a computer is just a pile of electronics that gives off heat. If the hardware is the heart of a computer, then the software is its soul. An operating system is a collection of system programs which allow the user to run application software. The operating system abstracts the real hardware of the system and presents the system's users and its applications with a virtual machine. In a very real sense the software provides the character of the system. Most PCs can run one or more operating systems and each one can have a very different look and feel. Linux is made up of a number of functionally separate pieces that, together, comprise the operating system. One obvious part of Linux is the kernel itself; but even that would be useless without libraries or shells.

In order to start understanding what an operating system is, consider what happens when you type an apparently simple command:

```
$ ls
Mail            c               images          perl
docs            tcl
$
```

The $ is a prompt put out by a login shell (in this case bash). This means that it is waiting for you, the user, to type some command. Typing **ls** causes the keyboard driver to recognize that characters have been typed. The keyboard driver passes them to the shell which processes that command by looking for an executable image of the same name. It finds that image, in **/bin/ls/**. Kernel services are called to pull the **ls** executable image into virtual memory and start executing it. The **ls** image makes calls to the file subsystem of the kernel to find out what files are available. The file system might make use of cached file system information or use the disk device driver to read this information from the disk. It might even cause a network driver to exchange information with a remote machine to find out details of remote files that this system has access to (file systems can be remotely mounted via the *Networked File System*, or NFS). Whichever way the information is located, **ls** writes that information out and the video driver displays it on the screen.

All of the above seems rather complicated, but it shows that even most simple commands reveal that an operating system is in fact a cooperating set of functions that together give you, the user, a coherent view of the system.

2.2.1   Memory Management

With infinite resources, for example, memory, many of the things that an operating system has to do would be redundant. One of the basic tricks of any operating system is the ability to make a small amount of physical memory behave like rather more memory. This apparently large memory is known as *virtual memory*. The idea is that the software running in the system is fooled into believing that it is running in a lot of memory. The system divides the memory into easily handled pages and swaps these pages onto a hard disk as the system runs. The software does not notice because of another trick, *multiprocessing*.

2.2.2   Processes

A process could be thought of as a program in action, each process is a separate entity that is running a particular program. If you look at the processes on your Linux system, you will see that there are rather a lot. For example, typing **ps** shows the following processes on my system:

```
$ ps
 PID TTY STAT   TIME COMMAND
 158 pRe 1      0:00 -bash
 174 pRe 1      0:00 sh /usr/X11R6/bin/startx
 175 pRe 1      0:00 xinit /usr/X11R6/lib/X11/xinit/xinitrc —
 178 pRe 1 N    0:00 bowman
 182 pRe 1 N    0:01 rxvt -geometry 120x35 -fg white -bg black
 184 pRe 1 <    0:00 xclock -bg grey -geometry -1500-1500 -padding 0
 185 pRe 1 <    0:00 xload -bg grey -geometry -0-0 -label xload
 187 pp6 1      9:26 /bin/bash
 202 pRe 1 N    0:00 rxvt -geometry 120x35 -fg white -bg black
 203 ppc 2      0:00 /bin/bash
1796 pRe 1 N    0:00 rxvt -geometry 120x35 -fg white -bg black
```

```
1797 v06 1      0:00 /bin/bash
3056 pp6 3 <    0:02 emacs intro/introduction.tex
3270 pp6 3      0:00 ps
$
```

If my system had many CPUs, then each process could (theoretically at least) run on a different CPU. Unfortunately, there is only one, so again the operating system resorts to trickery by running each process in turn for a short period. This period of time is known as a *time-slice*. This trick is known as multiprocessing or scheduling and it fools each process into thinking that it is the only process. Processes are protected from one another so that if one process crashes or malfunctions then it will not affect any others. The operating system achieves this by giving each process a separate address space which only they have access to.

2.2.3   Device Drivers

Device drivers make up the major part of the Linux kernel. Like other parts of the operating system, they operate in a highly privileged environment and can cause disaster if they get things wrong. Device drivers control the interaction between the operating system and the hardware device that they are controlling. For example, the file system makes use of a general block device interface when writing blocks to an IDE disk. The driver takes care of the details and makes device specific things happen. Device drivers are specific to the controller chip that they are driving which is why, for example, you need the NCR810 SCSI driver if your system has an NCR810 SCSI controller.

2.2.4   The File Systems

In Linux, as it is for Unix, the separate file systems that the system may use are not accessed by device identifiers (such as a drive number or a drive name) but instead they are combined into a single hierarchical tree structure that represents the file system as a single entity. Linux adds each new file system into this single file system tree as they are mounted onto a mount directory, for example `/mnt/cdrom /`. One of the most important features of Linux is its support for many different file systems. This makes it very flexible and well able to coexist with other operating systems. The most popular file system for Linux is the EXT2 file system and this is the file system supported by most of the Linux distributions.

A file system gives the user a sensible view of files and directories held on the hard disks of the system regardless of the file system type or the characteristics of the underlying physical device. Linux transparently supports many different file systems (for example MS-DOS and EXT2) and presents all of the mounted files and file systems as one integrated virtual file system. So, in general, users and processes do not need to know what sort of file system that any file is part of, they just use them.

The block device drivers hide the differences between the physical block device types (for example, IDE and SCSI) and, so far as each file system is concerned, the physical devices are just linear collections of blocks of data. The block sizes may vary between devices; for example, 512 bytes is common for floppy devices, whereas 1,024 bytes is common for IDE devices and, again, this is hidden from the users of the system. An EXT2 file system looks the same no matter what device holds it.

2.3   Kernel Data Structures

The operating system must keep a lot of information about the current state of the system. As things happen within the system these data structures must be changed to reflect the current reality. For example, a new process might be created when a user logs onto the system. The kernel must create a data structure representing the new process and link it with the data structures representing all of the other processes in the system.

Mostly, these data structures exist in physical memory and are accessible only by the kernel and its subsystems. Data structures contain data and pointers, addresses of other data structures, or the addresses of routines. Taken all together, the data structures used by the Linux kernel can look very confusing. Every data structure has a purpose and although some are used by several kernel subsystems, they are more simple than they appear at first sight.

Understanding the Linux kernel hinges on understanding its data structures and the use that the various functions within the Linux kernel makes of them. This book bases its description of the Linux kernel on its data structures. It talks about each kernel subsystem in terms of its algorithms, its methods of getting things done, and their usage of the kernel's data structures.

2.3.1   Linked Lists

Linux uses a number of software engineering techniques to link together its data structures. On a lot of occasions it uses *linked* or *chained* data structures. If each data structure describes a single instance or occurrence of something, for example, a process or a network device, the kernel must be able to find all of the instances. In a linked list a root pointer contains the address of the first data structure, or *element*, in the list and each data structure contains a pointer to the next element in the list. The last element's next pointer would be 0 or NULL to show that it is the end of the list. In a *doubly linked list* each element contains both a pointer to the next element in the list but also a pointer to the previous element in the list. Using doubly linked lists makes it easier to add or remove elements from the middle of list although you do need more memory accesses. This is a typical operating system trade off: memory accesses versus CPU cycles.

2.3.2   Hash Tables

Linked lists are handy ways of tying data structures together, but navigating linked lists can be inefficient. If you were searching for a particular element, you might easily have to look at the whole list before you find the one that you need. Linux uses another technique, *hashing*, to get around this restriction. A *hash table* is an *array* or *vector* of pointers. An array, or vector, is simply a set of things coming one after another in memory. A bookshelf could be said to be an array of books. Arrays are accessed by an *index*, the index is an offset into the array. Taking the bookshelf analogy a little further, you could describe each book by its position on the shelf; you might ask for the fifth book.

A hash table is an array of pointers to data structures and its index is derived from information in those data structures. If you had data structures describing the population of a village then you could use a person's age as an index. To find a particular person's data you could use their age as an index into the population hash table and then follow the pointer to the data structure containing the person's details. Unfortunately, many people in the village are likely to have the same age and so the hash table pointer becomes a pointer to a chain or list of data structures each describing people of the same age. However, searching these shorter chains is still faster than searching all of the data structures.

As a hash table speeds up access to commonly used data structures, Linux often uses hash tables to implement *caches*. Caches are handy information that needs to be accessed quickly and are usually a subset of the full set of information available. Data structures are put into a cache and kept there because the kernel often accesses them. There is a drawback to caches in that they are more complex to use and maintain than simple linked lists or hash tables. If the data structure can be found in the cache (this is known as a *cache hit*), then all well and good. If it cannot, then all of the relevant data structures must be searched and, if the data structure exists at all, it must be added into the cache. In adding new data structures into the cache an old cache entry may need discarding. Linux must decide which one to discard, the danger being that the discarded data structure may be the next one that Linux needs.

2.3.3   Abstract Interfaces

The Linux kernel often abstracts its interfaces. An *interface* is a collection of routines and data structures which operate in a particular way. For example, all network device drivers have to provide certain routines in which particular data structures are operated on. This way, there can be generic layers of code using the services (interfaces) of lower layers of specific code. The network layer is generic and it is supported by device-specific code that conforms to a standard interface.

Often these lower layers *register* themselves with the upper layer at boot time. This registration usually involves adding a data structure to a linked list. For example, each file system built into the kernel registers itself with the kernel at boot time or, if you are using modules, when the file system is first used. You can see which file systems have registered themselves by looking at the file `/proc/filesystems`. The registration data structure often includes pointers to functions. These are the addresses of software functions that perform particular tasks. Again, using file system registration as an example, the data structure that each file system passes to the Linux kernel as it registers includes the address of a file system-specific routine which must be called whenever that file system is mounted.

Chapter 3
Memory Management

The memory management subsystem is one of the most important parts of the operating system. Since the early days of computing, there has been a need for more memory than exists physically in a system. Strategies have been developed to overcome this limitation and the most successful of these is virtual memory. Virtual memory makes the system appear to have more memory than it actually has by sharing it between competing processes as they need it.

Virtual memory does more than just make your computer's memory go further. The memory management subsystem provides:

- Large Address Spaces—The operating system makes the system appear as if it has a larger amount of memory than it actually has. The virtual memory can be many times larger than the physical memory in the system.

- Protection—Each process in the system has its own virtual address space. These virtual address spaces are completely separate from each other, and so a process running one application cannot affect another. Also, the hardware virtual memory mechanisms allow areas of memory to be protected against writing. This protects code and data from being overwritten by rogue applications.

- Memory Mapping—Memory mapping is used to map image and data files into a processes address space. In memory mapping, the contents of a file are linked directly into the virtual address space of a process.

- Fair Physical Memory Allocation—The memory management subsystem allows each running process in the system a fair share of the physical memory of the system.

♦ Shared Virtual Memory—Although virtual memory allows processes to have separate (virtual) address spaces, there are times when you need processes to share memory. For example, there could be several processes in the system running the **bash** command shell. Rather than have several copies of **bash**, one in each process's virtual address space, it is better to have only one copy in physical memory and all of the processes running **bash** share it. Dynamic libraries are another common example of executing code shared between several processes.

Shared memory can also be used as an Inter-Process Communication (IPC) mechanism, with two or more processes exchanging information via memory common to all of them. Linux supports the Unix System V shared memory IPC.

3.1 An Abstract Model Of Virtual Memory

Before considering the methods that Linux uses to support virtual memory, it is useful to consider an abstract model that is not cluttered by too much detail.

As the processor executes a program, it reads an instruction from memory and decodes it. In decoding the instruction, it may need to fetch or store the contents of a location in memory. The processor then executes the instruction and moves onto the next instruction in the program. In this way the processor is always accessing memory either to fetch instructions or to fetch and store data.

In a virtual memory system, all of these addresses are virtual addresses and not physical addresses. These virtual addresses are converted into physical addresses by the processor based on information held in a set of tables maintained by the operating system.

To make this translation easier, virtual and physical memory are divided into handy-sized chunks called *pages*. These pages are all the same size; they need not be but if they were not, the system would be very hard to administer. Linux on Alpha AXP systems uses 8K pages and on Intel x86 systems, it uses 4K pages. Each of these pages is given a unique number: the *page frame number* (PFN).

In this paged model, a virtual address is composed of two parts: an offset and a virtual page frame number. If the page size is 4K, bits 11:0 of the virtual address contain the offset and bits 12 and above are the virtual page frame number. Each time the processor encounters a virtual address, it must extract the offset and the virtual page frame number. The processor must translate the virtual page frame number into a physical one and then access the location at the correct offset into that physical page. To do this, the processor uses *page tables*.

Figure 3.1 shows the virtual address spaces of two processes, process X and process Y, each with their own page tables. These page tables map each process's virtual pages into physical pages in memory. This shows that process X's virtual page frame number 0 is mapped into memory in physical page frame number 1 and that process Y's virtual page frame number 1 is mapped into physical page frame number 4. Each entry in the theoretical page table contains the following information:

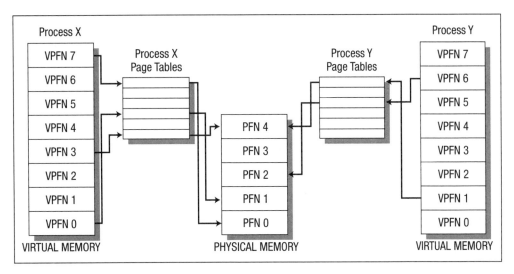

Figure 3.1
Abstract model of virtual to physical address mapping.

- ◆ Valid flag. This indicates if this page table entry is valid.
- ◆ The physical page frame number that this entry is describing.
- ◆ Access control information. This describes how the page may be used. Can it be written to? Does it contain executable code?

The page table is accessed using the virtual page frame number as an offset. Virtual page frame 5 would be the 6th element of the table (0 is the first element).

To translate a virtual address into a physical one, the processor must first work out the virtual addresses page frame number and the offset within that virtual page. By making the page size a power of 2, this can be easily done by masking and shifting. Looking again at Figure 3.1 and assuming a page size of *0x2000* bytes (which is decimal 8192) and an address of *0x2194* in process Y's virtual address space then the processor would translate that address into offset *0x194* into virtual page frame number 1.

The processor uses the virtual page frame number as an index into the process's page table to retrieve its page table entry. If the page table entry at that offset is valid, the processor takes the physical page frame number from this entry. If the entry is invalid, the process has accessed a nonexistent area of its virtual memory. In this case, the processor cannot resolve the address and must pass control to the operating system so that it can fix things up.

Just how the processor notifies the operating system that the correct process has attempted to access a virtual address for which there is no valid translation is specific to the processor. However the processor delivers it, this is known as a *page fault* and the operating system is notified of the faulting virtual address and the reason for the page fault.

Assuming that this is a valid page table entry, the processor takes that physical page frame number and multiplies it by the page size to get the address of the base of the page in physical memory. Finally, the processor adds in the offset to the instruction or data that it needs.

Using the above example again, process Y's virtual page frame number 1 is mapped to physical page frame number 4 which starts at $0x8000$ (4 x $0x2000$). Adding in the $0x194$ byte offset gives us a final physical address of $0x8194$.

By mapping virtual to physical addresses this way, the virtual memory can be mapped into the system's physical pages in any order. For example, in Figure 3.1 process X's virtual page frame number 0 is mapped to physical page frame number 1 whereas virtual page frame number 7 is mapped to physical page frame number 0 even though it is higher in virtual memory than virtual page frame number 0. This demonstrates an interesting by-product of virtual memory; the pages of virtual memory do not have to be present in physical memory in any particular order.

3.1.1 Demand Paging

As there is much less physical memory than virtual memory, the operating system must be careful that it does not use the physical memory inefficiently. One way to save physical memory is to only load virtual pages that are currently being used by the executing program. For example, a database program may be run to query a database. In this case, not all of the database needs to be loaded into memory, just those data records that are being examined. If the database query is a search query, then it does not make sense to load the code from the database program that deals with adding new records. This technique of only loading virtual pages into memory as they are accessed is known as *demand paging*.

When a process attempts to access a virtual address that is not currently in memory the processor cannot find a page table entry for the virtual page referenced. For example, in Figure 3.1, there is no entry in process X's page table for virtual page frame number 2 and so if process X attempts to read from an address within virtual page frame number 2, the processor cannot translate the address into a physical one. At this point, the processor notifies the operating system that a page fault has occurred.

If the faulting virtual address is invalid this means that the process has attempted to access a virtual address that it should not have. Maybe the application has gone wrong in some way, for example, writing to random addresses in memory. In this case the operating system will terminate it, protecting the other processes in the system from this rogue process.

If the faulting virtual address was valid but the page that it refers to is not currently in memory, the operating system must bring the appropriate page into memory from the image on disk. Disk access takes a long time, relatively speaking, and so the process must wait quite a while until the page has been fetched. If there are other processes that could run then the operating system will select one of them to run. The fetched page is written into a free physical page frame and an entry for the virtual page frame number is added to the processes page table. The process is then restarted at the machine instruction where the memory fault occurred. This time the virtual memory access is made, the processor can make the virtual to physical address translation and so the process continues to run.

Linux uses demand paging to load executable images into a process's virtual memory. Whenever a command is executed, the file containing it is opened and its contents are mapped into the process's virtual memory. This is done by modifying the data structures describing this process's memory map and is known as *memory mapping*. However, only the first part of the image is actually brought into physical memory. The rest of the image is left on disk. As the image executes, it generates page faults and Linux uses the process's memory map in order to determine which parts of the image to bring into memory for execution.

3.1.2   Swapping

If a process needs to bring a virtual page into physical memory and there are no free physical pages available, the operating system must make room for this page by discarding another page from physical memory.

If the page to be discarded from physical memory came from an image or data file and has not been written to then the page does not need to be saved. Instead it can be discarded, and if the process needs that page again it can be brought back into memory from the image or data file.

However, if the page has been modified, the operating system must preserve the contents of that page so that it can be accessed at a later time. This type of page is known as a *dirty* page and when it is removed from memory it is saved in a special sort of file called the *swap file*. Accesses to the swap file are very long relative to the speed of the processor and physical memory, and the operating system must juggle the need to write pages to disk with the need to retain them in memory to be used again.

If the algorithm used to decide which pages to discard or swap (the *swap algorithm*) is not efficient, then a condition known as *thrashing* occurs. In this case, pages are constantly being written to disk and then being read back, and the operating system is too busy to allow much real work to be performed. If, for example, physical page frame number 1 in Figure 3.1 is being regularly accessed then it is not a good candidate for swapping to hard disk. The set of pages that a process is currently using is called the *working set*. An efficient swap scheme would make sure that all processes have their working set in physical memory.

Linux uses a Least Recently Used (LRU) page aging technique to fairly choose pages which might be removed from the system. This scheme involves every page in the system having an age which changes as the page is accessed. The more that a page is accessed, the younger it is; the less that it is accessed the older and more stale it becomes. Old pages are good candidates for swapping.

3.1.3 Shared Virtual Memory

Virtual memory makes it easy for several processes to share memory. All memory access are made via page tables and each process has its own separate page table. For two processes sharing a physical page of memory, its physical page frame number must appear in a page table entry in both of their page tables.

Figure 3.1 shows two processes that each share physical page frame number 4. For process X, this is virtual page frame number 4, whereas for process Y, this is virtual page frame number 6. This illustrates an interesting point about sharing pages: the shared physical page does not have to exist at the same place in virtual memory for any or all of the processes sharing it.

3.1.4 Physical And Virtual Addressing Modes

It does not make much sense for the operating system itself to run in virtual memory. This would be a nightmare situation, where the operating system must maintain page tables for itself. Most multipurpose processors support the notion of a physical address mode as well as a virtual address mode. Physical addressing mode requires no page tables and the processor does not attempt to perform any address translations in this mode. The Linux kernel is linked to run in physical address space.

The Alpha AXP processor does not have a special physical addressing mode. Instead, it divides up the memory space into several areas and designates two of them as physically mapped addresses. This kernel address space is known as KSEG address space and it encompasses all addresses upwards from *0xfffffc0000000000*. In order to execute from code linked in KSEG (by definition, kernel code) or access data there, the code must be executing in kernel mode. The Linux kernel on Alpha is linked to execute from address *0xfffffc0000310000*.

3.1.5 Access Control

The page table entries also contain access control information. As the processor is already using the page table entry to map a process's virtual address to a physical one, it can easily use the access control information to check that the process is not accessing memory in a way that it should not.

There are many reasons why you would want to restrict access to areas of memory. Some memory, such as that containing executable code, is naturally read-only memory; the operating system should not allow a process to write data over its executable code. By contrast, pages containing data can be written to but attempts to execute that memory as instructions should fail. Most processors have at least two modes of execution: *kernel* and *user*. You would not want kernel code executing by a user or kernel data structures to be accessible except when the processor is running in kernel mode.

The access control information is held in the PTE and is processor specific; Figure 3.2 shows the PTE for Alpha AXP. The bit fields have the following meanings:

♦ V—Valid, if set this PTE is valid.

♦ FOE—"Fault on Execute." Whenever an attempt to execute instructions in this page occurs, the processor reports a page fault and passes control to the operating system.

♦ FOW—"Fault on Write." As above, but page fault on an attempt to write to this page.

♦ FOR—"Fault on Read." As above, but page fault on an attempt to read from this page.

♦ ASM—Address Space Match. This is used when the operating system wishes to clear only some of the entries from the translation buffer.

♦ KRE—Code running in kernel mode can read this page.

♦ URE—Code running in user mode can read this page.

♦ GH—Granularity hint used when mapping an entire block with a single translation buffer entry rather than many.

♦ KWE—Code running in kernel mode can write to this page.

♦ UWE—Code running in user mode can write to this page.

♦ page frame number—For PTEs with the V bit set, this field contains the physical Page Frame Number (page frame number) for this PTE. For invalid PTEs, if this field is not zero, it contains information about where the page is in the swap file.

The following two bits are defined and used by Linux:

♦ _PAGE_DIRTY—If set, the page needs to be written out to the swap file.

♦ _PAGE_ACCESSED—Used by Linux to mark a page as having been accessed.

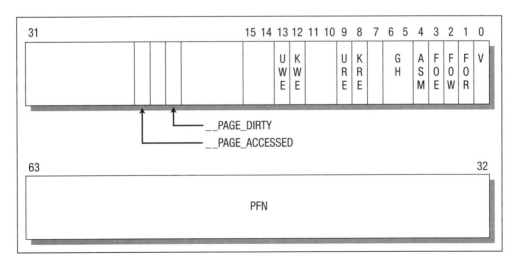

Figure 3.2
Alpha AXP page table entry.

3.2   Caches

If you were to implement a system using the above theoretical model, then it would work, but not particularly efficiently. Both operating system and processor designers try hard to extract more performance from the system. Apart from making the processors, memory and so on faster, the best approach is to maintain caches of useful information and data that make some operations faster. Linux uses a number of memory management-related caches:

♦ *Buffer cache*—The buffer cache contains data buffers that are used by the block device drivers.

These buffers are of fixed sizes (for example, 512 bytes) and contain blocks of information that have either been read from a block device or are being written to it. A block device is one that can only be accessed by reading and writing fixed-sized blocks of data. All hard disks are block devices.

The buffer cache is indexed via the device identifier and the desired block number and is used to quickly find a block of data. Block devices are only ever accessed via the buffer cache. If data can be found in the buffer cache, then it does not need to be read from the physical block device, for example, a hard disk, and access to it is much faster.

♦ *Page cache*—This is used to speed up access to images and data on disk.

It is used to cache the logical contents of a file a page at a time and is accessed via the file and offset within the file. As pages are read into memory from disk, they are cached in the page cache.

♦ *Swap cache*—Only modified (or dirty) pages are saved in the swap file.

So long as these pages are not modified after they have been written to the swap file, then the next time the page is swapped out there is no need to write it to the swap file as the page is already in the swap file. Instead, the page can simply be discarded. In a heavily swapping system, this saves many unnecessary and costly disk operations.

♦ *Hardware caches*—One commonly implemented hardware cache is in the processor; a cache of page table entries. In this case, the processor does not always read the page table directly but instead caches translations for pages as it needs them. These are the translation look-aside buffers (TLB) and contain cached copies of the page table entries from one or more processes in the system.

When the reference to the virtual address is made, the processor will attempt to find a matching TLB entry. If it finds one, it can directly translate the virtual address into a physical one and perform the correct operation on the data. If the processor cannot find a matching TLB entry, then it must get the operating system to help. It does this by signaling the operating system that a TLB miss has occurred. A system-specific mechanism is used to deliver that exception to the operating system code that can fix things up. The operating system generates a new TLB entry for the address mapping. When the exception has been cleared, the processor will make another attempt to translate the virtual address. This time it will work, because there is now a valid entry in the TLB for that address.

The drawback of using caches, hardware or otherwise, is that in order to save effort Linux must use more time and space maintaining these caches and, if the caches become corrupted, the system will crash.

3.3 Linux Page Tables

Linux assumes that there are three levels of page tables. Each page table accessed contains the page frame number of the next level of page table. Figure 3.3 shows how a virtual address can be broken into a number of fields, each field providing an offset into a particular page table. To translate a virtual address into a physical one, the processor must take the contents of each level field, convert it into an offset into the physical page containing the page table , and read the page frame number of the next level of page table . This is repeated three times until the page frame number of the physical page containing the virtual address is found. Now the final field in the virtual address, the byte offset, is used to find the data inside the page.

Each platform that Linux runs on must provide translation macros that allow the kernel to traverse the page tables for a particular process. This way, the kernel does not need to know the format of the page table entries or how they are arranged.

This is so successful that Linux uses the same page table manipulation code for the Alpha processor, which has three levels of page tables, and for Intel x86 processors, which have two levels of page tables.

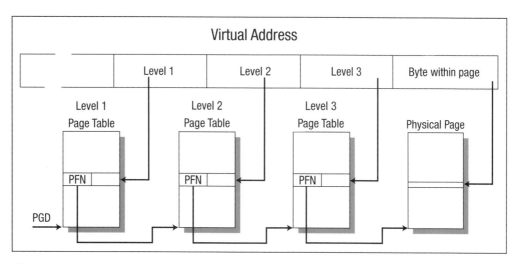

Figure 3.3
Three-level page tables.

3.4   Page Allocation And Deallocation

There are many demands on the physical pages in the system. For example, when an image is loaded into memory the operating system needs to allocate pages. These will be freed when the image has finished executing and is unloaded. Another use for physical pages is to hold kernel-specific data structures such as the page tables themselves. The mechanisms and data structures used for page allocation and deallocation are perhaps the most critical in maintaining the efficiency of the virtual memory subsystem.

All of the physical pages in the system are described by the mem_map data structure which is a list of mem_map_t (confusingly the structure is also known as the *page* structure) structures which is initialized at boot time. Each mem_map_t describes a single physical page in the system. Important fields (so far as memory management is concerned) are:

♦ count—This is a count of the number of users of this page. The count is greater than one when the page is shared between many processes.

♦ age—This field describes the age of the page and is used to decide if the page is a good candidate for discarding or swapping.

♦ map_nr—This is the physical page frame number that this mem_map_t describes.

The free_area vector is used by the page allocation code to find and free pages. The whole buffer management scheme is supported by this mechanism and so far as the code is concerned, the size of the page and physical paging mechanisms used by the processor are irrelevant.

Each element of free_area contains information about blocks of pages. The first element in the array describes single pages, the next blocks of two pages, the next blocks of four pages and so on upwards in powers of two. The list element is used as a queue head and has pointers to the page data structures in the mem_map array. Free blocks of pages are queued here. map is a pointer to a bitmap, which keeps track of allocated groups of pages of this size. Bit N of the bitmap is set if the Nth block of pages is free.

Figure 3.4 shows the free_area structure. Element 0 has one free page (page frame number 0) and element two has two free blocks of four pages, the first starting at page frame number 4 and the second at page frame number 56.

3.4.1   Page Allocation

Linux uses the Buddy algorithm to effectively allocate and deallocate blocks of pages. The page allocation code attempts to allocate a block of one or more physical pages. Pages are allocated in blocks which are powers of two in size. That means that it can allocate a block one page, two pages, four pages, and so on. So long as there are enough free pages in the system to grant this request (nr_free_pages > min_free_pages) the allocation code will search the free_area for a block of pages of the size requested. Each element of the free_area has a map of the allocated and free blocks of pages for that sized block. For example, element two of the array has a memory map that describes free and allocated blocks each of 4 pages long.

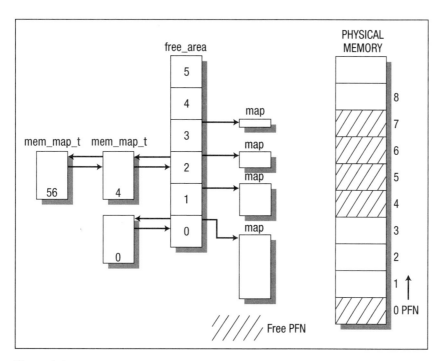

Figure 3.4
The `free_area` data structure.

The allocation algorithm first searches for blocks of pages of the size requested. It follows the chain of free pages that is queued on the *list* element of the `free_area` data structure. If no blocks of pages of the requested size are free, blocks of the next size (which is twice that of the size requested) are looked for. This process continues until all of the `free_area` has been searched or until a block of pages has been found. If the block of pages found is larger than that requested it must be broken down until there is a block of the right size. Because the blocks are each a power of two pages big, then this breaking down process is easy as you simply break the blocks in half. The free blocks are queued on the appropriate queue and the allocated block of pages is returned to the caller.

For example, in Figure 3.4, if a block of two pages was requested, the first block of four pages (starting at page frame number 4) would be broken into two two-page blocks. The first, starting at page frame number 4 would be returned to the caller as the allocated pages and the second block, starting at page frame number 6 would be queued as a free block of two pages onto element 1 of the free_area array.

3.4.2   Page Deallocation

Allocating blocks of pages tends to fragment memory with larger blocks of free pages being broken down into smaller ones. The page deallocation code recombines pages into larger blocks of free pages whenever it can. In fact, the page block size is important as it allows for easy combination of blocks into larger blocks.

Whenever a block of pages is freed, the adjacent or buddy block of the same size is checked to see if it is free. If it is, then it is combined with the newly freed block of pages to form a new free block of pages for the next size block of pages. Each time two blocks of pages are recombined into a bigger block of free pages the page deallocation code attempts to recombine that block into a still larger one. In this way, the blocks of free pages are as large as memory usage will allow.

For example, in Figure 3.4, if page frame number 1 were to be freed, then that would be combined with the already free page frame number 0 and queued onto element 1 of the `free_area` as a free block of size two pages.

3.5   Memory Mapping

When an image is executed, the contents of the executable image must be brought into the process's virtual address space. The same is also true of any shared libraries that the executable image has been linked to use. The executable file is not actually brought into physical memory; instead it is merely linked into the process's virtual memory. Then, as the parts of the program are referenced by the running application, the image is brought into memory from the executable image. This linking of an image into a process's virtual address space is known as *memory mapping*.

Every process's virtual memory is represented by an `mm_struct` data structure. This contains information about the image that it is currently executing (for example, `bash`) and also has pointers to a number of `vm_area_struct` data structures. Each `vm_area_struct` data structure describes the start and end of the area of virtual memory, the process's access rights to that memory, and a set of operations for that memory (see Figure 3.5). These operations are a set of routines that Linux must use when manipulating this area of virtual memory. For example, one of the virtual memory operations performs the correct actions when the process has attempted to access this virtual memory but finds (via a page fault) that the memory is not actually in physical memory. This operation is the nopage operation. The nopage operation is used when Linux demand pages the pages of an executable image into memory.

When an executable image is mapped into a process's virtual address a set of `vm_area_struct` data structures is generated. Each `vm_area_struct` data structure represents a part of the executable image; the executable code, initialized data (variables), uninitialized data, and so on. Linux supports a number of standard virtual memory operations and as the `vm_area_ struct` data structures are created, the correct set of virtual memory operations are associated with them.

3.6   Demand Paging

Once an executable image has been memory mapped into a processes virtual memory, it can start to execute. As only the very start of the image is physically pulled into memory, it will

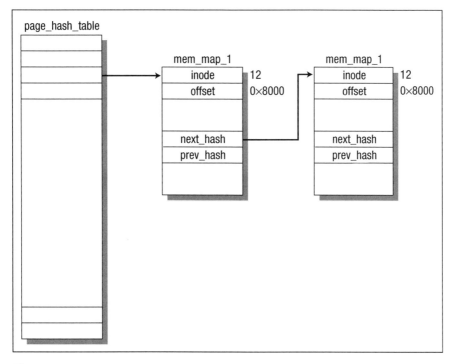

Figure 3.5
Areas of virtual memory.

soon access an area of virtual memory that is not yet in physical memory. When a process accesses a virtual address that does not have a valid page table entry, the processor will report a page fault to Linux.

The page fault describes the virtual address where the page fault occurred and the type of memory access that caused it.

Linux must find the `vm_area_struct` that represents the area of memory that the page fault occurred in. As searching through the `vm_area_struct` data structures is critical to the efficient handling of page faults, these are linked together in an AVL (Adelson-Velskii and Landis) tree structure. If there is no `vm_area_struct` data structure for this faulting virtual address, this process has accessed an illegal virtual address. Linux will signal the process, sending a `SIGSEGV` signal, and if the process does not have a handler for that signal it will be terminated.

Linux next checks the type of page fault that occurred against the types of accesses allowed for this area of virtual memory. If the process is accessing the memory in an illegal way, say, writing to an area that it is only allowed to read from, it is also signaled with a memory error.

Now that Linux has determined that the page fault is legal, it must deal with it.

Linux must differentiate between pages that are in the swap file and those that are part of an executable image on a disk somewhere. It does this by using the page table entry for this faulting virtual address.

If the page's page table entry is invalid but not empty, the page fault is for a page currently being held in the swap file. For Alpha AXP page table entries, these are entries which do not have their valid bit set but which have a non-zero value in their PFN field. In this case, the PFN field holds information about where in the swap (and which swap file) the page is being held. How pages in the swap file are handled is described later in this chapter.

Not all `vm_area_struct` data structures have a set of virtual memory operations and even those that do may not have a nopage operation. This is because by default Linux will fix up the access by allocating a new physical page and creating a valid page table entry for it. If there is a nopage operation for this area of virtual memory, Linux will use it.

The generic Linux nopage operation is used for memory-mapped executable images and it uses the page cache to bring the required image page into physical memory.

However the required page is brought into physical memory, the processes page tables are updated. It may be necessary for hardware specific actions to update those entries, particularly if the processor uses translation look aside buffers. Now that the page fault has been handled, it can be dismissed and the process is restarted at the instruction that made the faulting virtual memory access.

3.7   The Linux Page Cache

The role of the Linux page cache is to speed up access to files on disk. Memory-mapped files are read a page at a time and these pages are stored in the page cache. Figure 3.6 shows that the page cache consists of the `page_hash_table`, a vector of pointers to `mem_map_t` data structures.

Each file in Linux is identified by a VFS `inode` data structure (described in Chapter 9), and each VFS `inode` is unique and fully describes one and only one file. The index into the page table is derived from the file's VFS `inode` and the offset into the file.

Whenever a page is read from a memory-mapped file, for example, when it needs to be brought back into memory during demand paging, the page is read through the page cache. If the page is present in the cache, a pointer to the `mem_map_t` data structure representing it is returned to the page fault handling code. Otherwise, the page must be brought into memory from the file system that holds the image. Linux allocates a physical page and reads the page from the file on disk.

If it is possible, Linux will initiate a read of the next page in the file. This single page read ahead means that if the process is accessing the pages in the file serially, the next page will be waiting in memory for the process.

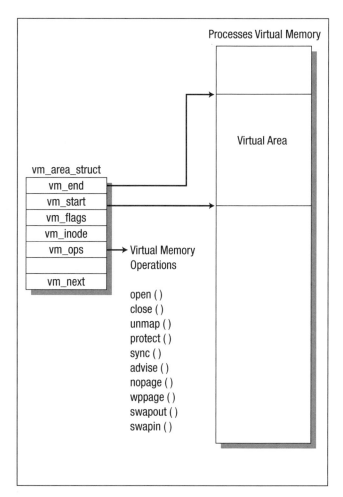

Figure 3.6
The Linux page cache.

Over time, the page cache grows as images are read and executed. Pages will be removed from the cache as they are no longer needed, say, as an image is no longer being used by any process. As Linux uses memory it can start to run low on physical pages. In this case, Linux will reduce the size of the page cache.

3.8   Swapping Out And Discarding Pages

When physical memory becomes scarce the Linux memory management subsystem must attempt to free physical pages. This task falls to the kernel swap daemon (*kswapd*).

The kernel swap daemon is a special type of process, a *kernel thread*. Kernel threads are processes have no virtual memory, instead they run in kernel mode in the physical address space. The kernel swap daemon is slightly misnamed in that it does more than merely swap pages out to the system's swap files. Its role is make sure that there are enough free pages in the system to keep the memory management system operating efficiently.

The kernel swap daemon (*kswapd*) is started by the kernel init process at startup time and sits waiting for the kernel swap timer to periodically expire.

Every time the timer expires, the swap daemon looks to see if the number of free pages in the system is getting too low. It uses two variables, *free_pages_high* and *free_pages_low* to decide if it should free some pages. So long as the number of free pages in the system remains above *free_pages_high*, the kernel swap daemon does nothing; it sleeps again until its timer next expires. For the purposes of this check the kernel swap daemon takes into account the number of pages currently being written out to the swap file. It keeps a count of these in *nr_async_pages*; this is incremented each time a page is queued waiting to be written out to the swap file and decremented when the write to the swap device has completed. *free_pages_low* and *free_pages_high* are set at system startup time and are related to the number of physical pages in the system. If the number of free pages in the system has fallen below *free_pages_high* or worse still *free_pages_low*, the kernel swap daemon will try three ways to reduce the number of physical pages being used by the system:

♦ Reducing the size of the buffer and page caches.

♦ Swapping out System V shared memory pages.

♦ Swapping out and discarding pages.

If the number of free pages in the system has fallen below *free_pages_low*, the kernel swap daemon will try to free six pages before it next runs. Otherwise it will try to free three pages. Each of the above methods are tried in turn until enough pages have been freed. The kernel swap daemon remembers which method it was using the last time that it attempted to free physical pages. Each time it runs it will start trying to free pages using this last successful method.

After it has free sufficient pages, the swap daemon sleeps again until its timer expires. If the reason that the kernel swap daemon freed pages was that the number of free pages in the system had fallen below *free_pages_low*, it only sleeps for half its usual time. Once the number of free pages is more than *free_pages_low* the kernel swap daemon goes back to sleeping longer between checks.

3.8.1 Reducing The Size Of The Page And Buffer Caches

The pages held in the page and buffer caches are good candidates for being freed into the `free_area` vector. The page cache, which contains pages of memory mapped files, may contain unneccessary pages that are filling up the system's memory. Likewise, the buffer cache, which contains buffers read from or being written to physical devices, may also contain unneeded buffers. When the physical pages in the system start to run out, discarding pages from these caches is relatively easy as it requires no writing to physical devices (unlike swapping pages out of memory). Discarding these pages does not have too many harmful side effects other than making access to physical devices and memory mapped files slower. However, if the discarding of pages from these caches is done fairly, all processes will suffer equally.

Every time the kernel swap daemon tries to shrink these caches, it examines a block of pages in the mem_map page vector to see if any can be discarded from physical memory. The size of the block of pages examined is higher if the kernel swap daemon is intensively swapping; that is if the number of free pages in the system has fallen dangerously low. The blocks of pages are examined in a cyclical manner; a different block of pages is examined each time an attempt is made to shrink the memory map. This is known as the *clock algorithm* as, rather like the minute hand of a clock, the whole mem_map page vector is examined a few pages at a time.

Each page being examined is checked to see if it is cached in either the page cache or the buffer cache. You should note that shared pages are not considered for discarding at this time and that a page cannot be in both caches at the same time. If the page is not in either cache then the next page in the mem_map page vector is examined.

Pages are cached in the buffer cache (or rather, the buffers within the pages are cached) to make buffer allocation and deallocation more efficient. The memory map shrinking code tries to free the buffers that are contained within the page being examined.

If all the buffers are freed, then the pages that contain them are also freed. If the examined page is in the Linux page cache, it is removed from the page cache and freed.

When enough pages have been freed on this attempt then the kernel swap daemon will wait until the next time it is periodically woken. As none of the freed pages were part of any process's virtual memory (they were cached pages), then no page tables need updating. If there were not enough cached pages discarded, then the swap daemon will try to swap out some shared pages.

3.8.2   Swapping Out System V Shared Memory Pages

System V shared memory is an interprocess communication mechanism which allows two or more processes to share virtual memory in order to pass information among them. How processes share memory in this way is described in more detail in Chapter 5. For now, it is enough to say that each area of System V shared memory is described by a shmid_ds data structure. This contains a pointer to a list of vm_area_struct data structures, one for each process sharing this area of virtual memory. The vm_area_struct data structures describe where in each processes virtual memory this area of System V shared memory goes. Each vm_area_struct data structure for this System V shared memory is linked together using the vm_next_shared and vm_prev_shared pointers. Each shmid_ds data structure also contains a list of page table entries each of which describes the physical page that a shared virtual page maps to.

The kernel swap daemon also uses a clock algorithm when swapping out System V shared memory pages. Each time it runs, it remembers which page of which shared virtual memory area it last swapped out. It does this by keeping two indices, the first is an index into the set of shmid_ds data structures, the second into the list of page table entries for this area of System V shared memory. This makes sure that it fairly victimizes the areas of System V shared memory.

As the physical page frame number for a given virtual page of System V shared memory is contained in the page tables of all of the processes sharing this area of virtual memory, the kernel swap daemon must modify all of these page tables to show that the page is no longer in memory but is now held in the swap file. For each shared page it is swapping out, the kernel swap daemon finds the page table entry in each of the sharing processes page tables (by following a pointer from each vm_area_struct data structure). If this processes page table entry for this page of System V shared memory is valid, it converts it into an invalid but swapped-out page table entry and reduces this (shared) page's count of users by one. The format of a swapped-out System V shared page table entry contains an index into the set of shmid_ds data structures and an index into the page table entries for this area of System V shared memory.

If the page's count is zero after the page tables of the sharing processes have all been modified, the shared page can be written out to the swap file. The page table entry in the list pointed at by the shmid_ds data structure for this area of System V shared memory is replaced by a swapped-out page table entry. A swapped-out page table entry is invalid but contains an index into the set of open swap files and the offset in that file where the swapped-out page can be found. This information will be used when the page has to be brought back into physical memory.

3.8.3   Swapping Out And Discarding Pages

The swap daemon looks at each process in the system in turn to see if it is a good candidate for swapping.

Good candidates are processes that can be swapped (some cannot) and that have one or more pages which can be swapped or discarded from memory. Pages are swapped out of physical memory into the system's swap files only if the data in them cannot be retrieved another way.

A lot of the contents of an executable image come from the image's file and can easily be re-read from that file. For example, the executable instructions of an image will never be modified by the image and so will never be written to the swap file. These pages can simply be discarded; when they are again referenced by the process, they will be brought back into memory from the executable image.

Once the process to swap has been located, the swap daemon looks through all of its virtual memory regions looking for areas which are not shared or locked.

Linux does not swap out all of the swappable pages of the process that it has selected; instead it removes only a small number of pages.

Pages cannot be swapped or discarded if they are locked in memory.

The Linux swap algorithm uses page aging. Each page has a counter (held in the `mem_map_t` data structure) that gives the kernel swap daemon some idea whether or not a page is worth swapping. Pages age when they are unused and rejuvenate on access; the swap daemon only swaps out old pages. The default action when a page is first allocated, is to give it an initial age of three. Each time it is touched, its age is increased by 3 to a maximum of 20. Every time the Kernel swap daemon runs it ages pages, decrementing their age by one. These default actions can be changed and for this reason they (and other swap-related information) are stored in the `swap_control` data structure.

If the page is old (age=0), the swap daemon will process it further. Dirty pages are pages which can be swapped out. Linux uses an architecture specific bit in the PTE to describe pages this way (Figure 3.2). However, not all dirty pages are necessarily written to the swap file. Every virtual memory region of a process may have its own swap operation (pointed at by the `vm_ops` pointer in the `vm_area_struct`) and that method is used. Otherwise, the swap daemon will allocate a page in the swap file and write the page out to that device.

The page's page table entry is replaced by one which is marked as invalid but which contains information about where the page is in the swap file. This is an offset into the swap file where the page is held and an indication of which swap file is being used. Whatever the swap method used, the original physical page is made free by putting it back into the `free_area`. Clean (or rather, not dirty) pages can be discarded and put back into the `free_area` for re-use.

If enough of the swappable processes pages have been swapped out or discarded, the swap daemon will again sleep. The next time it wakes it will consider the next process in the system. In this way, the swap daemon nibbles away at each process's physical pages until the system is again in balance. This is much fairer than swapping out whole processes.

3.9 The Swap Cache

When swapping pages out to the swap files, Linux avoids writing pages if it does not have to. There are times when a page is both in a swap file and in physical memory. This happens when a page that was swapped out of memory was then brought back into memory when it was again accessed by a process. So long as the page in memory is not written to, the copy in the swap file remains valid.

Linux uses the *swap cache* to track these pages. The swap cache is a list of page table entries, one per physical page in the system. This is a page table entry for a swapped-out page and describes which swap file the page is being held in together with its location in the swap file. If a swap cache entry is non-zero, it represents a page which is being held in a swap file that has not been modified. If the page is subsequently modified (by being written to), its entry is removed from the swap cache.

When Linux needs to swap a physical page out to a swap file, it consults the swap cache and, if there is a valid entry for this page, it does not need to write the page out to the swap file. This is because the page in memory has not been modified since it was last read from the swap file.

The entries in the swap cache are page table entries for swapped-out pages. They are marked as invalid, but contain information which allow Linux to find the right swap file and the right page within that swap file.

3.10   Swapping Pages In

The dirty pages saved in the swap files may be needed again, for example, when an application writes to an area of virtual memory whose contents are held in a swapped-out physical page. Accessing a page of virtual memory that is not held in physical memory causes a page fault to occur. The page fault is the processor signaling the operating system that it cannot translate a virtual address into a physical one. In this case this is because the page table entry describing this page of virtual memory was marked as invalid when the page was swapped out. The processor cannot handle the virtual to physical address translation and so hands control back to the operating system describing as it does so the virtual address that faulted and the reason for the fault. The format of this information and how the processor passes control to the operating system is processor specific.

The processor-specific page fault handling code must locate the `vm_area_struct` data structure that describes the area of virtual memory that contains the faulting virtual address. It does this by searching the `vm_area_struct` data structures for this process until it finds the one containing the faulting virtual address. This is very time-critical code and a processes `vm_area_struct` data structures are so arranged as to make this search take as little time as possible.

Having carried out the appropriate processor specific actions and found that the faulting virtual address is for a valid area of virtual memory, the page fault processing becomes generic and applicable to all processors that Linux runs on.

The generic page fault handling code looks for the page table entry for the faulting virtual address. If the page table entry it finds is for a swapped-out page, Linux must swap the page back into physical memory. The format of the page table entry for a swapped-out page is processor specific but all processors mark these pages as invalid and put the information necessary to locate the page within the swap file into the page table entry. Linux needs this information in order to bring the page back into physical memory.

At this point, Linux knows the faulting virtual address and has a page table entry containing information about where this page has been swapped to. The `vm_area_struct` data structure may contain a pointer to a routine which will swap any page of the area of virtual memory that it describes back into physical memory. This is its *swapin operation*. If there is a swapin operation for this area of virtual memory then Linux will use it. This is, in fact, how swapped-out System V shared memory pages are handled as it requires special handling because the format of a swapped-out System V shared page is a little different from that of an ordinary swapped-out page. There may not be a swapin operation, in which case Linux will assume that this is an ordinary page that does not need to be specially handled.

It allocates a free physical page and reads the swapped-out page back from the swap file. Information telling it where in the swap file (and which swap file) is taken from the invalid page table entry.

If the access that caused the page fault was not a write access then the page is left in the swap cache and its page table entry is not marked as writable. If the page is subsequently written to, another page fault will occur and, at that point, the page is marked as dirty and its entry is removed from the swap cache. If the page is not written to and it needs to be swapped out again, Linux can avoid the write of the page to its swap file because the page is already in the swap file.

If the access that caused the page to be brought in from the swap file was a write operation, this page is removed from the swap cache and its page table entry is marked as both dirty and writable.

Chapter 4
Processes

This chapter describes what a process is, and how the Linux kernel creates, manages, and deletes the processes in the system.

Processes carry out tasks within the operating system. A program is a set of machine code instructions and data stored in an executable image on disk and is, as such, a passive entity; a process can be thought of as a computer program in action.

It is a dynamic entity, constantly changing as the machine code instructions are executed by the processor. As well as the program's instructions and data, the process also includes the program counter and all of the CPU's registers, as well as the process stacks containing temporary data, such as routine parameters, return addresses, and saved variables. The current executing program, or process, includes all of the current activity in the microprocessor. Linux is a multiprocessing operating system. Processes are separate tasks, each with their own rights and responsibilities. If one process crashes, it will not cause another process in the system to crash. Each individual process runs in its own virtual address space and is not capable of interacting with another process except through secure, kernel-managed mechanisms.

During the lifetime of a process, it will use many system resources. It will use the CPUs in the system to run its instructions and the system's physical memory to hold it and its data. It will open and use files within the file systems and may directly or indirectly use the physical devices in the system. Linux must keep track of the process itself and of the system resources that it has so that it can manage it and the other processes in the system fairly. It would not be fair to the other processes in the system if one process monopolized most of the system's physical memory or its CPUs.

The most precious resource in the system is the CPU; usually there is only one. Linux is a multiprocessing operating system; its objective is to have a process running on each CPU in the system at all times, to maximize CPU utilization. If there are more processes than CPUs (and there usually are), the rest of the processes must wait before a CPU becomes free until they can be run. Multiprocessing is a simple idea; a process is executed until it must wait, usually for some system resource; when it has this resource, it may run again. In a uniprocessing system, for example, DOS, the CPU would simply sit idle and the waiting time would be wasted. In a multiprocessing system many processes are kept in memory at the same time. Whenever a process has to wait the operating system takes the CPU away from that process and gives it to another, more deserving process. It is the scheduler that chooses which is the most appropriate process to run next and Linux uses a number of scheduling strategies to ensure fairness.

Linux supports a number of different executable file formats: ELF is one, Java is another, and these must be managed transparently as must the processes use of the system's shared libraries.

4.1   Linux Processes

So that Linux can manage the processes in the system, each process is represented by a `task_struct` data structure (task and process are terms that Linux uses interchangeably). The `task` vector is an array of pointers to every `task_struct` data structure in the system.

This means that the maximum number of processes in the system is limited by the size of the `task` vector; by default it has 512 entries. As processes are created, a new `task_struct` is allocated from system memory and added into the `task` vector. To make it easy to find, the current, running, process is pointed to by the `current` pointer.

As well as the normal type of process, Linux supports realtime processes. These processes have to react very quickly to external events (hence the term "realtime") and they are treated differently from normal user processes by the scheduler. Although the `task_struct` data structure is quite large and complex, but its fields can be divided into a number of functional areas:

State

As a process executes, it changes state according to its circumstances. Linux processes have the following states:

◆ Running—The process is either running (it is the current process in the system) or it is ready to run (it is waiting to be assigned to one of the system's CPUs).

◆ Waiting—The process is waiting for an event or for a resource. Linux differentiates between two types of waiting process: *interruptible* and *uninterruptible*. Interruptible waiting processes can be interrupted by signals, whereas uninterruptible waiting processes are wait-ing directly on hardware conditions and cannot be interrupted under any circumstances.

♦ Stopped—The process has been stopped, usually by receiving a signal. A process that is being debugged can be in a stopped state.

♦ Zombie—This is a halted process which, for some reason, still has a `task_struct` data structure in the `task` vector. It is what it sounds like: a dead process.

♦ Scheduling Information—The scheduler needs this information in order to fairly decide which process in the system most deserves to run.

♦ Identifiers—Every process in the system has a process identifier. The process identifier is not an index into the `task` vector; it is simply a number. Each process also has user and group identifiers; these are used to control this processes access to the files and devices in the system.

♦ Interprocess Communication—Linux supports the classic Unix IPC mechanisms of sig-nals, pipes, and semaphores and also the System V IPC mechanisms of shared memory, semaphores and message queues. The IPC mechanisms supported by Linux are described in Chapter 5.

♦ Links—In a Linux system, no process is independent of any other process. Every process in the system, except the initial process has a parent process. New processes are not created; they are copied, or rather *cloned,* from previous processes. Every `task_struct` represent-ing a process keeps pointers to its parent process and to its siblings (those processes with the same parent process) as well as to its own child processes. You can see the family relation-ship between the running processes in a Linux system using the **pstree** command:

```
init(1)-+-crond(98)
        |-emacs(387)
        |-gpm(146)
        |-inetd(110)
        |-kerneld(18)
        |-kflushd(2)
        |-klogd(87)
        |-kswapd(3)
        |-login(160)—bash(192)—emacs(225)
        |-lpd(121)
        |-mingetty(161)
        |-mingetty(162)
        |-mingetty(163)
        |-mingetty(164)
        |-login(403)—bash(404)—pstree(594)
        |-sendmail(134)
        |-syslogd(78)
        '-update(166)
```

Additionally all of the processes in the system are held in a doubly linked list whose root is the init processes `task_struct` data structure. This list allows the Linux kernel to look at every process in the system. It needs to do this to provide support for commands such as **ps** or **kill**.

♦ Times and Timers—The kernel keeps track of a processes creation time as well as the CPU time that it consumes during its lifetime. Each clock tick, the kernel updates the amount of time in `jiffies` that the current process has spent in system and in user mode. Linux also supports process specific interval timers, processes can use system calls to set up timers to send signals to themselves when the timers expire. These timers can be single-shot or periodic timers.

♦ File System—Processes can open and close files as they wish, and the processes task_struct contains pointers to descriptors for each open file as well as pointers to two VFS inodes. Each VFS inode uniquely describes a file or directory within a file system and also provides a uniform interface to the underlying file systems. How file systems are supported under Linux is described in Chapter 9. The first is to the root of the process (its home directory) and the second is to its current or *pwd* directory. *pwd* is derived from the Unix command **pwd**, *print working directory*. These two VFS inodes have their `count` fields incremented to show that one or more processes are referencing them. This is why you cannot delete the directory that a process has as its *pwd* directory set to, or for that matter one of its subdirectories.

♦ Virtual Memory—Most processes have some virtual memory (kernel threads and daemons do not) and the Linux kernel must track how that virtual memory is mapped onto the system's physical memory.

♦ Processor-Specific Context—A process could be thought of as the sum total of the system's current state. Whenever a process is running it is using the processor's registers, stacks, and so on. This is the processes context and, when a process is suspended, all of that CPU specific context must be saved in the `task_struct` for the process. When a process is restarted by the scheduler, its context is restored from here.

4.2 Identifiers

Linux, like all Unix, uses user and group identifiers to check for access rights to files and images in the system. All of the files in a Linux system have ownership and permissions; these permissions describe what access the system's users have to that file or directory. Basic permissions are *read*, *write*, and *execute* and are assigned to three classes of user: the owner of the file, processes belonging to a particular group, and all of the processes in the system. Each class of user can have different permissions; for example, a file could have permissions which allow its owner to read and write it, the file's group to read it, and for all other processes in the system to have no access at all.

Groups are Linux's way of assigning privileges to files and directories for a group of users, rather than to a single user or to all processes in the system. You might, for example, create a group for all of the users in a software project and arrange it so that only they could read and write the source code for the project. A process can belong to several groups (a maximum of 32 is the default) and these are held in the `groups` vector in the `task_struct` for each process. So long as a file has access rights for one of the groups that a process belongs to, then that process will have appropriate group access rights to that file.

There are four pairs of process and group identifiers held in a process's `task_struct`:

♦ uid, gid—The user identifier and group identifier of the user that the process is running on behalf of.

♦ effective uid and gid—There are some programs which change the uid and gid from that of the executing process into their own (held as attributes in the VFS inode describing the executable image). These programs are known as *setuid* programs and they are useful because it is a way of restricting accesses to services, particularly those that run on behalf of someone else, for example, a network daemon. The effective uid and gid are those from the setuid program and the uid and gid remain as they were. The kernel checks the effective uid and gid whenever it checks for privilege rights.

♦ file system uid and gid—These are normally the same as the effective uid and gid, and are used when checking file system access rights. They are needed for NFS-mounted file systems where the user mode NFS server needs to access files as if it were a particular process. In this case, only the filesystem uid and gid are changed (not the effective uid and gid). This avoids a situation where malicious users could send a kill signal to the NFS server. Kill signals are delivered to processes with a particular effective uid and gid.

♦ saved uid and gid—These are mandated by the POSIX standard and are used by programs which change the process's uid and gid via system calls. They are used to save the real uid and gid during the time that the original uid and gid have been changed.

4.3   Scheduling

All processes run partially in user mode and partially in system mode. How these modes are supported by the underlying hardware differs, but generally there is a secure mechanism for getting from user mode into system mode and back again. User mode has far less privileges than system mode. Each time a process makes a system call, it swaps from user mode to system mode and continues executing. At this point the kernel is executing on behalf of the process. In Linux, processes do not preempt the current, running process, they cannot stop it from running so that they can run. Each process decides to relinquish the CPU that it is running on when it has to wait for some system event. For example, a process may have to wait for a character to be read from a file. This waiting happens within the system call, in system mode; the process used a library function to open and read the file and it, in turn made system calls to read bytes from the open file. In this case, the waiting process will be suspended and another, more deserving process will be chosen to run.

Processes are always making system calls, and so may often need to wait. Even so, if a process executes until it waits then it still might use a disproportionate amount of CPU time and so Linux uses preemptive scheduling. In this scheme, each process is allowed to run for a small amount of time, 200 ms, and, when this time has expired another process is selected to run and the original process is made to wait for a little while until it can run again. This small amount of time is known as a *time slice*.

It is the *scheduler* that must select the most deserving process to run out of all of the runnable processes in the system.

A runnable process is one which is waiting only for a CPU to run on. Linux uses a reasonably simple priority-based scheduling algorithm to choose between the current processes in the system. When it has chosen a new process, to run it saves the state of the current process, the processor specific registers and other context being saved in the processes `task_struct` data structure. It then restores the state of the new process (again, this is processor-specific) to run, and gives control of the system to that process. For the scheduler to fairly allocate CPU time between the runnable processes in the system it keeps information in the `task_struct` for each process:

♦ policy—This is the scheduling policy that will be applied to this process. There are two types of Linux process: normal and realtime. Realtime processes have a higher priority than all of the other processes. If there is a realtime process ready to run, it will always run first. Realtime processes may have two types of policy: round robin and first in first out. In round robin scheduling, each runnable realtime process is run in turn; and in first in, first out scheduling each runnable process is run in the order that it is in on the run queue and that order is never changed.

♦ priority—This is the priority that the scheduler will give to this process. It is also the amount of time (in `jiffies`) that this process will run for when it is allowed to run. You can alter the priority of a process by means of system calls and the **renice** command.

♦ rt_priority—Linux supports real time processes and these are scheduled to have a higher priority than all of the other non-real time processes in system. This field allows the scheduler to give each real time process a relative priority. The priority of a realtime processes can be altered using system calls.

♦ counter—This is the amount of time (in `jiffies`) that this process is allowed to run for. It is set to `priority` when the process is first run and is decremented each clock tick.

The scheduler is run from several places within the kernel. It is run after putting the current process onto a wait queue and it may also be run at the end of a system call, just before a process is returned to process mode from system mode. One reason that it might need to run is because the system timer has just set the current process's `counter` to zero. Each time the scheduler is run it does the following:

♦ Kernel work—The scheduler runs the bottom half handlers and processes the scheduler task queue. These lightweight kernel threads are described in detail in Chapter 11.

♦ Current process—The current process must be processed before another process can be selected to run.

If the scheduling policy of the current processes is round robin, then it is put onto the back of the run queue.

If the task is INTERRUPTIBLE and it has received a signal since the last time it was scheduled, then its state becomes RUNNING.

If the current process has timed out, then its state becomes RUNNING.

If the current process is RUNNING then it will remain in that state.

Processes that were neither RUNNING nor INTERRUPTIBLE are removed from the run queue. This means that they will not be considered for running when the scheduler looks for the most deserving process to run.

◆ Process selection—The scheduler looks through the processes on the run queue, looking for the most deserving process to run. If there are any realtime processes (those with a realtime scheduling policy), then those will get a higher weighting than ordinary processes. The weight for a normal process is its counter, but for a realtime process it is counter plus 1000. This means that if there are any runnable realtime processes in the system then these will always be run before any normal runnable processes. The current process, which has consumed some of its time slice (its counter has been decremented) is at a disadvantage if there are other processes with equal priority in the system; that is as it should be. If several processes have the same priority, the one nearest the front of the run queue is chosen. The current process will get put onto the back of the run queue. In a balanced system with many processes of the same priority, each one will run in turn. This is known as *round robin* scheduling. However, as processes wait for resources, their run order tends to get moved around.

◆ Swap processes—If the most deserving process to run is not the current process, then the current process must be suspended and the new one made to run. When a process is running it is using the registers and physical memory of the CPU and of the system. Each time it calls a routine it passes its arguments in registers and may stack saved values such as the address to return to in the calling routine. So, when the scheduler is running, it is running in the context of the current process. It will be in a privileged mode, kernel mode, but it is still the current process that is running. When that process comes to be suspended, all of its machine state, including the program counter (PC) and all of the processor's registers, must be saved in the processes task_struct data structure. Then, all of the machine state for the new process must be loaded. This is a system-dependent operation; no two CPUs do this in quite the same way, but there is usually some hardware assistance for this act.

This swapping of process context takes place at the end of the scheduler. The saved context for the previous process is, therefore, a snapshot of the hardware context of the system as it was for this process at the end of the scheduler. Equally, when the context of the new process is loaded, it too will be a snapshot of the way things were at the end of the scheduler, including this process's program counter and register contents.

If the previous process or the new current process uses virtual memory, then the system's page table entries may need to be updated. Again, this action is architecture specific. Processors like the Alpha AXP, which use translation look-aside tables or cached page table entries, must flush those cached table entries that belonged to the previous process.

4.3.1 Scheduling In Multiprocessor Systems

Systems with multiple CPUs are reasonably rare in the Linux world, but a lot of work has already gone into making Linux an SMP (symmetric multiprocessing) operating system. That is, one that is capable of evenly balancing work between the CPUs in the system. Nowhere is this balancing of work more apparent than in the scheduler.

In a multiprocessor system, hopefully, all of the processors are busily running processes. Each will run the scheduler separately as its current process exhausts its time slice or has to wait for a system resource. The first thing to notice about an SMP system is that there is not just one idle process in the system. In a single processor system, the idle process is the first task in the task vector, in an SMP system there is one idle process per CPU, and you could have more than one idle CPU. Additionally there is one current process per CPU, so SMP systems must keep track of the current and idle processes for each processor.

In an SMP system each process's `task_struct` contains the number of the processor that it is currently running on (`processor`) and its processor number of the last processor that it ran on (`last_processor`). There is no reason why a process should not run on a different CPU each time it is selected to run, but Linux can restrict a process to one or more processors in the system using the `processor_mask`. If bit N is set, then this process can run on processor N. When the scheduler is choosing a new process to run, it will not consider one that does not have the appropriate bit set for the current processor's number in its `processor_mask`. The scheduler also gives a slight advantage to a process that last ran on the current processor because there is often a performance overhead when moving a process to a different processor.

4.4 Files

Figure 4.1 shows that there are two data structures that describe file system specific information for each process in the system. The first, the `fs_struct`, contains pointers to this process's VFS inodes and its `umask`. The `umask` is the default mode that new files will be created in, and it can be changed via system calls.

The second data structure, the `files_struct`, contains information about all of the files that this process is currently using. Programs read from *standard input* and write to standard output. Any error messages should go to *standard error*. These may be files, terminal input/output, or a real device, but so far as the program is concerned they are all treated as files. Every file has its own descriptor, and the `files_struct` contains pointers to up to 256

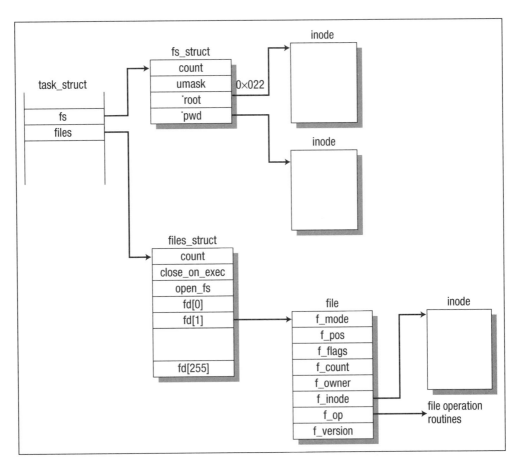

Figure 4.1
A process's files.

file data structures, each one describing a file being used by this process. The f_mode field describes what mode the file has been created in; read only, read and write, or write only. f_pos holds the position in the file where the next read or write operation will occur. f_inode points at the VFS inode describing the file and f_ops is a pointer to a vector of routine addresses; one for each function that you might wish to perform on a file. There is, for example, a write data function. This abstraction of the interface is very powerful and allows Linux to support a wide variety of file types. In Linux, pipes are implemented using this mechanism, as we shall see later.

Every time a file is opened, one of the free file pointers in the files_struct is used to point to the new file structure. Linux processes expect three file descriptors to be open when they start. These are known as *standard input, standard output,* and *standard error,* and they are usually inherited from the creating parent process. All accesses to files are via standard system calls which pass or return file descriptors. These descriptors are indices into the process's `fd` vector, so standard input, standard output, and standard error have file descriptors 0, 1 and 2. Each access to the file uses the `file` data structure's file operation routines to together with the VFS inode to achieve its needs.

4.5   Virtual Memory

A process's virtual memory contains executable code and data from many sources. First, there is the program image that is loaded; for example a command like ls. This command, like all executable images, is composed of both executable code and data. The image file contains all of the information necessary to load the executable code and associated program data into the virtual memory of the process. Secondly, processes can allocate (virtual) memory to use during their processing, say, to hold the contents of files that it is reading. This newly allocated, virtual, memory needs to be linked into the process's existing virtual memory so that it can be used. Third, Linux processes use libraries of commonly useful code, for example, file handling routines. It does not make sense that each process has its own copy of the library; Linux uses shared libraries that can be used by several running processes at the same time. The code and the data from these shared libraries must be linked into this process's virtual address space, and also into the virtual address space of the other processes sharing the library.

In any given time period, a process will not have used all of the code and data contained within its virtual memory. It could contain code that is only used during certain situations, such as during initialization or to process a particular event. It may only have used some of the routines from its shared libraries. It would be wasteful to load all of this code and data into physical memory where it would lie unused. Multiply this wastage by the number of processes in the system and the system would run very inefficiently. Instead, Linux uses a technique called *demand paging*, where the virtual memory of a process is brought into physical memory only when a process attempts to use it. So, instead of loading the code and data into physical memory straight away, the Linux kernel alters the process's page table, marking the virtual areas as existing but not in memory. When the process attempts to access the code or data, the system hardware will generate a page fault and hand control to the Linux kernel to fix things up. Therefore, for every area of virtual memory in the process's address space Linux needs to know where that virtual memory comes from and how to get it into memory so that it can fix up these page faults.

The Linux kernel needs to manage all of these areas of virtual memory, and the contents of each process's virtual memory is described by a `mm_struct` data structure pointed at from its `task_struct`. The process's `mm_struct` data structure also contains information about the loaded executable image and a pointer to the process's page tables. It contains pointers to a list of `vm_area_struct` data structures, each representing an area of virtual memory within this process.

This linked list is in ascending virtual memory order; Figure 4.2 shows the layout in virtual memory of a simple process together with the kernel data structures managing it. As those areas of virtual memory are from several sources, Linux abstracts the interface by having the `vm_area_struct` point to a set of virtual memory handling routines (via `vm_ops`). This way, all of the process's virtual memory can be handled in a consistent way no matter how the underlying services managing that memory differ. For example, there is a routine that will be called when the process attempts to access the memory and it does not exist; this is how page faults are handled.

The process's set of `vm_area_struct` data structures is accessed repeatedly by the Linux kernel as it creates new areas of virtual memory for the process and as it fixes up references to virtual memory not in the system's physical memory. This makes the time that it takes to find the correct `vm_area_struct` critical to the performance of the system. To speed up this access, Linux also arranges the `vm_area_struct` data structures into an AVL (Adelson-Velskii and Landis) tree. This tree is arranged so that each `vm_area_struct` (or node) has a left and a right pointer to its neighboring `vm_area_struct` structure. The left pointer points to node with a lower starting virtual address and the right pointer points to a node with a higher starting virtual address. To find the correct node, Linux goes to the root of the

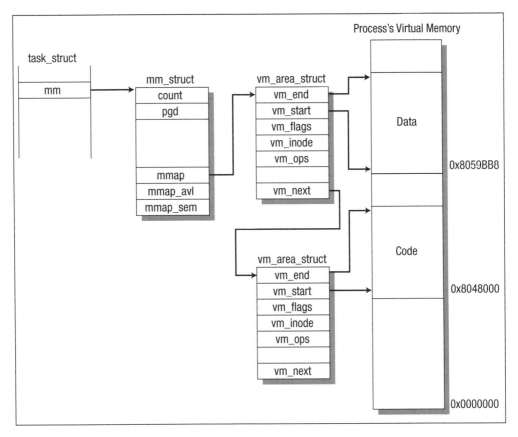

Figure 4.2
A process's virtual memory.

tree and follows each node's left and right pointers until it finds the right vm_area_struct. Of course, nothing is for free and inserting a new vm_area_struct into this tree takes additional processing time.

When a process allocates virtual memory, Linux does not actually reserve physical memory for the process. Instead, it describes the virtual memory by creating a new vm_area_struct data structure. This is linked into the process's list of virtual memory. When the process attempts to write to a virtual address within that new virtual memory region, then the system will page fault. The processor will attempt to decode the virtual address, but as there are no page table entries for any of this memory, it will give up and raise a page fault exception, leaving the Linux kernel to fix things up. Linux looks to see if the virtual address referenced is in the current process's virtual address space. If it is, Linux creates the appropriate PTEs and allocates a physical page of memory for this process. The code or data may need to be brought into that physical page from the file system or from the swap disk. The process can then be restarted at the instruction that caused the page fault and, this time as the memory physically exists, it may continue.

4.6   Creating A Process

When the system starts up, it is running in kernel mode and there is, in a sense, only one process, the initial process. Like all processes, the initial process has a machine state represented by stacks, registers, and so on. These will be saved in the initial process's task_struct data structure when other processes in the system are created and run. At the end of system initialization, the initial process starts up a kernel thread (called init) and then sits in an idle loop doing nothing. Whenever there is nothing else to do the scheduler will run this idle process. The idle process's task_struct is the only one that is not dynamically allocated; it is statically defined at kernel build time and is, rather confusingly, called init_task.

The init kernel thread or process has a process identifier of 1, as it is the system's first real process. It does some initial setting up of the system (such as opening the system console and mounting the root file system) and then executes the system initialization program. This is one of /etc/init, /bin/init, or /sbin/init, depending on your system. The init program uses /etc/inittab as a script file to create new processes within the system. These new processes may themselves go on to create new processes. For example, the getty process may create a login process when a user attempts to login. All of the processes in the system are descended from the init kernel thread.

New processes are created by cloning old processes, or rather by cloning the current process. A new task is created by a system call (*fork* or *clone*) and the cloning happens within the kernel in kernel mode. At the end of the system call, there is a new process waiting to run once the scheduler chooses it. A new task_struct data structure is allocated from the system's physical memory with one or more physical pages for the cloned process's stacks (user and kernel). A new process identifier may be created, one that is unique within the set of process identifiers in the system. However, it is perfectly reasonable for the cloned process to keep its parents' process identifier. The new `task_struct` is entered into the task vector and the contents of the old (current) process's `task_struct` are copied into the cloned `task_struct`.

When cloning processes, Linux allows the two processes to share resources rather than have two separate copies. This applies to the process's files, signal handlers, and virtual memory. When the resources are to be shared, their respective `count` fields are incremented so that Linux will not deallocate these resources until both processes have finished using them. So, for example, if the cloned process is to share virtual memory, its `task_struct` will contain a pointer to the `mm_struct` of the original process and that `mm_struct` has its count field incremented to show the number of current processes sharing it.

Cloning a process's virtual memory is rather tricky. A new set of `vm_area_struct` data structures must be generated, together with their owning `mm_struct` data structure, and the cloned process's page tables. None of the process's virtual memory is copied at this point. That would be a rather difficult and lengthy task for some of that virtual memory would be in physical memory, some in the executable image that the process is currently executing, and possibly some would be in the swap file. Instead Linux uses a technique called "copy on write," which means that virtual memory will only be copied when one of the two processes tries to write to it. Any virtual memory that is not written to, even if it can be, will be shared between the two processes without any harm occurring. The read-only memory, for example the executable code, will always be shared. For "copy on write" to work, the writeable areas have their page table entries marked as read-only and the `vm_area_struct` data structures describing them are marked as "copy on write." When one of the processes attempts to write to this virtual memory, a page fault will occur. It is at this point that Linux will make a copy of the memory and fix up the two processes' page tables and virtual memory data structures.

4.7   Times And Timers

The kernel keeps track of a process's creation time as well as the CPU time that it consumes during its lifetime. Each clock tick, the kernel updates the amount of time in `jiffies` that the current process has spent in system and in user mode.

In addition to these accounting timers, Linux supports process specific *interval* timers.

A process can use these timers to send itself various signals each time that they expire. Three sorts of interval timers are supported:

♦ Real—The timer ticks in real time, and when the timer has expired, the process is sent a `SIGALRM` signal.

♦ Virtual—This timer only ticks when the process is running and when it expires it sends a `SIGVTALRM` signal.

♦ Profile—This timer ticks both when the process is running and when the system is executing on behalf of the process itself. `SIGPROF` is signaled when it expires.

One or all of the interval timers may be running, and Linux keeps all of the necessary information in the process's `task_struct` data structure. System calls can be made to set up these interval timers and to start them, stop them, and read their current values. The virtual and profile timers are handled the same way.

Every clock tick, the current process's interval timers are decremented and, if they have expired, the appropriate signal is sent.

Realtime interval timers are a little different and for these Linux uses the timer mechanism described in Chapter 11. Each process has its own `timer_list` data structure and, when the real interval timer is running, this is queued on the system timer list. When the timer expires, the timer bottom half handler removes it from the queue and calls the interval timer handler.

This generates the `SIGALRM` signal and restarts the interval timer, adding it back into the system timer queue.

4.8   Executing Programs

In Linux, as in Unix, programs and commands are normally executed by a command interpreter. A command interpreter is a user process like any other process, and is called a *shell*. (Think of a nut: The kernel is the edible bit in the middle and the shell goes around it, providing an interface.)

There are many shells in Linux; some of the most popular are `sh`, `bash`, and `tcsh`. With the exception of a few built-in commands, such as **cd** and **pwd**, a command is an executable binary file. For each command entered, the shell searches the directories in the process's *search path*, held in the `PATH` environment variable, for an executable image with a matching name. If the file is found, it is loaded and executed. The shell clones itself using the *fork* mechanism described above, and then the new child process replaces the binary image that it was executing, the shell, with the contents of the executable image file just found. Normally, the shell waits for the command to complete, or rather for the child process to exit. You can cause the shell to run again by pushing the child process to the background by typing Ctrl+Z, which causes a `SIGSTOP` signal to be sent to the child process, stopping it. You then use the shell command **bg** to push it into a background, the shell sends it a `SIGCONT` signal to restart it, where it will stay until either it ends or it needs to do terminal input or output.

An executable file can have many formats, or even be a script file. Script files have to be recognized and the appropriate interpreter run to handle them; for example, `/bin/sh` interprets shell scripts. Executable object files contain executable code and data, together with enough information to allow the operating system to load them into memory and execute them. The most commonly used object file format used by Linux is ELF, but, in theory, Linux is flexible enough to handle almost any object file format.

As with file systems, the binary formats supported by Linux are either built into the kernel at kernel build time or available to be loaded as modules. The kernel keeps a list of supported binary formats (see Figure 4.3), and when an attempt is made to execute a file, each binary format is tried in turn until one works.

Commonly supported Linux binary formats are a.out and ELF. Executable files do not have to be read completely into memory; a technique known as demand loading is used. As each part of the executable image is used by a process it is brought into memory. Unused parts of the image may be discarded from memory.

4.8.1   ELF

The ELF (Executable and Linkable Format) object file format, designed by the Unix System Laboratories, is now firmly established as the most commonly used format in Linux. Whilst there is a slight performance overhead when compared with other object file formats such as ECOFF and a.out, ELF is felt to be more flexible. ELF executable files contain executable code, sometimes referred to as *text*, and *data*. Tables within the executable image describe how the program should be placed into the process'ss virtual memory. Statically linked images are built by the linker (**ld**), or link editor, into one single image containing all of the code and data needed to run this image. The image also specifies the layout in memory of this image and the address in the image of the first code to execute.

Figure 4.4 shows the layout of a statically linked ELF executable image.

It is a simple C program that prints "hello world" and then exits. The header describes it as an ELF image with two physical headers (**e_phnum** is 2) starting 52 bytes (**e_phoff**) from the start of the image file. The first physical header describes the executable code in the image. It goes at virtual address *0x8048000* and there is 65,532 bytes of it. This is because it is a statically linked image which contains all of the library code for the **printf()** call to output "hello world." The entry point for the image, the first instruction for the program, is not at the start of the image but at virtual address *0x8048090* (**e_entry**). The code starts immediately after the second physical header. This physical header describes the data for the program and is to be loaded into virtual memory at address *0x8059BB8*. This data is both readable and writeable. You will notice that the size of the data in the file is 2,200 bytes

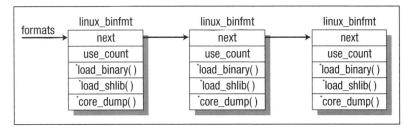

Figure 4.3
Registered binary formats.

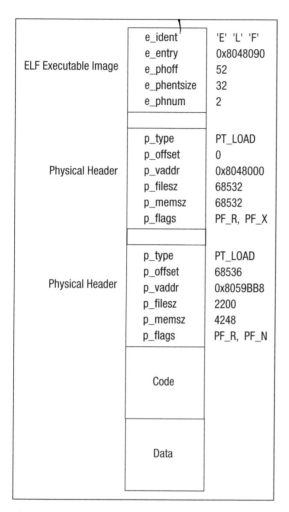

	e_ident	'E' 'L' 'F'
	e_entry	0x8048090
ELF Executable Image	e_phoff	52
	e_phentsize	32
	e_phnum	2
	p_type	PT_LOAD
	p_offset	0
Physical Header	p_vaddr	0x8048000
	p_filesz	68532
	p_memsz	68532
	p_flags	PF_R, PF_X
	p_type	PT_LOAD
	p_offset	68536
Physical Header	p_vaddr	0x8059BB8
	p_filesz	2200
	p_memsz	4248
	p_flags	PF_R, PF_N
	Code	
	Data	

Figure 4.4
ELF executable file format.

(p_filesz) whereas its size in memory is 4,248 bytes. This because the first 2,200 bytes contain pre-initialized data and the next 2,048 bytes contain data that will be initialized by the executing code.

When Linux loads an ELF executable image into the process's virtual address space, it does not actually load the image. It sets up the virtual memory data structures, the process's vm_area_struct tree, and its page tables. When the program is executed, page faults will cause the program's code and data to be fetched into physical memory. Unused portions of the program will never be loaded into memory. Once the ELF binary format loader is satisfied that the image is a valid ELF executable image, it flushes the process's current executable image from its virtual memory. As this process is a cloned image (*all* processes are) this old image is the program that the parent process was executing; for example, the command interpreter shell such as bash. This flushing of the old executable image discards the old virtual memory data structures and resets the process's page tables. It also clears away any signal handlers that were set up and closes any files that are open. At the end of the flush, the process is ready for the new executable image. No matter what format the executable image is in, the same information gets set up in the process's `mm_struct`. There are pointers to the start and end of the image's code and data. These values are found as the ELF executable images physical headers are read, and the sections of the program that they describe are mapped into the process's virtual address space. That is also when the `vm_area_struct` data structures are set up and the process's page tables are modified. The `mm_struct` data structure also contains pointers to the parameters to be passed to the program and to this process's environment variables.

4.8.1.2 ELF Shared Libraries

A dynamically linked image, on the other hand, does not contain all of the code and data required to run. Some of it is held in shared libraries that are linked into the image at run time. The ELF shared library's tables are also used by the *dynamic linker* when the shared library is linked into the image at run time. Linux uses several dynamic linkers, `ld.so.1`, `libc.so.1`, and `ld-linux.so.1`, all to be found in `/lib`. The libraries contain commonly used code, such as language subroutines. Without dynamic linking, all programs would need their own copy of the these libraries and would need far more disk space and virtual memory. In dynamic linking, information is included in the ELF image's tables for every library routine referenced. The information indicates to the dynamic linker how to locate the library routine and link it into the program's address space.

4.8.2 Script Files

Script files are executables that need an interpreter to run them. There are a wide variety of interpreters available for Linux; for example, **wish**, **perl**, and command shells, such as **tcsh**. Linux uses the standard Unix convention of having the first line of a script file contain the name of the interpreter. So, a typical script file would start:

```
#!/usr/bin/wish
```

The script binary loader tries to find the interpreter for the script.

It does this by attempting to open the executable file that is named in the first line of the script. If it can open it, it has a pointer to its VFS inode and it can go ahead and have it interpret the script file. The name of the script file becomes argument zero (the first argument) and all of the other arguments move up one place (the original first argument becomes the new second argument and so on). Loading the interpreter is done in the same way as Linux loads all of its executable files. Linux tries each binary format in turn until one works. This means that you could in theory stack several interpreters and binary formats, making the Linux binary format handler a very flexible piece of software.

Chapter 5
Interprocess Communication Mechanisms

Processes communicate with each other and with the kernel to coordinate their activities. Linux supports a number of Interprocess Communication (IPC) mechanisms. Signals and pipes are two of them, but Linux also supports the System V IPC mechanisms named after the Unix release in which they first appeared.

5.1 Signals

Signals are one of the oldest interprocess communication methods used by Unix systems. They are used to signal asynchronous events to one or more processes. A signal could be generated by a keyboard interrupt or an error condition, such as the process attempting to access a nonexistent location in its virtual memory. Signals are also used by the shells to signal job control commands to their child processes.

There are a set of defined signals that the kernel can generate or that can be generated by other processes in the system, provided that they have the correct privileges. You can list a system's set of signals using the **kill** command (**kill -l**); on my Intel Linux box this gives:

```
 1) SIGHUP      2) SIGINT     3) SIGQUIT     4) SIGILL
 5) SIGTRAP     6) SIGIOT     7) SIGBUS      8) SIGFPE
 9) SIGKILL    10) SIGUSR1   11) SIGSEGV    12) SIGUSR2
13) SIGPIPE    14) SIGALRM   15) SIGTERM    17) SIGCHLD
18) SIGCONT    19) SIGSTOP   20) SIGTSTP    21) SIGTTIN
22) SIGTTOU    23) SIGURG    24) SIGXCPU    25) SIGXFSZ
26) SIGVTALRM  27) SIGPROF   28) SIGWINCH   29) SIGIO
30) SIGPWR
```

The numbers are different for an Alpha AXP Linux box. Processes can choose to ignore most of the signals that are generated, with two notable exceptions: Neither the SIGSTOP signal, which causes a process to halt its execution, nor the SIGKILL signal, which causes a process to exit, can be ignored. Otherwise, though, a process can choose just how it wants to handle the various signals. Processes can block the signals and, if they do not block them, they can either choose to handle them themselves or allow the kernel to handle them. If the kernel handles the signals, it will do the default actions required for this signal. For example, the default action when a process receives the SIGFPE (floating point exception) signal is to core dump and then exit. Signals have no inherent relative priorities. If two signals are generated for a process at the same time then they may be presented to the process or handled in any order. Also, there is no mechanism for handling multiple signals of the same kind. There is no way that a process can tell if it received 1 or 42 SIGCONT signals.

Linux implements signals using information stored in the task_struct for the process. The number of supported signals is limited to the word size of the processor. Processes with a word size of 32 bits can have 32 signals, whereas 64-bit processors like the Alpha AXP may have up to 64 signals. The currently pending signals are kept in the signal field with a mask of blocked signals held in blocked. With the exception of SIGSTOP and SIGKILL, all signals can be blocked. If a blocked signal is generated, it remains pending until it is unblocked. Linux also holds information about how each process handles every possible signal, and this is held in an array of sigaction data structures pointed at by the task_struct for each process. Among other things, it contains either the address of a routine that will handle the signal or a flag which tells Linux that the process either wishes to ignore this signal or let the kernel handle the signal for it. The process modifies the default signal handling by making system calls, and these calls alter the sigaction for the appropriate signal as well as the blocked mask.

Not every process in the system can send signals to every other process; the kernel can and super-users can. Normal processes can only send signals to processes with the same uid and gid or to processes in the same process group. Signals are generated by setting the appropriate bit in the task_struct's signal field. If the process has not blocked the signal and is waiting but interruptible (in state Interruptible), then it is woken up by changing its state to Running and making sure that it is in the run queue. That way, the scheduler will consider it a candidate for running when the system next schedules. If the default handling is needed, then Linux can optimize the handling of the signal. For example, if the signal SIGWINCH (the X window changed focus) and the default handler is being used, then there is nothing to be done.

Signals are not presented to the process immediately they are generated. They must wait until the process is running again. Every time a process exits from a system call, its signal and blocked fields are checked and, if there are any unblocked signals, they can now be delivered. This might seem a very unreliable method, but every process in the system is making system calls—for example, to write a character to the terminal—all of the time. Processes can elect to wait for signals if they wish; they are suspended in state Interruptible until a signal is presented. The Linux signal processing code looks at the `sigaction` structure for each of the current unblocked signals.

If a signal's handler is set to the default action, then the kernel will handle it. The `SIGSTOP` signal's default handler will change the current process's state to Stopped and then run the scheduler to select a new process to run. The default action for the `SIGFPE` signal will core dump the process and then cause it to exit. Alternatively, the process may have specified its own signal handler. This is a routine which will be called whenever the signal is generated, and the `sigaction` structure holds the address of this routine. The kernel must call the process's signal handling routine, and how this happens is processor-specific, but all CPUs must cope with the fact that the current process is running in kernel mode and is just about to return to the process that called the kernel or system routine in user mode. The problem is solved by manipulating the stack and registers of the process. The process's program counter is set to the address of its signal handling routine, and the parameters to the routine are added to the call frame or passed in registers. When the process resumes operation, it appears as if the signal handling routine was called normally.

Linux is POSIX-compatible, and so the process can specify which signals are blocked when a particular signal handling routine is called. This means changing the `blocked` mask during the call to the processes signal handler. The `blocked` mask must be returned to its original value when the signal handling routine has finished. Therefore, Linux adds a call to a tidy-up routine, which will restore the original `blocked` mask onto the call stack of the signaled process. Linux also optimizes the case where several signal handling routines need to be called by stacking them, so that each time one handling routine exits, the next one is called until the tidy-up routine is called.

5.2   Pipes

The common Linux shells all allow redirection. For example,

```
$ ls | pr | lpr
```

pipes the output from the **ls** command listing the directory's files into the standard input of the **pr** command, which paginates them. Finally the standard output from the **pr** command is piped into the standard input of the **lpr** command, which prints the results on the default printer. Pipes then are unidirectional byte streams which connect the standard output from one process into the standard input of another process. Neither process is aware of this redirection, and behaves just as it would normally. It is the shell that sets up these temporary pipes between the processes.

In Linux, a pipe is implemented using two `file` data structures which both point at the same temporary VFS inode which itself points at a physical page within memory. Figure 5.1 shows that each `file` data structure contains pointers to different file operation routine vectors: one for writing to the pipe, the other for reading from the pipe.

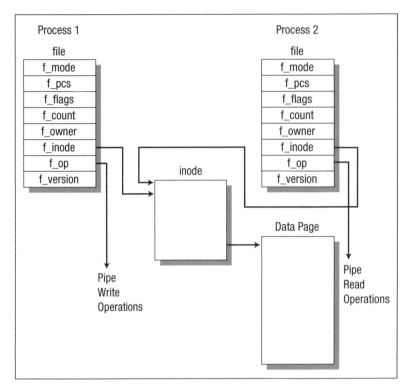

Figure 5.1
Pipes.

This hides the underlying differences from the generic system calls, which read and write to ordinary files. As the writing process writes to the pipe, bytes are copied into the shared data page, and when the reading process reads from the pipe, bytes are copied from the shared data page. Linux must synchronize access to the pipe. It must make sure that the reader and the writer of the pipe are in step, and to do this it uses locks, wait queues, and signals.

When the writer wants to write to the pipe, it uses the standard write library functions. These all pass file descriptors that are indices into the process's set of file data structures, each one representing an open file or, as in this case, an open pipe. The Linux system call uses the write routine pointed at by the file data structure describing this pipe. That write routine uses information held in the VFS inode representing the pipe to manage the write request.

If there is enough room to write all of the bytes into the pipe and, so long as the pipe is not locked by its reader, Linux locks it for the writer and copies the bytes to be written from the process's address space into the shared data page. If the pipe is locked by the reader or if there is not enough room for the data, then the current process is made to sleep on the pipe inode's wait queue and the scheduler is called so that another process can run. It is interruptible, so it can receive signals and it will be woken by the reader when there is enough room for the write data or when the pipe is unlocked. When the data has been written, the pipe's VFS inode is unlocked and any waiting readers sleeping on the inode's wait queue will themselves be woken up.

Reading data from the pipe is a very similar process to writing to it.

Processes are allowed to do nonblocking reads (it depends on the mode in which they opened the file or pipe) and, in this case, if there is no data to be read or if the pipe is locked, an error will be returned. This means that the process can continue to run. The alternative is to wait on the pipe inode's wait queue until the write process has finished. When both processes have finished with the pipe, the pipe inode is discarded along with the shared data page.

Linux also supports *named* pipes, also known as *FIFOs* because pipes operate on a First In, First Out principle. The first data written into the pipe is the first data read from the pipe. Unlike pipes, FIFOs are not temporary objects, they are entities in the file system and can be created using the **mkfifo** command. Processes are free to use a FIFO so long as they have appropriate access rights to it. The way that FIFOs are opened is a little different from pipes. A pipe (its two file data structures, its VFS inode and the shared data page) is created in one go, whereas a FIFO already exists and is opened and closed by its users. Linux must handle readers opening the FIFO before writers open it as well as readers reading before any writers have written to it. That aside, FIFOs are handled almost exactly the same way as pipes and they use the same data structures and operations.

5.3   Sockets

5.3.1   System V IPC Mechanisms

Linux supports three types of interprocess communication mechanisms that first appeared in Unix System V (1983). These are message queues, semaphores, and shared memory. These System V IPC mechanisms all share common authentication methods. Processes may access these resources only by passing a unique reference identifier to the kernel via system calls. Access to these System V IPC objects is checked using access permissions, much like accesses to files are checked. The access rights to the System V IPC object is set by the creator of the object via system calls. The object's reference identifier is used by each mechanism as an index into a table of resources. It is not a straightforward index, but requires some manipulation to generate the index.

All Linux data structures representing System V IPC objects in the system include an ipc_perm structure which contains the owner and creator process's user and group identifiers. The access mode for this object (owner, group, and other) and the IPC object's key. The key is used as a way of locating the System V IPC object's reference identifier. Two sets of keys are supported: public and private. If the key is public then any process in the system, subject to rights checking, can find the reference identifier for the System V IPC object. System V IPC objects can never be referenced with a key, only by their reference identifier.

5.3.2 Message Queues

Message queues (see Figure 5.2) allow one or more processes to write messages, which will be read by one or more reading processes. Linux maintains a list of message queues, the `msgque` vector; each element of which points to a `msqid_ds` data structure that fully describes the message queue. When message queues are created, a new `msqid_ds` data structure is allocated from system memory and inserted into the vector.

Each `msqid_ds` data structure contains an `ipc_perm` data structure and pointers to the messages entered onto this queue. In addition, Linux keeps queue modification times, such as the last time that this queue was written to and so on. The `msqid_ds` also contains two wait queues: one for the writers to the queue, and one for the readers of the message queue.

Each time a process attempts to write a message to the write queue, its effective user and group identifiers are compared with the mode in this queue's `ipc_perm` data structure. If the process can write to the queue, then the message may be copied from the process's address space into a `msg` data structure and put at the end of this message queue. Each message is tagged with an application-specific type, agreed on between the cooperating processes. However, there may be no room for the message, as Linux restricts the number and length of messages that can be written. In this case, the process will be added to this message queue's write wait queue, and the scheduler will be called to select a new process to run. It will be woken up when one or more messages have been read from this message queue.

Reading from the queue is a similar process. Again, the process's access rights to the write queue are checked. A reading process may choose to either get the first message in the queue regardless of its type, or select messages with particular types. If no messages match this criteria, the reading process will be added to the message queue's read wait queue and

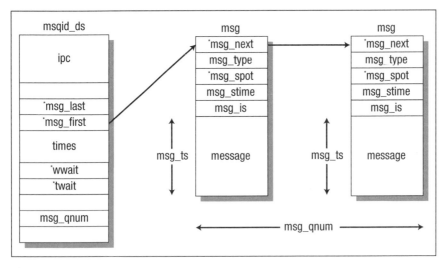

Figure 5.2
System V IPC message queues.

the scheduler run. When a new message is written to the queue this process will be woken up and run again.

5.3.3   Semaphores

In its simplest form, a *semaphore* is a location in memory whose value can be tested and set by more than one process. The test and set operation is, so far as each process is concerned, uninterruptible or atomic; once started, nothing can stop it. The result of the test and set operation is the addition of the current value of the semaphore and the set value, which can be positive or negative. Depending on the result of the test and set operation, one process may have to sleep until the semaphore's value is changed by another process. Semaphores can be used to implement *critical regions*, areas of critical code that only one process at a time should be executing (see Figure 5.3).

Say that you had many cooperating processes reading records from and writing records to a single data file. You would want that file access to be strictly coordinated. You could use a semaphore with an initial value of 1 and, around the file operating code, put two semaphore operations: the first to test and decrement the semaphore's value, and the second to test and increment it. The first process to access the file would try to decrement the semaphore's value and it would succeed, the semaphore's value now being 0. This process can now go

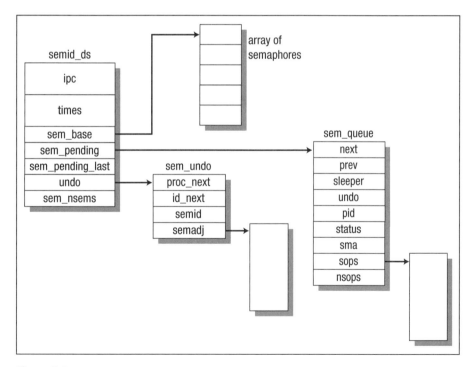

Figure 5.3
System V IPC semaphores.

ahead and use the data file, but if another process wishing to use it now tries to decrement the semaphore's value, it would fail as the result would be -1. That process will be suspended until the first process has finished with the data file. When the first process has finished with the data file, it will increment the semaphore's value, making it 1 again. Now the waiting process can be woken, and this time its attempt to increment the semaphore will succeed.

System V IPC semaphore objects each describe a semaphore array, and Linux uses the `semid_ds` data structure to represent this. All of the `semid_ds` data structures in the system are pointed at by the `semary`, a vector of pointers. There are `sem_nsems` in each semaphore array, each one described by a `sem` data structure pointed at by `sem_base`. All of the processes that are allowed to manipulate the semaphore array of a System V IPC semaphore object may make system calls that perform operations on them. The system call can specify many operations, and each operation is described by three inputs: the semaphore index, the operation value, and a set of flags. The *semaphore index* is an index into the semaphore array, and the *operation value* is a numerical value that will be added to the current value of the semaphore. First, Linux tests whether or not all of the operations would succeed. An operation will succeed if the operation value added to the semaphore's current value would be greater than zero, or if both the operation value and the semaphore's current value are zero. If any of the semaphore operations would fail, Linux may suspend the process—but only if the operation flags have not requested that the system call is nonblocking. If the process is to be suspended, then Linux must save the state of the semaphore operations to be performed and put the current process onto a wait queue. It does this by building a `sem_queue` data structure on the stack and filling it out. The new `sem_queue` data structure is put at the end of this semaphore object's wait queue (using the `sem_pending` and `sem_pending_last` pointers). The current process is put on the wait queue in the `sem_queue` data structure (`sleeper`) and the scheduler called to choose another process to run.

If all of the semaphore operations would have succeeded and the current process does not need to be suspended, Linux goes ahead and applies the operations to the appropriate members of the semaphore array. Now Linux must check that any waiting, suspended processes may now apply their semaphore operations. It looks at each member of the operations pending queue (`sem_pending`) in turn, testing to see if the semaphore operations will succeed this time. If they will, then it removes the `sem_queue` data structure from the operations pending list and applies the semaphore operations to the semaphore array. It wakes up the sleeping process, making it available to be restarted the next time the scheduler runs. Linux keeps looking through the pending list from the start until there is a pass where no semaphore operations can be applied, and so no more processes can be woken.

There is a problem with semaphores: *deadlocks*. These occur when one process has altered the semaphore's value as it enters a critical region, but then fails to leave the critical region because it crashed or was killed. Linux protects against this by maintaining lists of adjustments to the semaphore arrays. The idea is that when these adjustments are applied, the semaphores will be put back to the state that they were in before the process's set of semaphore operations were applied. These adjustments are kept in sem_undo data structures queued both on the semid_ds data structure and on the task_struct data structure for the processes using these semaphore arrays.

Each individual semaphore operation may request that an adjustment be maintained. Linux will maintain at most one sem_undo data structure per process for each semaphore array. If the requesting process does not have one, then one is created when it is needed. The new sem_undo data structure is queued both onto this process's task_struct data structure and onto the semaphore array's semid_ds data structure. As operations are applied to the semaphores in the semaphore array, the negation of the operation value is added to this semaphore's entry in the adjustment array of this process's sem_undo data structure. So, if the operation value is 2, then -2 is added to the adjustment entry for this semaphore.

When processes are deleted, as they exit Linux works through their set of sem_undo data structures, applying the adjustments to the semaphore arrays. If a semaphore set is deleted, the sem_undo data structures are left queued on the process's task_struct, but the semaphore array identifier is made invalid. In this case, the semaphore clean up code simply discards the sem_undo data structure.

5.3.4   Shared Memory

Shared memory allows one or more processes to communicate via memory that appears in all of their virtual address spaces (see Figure 5.4). The pages of the virtual memory is referenced by page table entries in each of the sharing processes' page tables. It does not have to be at the same address in all of the processes' virtual memory. As with all System V IPC objects, access to shared memory areas is controlled via keys and access rights checking. Once the memory is being shared, there are no checks on how the processes are using it. They must rely on other mechanisms, for example System V semaphores, to synchronize access to the memory.

Each newly created shared memory area is represented by a shmid_ds data structure. These are kept in the shm_segs vector.

The shmid_ds data structure describes how big the area of shared memory is, how many processes are using it, and information about how that shared memory is mapped into their address spaces. It is the creator of the shared memory that controls the access permissions to that memory and whether its key is public or private. If it has enough access rights, it may also lock the shared memory into physical memory.

Each process that wishes to share the memory must attach to that virtual memory via a system call. This creates a new vm_area_struct data structure describing the shared memory for this process. The process can choose where in its virtual address space the shared memory goes, or it can let Linux choose a free area large enough. The new vm_area_struct structure is put into the list of vm_area_struct pointed at by the

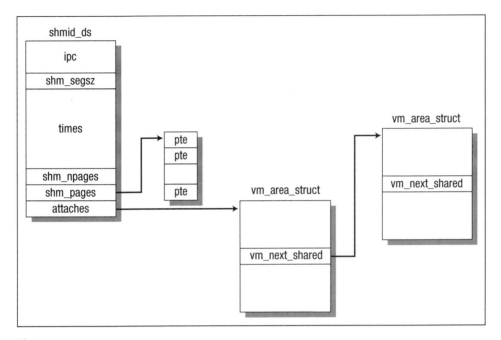

Figure 5.4
System V IPC shared memory.

`shmid_ds`. The `vm_next_shared` and `vm_prev_shared` pointers are used to link them together. The virtual memory is not actually created during the attach; it happens when the first process attempts to access it.

The first time that a process accesses one of the pages of the shared virtual memory, a page fault will occur. When Linux fixes up that page fault, it finds the `vm_area_struct` data structure describing it. This contains pointers to handler routines for this type of shared virtual memory. The shared memory page fault handling code looks in the list of page table entries for this `shmid_ds` to see if one exists for this page of the shared virtual memory. If it does not exist, it will allocate a physical page and create a page table entry for it. As well as going into the current process's page tables, this entry is saved in the `shmid_ds`. This means that when the next process that attempts to access this memory gets a page fault, the shared memory fault handling code will use this newly created physical page for that process, too. So, the first process that accesses a page of the shared memory causes it to be created, and thereafter access by the other processes cause that page to be added into their virtual address spaces.

When processes no longer wish to share the virtual memory, they detach from it. So long as other processes are still using the memory the detach only affects the current process. Its `vm_area_struct` is removed from the `shmid_ds` data structure and deallocated. The current process's page tables are updated to invalidate the area of virtual memory that it used to share. When the last process sharing the memory detaches from it, the pages of the shared memory current in physical memory are freed, as is the `shmid_ds` data structure for this shared memory.

Further complications arise when shared virtual memory is not locked into physical memory. In this case the pages of the shared memory may be swapped out to the system's swap disk during periods of high memory usage. How shared memory is swapped into and out of physical memory is described in Chapter 3.

Chapter 6
PCI

Peripheral Component Interconnect (PCI), as its name implies, is a standard that describes how to connect the peripheral components of a system together in a structured and controlled way. The standard describes the way that the system components are electrically connected and the way that they should behave. This chapter looks at how the Linux kernel initializes the system's PCI buses and devices.

Figure 6.1 is a logical diagram of an example PCI-based system. The PCI buses and PCI-PCI bridges are the glue connecting the system components together; the CPU is connected to PCI bus 0, the primary PCI bus, as is the video device. A special PCI device, a PCI-PCI bridge, connects the primary bus to the secondary PCI bus, PCI bus 1. In the jargon of the PCI specification, PCI bus 1 is described as being *downstream* of the PCI-PCI bridge and PCI bus 0 is *upstream* of the bridge. Connected to the secondary PCI bus are the SCSI and Ethernet devices for the system. Physically, the bridge, secondary PCI bus, and two devices would all be contained on the same combination PCI card. The PCI-ISA bridge in the system supports older, legacy ISA devices, and the diagram shows a super I/O controller chip, which controls the keyboard, mouse and floppy.

6.1   PCI Address Spaces

The CPU and the PCI devices need to access memory that is shared between them. This memory is used by device drivers to control the PCI devices and to pass information between them. Typically, the shared memory contains control and status registers

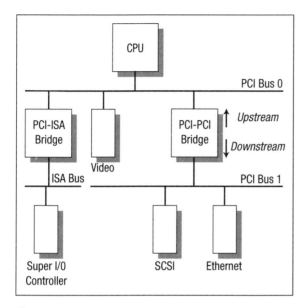

Figure 6.1
Example of PCI-based system.

for the device. These registers are used to control the device and to read its status. For example, the PCI SCSI device driver would read its status register to find out if the SCSI device was ready to write a block of information to the SCSI disk. Or it might write to the control register to start the device running after it has been turned on.

The CPU's system memory could be used for this shared memory, but if it were, then every time a PCI device accessed memory the CPU would have to stall, waiting for the PCI device to finish. Access to memory is generally limited to one system component at a time. This would slow the system down. It is also not a good idea to allow the system's peripheral devices to access main memory in an uncontrolled way. This would be very dangerous; a rogue device could make the system very unstable.

Peripheral devices have their own memory spaces. The CPU can access these spaces but access by the devices into the system's memory is very strictly controlled using DMA (direct memory access) channels. ISA devices have access to two address spaces: ISA I/O (input/output) and ISA memory. PCI has three: PCI I/O, PCI Memory, and PCI Configuration space. All of these address spaces are also accessible by the CPU with the PCI I/O and PCI Memory address spaces being used by the device drivers and the PCI Configuration space being used by the PCI initialization code within the Linux kernel.

The Alpha AXP processor does not have natural access to addresses spaces other than the system address space. It uses support chipsets to access other address spaces, such as PCI Configuration space. It uses a sparse address mapping scheme which steals part of the large virtual address space and maps it to the PCI address spaces.

6.2 PCI Configuration Headers

Every PCI device in the system, including the PCI-PCI bridges, has a configuration data structure that is somewhere in the PCI configuration address space. The PCI Configuration header allows the system to identify and control the device. Exactly where the header is in the PCI Configuration address space depends on where in the PCI topology that device is. For example, a PCI video card plugged into one PCI slot on the PC motherboard will have its configuration header at one location; and if it is plugged into another PCI slot, then its header will appear in another location in PCI Configuration memory. This does not matter, for wherever the PCI devices and bridges are, the system will find and configure them using the status and configuration registers in their configuration headers.

Typically, systems are designed so that every PCI slot has its PCI Configuration header in an offset that is related to its slot on the board. So, for example, the first slot on the board might have its PCI Configuration at offset 0 and the second slot at offset 256 (all headers are the same length, 256 bytes), and so on. A system-specific hardware mechanism is defined so that the PCI Configuration code can attempt to examine all possible PCI Configuration headers for a given PCI bus and know which devices are present and which devices are absent simply by trying to read one of the fields in the header (usually the *Vendor Identification* field) and getting some sort of error. The describes one possible error message as returning *0xFFFFFFFF* when attempting to read the *Vendor Identification* and *Device Identification* fields for an empty PCI slot.

Figure 6.2 shows the layout of the 256-byte PCI configuration header. It contains the following fields:

♦ Vendor Identification—A unique number describing the originator of the PCI device. Digital's PCI vendor identification is *0x1011* and Intel's is *0x8086*.

♦ Device Identification—A unique number describing the device itself. For example, Digital's 21141 fast Ethernet device has a device identification of *0x0009*.

♦ Status—This field gives the status of the device with the meaning of the bits of this field set by the standard.

♦ Command—By writing to this field the system controls the device, for example, allowing the device to access PCI I/O memory.

♦ Class Code—This identifies the type of device that this is. There are standard classes for every sort of device: video, SCSI, and so on. The class code for SCSI is *0x0100*.

♦ Base Address Register—These registers are used to determine and allocate the type, amount, and location of PCI I/O and PCI memory space that the device can use.

♦ Interrupt Pin—Four of the physical pins on the PCI card carry interrupts from the card to the PCI bus. The standard labels these as A, B, C, and D. The *Interrupt Pin* field describes which of these pins this PCI device uses. Generally, it is hardwired for a particular device. That is, every time the system boots, the device uses the same interrupt pin. This information allows the interrupt handling subsystem to manage interrupts from this device.

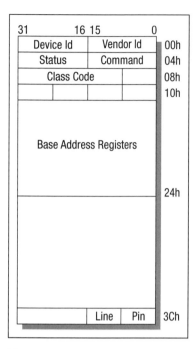

Figure 6.2
The PCI Configuration header.

♦ Interrupt Line—The *Interrupt Line* field of the device's PCI Configuration header is used to pass an interrupt handle between the PCI initialization code, the device's driver and Linux's interrupt handling subsystem. The number written there is meaningless to the device driver, but it allows the interrupt handler to correctly route an interrupt from the PCI device to the correct device driver's interrupt handling code within the Linux operating system. See Chapter 7 for details on how Linux handles interrupts.

6.3   PCI I/O And PCI Memory Addresses

These two address spaces are used by the devices to communicate with their device drivers running in the Linux kernel on the CPU. For example, the DECchip 21141 fast Ethernet device maps its internal registers into PCI I/O space. Its Linux device driver then reads and writes those registers to control the device. Video drivers typically use large amounts of PCI memory space to contain video information.

Until the PCI system has been set up and the device's access to these address spaces has been turned on using the *Command* field in the PCI Configuration header, nothing can access them. It should be noted that only the PCI Configuration code reads and writes PCI Configuration addresses; the Linux device drivers only read and write PCI I/O and PCI Memory addresses.

6.4   PCI-ISA Bridges

These bridges support legacy ISA devices by translating PCI I/O and PCI Memory space accesses into ISA I/O and ISA Memory accesses. A lot of systems now sold contain several ISA bus slots and several PCI bus slots. Over time, the need for this backward compatibility will dwindle and PCI only systems will be sold. Where in the ISA address spaces (I/O and Memory) the ISA devices of the system have their registers was fixed in the dim mists of time by the early Intel 8080-based PCs. Even a $5,000 Alpha AXP-based computer system will have its ISA floppy controller at the same place in ISA I/O space as the first IBM PC. The PCI specification copes with this by reserving the lower regions of the PCI I/O and PCI Memory address spaces for use by the ISA peripherals in the system and using a single PCI-ISA bridge to translate any PCI memory accesses to those regions into ISA accesses.

6.5   PCI-PCI Bridges

PCI-PCI bridges are special PCI devices that glue the PCI buses of the system together. Simple systems have a single PCI bus, but there is an electrical limit on the number of PCI devices that a single PCI bus can support. Using PCI-PCI bridges to add more PCI buses allows the system to support many more PCI devices. This is particularly important for a high-performance server. Of course, Linux fully supports the use of PCI-PCI bridges.

6.5.1   PCI-PCI Bridges: PCI I/O And PCI Memory Windows

PCI-PCI bridges only pass a subset of PCI I/O and PCI memory read and write requests downstream. For example, in Figure 6.1, the PCI-PCI bridge will only pass read and write addresses from PCI bus 0 to PCI bus 1 if they are for PCI I/O or PCI memory addresses owned by either the SCSI or Ethernet device; all other PCI I/O and memory addresses are ignored. This filtering stops addresses propagating needlessly throughout the system. To do this, the PCI-PCI bridges must be programmed with a base and limit for PCI I/O and PCI Memory space access that they have to pass from their primary bus onto their secondary bus. Once the PCI-PCI bridges in a system have been configured, then so long as the Linux device drivers only access PCI I/O and PCI Memory space via these windows, the PCI-PCI bridges are invisible. This is an important feature that makes life easier for Linux PCI device driver writers. However, it also makes PCI-PCI bridges somewhat tricky for Linux to configure, as we shall see later on.

6.5.2   PCI-PCI Bridges: PCI Configuration Cycles And PCI Bus Numbering

So that the CPU's PCI initialization code can address devices that are not on the main PCI bus, there has to be a mechanism that allows bridges to decide whether or not to pass configuration cycles from their primary interface to their secondary interface. A *cycle* is just an address as it appears on the PCI bus. The PCI specification defines two formats for the PCI Configuration addresses; Type 0 and Type 1; these are shown in Figure 6.3 and Figure 6.4, respectively. Type 0 PCI Configuration cycles do not contain a bus number and these are interpreted by all devices as being for PCI configuration addresses on this PCI bus. Bits 31:11 of the Type 0 configuration cycles are treated as the device select field. One way to design a system is to have each bit select a different device. In this case, bit 11 would select the PCI device in slot 0, bit 12 would select the PCI device in slot 1, and so on. Another way is to write the device's slot number directly into bits 31:11. Which mechanism is used in a system depends on the system's PCI memory controller.

Type 1 PCI Configuration cycles contain a PCI bus number, and this type of configuration cycle is ignored by all PCI devices except the PCI-PCI bridges. All of the PCI-PCI bridges seeing Type 1 configuration cycles may choose to pass them to the PCI buses downstream of themselves. Whether the PCI-PCI bridge ignores the Type 1 configuration cycle or passes it onto the downstream PCI bus depends on how the PCI-PCI bridge has been configured. Every PCI-PCI bridge has a primary bus interface number and a secondary bus interface number. The primary bus interface being the one nearest the CPU and the secondary bus interface being the one furthest away. Each PCI-PCI bridge also has a subordinate bus number, and this is the maximum bus number of all the PCI buses that are bridged beyond the secondary bus interface. Or to put it another way, the subordinate bus number is the highest numbered PCI bus downstream of the PCI-PCI bridge. When the PCI-PCI bridge sees a Type 1 PCI configuration cycle it does one of the following things:

♦ Ignore it, if the bus number specified is not in between the bridge's secondary bus number and subordinate bus number (inclusive).

♦ Convert it to a Type 0 configuration command, if the bus number specified matches the secondary bus number of the bridge.

♦ Pass it onto the secondary bus interface unchanged, if the bus number specified is greater than the secondary bus number and less than or equal to the subordinate bus number.

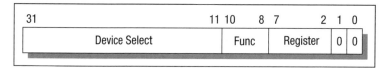

Figure 6.3
Type 0 PCI Configuration cycle.

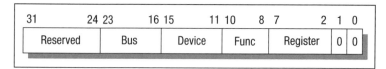

Figure 6.4
Type 1 PCI Configuration cycle.

So, if we want to address Device 1 on bus 3 of the topology (see Figure 6.9), we must generate a Type 1 Configuration command from the CPU. Bridge 1 passes this unchanged onto bus 1. Bridge 2 ignores it but bridge 3 converts it into a Type 0 Configuration command and sends it out on bus 3 where device 1 responds to it.

It is up to each individual operating system to allocate bus numbers during PCI configuration, but whatever the numbering scheme used the following statement must be true for all of the PCI-PCI bridges in the system.

Note

All PCI buses located behind a PCI-PCI bridge must reside between the secondary bus number and the subordinate bus number (inclusive).

If this rule is broken, then the PCI-PCI bridges will not pass and translate Type 1 PCI configuration cycles correctly and the system will fail to find and initialize the PCI devices in the system. To achieve this numbering scheme, Linux configures these special devices in a particular order. Section 6.6.2 describes Linux's PCI bridge and bus numbering scheme in detail, together with a worked example.

6.6   Linux PCI Initialization

The PCI initialization code in Linux is broken into three logical parts:

- ♦ PCI device driver—This pseudo-device driver searches the PCI system starting at bus 0 and locates all PCI devices and bridges in the system. It builds a linked list of data structures describing the topology of the system. Additionally, it numbers all of the bridges that it finds.

- ♦ PCI BIOS—This software layer provides the services described in bib-pci bios specification. Even though Alpha AXP does not have BIOS services, there is equivalent code in the Linux kernel providing the same functions.

- ♦ PCI fixup—System-specific fixup code tidies up the system specific loose ends of PCI initialization.

6.6.1   The Linux Kernel PCI Data Structures

As the Linux kernel initializes the PCI system, it builds data structures mirroring the real PCI topology of the system. Figure 6.5 shows the relationships of the data structures that it would build for the example PCI system in Figure 6.1.

Each PCI device (including the PCI-PCI bridges) is described by a `pci_dev` data structure. Each PCI bus is described by a `pci_bus` data structure. The result is a tree structure of PCI buses, each of which has a number of child PCI devices attached to it. As a PCI bus can only be reached using a PCI-PCI bridge (except the primary PCI bus, bus 0), each `pci_bus` contains a pointer to the PCI device (the PCI-PCI bridge) that it is accessed through. That PCI device is a child of the PCI bus's parent PCI bus.

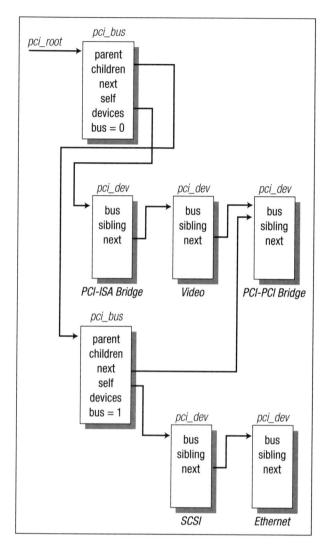

Figure 6.5
Linux kernel PCI data structures.

Not shown in Figure 6.5 is a pointer to all of the PCI devices in the system, `pci_devices`. All of the PCI devices in the system have their `pci_dev` data structures queued onto this queue. This queue is used by the Linux kernel to quickly find all of the PCI devices in the system.

6.6.2 The PCI Device Driver

The PCI device driver is not really a device driver at all, but a function of the operating system called at system initialization time. The PCI initialization code must scan all of the PCI buses in the system looking for all PCI devices in the system (including PCI-PCI bridge devices).

It uses the PCI BIOS code to find out if every possible slot in the current PCI bus that it is scanning is occupied. If the PCI slot is occupied, it builds a `pci_dev` data structure describing the device and links into the list of known PCI devices (pointed at by `pci_devices`).

The PCI initialization code starts by scanning PCI bus 0. It tries to read the *Vendor Identification* and *Device Identification* fields for every possible PCI device in every possible PCI slot. When it finds an occupied slot, it builds a `pci_dev` data structure describing the device. All of the `pci_dev` data structures built by the PCI initialization code (including all of the PCI-PCI bridges) are linked into a singly linked list; `pci_devices`.

If the PCI device that was found was a PCI-PCI bridge, then a `pci_bus` data structure is built and linked into the tree of `pci_bus` and `pci_dev` data structures pointed at by `pci_root`. The PCI initialization code can tell if the PCI device is a PCI-PCI bridge because it has a class code of *0x060400*. The Linux kernel then configures the PCI bus on the other (downstream) side of the PCI-PCI bridge that it has just found. If more PCI-PCI Bridges are found, then these are also configured. This process is known as a depthwise algorithm; the system's PCI topology is fully mapped depthwise before searching breadthwise. Looking at Figure 6.1, Linux would configure PCI bus 1 with its Ethernet and SCSI device before it configured the video device on PCI bus 0.

As Linux searches for downstream PCI buses, it must also configure the intervening PCI-PCI bridges' secondary and subordinate bus numbers. This is described in detail below.

6.6.2.2 *Configuring PCI-PCI Bridges: Assigning PCI Bus Numbers*

For PCI-PCI bridges to pass PCI I/O, PCI Memory, or PCI Configuration address space reads and writes across them, they need to know the following:

♦ Primary bus number—The bus number immediately upstream of the PCI-PCI bridge.

♦ Secondary bus number—The bus number immediately downstream of the PCI-PCI bridge.

♦ Subordinate bus number—The highest bus number of all of the buses that can be reached downstream of the bridge.

♦ PCI I/O and PCI Memory windows—The window base and size for PCI I/O address space and PCI Memory address space for all addresses downstream of the PCI-PCI bridge.

The problem is that at the time when you wish to configure any given PCI-PCI bridge, you do not know the subordinate bus number for that bridge. You do not know if there are further PCI-PCI bridges downstream—and if you did, you do not know what numbers will be assigned to them. The answer is to use a depthwise recursive algorithm and scan each bus for any PCI-PCI bridges assigning them numbers as they are found. As each PCI-PCI bridge is found and its secondary bus numbered, assign it a temporary subordinate number of *0xFF* and scan and assign numbers to all PCI-PCI bridges downstream of it. This all seems complicated, but the worked example below makes this process clearer.

1. PCI-PCI Bridge Numbering: Step 1

    Taking the topology in Figure 6.6, the first bridge the scan would find is bridge. The PCI bus downstream of bridge 1 would be numbered as 1 and bridge 1 assigned a secondary bus number of 1 and a temporary subordinate bus number of 0xFF. This means that all Type 1 PCI Configuration addresses specifying a PCI bus number of 1 or higher would be passed across bridge 1 and onto PCI bus 1. They would be translated into Type 0 Configuration cycles if they have a bus number of 1 but left untranslated for all other bus numbers. This is exactly what the Linux PCI initialization code needs to do in order to go and scan PCI bus 1.

2. PCI-PCI Bridge Numbering: Step 2

    Linux uses a depthwise algorithm, and so the initialization code goes on to scan PCI bus 1. Here it finds PCI-PCI bridge 2. There are no further PCI-PCI bridges beyond PCI-PCI bridge 2, so it is assigned a subordinate bus number of 2 which matches the number assigned to its secondary interface. Figure 6.7 shows how the buses and PCI-PCI bridges are numbered at this point.

    The PCI initialization code returns to scanning PCI bus 1 and finds another PCI-PCI bridge, bridge 3. It is assigned 1 as its primary bus interface number, 3 as its secondary bus interface number and *0xFF* as its subordinate bus number. Figure 6.8 shows how the system is configured now. Type 1 PCI configuration cycles with a bus number of 1, 2, or 3 will be correctly delivered to the appropriate PCI buses.

4. PCI-PCI Bridge Numbering: Step 4

    Linux starts scanning PCI Bus 3, downstream of PCI-PCI bridge 3. PCI bus 3 has another PCI-PCI bridge (bridge 4) on it, it is assigned 3 as its primary bus number and 4 as its secondary bus number. It is the last bridge on this branch, and so it is assigned a subordinate bus interface number of 4. The initialization code returns to PCI-PCI bridge 3 and assigns it a subordinate bus number of 4. Finally, the PCI initialization code can assign 4 as the subordinate bus number for PCI-PCI bridge 1. Figure 6.9 shows the final bus numbers.

6.6.3   PCI BIOS Functions

The PCI BIOS functions are a series of standard routines which are common across all platforms. For example, they are the same for both Intel- and Alpha AXP-based systems. They allow the CPU controlled access to all of the PCI address spaces.

Only Linux kernel code and device drivers may use them.

6.6.4   PCI Fixup

The PCI fixup code for Alpha AXP does rather more than that for Intel (which basically does nothing).

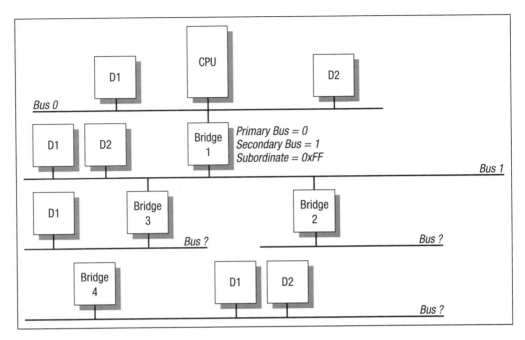

Figure 6.6
Configuring a PCI system: Part 1.

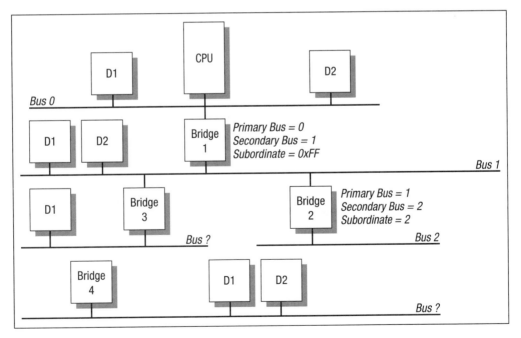

Figure 6.7
Configuring a PCI system: Part 2.

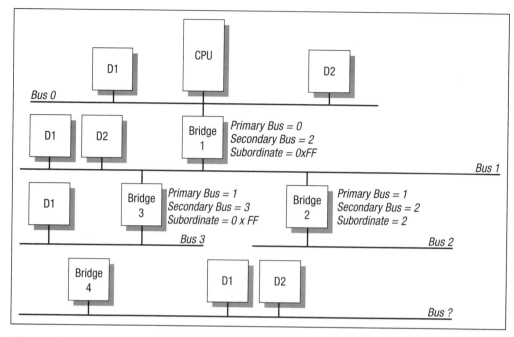

Figure 6.8
Configuring a PCI system: Part 3 (PCI-PCI bridge numbering: Step 3).

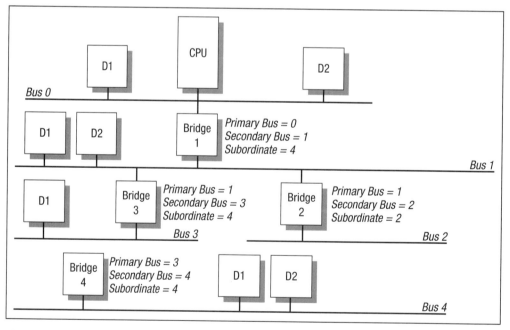

Figure 6.9
Configuring a PCI system: Part 4.

For Intel-based systems the system BIOS, which ran at boot time, has already fully configured the PCI system. This leaves Linux with little to do other than map that configuration. For non-Intel-based systems further configuration needs to happen to:

♦ Allocate PCI I/O and PCI Memory space to each device.

♦ Configure the PCI I/O and PCI Memory address windows for each PCI-PCI bridge in the system.

♦ Generate *Interrupt Line* values for the devices; these control interrupt handling for the device.

The next subsections describe how that code works.

6.6.4.2   *Finding Out How Much PCI I/O And PCI Memory Space A Device Needs*

Each PCI device found is queried to find out how much PCI I/O and PCI Memory address space it requires. To do this, each Base Address Register has all ones written to it and then read. The device will return zeros in the don't-care address bits, effectively specifying the address space required.

There are two basic types of Base Address Register; the first indicates within which address space the devices registers must reside: either PCI I/O or PCI Memory space. This is indicated by bit 0 of the register. Figure 6.10 shows the two forms of the Base Address Register for PCI Memory and for PCI I/O.

To find out just how much of each address space a given Base Address Register is requesting, you write all ones into the register and then read it back. The device will specify zeros in the don't-care address bits, effectively specifying the address space required. This design implies that all address spaces used are a power of two and are naturally aligned.

For example, when you initialize the DECChip 21142 PCI Fast Ethernet device, it tells you that it needs 0x100 bytes of space of either PCI I/O or PCI Memory. The initialization code allocates it space. The moment that it allocates space, the 21142's control and status registers can be seen at those addresses.

6.6.4.6   *Allocating PCI I/O And PCI Memory To PCI-PCI Bridges And Devices*

Like all memory the PCI I/O and PCI Memory spaces are finite, and to some extent scarce. The PCI fixup code for non-Intel systems (and the BIOS code for Intel systems) has to allocate each device the amount of memory that it is requesting in an efficient manner. Both PCI I/O and PCI Memory must be allocated to a device in a naturally aligned way. For example, if a device asks for 0xB0 of PCI I/O space, then it must be aligned on an address that is a multiple of 0xB0. In addition to this, the PCI I/O and PCI Memory bases for any given bridge must be aligned on 4K and on 1MB boundaries, respectively. Given that the address spaces for downstream devices must lie within all of the upstream PCI-PCI bridge's memory ranges for any given device, it is a somewhat difficult problem to allocate space efficiently.

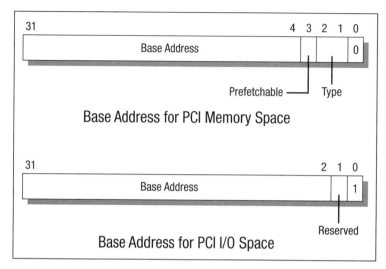

Figure 6.10
PCI configuration header: Base Address Registers.

The algorithm that Linux uses relies on each device described by the bus/device tree built by the PCI Device Driver being allocated address space in ascending PCI I/O memory order. Again, a recursive algorithm is used to walk the `pci_bus` and `pci_dev` data structures built by the PCI initialization code. Starting at the root PCI bus (pointed at by `pci_root`) the BIOS fixup code:

◆ Aligns the current global PCI I/O and Memory bases on 4K and 1MB boundaries respectively.

◆ For every device on the current bus (in ascending PCI I/O memory needs),

  ◆ allocates it space in PCI I/O and/or PCI Memory,

  ◆ moves on the global PCI I/O and Memory bases by the appropriate amounts, and

  ◆ enables the device's use of PCI I/O and PCI Memory.

◆ Allocates space recursively to all of the buses downstream of the current bus. Note that this will change the global PCI I/O and Memory bases.

◆ Aligns the current global PCI I/O and Memory bases on 4K and 1MB boundaries respectively, and in doing so figure out the size and base of PCI I/O and PCI Memory windows required by the current PCI-PCI bridge.

◆ Programs the PCI-PCI bridge that links to this bus with its PCI I/O and PCI Memory bases and limits.

◆ Turns on bridging of PCI I/O and PCI Memory accesses in the PCI-PCI bridge. This means that if any PCI I/O or PCI Memory addresses seen on the bridge's primary PCI bus that are within its PCI I/O and PCI Memory address, windows will be bridged onto its secondary PCI bus.

Taking the PCI system in Figure 6.1 as our example, the PCI fixup code would set up the system in the following way:

- Align the PCI bases—PCI I/O is *0x4000* and PCI Memory is *0x100000*. This allows the PCI-ISA bridges to translate all addresses below these into ISA address cycles.

- The video device—This is asking for *0x200000* of PCI Memory, and so we allocate it that amount starting at the current PCI Memory base of *0x200000* as it has to be naturally aligned to the size requested. The PCI Memory base is moved to *0x400000* and the PCI I/O base remains at *0x4000*.

- The PCI-PCI bridge—We now cross the PCI-PCI bridge and allocate PCI memory there, note that we do not need to align the bases as they are already correctly aligned.

- The Ethernet device—This is asking for *0xB0* bytes of both PCI I/O and PCI Memory space. It gets allocated PCI I/O at *0x4000* and PCI Memory at *0x400000*. The PCI Memory base is moved to *0x4000B0* and the PCI I/O base to *0x40B0*.

- The SCSI device—This is asking for *0x1000* PCI Memory, and so it is allocated it at *0x401000* after it has been naturally aligned. The PCI I/O base is still 0x40B0 and the PCI Memory base has been moved to *0x402000*.

- The PCI-PCI bridge's PCI I/O and Memory windows—We now return to the bridge and set its PCI I/O window at between *0x4000* and *0x40B0* and its PCI Memory window at between *0x400000* and *0x402000*. This means that the PCI-PCI bridge will ignore the PCI Memory accesses for the video device and pass them on if they are for the Ethernet or SCSI devices.

Chapter 7
Interrupts And Interrupt Handling

This chapter looks at how interrupts are handled by the Linux kernel. While the kernel has generic mechanisms and interfaces for handling interrupts, most of the interrupt handling details are architecture-specific.

Linux uses a lot of different pieces of hardware to perform many different tasks. The video device drives the monitor, the IDE device drives the disks, and so on. You could drive these devices synchronously; that is, you could send a request for some operation (say writing a block of memory out to disk) and then wait for the operation to complete. That method, although it would work, is very inefficient, and the operating system would spend a lot of time being "busy doing nothing" as it waited for each operation to complete. A better, more efficient way is to make the request and then do other, more useful work and later be interrupted by the device when it has finished the request. With this scheme, there may be many outstanding requests to the devices in the system all happening at the same time.

There has to be some hardware support for the devices to interrupt whatever the CPU is doing. Most, if not all, general purpose processors, such as the Alpha AXP, use a similar method. Some of the physical pins of the CPU are wired such that changing the voltage (for example, changing it from +5V to –5V) causes the CPU to stop what it is doing and to start executing special code to handle the interruption—the *interrupt handling code*. One of these pins might be connected to an interval timer and receive an interrupt every 1,000th of a second; others may be connected to the other devices in the system, such as the SCSI controller.

Systems often use an interrupt controller to group the device interrupts together before passing on the signal to a single interrupt pin on the CPU. This saves interrupt pins on the CPU and also gives flexibility when designing systems. The interrupt controller has mask and status registers that control the interrupts. Setting the bits in the mask register enables and disables interrupts and the status register returns the currently active interrupts in the system.

Some of the interrupts in the system may be hard-wired; for example, the realtime clock's interval timer may be permanently connected to pin 3 on the interrupt controller. However, what some of the pins are connected to may be determined by what controller card is plugged into a particular ISA or PCI slot. For example, pin 4 on the interrupt controller may be connected to PCI slot number 0 which might one day have an Ethernet card in it but the next have a SCSI controller in it. The bottom line is that each system has its own interrupt routing mechanisms and the operating system must be flexible enough to cope.

Most modern general-purpose microprocessors handle the interrupts the same way. When a hardware interrupt occurs, the CPU stops executing the instructions that it was executing and jumps to a location in memory that either contains the interrupt handling code or an instruction branching to the interrupt handling code. This code usually operates in a special mode for the CPU, *interrupt mode*, and, normally, no other interrupts can happen in this mode. There are exceptions though; some CPUs rank the interrupts in priority and higher-level interrupts may happen. This means that the first-level interrupt handling code must be very carefully written and it often has its own stack, which it uses to store the CPU's execution state (all of the CPU's normal registers and context) before it goes off and handles the interrupt. Some CPUs have a special set of registers that only exist in interrupt mode, and the interrupt code can use these registers to do most of the context saving it needs to do.

When the interrupt has been handled, the CPU's state is restored, and the interrupt is dismissed. The CPU will then continue to do whatever it was doing before being interrupted. It is important that the interrupt processing code is as efficient as possible and that the operating system does not block interrupts too often or for too long.

7.1   Programmable Interrupt Controllers

Systems designers are free to use whatever interrupt architecture they wish, but IBM PCs use the Intel 82C59A-2 CMOS Programmable Interrupt Controller or its derivatives. This controller has been around since the dawn of the PC and it is programmable with its registers being at well-known locations in the ISA address space. Even very modern support logic chip sets keep equivalent registers in the same place in ISA memory. Non-Intel-based systems, such as Alpha AXP-based PCs, are free from these architectural constraints and so often use different interrupt controllers.

Figure 7.1 shows that there are two 8-bit controllers chained together; each having a mask and an interrupt status register, PIC1 and PIC2. The mask registers are at addresses *0x21*

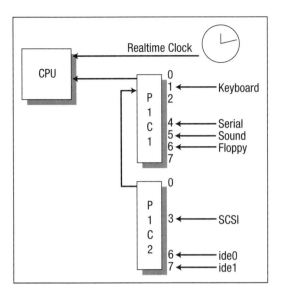

Figure 7.1
A logical diagram of interrupt routing.

and $0xA1$ and the status registers are at $0x20$ and $0xA0$. Writing a 1 to a particular bit of the mask register enables an interrupt; writing a 0 disables it. So, writing one to bit 3 would enable interrupt 3, writing zero would disable it. Unfortunately (and irritatingly), the interrupt mask registers are write-only; you cannot read back the value that you wrote. This means that Linux must keep a local copy of what it has set the mask registers to. It modifies these saved masks in the interrupt enable and disable routines, and writes the full masks to the registers every time.

When an interrupt is signaled, the interrupt handling code reads the two interrupt status registers (ISRs). It treats the ISR at $0x20$ as the bottom 8 bits of a 16-bit interrupt register and the ISR at $0xA0$ as the top 8 bits. So, an interrupt on bit 1 of the ISR at $0xA0$ would be treated as system interrupt 9. Bit 2 of PIC1 is not available as this is used to chain interrupts from PIC2; any interrupt on PIC2 results in bit 2 of PIC1 being set.

7.2   Initializing The Interrupt Handling Data Structures

The kernel's interrupt handling data structures are set up by the device drivers as they request control of the system's interrupts. To do this, the device driver uses a set of Linux kernel services that are used to request an interrupt, enable it, and disable it.

The individual device drivers call these routines to register their interrupt handling routine addresses.

Some interrupts are fixed by convention for the PC architecture, and so the driver simply requests its interrupt when it is initialized. This is what the floppy disk device driver does; it always requests IRQ 6. There may be occasions when a device driver does not know which interrupt the device will use. This is not a problem for PCI device drivers, as they always know what their interrupt number is. Unfortunately, there is no easy way for ISA device drivers to find their interrupt number. Linux solves this problem by allowing device drivers to probe for their interrupts.

First, the device driver does something to the device that causes it to interrupt. Then all of the unassigned interrupts in the system are enabled. This means that the device's pending interrupt will now be delivered via the programmable interrupt controller. Linux reads the interrupt status register and returns its contents to the device driver. A non-zero result means that one or more interrupts occurred during the probe. The driver now turns probing off and the unassigned interrupts are all disabled.

If the ISA device driver has successfully found its IRQ number, then it can now request control of it as normal.

PCI-based systems are much more dynamic than ISA-based systems. The interrupt pin that an ISA device uses is often set using jumpers on the hardware device and fixed in the device driver. On the other hand, PCI devices have their interrupts allocated by the PCI BIOS or the PCI subsystem as PCI is initialized when the system boots. Each PCI device may use one of four interrupt pins: A, B, C, or D. This was fixed when the device was built and most devices default to interrupt on pin A. The PCI interrupt lines A, B, C, and D for each PCI slot are routed to the interrupt controller. So, pin A from PCI slot 4 might be routed to pin 6 of the interrupt controller, pin B of PCI slot 4 to pin 7 of the interrupt controller, and so on.

How the PCI interrupts are routed is entirely system-specific, and there must be some setup code which understands this PCI interrupt routing topology. On Intel-based PCs, this is the system BIOS code that runs at boot time but for systems without BIOS (for example, Alpha AXP-based systems) the Linux kernel does this setup.

The PCI setup code writes the pin number of the interrupt controller into the PCI Configuration header for each device. It determines the interrupt pin (or IRQ), number using its knowledge of the PCI interrupt routing topology together with the device's PCI slot number and which PCI interrupt pin that it is using. The interrupt pin that a device uses is fixed and is kept in a field in the PCI configuration header for this device. It writes this information into the *interrupt line* field that is reserved for this purpose. When the device driver runs, it reads this information and uses it to request control of the interrupt from the Linux kernel.

There may be many PCI interrupt sources in the system, for example, when PCI-PCI bridges are used. The number of interrupt sources may exceed the number of pins on the system's programmable interrupt controllers. In this case, PCI devices may share interrupts, one pin on the interrupt controller taking interrupts from more than one PCI device. Linux supports this by allowing the first requestor of an interrupt source declare whether it may be shared. Sharing interrupts results in several `irqaction` data structures being pointed at by one entry in the `irq_action vector` vector. When a shared interrupt happens, Linux will call all of the interrupt handlers for that source. Any device driver that can share interrupts (which should be all PCI device drivers) must be prepared to have its interrupt handler called when there is no interrupt to be serviced.

7.3   Interrupt Handling

One of the principal tasks of Linux's interrupt handling subsystem is to route the interrupts to the right pieces of interrupt handling code. This code must understand the interrupt topology of the system. If, for example, the floppy controller interrupts on pin 6 (actually, the floppy controller is one of the fixed interrupts in a PC system as, by convention, the floppy controller is always wired to interrupt 6) of the interrupt controller, then it must recognize the interrupt as coming from the floppy and route it to the floppy device driver's interrupt handling code. Linux uses a set of pointers to data structures containing the addresses of the routines that handle the system's interrupts. These routines belong to the device drivers for the devices in the system and it is the responsibility of each device driver to request the interrupt that it wants when the driver is initialized. Figure 7.2 shows that `irq_action` is a vector of pointers to the `irqaction` data structure. Each `irqaction` data structure contains information about the handler for this interrupt, including the address of the interrupt handling routine. As the number of interrupts and how they are handled varies between architectures and, sometimes, between systems, the Linux interrupt handling code is architecture-specific. This means that the size of the `irq_action vector` vector varies depending on the number of interrupt sources that there are.

When the interrupt happens, Linux must first determine its source by reading the interrupt status register of the system's programmable interrupt controllers. It then translates that

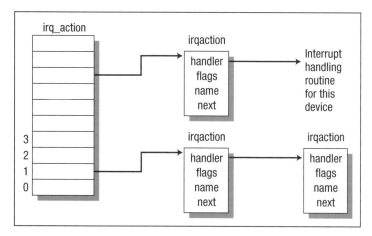

Figure 7.2
Linux interrupt handling data structures.

source into an offset into the `irq_action vector` vector. So, for example, an interrupt on pin 6 of the interrupt controller from the floppy controller would be translated into the seventh pointer in the vector of interrupt handlers. If there is not an interrupt handler for the interrupt that occurred then the Linux kernel will log an error, otherwise it will call into the interrupt handling routines for all of the `irqaction` data structures for this interrupt source.

When the device driver's interrupt handling routine is called by the Linux kernel, it must efficiently work out why it was interrupted and respond. To find the cause of the interrupt, the device driver would read the status register of the device that interrupted. The device may be reporting an error or that a requested operation has completed. For example, the floppy controller may be reporting that it has completed the positioning of the floppy's read head over the correct sector on the floppy disk. Once the reason for the interrupt has been determined, the device driver may need to do more work. If it does, the Linux kernel has mechanisms that allow it to postpone that work until later. This avoids the CPU spending too much time in interrupt mode. See Chapter 8 for more details.

Chapter 8
Device Drivers

O ne of the purposes of an operating system is to hide the peculiarities of the system's hardware devices from its users. For example, the Virtual File System presents a uniform view of the mounted file systems, irrespective of the underlying physical devices. This chapter describes how the Linux kernel manages the physical devices in the system.

The CPU is not the only intelligent device in the system; every physical device has its own hardware controller. The keyboard, mouse and serial ports are controlled by a SuperIO chip, the IDE disks by an IDE controller, SCSI disks by a SCSI controller, and so on. Each hardware controller has its own control and status registers (CSRs) and these differ between devices. The CSRs for an Adaptec 2940 SCSI controller are completely different from those of an NCR 810 SCSI controller. The CSRs are used to start and stop the device, to initialize it and to diagnose any problems with it. Instead of putting code to manage the hardware controllers in the system into every application, the code is kept in the Linux kernel. The software that handles or manages a hardware controller is known as a *device driver*. The Linux kernel device drivers are, essentially, a shared library of privileged, memory resident, low-level hardware handling routines. It is Linux's device drivers that handle the peculiarities of the devices they are managing.

One of the basic features of Linux is that it abstracts the handling of devices. All hardware devices look like regular files; they can be opened, closed, read and written using the same, standard, system calls that are used to manipulate files. Every device in the system is represented by a *device special file*, for example, the first IDE disk in the system is represented by /dev/hda. For block

101

(disk) and character devices, these device special files are created by the **mknod** command, and they describe the device using major and minor device numbers. Network devices are also represented by device special files, but they are created by Linux as it finds and initializes the network controllers in the system. All devices controlled by the same device driver have a common major device number. The minor device numbers are used to distinguish between different devices and their controllers, for example each partition on the primary IDE disk has a different minor device number. So, /dev/hda2, the second partition of the primary IDE disk, has a major number of 3 and a minor number of 2. Linux maps the device special file passed in system calls (say, to mount a file system on a block device) to the device's device driver using the major device number and a number of system tables, for example, the character device table, chrdevs.

Linux supports three types of hardware device: character, block, and network. *Character* devices are read and written directly without buffering; for example, the system's serial ports /dev/cua0 and /dev/cua1. *Block* devices can only be written to and read from in multiples of the block size, typically 512 or 1,024 bytes. Block devices are accessed via the buffer cache and may be randomly accessed, that is to say, any block can be read or written no matter where it is on the device. Block devices can be accessed via their device special file but more commonly they are accessed via the file system. Only a block device can support a mounted file system. *Network* devices are accessed via the BSD socket interface and the networking subsystems described in Chapter 10. There are many different device drivers in the Linux kernel (that is one of Linux's strengths), but they all share some common attributes:

♦ Kernel code—Device drivers are part of the kernel and, like other code within the kernel, if they go wrong they can seriously damage the system. A badly written driver may even crash the system, possibly corrupting file systems and losing data.

♦ Kernel interfaces—Device drivers must provide a standard interface to the Linux kernel or to the subsystem that they are part of. For example, the terminal driver provides a file I/O interface to the Linux kernel and a SCSI device driver provides a SCSI device interface to the SCSI subsystem which, in turn, provides both file I/O and buffer cache interfaces to the kernel.

♦ Kernel mechanisms and services—Device drivers make use of standard kernel services such as memory allocation, interrupt delivery and wait queues to operate.

♦ Loadable—Most of the Linux device drivers can be loaded on demand as kernel modules when they are needed and unloaded when they are no longer being used. This makes the kernel very adaptable and efficient with the system's resources.

♦ Configurable—Linux device drivers can be built into the kernel. Which devices are built is configurable when the kernel is compiled.

♦ Dynamic—As the system boots and each device driver is initialized, it looks for the hardware devices that it is controlling. It does not matter if the device being controlled by a particular device driver does not exist. In this case the device driver is simply redundant and causes no harm apart from occupying a little of the system's memory.

8.1   Polling And Interrupts

Each time the device is given a command, for example *"move the read head to sector 42 of the floppy disk,"* the device driver has a choice as to how it finds out that the command has completed. The device drivers can either poll the device or they can use interrupts.

Polling the device usually means reading its status register every so often until the device's status changes to indicate that it has completed the request. As a device driver is part of the kernel, it would be disastrous if a driver were to poll, as nothing else in the kernel would run until the device had completed the request. Instead polling device drivers use system timers to have the kernel call a routine within the device driver at some later time. This timer routine would check the status of the command and this is exactly how Linux's floppy driver works. Polling by means of timers is at best approximate; a much more efficient method is to use interrupts.

An interrupt-driven device driver is one where the hardware device being controlled will raise a hardware interrupt whenever it needs to be serviced. For example, an Ethernet device driver would interrupt whenever it receives an Ethernet packet from the network. The Linux kernel needs to be able to deliver the interrupt from the hardware device to the correct device driver. This is achieved by the device driver registering its usage of the interrupt with the kernel. It registers the address of an interrupt handling routine and the interrupt number that it wishes to own. You can see which interrupts are being used by the device drivers, as well as how many of each type of interrupts there have been, by looking at `/proc/interrupts`:

```
 0:    727432    timer
 1:     20534    keyboard
 2:         0    cascade
 3:     79691 +  serial
 4:     28258 +  serial
 5:         1    sound blaster
11:     20868 +  aic7xxx
13:         1    math error
14:       247 +  ide0
15:       170 +  ide1
```

This requesting of interrupt resources is done at driver initialization time. Some of the interrupts in the system are fixed; this is a legacy of the IBM PC's architecture. So, for example, the floppy disk controller always uses interrupt 6. Other interrupts, for example the interrupts from PCI devices, are dynamically allocated at boot time. In this case, the device driver must first discover the interrupt number (IRQ) of the device that it is controlling before it requests ownership of that interrupt. For PCI interrupts Linux supports standard PCI BIOS callbacks to determine information about the devices in the system, including their IRQ numbers.

How an interrupt is delivered to the CPU itself is architecture dependent, but on most architectures the interrupt is delivered in a special mode that stops other interrupts from happening in the system. A device driver should do as little as possible in its interrupt handling routine, so that the Linux kernel can dismiss the interrupt and return to what it was doing before it was interrupted. Device drivers that need to do a lot of work as a result of receiving an interrupt can use the kernel's bottom half handlers or task queues to queue routines to be called later on.

8.2 Direct Memory Access (DMA)

Using interrupt-driven device drivers to transfer data to or from hardware devices works well when the amount of data is reasonably low. For example, a 9,600-baud modem can transfer approximately one character every millisecond (1/1,000th second). If the interrupt latency—the amount of time that it takes between the hardware device raising the interrupt and the device driver's interrupt handling routine being called—is low (say two milliseconds), then the overall system impact of the data transfer is very low. The 9,600-baud modem data transfer would only take 0.002% of the CPU's processing time. For high-speed devices, such as hard disk controllers or Ethernet devices, the data transfer rate is a lot higher. A SCSI device can transfer up to 40MB of information per second.

Direct Memory Access, or DMA, was invented to solve this problem. A DMA controller allows devices to transfer data to or from the system's memory without the intervention of the processor. A PC's ISA DMA controller has eight DMA channels of which seven are available for use by the device drivers. Each DMA channel has associated with it a 16-bit address register and a 16-bit count register. To initiate a data transfer the device driver sets up the DMA channel's address and count registers together with the direction of the data transfer, read, or write. It then tells the device that it may start the DMA when it wishes. When the transfer is complete the device interrupts the PC. While the transfer is taking place, the CPU is free to do other things.

Device drivers have to be careful when using DMA. First of all, the DMA controller knows nothing of virtual memory; it only has access to the physical memory in the system. Therefore the memory that is being DMA'd to or from must be a contiguous block of physical memory. This means that you cannot DMA directly into the virtual address space of a process. You can, however, lock the process's physical pages into memory, preventing them from being swapped out to the swap device during a DMA operation. Secondly, the DMA controller cannot access the whole of physical memory. The DMA channel's address register represents the first 16 bits of the DMA address, the next 8 bits come from the page register. This means that DMA requests are limited to the bottom 16MB of memory.

DMA channels are scarce resources; there are only seven of them, and they cannot be shared between device drivers. Just like interrupts, the device driver must be able to work out which DMA channel it should use. Like interrupts, some devices have a fixed DMA channel. The floppy device, for example, always uses DMA channel 2. Sometimes the DMA channel for a device can be set by jumpers; a number of Ethernet devices use this technique. The more flexible devices can be told (via their CSRs) which DMA channels to use and, in this case, the device driver can simply pick a free DMA channel to use.

Linux tracks the usage of the DMA channels using a vector of `dma_chan` data structures (one per DMA channel). The `dma_chan` data structure contains just two fields: a pointer to a string describing the owner of the DMA channel, and a flag indicating if the DMA channel is allocated or not. It is this vector of `dma_chan` data structures that is printed when you `cat /proc/dma`.

8.3   Memory

Device drivers have to be careful when using memory. As they are part of the Linux kernel, they cannot use virtual memory. Each time a device driver runs, maybe as an interrupt is received or as a bottom half or task queue handler is scheduled, the `current` process may change. The device driver cannot rely on a particular process running, even if it is doing work on its behalf. Like the rest of the kernel, device drivers use data structures to keep track of the device that it is controlling. These data structures can be statically allocated, part of the device driver's code, but that would be wasteful as it makes the kernel larger than it need be. Most device drivers allocate kernel, nonpaged memory to hold their data.

Linux provides kernel memory allocation and deallocation routines, and it is these that the device drivers use. Kernel memory is allocated in chunks that are powers of 2. For example, 128 or 512 bytes, even if the device driver asks for less. The number of bytes that the device driver requests is rounded up to the next block size boundary. This makes kernel memory deallocation easier as the smaller free blocks can be recombined into bigger blocks.

It may be that Linux needs to do quite a lot of extra work when the kernel memory is requested. If the amount of free memory is low, physical pages may need to be discarded or written to the swap device. Normally, Linux would suspend the requestor, putting the process onto a wait queue until there is enough physical memory. Not all device drivers (or indeed Linux kernel code) may want this to happen and so the kernel memory allocation routines can be requested to fail if they cannot immediately allocate memory. If the device driver wishes to DMA to or from the allocated memory it can also specify that the memory is DMA'able. This way it is the Linux kernel that needs to understand what constitutes DMA'able memory for this system, and not the device driver.

8.4   Interfacing Device Drivers With The Kernel

The Linux kernel must be able to interact with device drivers in standard ways. Each class of device driver—character, block and network—provides common interfaces that the kernel uses when requesting services from them. These common interfaces mean that the kernel can treat often very different devices and their device drivers absolutely the same. For example, SCSI and IDE disks behave very differently, but the Linux kernel uses the same interface to both of them.

Linux is very dynamic; every time a Linux kernel boots, it may encounter different physical devices and thus need different device drivers. Linux allows you to include device drivers at kernel build time via its configuration scripts. When these drivers are initialized at boot time they may not discover any hardware to control. Other drivers can be loaded as kernel modules when they are needed. To cope with this dynamic nature of device drivers, device drivers register themselves with the kernel as they are initialized. Linux maintains tables of registered device drivers as part of its interfaces with them. These tables include pointers to routines and information that support the interface with that class of devices.

8.4.1   Character Devices

Character devices, the simplest of Linux's devices, are accessed as files; applications use standard system calls to open them, read from them, write to them, and close them, exactly as if the device were a file (see Figure 8.1). This is true even if the device is a modem being used by the PPP daemon to connect a Linux system onto a network. As a character device is initialized, its device driver registers itself with the Linux kernel by adding an entry into the `chrdevs` vector of `device_struct` data structures. The device's major device identifier (for example, 4 for the `tty` device) is used as an index into this vector. The major device identifier for a device is fixed.

Each entry in the `chrdevs` vector, a `device_struct` data structure contains two elements: a pointer to the name of the registered device driver, and a pointer to a block of file operations. This block of file operations is itself the addresses of routines within the device character device driver each of which handles specific file operations, such as open, read, write, and close. The contents of `/proc/devices` for character devices is taken from the `chrdevs` vector.

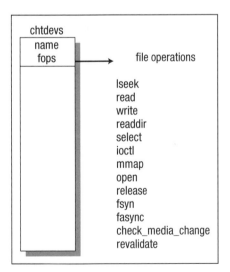

Figure 8.1
Character devices.

When a character special file representing a character device (for example /dev/cua0) is opened, the kernel must set things up so that the correct character device driver's file operation routines will be called. Just like an ordinary file or directory, each device special file is represented by a VFS inode. The VFS inode for a character special file, indeed for all device special files, contains both the major and minor identifiers for the device. This VFS inode was created by the underlying file system, for example EXT2, from information in the real filesystem when the device special file's name was looked up.

Each VFS inode has associated with it a set of file operations and these are different depending on the file system object that the inode represents. Whenever a VFS inode representing a character special file is created, its file operations are set to the default character device operations. This has only one file operation, the open file operation. When the character special file is opened by an application the generic open file operation uses the device's major identifier as an index into the chrdevs vector to retrieve the file operations block for this particular device. It also sets up the file data structure describing this character special file, making its file operations pointer point to those of the device driver. Thereafter, all of the applications file operations will be mapped to calls to the character devices set of file operations.

8.4.2   Block Devices

Block devices also support being accessed like files. The mechanisms used to provide the correct set of file operations for the opened block special file are very much the same as for character devices. Linux maintains the set of registered block devices as the blkdevs vector. It, like the chrdevs vector, is indexed using the device's major device number. Its entries are also device_struct data structures. Unlike character devices, there are classes of block devices. SCSI devices are one such class and IDE devices are another. It is the class that registers itself with the Linux kernel and provides file operations to the kernel. The device drivers for a class of block device provide class-specific interfaces to the class. So, for example, a SCSI device driver has to provide interfaces to the SCSI subsystem which the SCSI subsystem uses to provide file operations for this device to the kernel.

Every block device driver must provide an interface to the buffer cache as well as the normal file operations interface. Each block device driver fills in its entry in the blk_dev vector of blk_dev_struct data structures. The index into this vector is, again, the device's major number. The blk_dev_struct data structure consists of the address of a request routine and a pointer to a list of request data structures, each one representing a request from the buffer cache for the driver to read or write a block of data.

Each time the buffer cache wishes to read or write a block of data to or from a registered device, it adds a request data structure onto its blk_dev_struct. Figure 8.2 shows that each request has a pointer to one or more buffer_head data structures, each one a request to read or write a block of data. The buffer_head structures are locked (by the buffer cache) and there may be a process waiting on the block operation to this buffer to

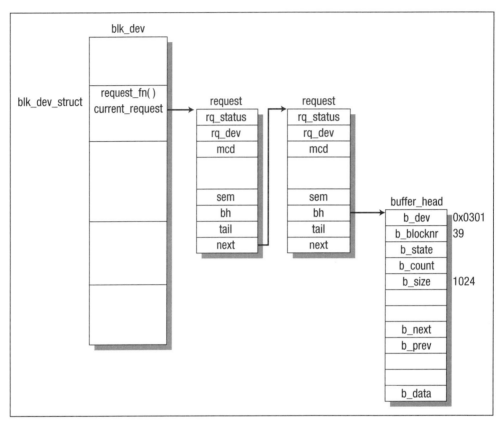

Figure 8.2
Buffer cache block device requests.

complete. Each `request` structure is allocated from a static list, the `all_requests` list. If the request is being added to an empty request list, the driver's request function is called to start processing the request queue. Otherwise, the driver will simply process every `request` on the request list.

Once the device driver has completed a request it must remove each of the `buffer_head` structures from the `request` structure, mark them as up to date, and unlock them. This unlocking of the `buffer_head` will wake up any process that has been sleeping waiting for the block operation to complete. An example of this would be where a file name is being resolved and the EXT2 file system must read the block of data that contains the next EXT2 directory entry from the block device that holds the file system. The process sleeps on the `buffer_head` that will contain the directory entry until the device driver wakes it up. The `request` data structure is marked as free so that it can be used in another block request.

8.5   Hard Disks

Disk drives provide a more permanent method for storing data, keeping it on spinning disk platters. To write data, a tiny head magnetizes minute particles on the platter's surface. The data is read by a head, which can detect whether a particular minute particle is magnetized.

A disk drive consists of one or more platters, each made of finely polished glass or ceramic composites and coated with a fine layer of iron oxide. The platters are attached to a central spindle and spin at a constant speed that can vary between 3,000 and 10,000 RPM depending on the model. Compare this to a floppy disk, which only spins at 360 RPM. The disk's read/ write heads are responsible for reading and writing data, and there is a pair for each platter, one head for each surface. The read/write heads do not physically touch the surface of the platters; instead they float on a very thin (10 millionths of an inch) cushion of air. The read/ write heads are moved across the surface of the platters by an actuator. All of the read/write heads are attached together; they all move across the surfaces of the platters together.

Each surface of the platter is divided into narrow, concentric circles called *tracks*. Track 0 is the outermost track and the highest numbered track is the track closest to the central spindle. A *cylinder* is the set of all tracks with the same number. So all of the fifth tracks from each side of every platter in the disk is known as cylinder 5. As the number of cylinders is the same as the number of tracks, you often see disk geometries described in terms of cylinders. Each track is divided into *sectors*. A sector is the smallest unit of data that can be written to or read from a hard disk and it is also the disk's block size. A common sector size is 512 bytes, and the sector size was set when the disk was formatted, usually when the disk is manufactured.

A disk is usually described by its geometry: the number of cylinders, heads and sectors. For example, at boot time Linux describes one of my IDE disks as:

```
hdb: Conner Peripherals 540MB - CFS540A, 516MB w/64kB Cache, CHS=1050/16/63
```

This means that it has 1,050 cylinders (tracks), 16 heads (8 platters), and 63 sectors per track. With a sector, or block, size of 512 bytes this gives the disk a storage capacity of 529,200 bytes. This does not match the disk's stated capacity of 516MB as some of the sectors are used for disk partitioning information. Some disks automatically find bad sectors and re-index the disk to work around them.

Hard disks can be further subdivided into partitions. A partition is a large group of sectors allocated for a particular purpose. Partitioning a disk allows the disk to be used by several operating system or for several purposes. A lot of Linux systems have a single disk with three partitions: one containing a DOS file system, another an EXT2 file system, and a third for the swap partition. The partitions of a hard disk are described by a partition table; each entry describing where the partition starts and ends in terms of heads, sectors, and cylinder numbers. For DOS-formatted disks, those formatted by **fdisk**, there are four primary disk partitions. Not all four entries in the partition table have to be used. There are three types of partition supported by **fdisk**, primary, extended, and logical. *Extended partitions* are not real partitions at all; they contain any number of logical partitions. Extended and *logical partitions* were invented as a way around the limit of four primary partitions. The following is the output from **fdisk** for a disk containing two primary partitions:

```
Disk /dev/sda: 64 heads, 32 sectors, 510 cylinders
Units = cylinders of 2048 * 512 bytes

    Device Boot    Begin    Start      End    Blocks   Id  System
/dev/sda1                 1        1      478    489456   83  Linux native
/dev/sda2               479      479      510     32768   82  Linux swap

Expert command (m for help): p

Disk /dev/sda: 64 heads, 32 sectors, 510 cylinders

Nr AF  Hd Sec  Cyl  Hd Sec  Cyl   Start      Size ID
 1 00   1   1    0  63  32  477      32    978912 83
 2 00   0   1  478  63  32  509  978944     65536 82
 3 00   0   0    0   0   0    0       0         0 00
 4 00   0   0    0   0   0    0       0         0 00
```

This shows that the first partition starts at cylinder or track 0, head 1, and sector 1 and extends to include cylinder 477, sector 32, and head 63. As there are 32 sectors in a track and 64 read/write heads, this partition is a whole number of cylinders in size. **fdisk** aligns partitions on cylinder boundaries by default. It starts at the outermost cylinder (0) and extends inward, toward the spindle, for 478 cylinders. The second partition, the swap partition, starts at the next cylinder (478) and extends to the innermost cylinder of the disk.

During initialization, Linux maps the topology of the hard disks in the system. It finds out how many hard disks there are and of what type. Additionally, Linux discovers how the individual disks have been partitioned. This is all represented by a list of gendisk data structures pointed at by the gendisk_head list pointer. As each disk subsystem, for example, IDE, is initialized, it generates gendisk data structures representing the disks that it finds. It does this at the same time as it registers its file operations and adds its entry into the blk_dev data structure. Each gendisk data structure has a unique major device number and these match the major numbers of the block special devices. For example, the SCSI disk subsystem creates a single gendisk entry ("sd") with a major number of 8, the major number of all SCSI disk devices. Figure 8.3 shows two gendisk entries, the first one for the SCSI disk subsystem and the second for an IDE disk controller. This is ide0, the primary IDE controller.

Although the disk subsystems build the gendisk entries during their initialization, they are only used by Linux during partition checking. Instead, each disk subsystem maintains its

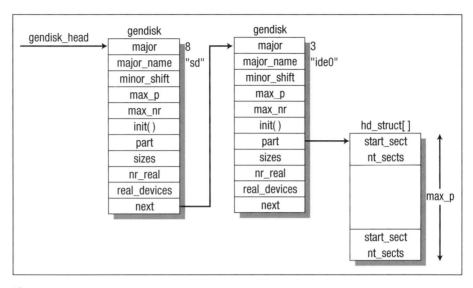

Figure 8.3
Linked list of disks.

own data structures which allow it to map device special major and minor device numbers to partitions within physical disks. Whenever a block device is read from or written to, either via the buffer cache or file operations, the kernel directs the operation to the appropriate device using the major device number found in its block special device file (for example, /dev/sda2). It is the individual device driver or subsystem that maps the minor device number to the real physical device.

8.5.1   IDE Disks

The most common disks used in Linux systems today are Integrated Disk Electronic or IDE disks. IDE is a disk interface, rather than an I/O bus like SCSI. Each IDE controller can support up to two disks, one the master disk and the other the slave disk. The master and slave functions are usually set by jumpers on the disk. The first IDE controller in the system is known as the primary IDE controller, the next the secondary controller and so on. IDE can manage about 3.3MB per second of data transfer to or from the disk and the maximum IDE disk size is 538MB. Extended IDE, or EIDE, has raised the disk size to a maximum of 8.6GB and the data transfer rate up to 16.6MB per second. IDE and EIDE disks are cheaper than SCSI disks and most modern PCs contain one or more onboard IDE controllers.

Note
Note from publisher: This data rate has of course been doubled twice more (to 33MB and 66MB respectively) and the biggest IDE disks are 20GB.

Linux names IDE disks in the order in which it finds their controllers. The master disk on the primary controller is /dev/hda and the slave disk is /dev/hdb. /dev/hdc is the master disk on the secondary IDE controller. The IDE subsystem registers IDE controllers and not disks with the Linux kernel. The major identifier for the primary IDE controller is 3 and is 22 for the secondary IDE controller. This means that if a system has two IDE controllers, there will be entries for the IDE subsystem at indices at 3 and 22 in the `blk_dev` and `blkdevs` vectors. The block special files for IDE disks reflect this numbering, disks `/dev/hda` and `/dev/hdb`, both connected to the primary IDE controller, have a major identifier of 3. Any file or buffer cache operations for the IDE subsystem operations on these block special files will be directed to the IDE subsystem as the kernel uses the major identifier as an index. When the request is made, it is up to the IDE subsystem to work out which IDE disk the request is for. To do this, the IDE subsystem uses the minor device number from the device special identifier, this contains information that allows it to direct the request to the correct partition of the correct disk. The device identifier for `/dev/hdb`, the slave IDE drive on the primary IDE controller is *(3,64)*. The device identifier for the first partition of that disk (`/dev/hdb1`) is *(3,65)*.

8.5.2   Initializing The IDE Subsystem

IDE disks have been around for much of the IBM PC's history. Throughout this time, the interface to these devices has changed. This makes the initialization of the IDE subsystem more complex than it might at first appear.

The maximum number of IDE controllers that Linux can support is four. Each controller is represented by an `ide_hwif_t` data structure in the `ide_hwifs` vector. Each `ide_hwif_t` data structure contains two `ide_drive_t` data structures, one per possible supported master and slave IDE drive. During the initializing of the IDE subsystem, Linux first looks to see if there is information about the disks present in the system's CMOS memory. This is battery-backed memory that does not lose its contents when the PC is powered off. This CMOS memory is actually in the system's realtime clock device which always runs no matter if your PC is on or off. The CMOS memory locations are set up by the system's BIOS and tell Linux what IDE controllers and drives have been found. Linux retrieves the found disk's geometry from BIOS and uses the information to set up the `ide_hwif_t` data structure for this drive. More modern PCs use PCI chipsets such as Intel's 82430 VX chipset which includes a PCI EIDE controller. The IDE subsystem uses PCI BIOS callbacks to locate the PCI (E)IDE controllers in the system. It then calls PCI specific interrogation routines for those chipsets that are present.

Once each IDE interface or controller has been discovered, its `ide_hwif_t` is set up to reflect the controllers and attached disks. During operation the IDE driver writes commands to IDE command registers that exist in the I/O Memory space. The default I/O address for the primary IDE controller's control and status registers is *0x1F0-0x1F7*. These addresses were set by convention in the early days of the IBM PC. The IDE driver registers each controller with the Linux block buffer cache and VFS, adding it to the `blk_dev` and `blkdevs` vectors respectively. The IDE drive will also request control of the appropriate interrupt. Again, these interrupts are set by convention to be 14 for the primary IDE controller and 15 for the secondary IDE controller. However, they like all IDE details, can be overridden by command line options to the kernel. The IDE driver also adds a `gendisk` entry into the list of `gendisk`'s discovered during boot for each IDE controller found. This list will later be used to discover the partition tables of all of the hard disks found at boot time. The partition checking code understands that IDE controllers may each control two IDE disks.

8.5.3   SCSI Disks

The SCSI (small computer system interface) bus is an efficient peer-to-peer data bus that supports up to eight devices per bus, including one or more hosts. Each device has to have a unique identifier and this is usually set by jumpers on the disks. Data can be transferred synchronously or asynchronously between any two devices on the bus, and with 32 bit wide data transfers up to 40MB per second are possible. The SCSI bus transfers both data and state information between devices, and a single transaction between an *initiator* and a *target* can involve up to eight distinct phases. You can tell the current phase of a SCSI bus from five signals from the bus. The eight phases are:

- BUS FREE—No device has control of the bus, and there are no transactions currently happening.
- ARBITRATION—A SCSI device has attempted to get control of the SCSI bus. It does this by asserting its SCSI identifier onto the address pins. The highest number SCSI identifier wins.
- SELECTION—When a device has succeeded in getting control of the SCSI bus through arbitration, it must now signal the target of this SCSI request that it wants to send a command to it. It does this by asserting the SCSI identifier of the target on the address pins.
- RESELECTION—SCSI devices may disconnect during the processing of a request. The target may then reselect the initiator. Not all SCSI devices support this phase.
- COMMAND—6,10, or 12 bytes of command can be transferred from the initiator to the target.
- DATA IN, DATA OUT—During these phases data is transferred between the initiator and the target.
- STATUS—This phase is entered after completion of all commands, and allows the target to send a status byte indicating success or failure to the initiator.
- MESSAGE IN, MESSAGE OUT—Additional information is transferred between the initiator and the target.

The Linux SCSI subsystem is made up of two basic elements, each of which is represented by data structures:

- Host—A SCSI host is a physical piece of hardware, a SCSI controller. The NCR810 PCI SCSI controller is an example of a SCSI host. If a Linux system has more than one SCSI controller of the same type, each instance will be represented by a separate SCSI host. This means that a SCSI device driver may control more than one instance of its controller. SCSI hosts are almost always the *initiator* of SCSI commands.

♦ Device—The most common set of SCSI device is a SCSI disk, but the SCSI standard supports several more types: tape, CD-ROM, and also a generic SCSI device. SCSI devices are almost always the *targets* of SCSI commands. These devices must be treated differently, for example, with removable media such as CD-ROMs or tapes, Linux needs to detect if the media was removed. The different disk types have different major device numbers, allowing Linux to direct block device requests to the appropriate SCSI type.

8.5.3.a   *Initializing The SCSI Subsystem*

Initializing the SCSI subsystem is quite complex, reflecting the dynamic nature of SCSI buses and their devices. Linux initializes the SCSI subsystem at boot time; it finds the SCSI controllers (known as SCSI hosts) in the system and then probes each of their SCSI buses finding all of their devices. It then initializes those devices and makes them available to the rest of the Linux kernel via the normal file and buffer cache block device operations. This initialization is done in four phases:

First, Linux finds out which of the SCSI host adapters, or controllers, that were built into the kernel at kernel build time have hardware to control. Each built in SCSI host has a `Scsi_Host_Template` entry in the `builtin_scsi_hosts` vector. The `Scsi_Host_Template` data structure contains pointers to routines that carry out SCSI host-specific actions, such as detecting what SCSI devices are attached to this SCSI host. These routines are called by the SCSI subsystem as it configures itself, and they are part of the SCSI device driver supporting this host type. Each detected SCSI host, those for which there are real SCSI devices attached, has its `Scsi_Host_Template` data structure added to the `scsi_hosts` list of active SCSI hosts. Each instance of a detected host type is represented by a `Scsi_Host` data structure held in the `scsi_hostlist` list. For example a system with two NCR810 PCI SCSI controllers would have two `Scsi_Host` entries in the list, one per controller. Each `Scsi_Host` points at the `Scsi_Host_Template` representing its device driver.

Now that every SCSI host has been discovered, the SCSI subsystem must find out what SCSI devices are attached to each host's bus. SCSI devices are numbered between 0 and 7 inclusively, each device's number or SCSI identifier being unique on the SCSI bus to which it is attached. SCSI identifiers are usually set by jumpers on the device. The SCSI initialization code finds each SCSI device on a SCSI bus by sending it a TEST_UNIT_READY command. When a device responds, its identification is read by sending it an ENQUIRY command. This gives Linux the vendor's name and the device's model and revision names. SCSI commands are represented by a `Scsi_Cmnd` data structure and these are passed to the device driver for this SCSI host by calling the device driver routines within its `Scsi_Host_Template` data structure. Every SCSI device that is found is represented by a `Scsi_Device` data structure, each of which points to its parent `Scsi_Host`. All of the `Scsi_Device` data structures are added to the `scsi_devices` list. Figure 8.4 shows how the main data structures relate to one another.

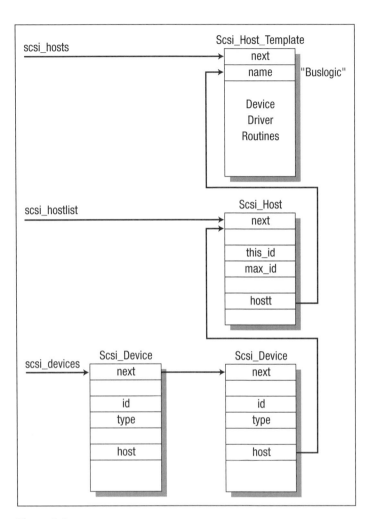

Figure 8.4
SCSI data structures.

There are four SCSI device types: disk, tape, CD, and generic. Each of these SCSI types are individually registered with the kernel as different major block device types. However, they will only register themselves if one or more of a given SCSI device type has been found. Each SCSI type, for example SCSI disk, maintains its own tables of devices. It uses these tables to direct kernel block operations (file or buffer cache) to the correct device driver or SCSI host. Each SCSI type is represented by a `Scsi_Device_Template` data structure. This contains information about this type of SCSI device and the addresses of routines to perform various tasks. The SCSI subsystem uses these templates to call the SCSI type routines for each type of SCSI device. In other words, if the SCSI subsystem wishes to attach a SCSI disk device, it will call the SCSI disk type attach routine. The `Scsi_Type_Template` data structures are added to the `scsi_devicelist` list if one or more SCSI devices of that type have been detected.

The final phase of the SCSI subsystem initialization is to call the finish functions for each registered Scsi_Device_Template. For the SCSI disk type this spins up all of the SCSI disks that were found and then records their disk geometry. It also adds the gendisk data structure representing all SCSI disks to the linked list of disks shown in Figure 8.3.

8.5.3.6 *Delivering Block Device Requests*

Once Linux has initialized the SCSI subsystem, the SCSI devices may be used. Each active SCSI device type registers itself with the kernel so that Linux can direct block device requests to it. There can be buffer cache requests via blk_dev or file operations via blkdevs. Taking a SCSI disk driver that has one or more EXT2 file system partitions as an example, how do kernel buffer requests get directed to the right SCSI disk when one of its EXT2 partitions is mounted?

Each request to read or write a block of data to or from a SCSI disk partition results in a new request structure being added to the SCSI disks current_request list in the blk_dev vector. If the request list is being processed, the buffer cache need not do anything else; otherwise it must nudge the SCSI disk subsystem to go and process its request queue. Each SCSI disk in the system is represented by a Scsi_Disk data structure. These are kept in the rscsi_disks vector that is indexed using part of the SCSI disk partition's minor device number. For exmaple, /dev/sdb1 has a major number of 8 and a minor number of 17; this generates an index of 1. Each Scsi_Disk data structure contains a pointer to the Scsi_Device data structure representing this device. That in turn points at the Scsi_Host data structure which "owns" it. The request data structures from the buffer cache are translated into Scsi_Cmd structures describing the SCSI command that needs to be sent to the SCSI device and this is queued onto the Scsi_Host structure representing this device. These will be processed by the individual SCSI device driver once the appropriate data blocks have been read or written.

8.6   Network Devices

A *network device* is, so far as Linux's network subsystem is concerned, an entity that sends and receives packets of data. This is normally a physical device, such as an Ethernet card. Some network devices, though, are software only, such as the loopback device which is used for sending data to yourself. Each network device is represented by a device data structure. Network device drivers register the devices that they control with Linux during network initialization at kernel boot time. The device data structure contains information about the device and the addresses of functions that allow the various supported network protocols to use the device's services. These functions are mostly concerned with transmitting data using the network device. The device uses standard networking support mechanisms to pass received data up to the appropriate protocol layer. All network data (packets) transmitted and received are represented by sk_buff data structures, these are flexible data structures that allow network protocol headers to be easily added and removed. How the network protocol layers use the network devices, and how they pass data back and forth using sk_buff data structures is described in detail in the Networks chapter. This chapter concentrates on the device data structure and on how network devices are discovered and initialized.

The device data structure contains information about the network device:

♦ Name—Unlike block and character devices which have their device special files created using the **mknod** command, network device special files appear spontaneously as the system's network devices are discovered and initialized. Their names are standard, each name representing the type of device that it is. Multiple devices of the same type are numbered upward from 0. Thus the Ethernet devices are known as /dev/eth0,/dev/eth1,/dev/eth2 and so on. Some common network devices are:

  ♦ /dev/ethN   Ethernet devices
  ♦ /dev/slN   SLIP devices
  ♦ /dev/pppN   PPP devices
  ♦ /dev/lo   Loopback devices

♦ Bus information—This is information that the device driver needs in order to control the device. The IRQ number is the interrupt that this device is using. The *base address* is the address of any of the device's control and status registers in I/O memory. The *DMA channel* is the DMA channel number that this network device is using. All of this information is set at boot time as the device is initialized.

♦ Interface flags—These describe the characteristics and abilities of the network device:

IFF_UP	Interface is up and running
IFF_BROADCAST	Broadcast address in device is valid
IFF_DEBUG	Device debugging turned on
IFF_LOOPBACK	This is a loopback device
IFF_POINTTOPOINT	This is point-to-point link (SLIP and PPP)
IFF_NOTRAILERS	No network trailers
IFF_RUNNING	Resources allocated
IFF_NOARP	Does not support ARP protocol
IFF_PROMISC	Device in promiscuous receive mode, it will receive all packets no matter whom they are addressed to
IFF_ALLMULTI	Receive all IP multicast frames
IFF_MULTICAST	Can receive IP multicast frames

♦ Protocol information—Each device describes how it may be used by the network protocol layers:

♦ mtu—The size of the largest packet that this network can transmit, not including any link layer headers that it needs to add. This maximum is used by the protocol layers, for example, IP, to select suitable packet sizes to send.

♦ Family—The family indicates the protocol family that the device can support. The family for all Linux network devices is AF_INET, the Internet address family.

- Type—The hardware interface type describes the media that this network device is attached to. There are many different types of media that Linux network devices support. These include Ethernet, X.25, token ring, SLIP, PPP, and Apple Localtalk.

- Addresses—The `device` data structure holds a number of addresses that are relevant to this network device, including its IP addresses.

- Packet queue—This is the queue of `sk_buff` packets queued waiting to be transmitted on this network device.

- Support functions—Each device provides a standard set of routines that protocol layers call as part of their interface to this device's link layer. These include setup and frame transmit routines, as well as routines to add standard frame headers and collect statistics. These statistics can be seen using the **ifconfig** command.

8.6.1   Initializing Network Devices

Network device drivers can, like other Linux device drivers, be built into the Linux kernel. Each potential network device is represented by a `device` data structure within the network device list pointed at by `dev_base` list pointer. The network layers call one of a number of network device service routines whose addresses are held in the `device` data structure if they need device specific work performing. Initially though, each `device` data structure holds only the address of an initialization or probe routine.

There are two problems to be solved for network device drivers. First, not all of the network device drivers built into the Linux kernel will have devices to control. Second, the Ethernet devices in the system are always called `/dev/eth0`, `/dev/eth1` and so on, no matter what their underlying device drivers are. The problem of "missing" network devices is easily solved. As the initialization routine for each network device is called, it returns a status indicating whether or not it located an instance of the controller that it is driving. If the driver could not find any devices, its entry in the `device` list pointed at by `dev_base` is removed. If the driver could find a device, it fills out the rest of the `device` data structure with information about the device and the addresses of the support functions within the network device driver.

The second problem, that of dynamically assigning Ethernet devices to the standard `/dev/ethN` device special files, is solved more elegantly. There are eight standard entries in the devices list; one for `eth0`, `eth1`, and so on to `eth7`. The initialization routine is the same for all of them, it tries each Ethernet device driver built into the kernel in turn until one finds a device. When the driver finds its Ethernet device it fills out the `ethN device` data structure, which it now owns. It is also at this time that the network device driver initializes the physical hardware that it is controlling and works out which IRQ it is using, which DMA channel (if any), and so on. A driver may find several instances of the network device that it is controlling and, in this case, it will take over several of the `/dev/ethN` `device` data structures. Once all eight standard `/dev/ethN` have been allocated, no more Ethernet devices will be probed for.

Chapter 9
The File System

This chapter describes how the Linux kernel maintains the files in the file systems that it supports. It describes the Virtual File System (VFS), and explains how the Linux kernel's real file systems are supported.

One of the most important features of Linux is its support for many different file systems. This makes it very flexible and well able to coexist with many other operating systems. At the time of writing, Linux supports 15 file systems: ext, ext2, xia, minix, umsdos, msdos, vfat, proc, smb, ncp, iso9660, sysv, hpfs, affs and ufs; and, no doubt, over time more will be added

Note
Note from publisher: For example, NTFS is now available read-only.

In Linux, as it is for Unix, the separate file systems the system may use are not accessed by device identifiers (such as a drive number or a drive name), but instead they are combined into a single hierarchical tree structure that represents the file system as one whole single entity. Linux adds each new file system into this single file system tree as it is mounted. All file systems, of whatever type, are mounted onto a directory and the files of the mounted file system cover up the existing contents of that directory. This directory is known as the *mount directory* or *mount point*. When the file system is unmounted, the mount directory's own files are once again revealed.

When disks are initialized (using **fdisk**, say) they have a partition structure imposed on them that divides the physical disk into a number of logical partitions. Each partition may hold a single file system, for example, an EXT2 file system. File systems organize files into logical hierarchical structures with directories, soft links, and so on held in blocks on physical devices. Devices that can contain file systems are known as block devices. The IDE disk partition `/dev/hda1`, the first partition of the first IDE disk drive in the system, is a block device. The Linux file systems regard these block devices as simply linear collections of blocks; they do not know or care about the underlying physical disk's geometry. It is the task of each block device driver to map a request to read a particular block of its device into terms meaningful to its device; the particular track, sector, and cylinder of its hard disk where the block is kept. A file system has to look, feel, and operate in the same way, no matter what device is holding it. Moreover, using Linux's file systems, it does not matter (at least to the system user) that these different file systems are on different physical media controlled by different hardware controllers. The file system might not even be on the local system, it could just as well be a disk remotely mounted over a network link. Consider the following example where a Linux system has its root file system on a SCSI disk:

A	E	boot	etc	lib	opt	tmp	usr
C	F	cdrom	fd	proc	root	var	sbin
D	bin	dev	home	mnt	lost+found		

Neither the users nor the programs that operate on the files themselves need know that /C is in fact a mounted VFAT file system that is on the first IDE disk in the system. In the example (which is actually my home Linux system), /E is the master IDE disk on the second IDE controller. It does not matter either that the first IDE controller is a PCI controller and that the second is an ISA controller which also controls the IDE CDROM. I can dial into the network where I work using a modem and the PPP network protocol using a modem and in this case I can remotely mount my Alpha AXP Linux system's file systems on `/mnt/remote`.

The files in a file system are collections of data; the file holding the sources to this chapter is an ASCII file called `file systems.tex`. A file system not only holds the data that is contained within the files of the file system but also the structure of the file system. It holds all of the information that Linux users and processes see as files, directories soft links, file protection information, and so on. Moreover, it must hold that information safely and securely; the basic integrity of the operating system depends on its file systems. Nobody would use an operating system that randomly lost data and files. (Well, not knowingly, although I have been bitten by operating systems with more lawyers than Linux has developers.)

Minix, the first file system that Linux had, is rather restrictive and lacking in performance. Its filenames cannot be longer than 14 characters (which is still better than 8.3 file names) and the maximum file size is 64MB. 64MB might, at first glance, seem large enough, but large file sizes are necessary to hold even modest databases. The first file system designed specifically for Linux, the Extended File system, or EXT, was introduced in April 1992 and cured a lot of the problems, but it was still felt to lack performance.

So, in 1993, the Second Extended File system, or EXT2, was added.

It is this file system that is described in detail, later on in this chapter.

An important development took place when the EXT file system was added into Linux. The real file systems were separated from the operating system and system services by an interface layer known as the *Virtual File System*, or *VFS*.

VFS allows Linux to support many, often very different file systems, each presenting a common software interface to the VFS. All of the details of the Linux file systems are translated by software, so that all file systems appear identical to the rest of the Linux kernel and to programs running in the system. Linux's VFS layer allows you to transparently mount the many different file systems at the same time.

The Linux VFS is implemented so that access to its files is as fast and efficient as possible. It must also make sure that the files and their data are kept correctly. These two requirements can be at odds with each other. The Linux VFS caches information in memory from each file system as it is mounted and used. A lot of care must be taken to update the file system correctly as data within these caches is modified as files and directories are created, written to, and deleted. If you could see the file system's data structures within the running kernel, you would be able to see data blocks being read and written by the file system. Data structures, describing the files and directories being accessed, would be created and destroyed—and all the time the device drivers would be working away, fetching and saving data. The most important of these caches is the *buffer cache*, which is integrated into the way that the individual file systems access their underlying block devices. As blocks are accessed, they are put into the buffer cache and kept on various queues depending on their states. The buffer cache not only caches data buffers, it also helps manage the asynchronous interface with the block device drivers.

9.1   The Second Extended File System (EXT2)

The Second Extended File System was devised (by Rémy Card) as an extensible and powerful file system for Linux. It is also the most successful file system so far in the Linux community and is the basis for all of the currently shipping Linux distributions.

The EXT2 file system, like a lot of the file systems, is built on the premise that the data held in files is kept in data blocks. These data blocks are all of the same length and, although that length can vary between different EXT2 file systems, the block size of a particular EXT2 file system is set when it is created (using **mke2fs**). Every file's size is rounded up to an integral number of blocks. If the block size is 1,024 bytes, then a file of 1,025 bytes will occupy two 1,024-byte blocks. Unfortunately, this means that on average you waste half a block per file. Usually, in computing, you trade off CPU usage for memory and disk space utilization. In this case, Linux, along with most operating systems, trades off a relatively inefficient disk usage in order to reduce the workload on the CPU. Not all of the blocks in the file system hold data; some must be used to contain the information that describes the structure of the file system. EXT2 defines the file system topology by describing each file in the system with an inode data structure. An *inode* describes which blocks the data within a file occupies, as well as the access rights of the file, the file's modification times, and the type of the file. Every file in the EXT2 file system is described by a single inode and each inode has a single unique number identifying it. The inodes for the file system are all kept together in inode tables. EXT2 directories are simply special files (themselves described by inodes) which contain pointers to the inodes of their directory entries.

Figure 9.1 shows the layout of the EXT2 file system as occupying a series of blocks in a block structured device. So far as each file system is concerned, block devices are just a series of blocks that can be read and written. A file system does not need to concern itself with where on the physical media a block should be put; that is the job of the device's driver. Whenever a file system needs to read information or data from the block device containing it, it requests that its supporting device driver reads an integral number of blocks. The EXT2 file system divides the logical partition that it occupies into Block Groups.

Each group duplicates information critical to the integrity of the file system, as well as holding real files and directories as blocks of information and data. This duplication is necessary should a disaster occur and the file system need recovering. The subsections describe in more detail the contents of each Block Group.

9.1.1   The EXT2 Inode

In the EXT2 file system, the inode is the basic building block; every file and directory in the file system is described by one and only one inode. The EXT2 inodes for each Block Group are kept in the inode table together with a bitmap that allows the system to keep track of allocated and unallocated inodes. Figure 9.2 shows the format of an EXT2 inode; among other information, it contains the following fields:

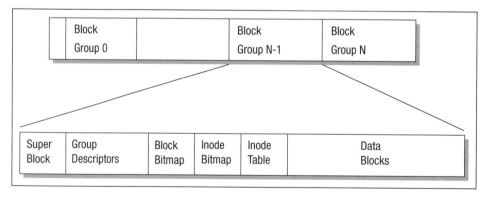

Figure 9.1
Physical layout of the EXT2 file system.

- Mode—This holds two pieces of information: what this inode describes, and the permissions that users have to it. For EXT2, an inode can describe one of file, directory, symbolic link, block device, character device, or FIFO.

- Owner information—The user and group identifiers of the owners of this file or directory. This allows the file system to correctly allow the right sort of accesses.

- Size—The size of the file in bytes.

- Timestamps—The time that the inode was created, and the last time that it was modified.

- Datablocks—Pointers to the blocks that contain the data that this inode is describing. The first 12 are pointers to the physical blocks containing the data described by this inode, and the last 3 pointers contain more and more levels of indirection. For example, the double indirect blocks pointer points at a block of pointers to blocks of pointers to data blocks. This means that files less than or equal to 12 data blocks in length are more quickly accessed than larger files.

You should note that EXT2 inodes can describe special device files. These are not real files, but handles that programs can use to access devices. All of the device files in /dev are there to allow programs to access Linux's devices. For example, the **mount** program takes as an argument the device file that it wishes to mount.

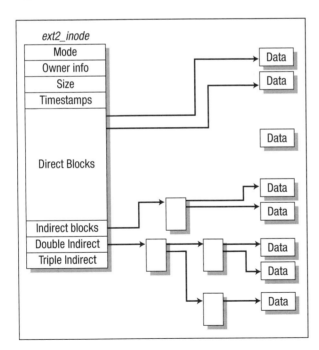

Figure 9.2
EXT2 inode.

9.1.2 The EXT2 Superblock

The Superblock contains a description of the basic size and shape of this file system. The information within it allows the file system manager to use and maintain the file system. Usually, only the Superblock in Block Group 0 is read when the file system is mounted, but each Block Group contains a duplicate copy in case of file system corruption. Among other information it holds the:

♦ Magic number—This allows the mounting software to check that this is indeed the Superblock for an EXT2 file system. For the current version of EXT2 this is *0xEF53*.

♦ Revision level—The major and minor revision levels allow the mounting code to determine whether or not this file system supports features that are only available in particular revisions of the file system. There are also feature compatibility fields which help the mounting code to determine which new features can safely be used on this file system.

♦ Mount count and maximum mount count—Together, these allow the system to determine if the file system should be fully checked. The mount count is incremented each time the file system is mounted; and when it equals the maximum mount count, the warning message "maximal mount count reached, running e2fsck is recommended" is displayed.

♦ Block Group number—The Block Group number that holds this copy of the Superblock.

♦ Block size—The size of the block for this file system in bytes, for example, 1,024 bytes.

♦ Blocks per group—The number of blocks in a group. Like the block size, this is fixed when the file system is created.

♦ Free inodes—The number of free inodes in the file system.

♦ First inode—This is the inode number of the first inode in the file system. The first inode in an EXT2 root file system would be the directory entry for the / directory.

9.1.3 The EXT2 Group Descriptor

Each Block Group has a data structure describing it. Like the Superblock, all the group descriptors for all of the Block Groups are duplicated in each Block Group in case of file system corruption.

Each Group Descriptor contains the following information:

♦ Blocks bitmap—The block number of the block allocation bitmap for this Block Group. This is used during block allocation and deallocation.

♦ Inode bitmap—The block number of the inode allocation bitmap for this Block Group. This is used during inode allocation and deallocation.

♦ Inode table—The block number of the starting block for the inode table for this Block Group. Each inode is represented by the EXT2 inode data structure, described below.

♦ Free blocks count, Free inodes count, Used directory count—The group descriptors are placed one after another, and together they make the group descriptor table. Each Block

Group contains the entire table of group descriptors after its copy of the Superblock. Only the first copy (in Block Group 0) is actually used by the EXT2 file system. The other copies are there, like the copies of the Superblock, in case the main copy is corrupted.

9.1.4   EXT2 Directories

In the EXT2 file system, directories are special files that are used to create and hold access paths to the files in the file system. Figure 9.3 shows the layout of a directory entry in memory.

A directory file is a list of directory entries, each one containing the following information:

♦ inode—The inode for this directory entry. This is an index into the array of inodes held in the inode table of the Block Group. In Figure 9.3, the directory entry for the file called `file` has a reference to inode number `i1`.

♦ name length—The length of this directory entry in bytes.

♦ name—The name of this directory entry.

The first two entries for every directory are always the standard "." and ".." entries, meaning "this directory" and "the parent directory," respectively.

9.1.5   Finding A File In An EXT2 File System

A Linux file name has the same format all Unix file names have. It is a series of directory names separated by forward slashes ("/") and ending in the file's name. One example file name would be `/home/rusling/.cshrc`, where `/home` and `/rusling` are directory names and the file's name is `.cshrc`. Like all other Unix systems, Linux does not care

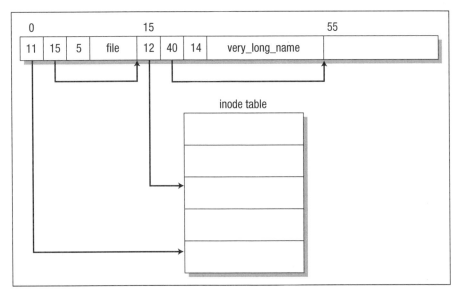

Figure 9.3
EXT2 directory.

about the format of the file name itself; it can be any length and consist of any of the printable characters. To find the inode representing this file within an EXT2 file system, the system must parse the file name a directory at a time until we get to the file itself.

The first inode we need is the inode for the root of the file system; and we find its number in the file system's Superblock. To read an EXT2 inode, we must look for it in the inode table of the appropriate Block Group. If, for example, the root inode number is 42, then we need the 42nd inode from the inode table of Block Group 0. The root inode is for an EXT2 directory; in other words, the mode of the root inode describes it as a directory and its data blocks contain EXT2 directory entries.

home is just one of the many directory entries, and this directory entry gives us the number of the inode describing the /home directory. We have to read this directory (by first reading its inode and then reading the directory entries from the data blocks described by its inode) to find the rusling entry which gives us the number of the inode describing the /home/rusling directory. Finally we read the directory entries pointed at by the inode describing the /home/rusling directory to find the inode number of the .cshrc file—and from this we get the data blocks containing the information in the file.

9.1.6   Changing The Size Of A File In An EXT2 File System

One common problem with a file system is its tendency to fragment. The blocks that hold the file's data get spread all over the file system, and this makes sequentially accessing the data blocks of a file more and more inefficient the further apart the data blocks are. The EXT2 file system tries to overcome this by allocating the new blocks for a file physically close to its current data blocks, or at least in the same Block Group as its current data blocks. Only when this fails does it allocate data blocks in another Block Group.

Whenever a process attempts to write data into a file, the Linux file system checks to see if the data has gone off the end of the file's last allocated block. If it has, then it must allocate a new data block for this file. Until the allocation is complete, the process cannot run; it must wait for the file system to allocate a new data block and write the rest of the data to it before it can continue. The first thing that the EXT2 block allocation routines do is to lock the EXT2 superblock for this file system. Allocating and deallocating changes fields within the Superblock, and the Linux file system cannot allow more than one process to do this at the same time. If another process needs to allocate more data blocks, it will have to wait until this process has finished. Processes waiting for the Superblock are suspended, unable to run, until control of the Superblock is relinquished by its current user. Access to the superblock is granted on a first come, first served basis, and once a process has control of the Superblock, it keeps control until it has finished. Having locked the Superblock, the process checks that there are enough free blocks left in this file system. If there are not enough free blocks, then this attempt to allocate more will fail and the process will relinquish control of this file system's Superblock.

If there are enough free blocks in the file system, the process tries to allocate one.

If the EXT2 file system has been built to preallocate data blocks, then we may be able to take one of those. The preallocated blocks do not actually exist; they are just reserved within the allocated block bitmap. The VFS inode representing the file that we are trying to allocate a new data block for has two EXT2-specific fields, `prealloc_block` and `prealloc_count`, which are the block number of the first preallocated data block and how many of them there are, respectively. If there were no preallocated blocks or block preallocation is not enabled, the EXT2 file system must allocate a new block. The EXT2 file system first looks to see if the data block after the last data block in the file is free. Logically, this is the most efficient block to allocate, as it makes sequential accesses much quicker. If this block is not free, then the search widens and it looks for a data block within 64 blocks of the of the ideal block. This block, although not ideal, is at least fairly close and within the same Block Group as the other data blocks belonging to this file.

If even that block is not free, the process starts looking in all of the other Block Groups in turn until it finds some free blocks. The block allocation code looks for a cluster of eight free data blocks somewhere in one of the Block Groups. If it cannot find eight together, it will settle for less. If block preallocation is wanted and enabled it will update `prealloc_block` and `prealloc_count` accordingly.

Wherever it finds the free block, the block allocation code updates the Block Group's block bitmap and allocates a data buffer in the buffer cache. That data buffer is uniquely identified by the file system's supporting device identifier and the block number of the allocated block. The data in the buffer is zeroed and the buffer is marked as "dirty" to show that its contents have not been written to the physical disk. Finally, the Superblock itself is marked as "dirty" to show that it has been changed, and it is unlocked. If there were any processes waiting for the Superblock, the first one in the queue is allowed to run again, and will gain exclusive control of the Superblock for its file operations. The process's data is written to the new data block and, if that data block is filled, the entire process is repeated and another data block allocated.

9.2   The Virtual File System (VFS)

Figure 9.4 shows the relationship between the Linux kernel's Virtual File System and its real file systems. The virtual file system must manage all of the different file systems that are mounted at any given time. To do this, it maintains data structures that describe the whole (virtual) file system and the real, mounted, file systems.

Rather confusingly, the VFS describes the system's files in terms of Superblocks and inodes in much the same way as the EXT2 file system uses Superblocks and inodes. Like the EXT2 inodes, the VFS inodes describe files and directories within the system: the contents and topology of the Virtual File System. From now on, to avoid confusion, I will write about VFS inodes and VFS Superblocks to distinguish them from EXT2 inodes and Superblocks.

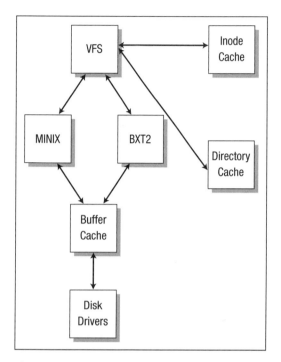

Figure 9.4
A logical diagram of the Virtual File System.

As each file system is initialized, it registers itself with the VFS. This happens as the operating system initializes itself at system boot time. The real file systems are either built into the kernel itself, or are built as loadable modules. File system modules are loaded as the system needs them, so, for example, if the VFAT file system is implemented as a kernel module, then it is only loaded when a VFAT file system is mounted. When a block device based file system is mounted, and this includes the root file system, the VFS must read its Superblock. Each file system type's Superblock read routine must work out the file system's topology and map that information onto a VFS Superblock data structure. The VFS keeps a list of the mounted file systems in the system together with their VFS superblocks. Each VFS Superblock contains information and pointers to routines that perform particular functions. So, for example, the Superblock representing a mounted EXT2 file system contains a pointer to the EXT2-specific inode reading routine. This EXT2 inode read routine, like all of the file system-specific inode read routines, fills out the fields in a VFS inode. Each VFS Superblock contains a pointer to the first VFS inode on the file system. For the root file system, this is the inode that represents the "/" directory. This mapping of information is very efficient for the EXT2 file system, but moderately less so for other file systems.

As the system's processes access directories and files, system routines are called that traverse the VFS inodes in the system.

For example, typing **ls** for a directory or **cat** for a file causes the Virtual File System to search through the VFS inodes that represent the file system. As every file and directory on the system is represented by a VFS inode, then a number of inodes will be being repeatedly accessed. These inodes are kept in the inode cache which makes access to them quicker. If an inode is not in the inode cache, then a file system-specific routine must be called in order to read the appropriate inode. The action of reading the inode causes it to be put into the inode cache, and further accesses to the inode keep it in the cache. The less-used VFS inodes get removed from the cache.

All of the Linux file systems use a common buffer cache to cache data buffers from the underlying devices to help speed up access by all of the file systems to the physical devices holding the file systems.

This buffer cache is independent of the file systems and is integrated into the mechanisms that the Linux kernel uses to allocate and read and write data buffers. It has the distinct advantage of making the Linux file systems independent from the underlying media and from the device drivers that support them. All block-structured devices register themselves with the Linux kernel and present a uniform, block-based, usually asynchronous interface. Even relatively complex block devices, such as SCSI devices, do this. As the real file systems read data from the underlying physical disks, this results in requests to the block device drivers to read physical blocks from the device that they control. Integrated into this block device interface is the buffer cache. As blocks are read by the file systems they are saved in the global buffer cache shared by all of the file systems and the Linux kernel. Buffers within it are identified by their block number and a unique identifier for the device that read it. So, if the same data is needed often, it will be retrieved from the buffer cache rather than read from the disk, which would take somewhat longer. Some devices support read ahead where data blocks are speculatively read just in case they are needed.

The VFS also keeps a cache of directory lookups so that the inodes for frequently used directories can be quickly found.

As an experiment, try listing a directory that you have not listed recently. The first time you list it, you may notice a slight pause, but the second time you list its contents the result is immediate. The directory cache does not store the inodes for the directories itself; these should be in the inode cache, the directory cache simply stores the mapping between the full directory names and their inode numbers.

9.2.1   The VFS Superblock

Every mounted file system is represented by a VFS Superblock; among other information, the VFS Superblock contains the:

♦ Device—This is the device identifier for the block device that this file system is contained in. For example, /dev/hda1, the first IDE hard disk in the system has a device identifier of *0x301*,

♦ Inode pointers—The `mounted` inode pointer points at the first inode in this file system. The `covered` inode pointer points at the inode representing the directory that this file system is mounted on. The root file system's VFS Superblock does not have a `covered` pointer.

♦ Block size—The block size in bytes of this file system, for example, 1,024 bytes.

♦ Superblock operations—A pointer to a set of Superblock routines for this file system. Among other things, these routines are used by the VFS to read and write inodes and Superblocks.

♦ File system type—A pointer to the mounted file system's `file_system_type` data structure.

♦ File system specific—A pointer to information needed by this file system.

9.2.2 The VFS Inode

Like the EXT2 file system, every file, directory, and so on in the VFS is represented by one and only one VFS inode.

The information in each VFS inode is built from information in the underlying file system by file system-specific routines. VFS inodes exist only in the kernel's memory and are kept in the VFS inode cache as long as they are useful to the system. Among other information, VFS inodes contain the following fields:

♦ Device—This is the device identifer of the device holding the file or whatever that this VFS inode represents.

♦ Inode number—This is the number of the inode and is unique within this file system. The combination of `device` and `inode number` is unique within the Virtual File System.

♦ Mode—Like EXT2 this field describes what this VFS inode represents as well as access rights to it.

♦ User IDs—The owner identifiers.

♦ Times—The creation, modification, and write times.

♦ Block size—The size of a block for this file in bytes, for example, 1,024 bytes.

♦ Inode operations—A pointer to a block of routine addresses. These routines are specific to the file system and they perform operations for this inode, for example, truncate the file that is represented by this inode.

♦ Count—The number of system components currently using this VFS inode. A count of zero means that the inode is free to be discarded or reused.

♦ Lock—This field is used to lock the VFS inode, for example, when it is being read from the file system.

♦ Dirty—Indicates whether this VFS inode has been written to; if so, the underlying file system will need modifying, file system-specific information.

9.2.3   Registering The File Systems

When you build the Linux kernel you are asked if you want each of the supported file systems. When the kernel is built, the file system startup code contains calls to the initialization routines of all of the built-in file systems.

Linux file systems may also be built as modules and, in this case, they may be demand loaded as they are needed or loaded by hand using **insmod**. Whenever a file system module is loaded it registers itself with the kernel and unregisters itself when it is unloaded. Each file system's initialization routine registers itself with the Virtual File System and is represented by a `file_system_type` data structure which contains the name of the file system and a pointer to its VFS Superblock read routine. Figure 9.5 shows that the `file_system_type` data structures are put into a list pointed at by the `file_systems` pointer. Each `file_system_type` data structure contains the following information:

- ♦ Superblock read routine—This routine is called by the VFS when an instance of the file system is mounted.

- ♦ File System name—The name of this file system, for example, EXT2.

- ♦ Device needed—Does this file system need a device to support? Not all file system need a device to hold them. The `/proc` file system, for example, does not require a block device.

You can see which file systems are registered by looking in at `/proc/file systems`. For example:

```
      ext2
nodev proc
      iso9660
```

9.2.4   Mounting A File System

When the super-user attempts to mount a file system, the Linux kernel must first validate the arguments passed in the system call. Although **mount** does some basic checking, it does not know which file systems this kernel has been built to support or that the proposed mount point actually exists. Consider the following **mount** command:

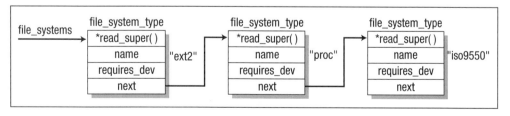

Figure 9.5
Registered file systems.

```
$ mount -t iso9660 -o ro /dev/cdrom /mnt/cdrom
```

This **mount** command will pass the kernel three pieces of information: the name of the file system, the physical block device that contains the file system, and, third, where in the existing file system topology the new file system is to be mounted.

The first thing that the Virtual File System must do is to find the file system.

To do this it searches through the list of known file systems by looking at each `file_system_type` data structure in the list pointed at by `file_systems`.

If it finds a matching name it now knows that this file system type is supported by this kernel and it has the address of the file system specific routine for reading this file system's superblock. If it cannot find a matching file system name then all is not lost if the kernel is built to demand load kernel modules (see Chapter 12). In this case the kernel will request that the kernel daemon loads the appropriate file system module before continuing as before.

Next if the physical device passed by **mount** is not already mounted, it must find the VFS inode of the directory that is to be the new file system's mount point. This VFS inode may be in the inode cache or it might have to be read from the block device supporting the file system of the mount point. Once the inode has been found it is checked to see that it is a directory and that there is not already some other file system mounted there. The same directory cannot be used as a mount point for more than one file system.

At this point the VFS mount code must allocate a VFS Superblock and pass it the mount information to the superblock read routine for this file system. All of the system's VFS Superblocks are kept in the `super_blocks` vector of `super_block` data structures and one must be allocated for this mount. The Superblock read routine must fill out the VFS Superblock fields based on information that it reads from the physical device. For the EXT2 file system this mapping or translation of information is quite easy, it simply reads the EXT2 Superblock and fills out the VFS Superblock from there. For other file systems, such as the MS DOS file system, it is not quite such an easy task. Whatever the file system, filling out the VFS Superblock means that the file system must read whatever describes it from the block device that supports it. If the block device cannot be read from or if it does not contain this type of file system then the **mount** command will fail.

Each mounted file system is described by a `vfsmount` data structure; see Figure 9.6. These are queued on a list pointed at by `vfsmntlist`.

Another pointer, `vfsmnttail`, points at the last entry in the list and the `mru_vfsmnt` pointer points at the most recently used file system. Each `vfsmount` structure contains the device number of the block device holding the file system, the directory where this file system is mounted and a pointer to the VFS Superblock allocated when this file system was mounted. In turn the VFS Superblock points at the `file_system_type` data structure for this sort of file system and to the root inode for this file system. This inode is kept resident in the VFS inode cache all of the time that this file system is loaded.

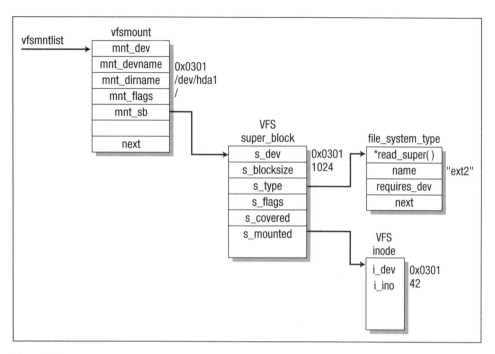

Figure 9.6
A mounted file system.

9.2.5   Finding A File In The Virtual File System

To find the VFS inode of a file in the Virtual File System, VFS must resolve the name a directory at a time, looking up the VFS inode representing each of the intermediate directories in the name. Each directory lookup involves calling the file system-specific lookup whose address is held in the VFS inode representing the parent directory. This works because we always have the VFS inode of the root of each file system available and pointed at by the VFS Superblock for that system. Each time an inode is looked up by the real file system it checks the directory cache for the directory. If there is no entry in the directory cache, the real file system gets the VFS inode either from the underlying file system or from the inode cache.

9.2.6   Creating A File In The Virtual File System

9.2.7   Unmounting A File System

The workshop manual for my MG usually describes assembly as the reverse of disassembly and the reverse is more or less true for unmounting a file system.

A file system cannot be unmounted if something in the system is using one of its files. So, for example, you cannot umount /mnt/cdrom if a process is using that directory or any of its children. If anything is using the file system to be unmounted there may be VFS inodes from it in the VFS inode cache, and the code checks for this by looking through the list of inodes looking for inodes owned by the device that this file system occupies. If the VFS Superblock for the mounted file system is dirty, that is it has been modified, then it must be written back to the file system on disk. Once it has been written to disk, the memory occupied by the VFS Superblock is returned to the kernel's free pool of memory. Finally, the `vfsmount` data structure for this mount is unlinked from `vfsmntlist` and freed.

9.2.8 The VFS Inode Cache

As the mounted file systems are navigated, their VFS inodes are being continually read and, in some cases, written. The Virtual File System maintains an inode cache to speed up accesses to all of the mounted file systems. Every time a VFS inode is read from the inode cache the system saves an access to a physical device.

The VFS inode cache is implemented as a hash table whose entries are pointers to lists of VFS inodes that have the same hash value. The hash value of an inode is calculated from its inode number and from the device identifier for the underlying physical device containing the file system. Whenever the Virtual File System needs to access an inode, it first looks in the VFS inode cache. To find an inode in the cache, the system first calculates its hash value and then uses it as an index into the inode hash table. This gives it a pointer to a list of inodes with the same hash value. It then reads each inode in turn until it finds one with both the same inode number and the same device identifier as the one that it is searching for.

If it can find the inode in the cache, its count is incremented to show that it has another user and the file system access continues. Otherwise, a free VFS inode must be found so that the file system can read the inode from memory. VFS has a number of choices about how to get a free inode. If the system may allocate more VFS inodes then this is what it does; it allocates kernel pages and breaks them up into new, free inodes and puts them into the inode list. All of the system's VFS inodes are in a list pointed at by `first_inode` as well as in the inode hash table. If the system already has all of the inodes that it is allowed to have, it must find an inode that is a good candidate to be reused. Good candidates are inodes with a usage count of zero; this indicates that the system is not currently using them. Really important VFS inodes, for example, the root inodes of file systems, always have a usage count greater than zero and so are never candidates for reuse. Once a candidate for reuse has been located it is cleaned up. The VFS inode might be dirty and in this case it needs to be written back to the file system or it might be locked and in this case the system must wait for it to be unlocked before continuing. The candidate VFS inode must be cleaned up before it can be reused.

However the new VFS inode is found, a file system-specific routine must be called to fill it out from information read from the underlying real file system. While it is being filled out, the new VFS inode has a usage count of one and is locked so that nothing else accesses it until it contains valid information.

To get the VFS inode that is actually needed, the file system may need to access several other inodes. This happens when you read a directory; only the inode for the final directory is needed, but the inodes for the intermediate directories must also be read. As the VFS inode cache is used and filled up, the less used inodes will be discarded and the more used inodes will remain in the cache.

9.2.9   The Directory Cache

To speed up accesses to commonly used directories, the VFS maintains a cache of directory entries.

As directories are looked up by the real file systems their details are added into the directory cache. The next time the same directory is looked up, for example to list it or open a file within it, then it will be found in the directory cache. Only short directory entries (up to 15 characters long) are cached, but this is reasonable as the shorter directory names are the most commonly used ones. For example, /usr/X11R6/bin is very commonly accessed when the X server is running.

The directory cache consists of a hash table, each entry of which points at a list of directory cache entries that have the same hash value. The hash function uses the device number of the device holding the file system and the directory's name to calculate the offset, or *index*, into the hash table. It allows cached directory entries to be quickly found. It is no use having a cache when lookups within the cache take too long to find entries, or even not to find them.

In an effort to keep the caches valid and up to date the VFS keeps lists of least recently used (LRU) directory cache entries. When a directory entry is first put into the cache, which is when it is first looked up, it is added onto the end of the first-level LRU list. In a full cache this will displace an existing entry from the front of the LRU list. As the directory entry is accessed again it is promoted to the back of the second LRU cache list. Again, this may displace a cached level-two directory entry at the front of the level-two LRU cache list. This displacing of entries at the front of the level-one and level-two LRU lists is fine. The only reason that entries are at the front of the lists is that they have not been recently accessed. If they had, they would be nearer the back of the lists. The entries in the second-level LRU cache list are safer than entries in the level-one LRU cache list. This is the intention as these entries have not only been looked up but also they have been repeatedly referenced.

9.3   The Buffer Cache

As the mounted file systems are used, they generate a lot of requests to the block devices to read and write data blocks. All block data read and write requests are given to the device drivers in the form of buffer_head data structures via standard kernel routine calls. These give all of the information that the block device drivers need; the device identifier uniquely identifies the device, and the block number tells the driver which block to read. All block devices are viewed as linear collections of blocks of the same size. To speed up access to the physical block devices, Linux maintains a cache of block buffers. All of the block buffers in the system are kept somewhere in this buffer cache, even the new, unused buffers. This cache is shared between all of the physical block devices; at any one time there are many block buffers in the cache, belonging to any one of the system's block devices and often in many different states. If valid data is available from the buffer cache this saves the system an access to a physical device. Any block buffer that has been used to read data from a block device or to write data to it goes into the buffer cache. Over time, it may be removed from the cache to make way for a more deserving buffer, or it may remain in the cache as it is frequently accessed.

Block buffers within the cache are uniquely identified by the owning device identifier and the block number of the buffer. The buffer cache is composed of two functional parts. The first part is the lists of free block buffers. There is one list per supported buffer size, and the system's free block buffers are queued onto these lists when they are first created or when they have been discarded. The currently supported buffer sizes are 512, 1,024, 2,048, 4,096, and 8,192 bytes.

The second functional part is the cache itself. This is a hash table, which is a vector of pointers to chains of buffers that have the same hash index. The hash index is generated from the owning device identifier and the block number of the data block. Figure 9.7 shows the hash table together with a few entries. Block buffers are either in one of the free lists or they are in the buffer cache. When they are in the buffer cache they are also queued onto LRU lists. There is an LRU list for each buffer type; and these are used by the system to perform work on buffers of a type, for example, writing buffers with new data in them out to disk. The buffer's type reflects its state; and Linux currently supports the following types:

♦ Clean—Unused, new buffers.

♦ Locked—Buffers that are locked, waiting to be written.

♦ Dirty—Dirty buffers. These contain new, valid data, and will be written but so far have not been scheduled to write.

♦ Shared—Shared buffers.

♦ Unshared—Buffers that were once shared but which are now not shared.

Whenever a file system needs to read a buffer from its underlying physical device, it tries to get a block from the buffer cache. If it cannot get a buffer from the buffer cache, then it will get a clean one from the appropriate-sized free list; and this new buffer will go into the buffer cache. If the buffer that it needed is in the buffer cache, then it may or may not be up to date. If it is not up to date or if it is a new block buffer, the file system must request that the device driver read the appropriate block of data from the disk.

Like all caches, the buffer cache must be maintained so that it runs efficiently and fairly allocates cache entries between the block devices using the buffer cache. Linux uses the

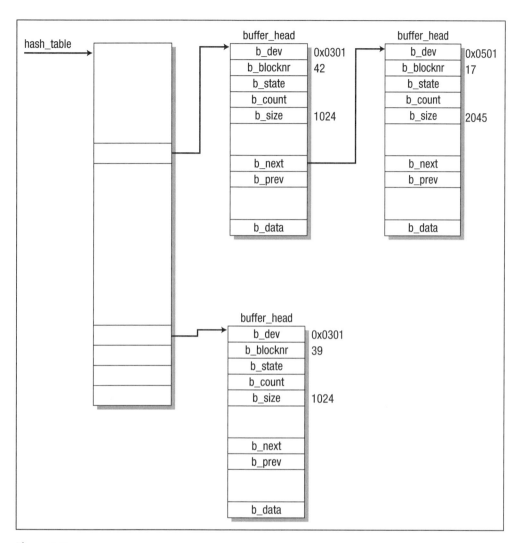

Figure 9.7
The buffer cache.

bdflush kernel daemon to perform a lot of housekeeping duties on the cache, but some happen automatically as a result of the cache being used.

9.3.1   The bdflush Kernel Daemon

The bdflush kernel daemon is a simple kernel daemon that provides a dynamic response to the system having too many dirty buffers, buffers that contain data that must be written out to disk at some time. It is started as a kernel thread at system startup time and, rather confusingly, it calls itself "kflushd"; that is the name that you will see if you use the ps command to show the processes in the system. Mostly, this daemon sleeps, waiting for the number of dirty buffers in the system to grow too large. As buffers are allocated and discarded, the number of dirty buffers in the system is checked. If there are too many, as a percentage of the total number of buffers in the system, then bdflush is woken up. The default threshold is 60 percent, but, if the system is desperate for buffers, bdflush will be woken up anyway. This value can be seen and changed using the **update** command:

```
# update -d

bdflush version 1.4
0:     60 Max fraction of LRU list to examine for dirty blocks
1:    500 Max number of dirty blocks to write each time bdflush activated
2:     64 Num of clean buffers to be loaded onto free list by refill_freelist
3:    256 Dirty block threshold for activating bdflush in refill_freelist
4:     15 Percentage of cache to scan for free clusters
5:   3000 Time for data buffers to age before flushing
6:    500 Time for non-data (dir, bitmap, etc) buffers to age before flushing
7:   1884 Time buffer cache load average constant
8:      2 LAV ratio (used to determine threshold for buffer fratricide).
```

All of the dirty buffers are linked into the BUF_DIRTY LRU list whenever they are made dirty by having data written to them, and bdflush tries to write a reasonable number of them out to their owning disks. Again, this number can be seen and controlled by the **update** command, and the default is 500 (see above).

9.3.2   The update Process

The **update** command is more than just a command; it is also a daemon. When run as super-user (during system initialization), it will periodically flush all of the older dirty buffers out to disk. It does this by calling a system service routine that does more or less the same thing as bdflush. Whenever a dirty buffer is finished with, it is tagged with the system time that it should be written out to its owning disk. Every time that **update** runs, it looks at all of the dirty buffers in the system looking for ones with an expired flush time. Every expired buffer is written out to disk.

9.4   The /proc File System

The /proc file system really shows the power of the Linux Virtual File System. It does not really exist (yet another of Linux's conjuring tricks); neither the /proc directory nor its subdirectories and its files actually exist. So how can you cat /proc/devices? The /proc file system, like a real file system, registers itself with the Virtual File System. However, when the VFS makes calls to it, requesting inodes as its files and directories are opened, the /proc file system creates those files and directories from information within the kernel. For example, the kernel's /proc/devices file is generated from the kernel's data structures describing its devices.

The /proc file system presents a user-readable window into the kernel's inner workings. Several Linux subsystems, such as Linux kernel modules described in Chapter 12, create entries in the the /proc file system.

9.5   Device Special Files

Linux, like all versions of Unix, presents its hardware devices as special files. So, for example, /dev/null is the null device. A device file does not use any data space in the file system; it is only an access point to the device driver. The EXT2 file system and the Linux VFS both implement device files as special types of inode.

There are two types of device file: character and block special files. Within the kernel itself, the device drivers implement file semantics: you can open them, close them, and so on. Character devices allow I/O operations in character mode, and block devices require that all I/O is via the buffer cache. When an I/O request is made to a device file, it is forwarded to the appropriate device driver within the system. Often this is not a real device driver, but a pseudo-device driver for some subsystem, such as the SCSI device driver layer. Device files are referenced by a major number, which identifies the device type, and a minor type, which identifies the unit, or instance, of that major type. For example, the IDE disks on the first IDE controller in the system have a major number of 3 and the first partition of an IDE disk would have a minor number of 1. So, ls -l of /dev/hda1 gives:

```
$ brw-rw—  1 root    disk      3,  1  Nov 24  15:09 /dev/hda1
```

Within the kernel, every device is uniquely described by a kdev_t data type; this is 2 bytes long, the first byte containing the minor device number and the second byte holding the major device number.

The IDE device above is held within the kernel as *0x0301*. An EXT2 inode that represents a block or character device keeps the device's major and minor numbers in its first direct block pointer. When it is read by the VFS, the VFS inode data structure representing it has its i_rdev field set to the correct device identifier.

Chapter 10
Networks

Networking and *Linux* are terms that are almost synonymous. In a very real sense, Linux is a product of the Internet or the World Wide Web (WWW). Its developers and users use the Web to exchange information, ideas, and code, and Linux itself is often used to support the networking needs of organizations. This chapter describes how Linux supports the network protocols known collectively as TCP/IP.

The TCP/IP protocols were designed to support communications between computers connected to the ARPANET, an American research network funded by the U.S. government. The ARPANET pioneered networking concepts such as packet switching and protocol layering where one protocol uses the services of another. ARPANET was retired in 1988, but its successors (NSF, otherwise known as the National Science Foundation, NET, and the Internet) have grown even larger. What is now known as the World Wide Web grew from the ARPANET and is itself supported by the TCP/IP protocols. Unix was extensively used on the ARPANET, and the first released networking version of Unix was 4.3 BSD. Linux's networking implementation is modeled on 4.3 BSD, in that it supports BSD sockets (with some extensions) and the full range of TCP/IP networking. This programming interface was chosen because of its popularity and to help applications be portable between Linux and other Unix platforms.

10.1 An Overview Of TCP/IP Networking

This section gives an overview of the main principles of TCP/IP networking. In an IP network, every machine is assigned an IP address; this is a 32-bit number that uniquely identifies the machine. The Web is a very large, and growing, IP network, and every machine that is connected to it has to have a unique IP address assigned to it. IP addresses are represented by four numbers separated by dots, for example, 16.42.0.9. This IP address is actually in two parts: the network address and the host address. The sizes of these parts may vary (there are several classes of IP addresses), but, using 16.42.0.9 as an example, the network address would be 16.42 and the host address 0.9. The host address is further subdivided into a subnetwork and a host address. Again, using 16.42.0.9 as an example, the subnetwork address would be 16.42.0 and the host address 16.42.0.9. This subdivision of the IP address allows organizations to subdivide their networks. For example, 16.42 could be the network address of the ACME Computer Company; 16.42.0 would be subnet 0 and 16.42.1 would be subnet 1. These subnets might be in separate buildings, perhaps connected by leased telephone lines or even microwave links. IP addresses are assigned by the network administrator, and having IP subnetworks is a good way of distributing the administration of the network. IP subnet administrators are free to allocate IP addresses within their IP subnetworks.

Generally, though, IP addresses are somewhat hard to remember. Names are much easier. `linux.acme.com` is much easier to remember than 16.42.0.9, but there must be some mechanism to convert the network names into an IP address. These names can be statically specified in the `/etc/hosts` file, or Linux can ask a *domain name server* (DNS, or DNS server) to resolve the name for it. In this case, the local host must know the IP address of one or more DNS servers; and these are specified in `/etc/resolv.conf`.

Whenever you connect to another machine, say, when reading a Web page, its IP address is used to exchange data with that machine. This data is contained in IP packets, each of which have an IP header containing the IP addresses of the source and destination machine's IP addresses, a checksum, and other useful information. The *checksum* is derived from the data in the IP packet, and allows the receiver of IP packets to tell if the IP packet was corrupted during transmission, perhaps by a noisy telephone line. The data transmitted by an application may have been broken down into smaller packets which are easier to handle.

The size of the IP data packets varies depending on the connection media; EEthernet packets are generally bigger than PPP packets. The destination host must reassemble the data packets before giving the data to the receiving application. You can see this fragmentation and re-assembly of data graphically, if you access a Web page containing a lot of graphical images via a moderately slow serial link.

Hosts connected to the same IP subnet can send IP packets directly to each other; all other IP packets will be sent to a special host, a *gateway*. Gateways (or routers) are connected to more than one IP subnet, and they will re-send IP packets received on one subnet, but destined for another, onward. For example, if subnets 16.42.1.0 and 16.42.0.0 are connected together by a gateway, then any packets sent from subnet 0 to subnet 1 would have to be directed to the gateway, so that it could route them. The local host builds up routing tables, which allow it to route IP packets to the correct machine. For every IP destination, there is an entry in the routing tables which tells Linux which host to send IP packets to, in order that they reach their destination. These routing tables are dynamic and change over time as applications use the network and as the network topology changes.

The IP protocol is a transport layer that is used by other protocols to carry their data. The *Transmission Control Protocol* (TCP) is a reliable end-to-end protocol that uses IP to transmit and receive its own packets (see Figure 10.1). Just as IP packets have their own header, TCP has its own header. TCP is a connection-based protocol where two networking applications are connected by a single, virtual connection, even though there may be many subnetworks, gateways, and routers between them. TCP reliably transmits and receives data between the two applications, and guarantees that there will be no lost or duplicated data. When TCP transmits its packet using IP, the data contained within the IP packet is the TCP packet itself. The IP layer on each communicating host is responsible for transmitting and receiving IP packets.

User Datagram Protocol (UDP) also uses the IP layer to transport its packets; unlike TCP, UDP is not a reliable protocol, but it offers a datagram service. This use of IP by other protocols means that when IP packets are received, the receiving IP layer must know to which upper protocol layer to give the data contained in this IP packet. To facilitate this, every IP packet header has a byte containing a protocol identifier. When TCP asks the IP layer to transmit an IP packet, that IP packet's header states that it contains a TCP packet.

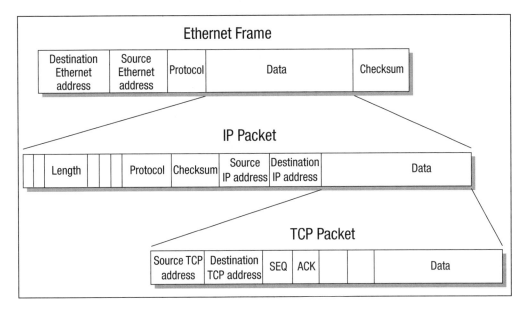

Figure 10.1
TCP/IP protocol layers.

The receiving IP layer uses that protocol identifier to decide which layer to pass the received data up to, in this case the TCP layer.

When applications communicate via TCP/IP, they must specify not only the target's IP address but also the port address of the application. A *port address* uniquely identifies an application, and standard network applications use standard port addresses. For example, Web servers use port 80. These registered port addresses can be seen in `/etc/services`.

This layering of protocols does not stop with TCP, UDP, and IP. The IP protocol layer itself uses many different physical media to transport IP packets to other IP hosts. These media may themselves add their own protocol headers. One such example is the EEthernet layer, but PPP and SLIP are others. An Ethernet network allows many hosts to be simultaneously connected to a single physical cable. Every transmitted Ethernet frame can be seen by all connected hosts, and so every Ethernet device has a unique address. Any Ethernet frame transmitted to that address will be received by the addressed host but ignored by all the other hosts connected to the network. These unique addresses are built into each Ethernet device when they are manufactured; and it is usually kept in an *SROM* (synchronous read only memory) on the Ethernet card. Ethernet addresses are six bytes long; an example would be `08-00-2b-00-49-A4`. Some Ethernet addresses are reserved for multicast purposes, and Ethernet frames sent with these destination addresses will be received by all hosts on the network. As Ethernet frames can carry many different protocols (as data) they, like IP packets, contain a protocol identifier in their headers. This allows the Ethernet layer to correctly receive IP packets and to pass them onto the IP layer.

In order to send an IP packet via a multiconnection protocol such as Ethernet, the IP layer must find the Ethernet address of the IP host. This is because IP addresses are simply an addressing concept; the Ethernet devices themselves have their own physical addresses. IP addresses, on the other hand, can be assigned and reassigned by network administrators at will, but the network hardware responds only to Ethernet frames with its own physical address or to special multicast addresses which all machines must receive. Linux uses the *Address Resolution Protocol* (ARP) to allow machines to translate IP addresses into real hardware addresses such as Ethernet addresses. A host wishing to know the hardware address associated with an IP address sends an ARP request packet, containing the IP address that needs translating, to all nodes on the network by sending it to a multicast address. The target host that owns the IP address responds with an ARP reply that contains its physical hardware address.

ARP is not just restricted to Ethernet devices; it can resolve IP addresses for other physical media, for example, FDDI. Those network devices that cannot ARP are marked so that Linux does not attempt to ARP. There is also the reverse function, *Reverse ARP* or RARP, which translates physical network addresses into IP addresses. This is used by gateways, which respond to ARP requests on behalf of IP addresses that are in the remote network.

10.2   The Linux TCP/IP Networking Layers

Just like the network protocols themselves, Figure 10.2 shows that Linux implements the internet protocol address family as a series of connected layers of software. BSD sockets are supported by a generic socket management software concerned only with BSD sockets. Supporting this is the INET socket layer; this manages the communication endpoints for the IP-based protocols, TCP and UDP. UDP is a connectionless protocol, whereas TCP is a reliable end-to-end protocol.

When UDP packets are transmitted, Linux neither knows nor cares if they arrive safely at their destination. TCP packets are numbered, and both ends of the TCP connection make sure that transmitted data is received correctly. The IP layer contains code implementing the Internet Protocol. This code prepends IP headers to transmitted data, and understands how to route incoming IP packets to either the TCP or UDP layers. Underneath the IP layer, supporting all of Linux's networking are the network devices, for example, PPP and Ethernet. Network devices do not always represent physical devices; some, like the loopback device, are purely software devices. Unlike standard Linux devices that are created via the

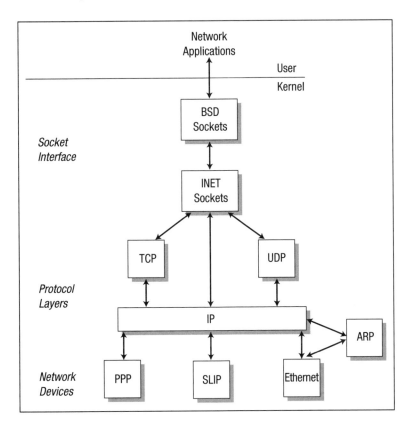

Figure 10.2
Linux networking layers.

mknod command, network devices appear only if the underlying software has found and initialized them. You will only see /dev/eth0 when you have built a kernel with the appropriate Ethernet device driver in it. The ARP protocol sits between the IP layer and the protocols that support ARPing for addresses.

10.3 The BSD Socket Interface

This is a general interface which not only supports various forms of networking but is also an interprocess communications mechanism. A socket describes one end of a communications link; two communicating processes would each have a socket describing their end of the communication link between them. Sockets could be thought of as a special case of pipes, but, unlike pipes, sockets have no limit on the amount of data that they can contain. Linux supports several classes of socket, and these are known as *address families*. This is because each class has its own method of addressing its communications. Linux supports the following socket address families, or domains:

UNIX	Unix domain sockets
INET	The Internet address family supports communications via TCP/IP protocols
AX25	Amateur radio X25
IPX	Novell IPX
APPLETALK	Appletalk DDP
X25	X25

There are several socket types, and these represent the type of service that supports the connection. Not all address families support all types of service. Linux BSD sockets support a number of socket types:

♦ Stream—These sockets provide reliable two-way sequenced data streams with a guarantee that data cannot be lost, corrupted, or duplicated in transit. Stream sockets are supported by the TCP protocol of the Internet (INET) address family.

♦ Datagram—These sockets also provide two-way data transfer, but, unlike stream sockets, there is no guarantee that the messages will arrive. Even if they do arrive, there is no guarantee that they will arrive in order or even not be duplicated or corrupted. This type of socket is supported by the UDP protocol of the Internet address family.

♦ Raw—This allows processes direct (hence "raw") access to the underlying protocols. It is, for example, possible to open a raw socket to an Ethernet device and see raw IP data traffic.

♦ Reliable Delivered Messages—These are very like datagram sockets, but the data is guaranteed to arrive.

♦ Sequenced Packets—These are like stream sockets, except that the data packet sizes are fixed.

♦ Packet—This is not a standard BSD socket type; it is a Linux-specific extension that allows processes to access packets directly at the device level.

Processes that communicate using sockets use a *client/server model*. A server provides a service, and clients make use of that service. One example would be a Web server, which provides Web pages, and a Web client, or browser, which reads those pages.

A server using sockets first creates a socket, and then binds a name to it. The format of this name is dependent on the socket's address family and it is, in effect, the local address of the server. The socket's name or address is specified using the `sockaddr` data structure. An INET socket would have an IP port address bound to it. The registered port numbers can be seen in `/etc/services`; for example, the port number for a Web server is 80. Having bound an address to the socket, the server then listens for incoming connection requests specifying the bound address. The originator of the request, the client, creates a socket and makes a connection request on it, specifying the target address of the server. For an INET socket, the address of the server is its IP address and its port number. These incoming requests must find their way up through the various protocol layers and then wait on the server's listening socket. Once the server has received the incoming request, it either accepts or rejects it. If the incoming request is to be accepted, the server must create a new socket to accept it on. Once a socket has been used for listening for incoming connection requests, it cannot be used to support a connection. With the connection established, both ends are free to send and receive data. Finally, when the connection is no longer needed, it can be shut down. Care is taken to ensure that data packets in transit are correctly dealt with.

The exact meaning of operations on a BSD socket depends on its underlying address family. Setting up TCP/IP connections is very different from setting up an amateur radio X.25 connection. Like the Virtual File System, Linux abstracts the socket interface with the BSD socket layer, being concerned with the BSD socket interface to the application programs, which is in turn supported by independent address family-specific software. At kernel initialization time, the address families built into the kernel register themselves with the BSD socket interface. Later on, as applications create and use BSD sockets, an association is made between the BSD socket and its supporting address family. This association is made via cross-linking data structures and tables of address family-specific support routines. For example, there is an address family-specific socket creation routine, which the BSD socket interface uses when an application creates a new socket.

When the kernel is configured, a number of address families and protocols are built into the `protocols` vector. Each is represented by its name, for example, "INET" and the address of its initialization routine. When the socket interface is initialized at boot time, each protocol's initialization routine is called. For the socket address families, this results in them registering a set of protocol operations. This is a set of routines, each of which performs a particular operation specific to that address family. The registered protocol operations are kept in the `pops` vector, a vector of pointers to `proto_ops` data structures.

The `proto_ops` data structure consists of the address family type and a set of pointers to socket operation routines specific to a particular address family. The `pops` vector is indexed by the address family identifier, for example, the Internet address family identifier (AF_INET is 2).

10.4   The INET Socket Layer

The INET socket layer supports the Internet address family, which contains the TCP/IP protocols. As discussed above, these protocols are layered, one protocol using the services of another. Linux's TCP/IP code and data structures reflect this layering. Its interface with the BSD socket layer is through the set of Internet address family socket operations, which it registers with the BSD socket layer during network initialization. These are kept in the pops vector along with the other registered address families. The BSD socket layer calls the INET layer socket support routines from the registered INET proto_ops data structure to perform work for it. For example, a BSD socket create request that gives the address family as INET will use the underlying INET socket create function. The BSD socket layer passes the socket data structure representing the BSD socket to the INET layer in each of these operations. Rather than clutter the BSD socket with TCP/IP specific information, the INET socket layer uses its own data structure, the sock which it links to the BSD socket data structure. This linkage can be seen in Figure 10.3. It links the sock data structure to the BSD socket data structure, using the data pointer in the BSD socket. This means that subsequent INET socket calls can easily retrieve the sock data structure. The sock data structure's protocol operations pointer is also set up at creation time and it depends on the protocol requested. If TCP is requested, then the sock data structure's protocol operations pointer will point to the set of TCP protocol operations needed for a TCP connection.

10.4.1   Creating A BSD Socket

The system call to create a new socket passes identifiers for its address family, socket type, and protocol.

First, the requested address family is used to search the pops vector for a matching address family. It may be that a particular address family is implemented as a kernel module and, in this case, the kerneld daemon must load the module before we can continue. A new socket data structure is allocated to represent the BSD socket. Actually the socket data structure is physically part of the VFS inode data structure and allocating a socket really means allocating a VFS inode. This may seem strange, unless you consider that sockets can be operated on in just the same way that ordinary files can. As all files are represented by a VFS inode data structure, then in order to support file operations, BSD sockets must also be represented by a VFS inode data structure.

The newly created BSD socket data structure contains a pointer to the address family-specific socket routines, and this is set to the proto_ops data structure retrieved from the pops vector. Its type is set to the socket type requested; one of SOCK_STREAM, SOCK_DGRAM, and so on. The address family specific creation routine is called using the address kept in the proto_ops data structure.

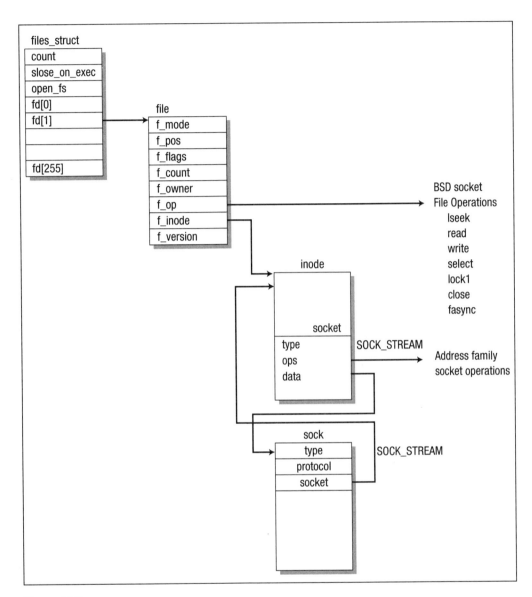

Figure 10.3
Linux BSD socket data structures.

A free file descriptor is allocated from the current processes fd vector and the file data structure that it points at is initialized. This includes setting the file operations pointer to point to the set of BSD socket file operations supported by the BSD socket interface. Any future operations will be directed to the socket interface, and it will, in turn, pass them to the supporting address family by calling its address family operation routines.

10.4.2   Binding An Address To An INET BSD Socket

In order to be able to listen for incoming Internet connection requests, each server must create an INET BSD socket and bind its address to it. The bind operation is mostly handled within the INET socket layer, with some support from the underlying TCP and UDP protocol layers. The socket having an address bound to it cannot be being used for any other communication. This means that the socket's state must be TCP_CLOSE. The sockaddr pass to the bind operation contains the IP address to be bound to and, optionally, a port number. Normally, the IP address bound to would be one that has been assigned to a network device that supports the INET address family, and whose interface is up and able to be used. You can see which network interfaces are currently active in the system by using the **ifconfig** command. The IP address may also be the IP broadcast address of either all ones or all zeros. These are special addresses that mean "send to everybody." The IP address could also be specified as any IP address, if the machine is acting as a transparent proxy or firewall, but only processes with super-user privileges can bind to any IP address. The IP address bound to is saved in the sock data structure in the recv_addr and saddr fields. These are used in hash lookups and as the sending IP address, respectively. The port number is optional and, if it is not specified, the supporting network is asked for a free one. By convention, port numbers less than 1,024 cannot be used by processes without super-user privileges. If the underlying network does allocate a port number, it always allocates ones greater than 1,024.

As packets are being received by the underlying network devices, they must be routed to the correct INET and BSD sockets so that they can be processed. For this reason, UDP and TCP maintain hash tables which are used to look up the addresses within incoming IP messages and direct them to the correct socket/sock pair. TCP is a connection-oriented protocol, and so there is more information involved in processing TCP packets than there is in processing UDP packets.

UDP maintains a hash table of allocated UDP ports, the udp_hash table. This consists of pointers to sock data structures, indexed by a hash function based on the port number. As the UDP hash table is much smaller than the number of permissible port numbers (udp_hash is only 128 or UDP_HTABLE_SIZE entries long) some entries in the table point to a chain of sock data structures linked together using each sock's next pointer.

TCP is much more complex, as it maintains several hash tables. However, TCP does not actually add the binding sock data structure into its hash tables during the bind operation; it merely checks that the port number requested is not currently being used. The sock data structure is added to TCP's hash tables during the listen operation.

10.4.3   Making A Connection On An INET BSD Socket

Once a socket has been created, provided it has not been used to listen for inbound connection requests, it can be used to make outbound connection requests. For connectionless protocols like UDP, this socket operation does not do a whole lot, but for connection-orientated protocols like TCP, it involves building a virtual circuit between two applications.

An outbound connection can only be made on an INET BSD socket that is in the right state; that is to say, one that does not already have a connection established, and one that is not being used for listening for inbound connections. This means that the BSD `socket` data structure must be in state `SS_UNCONNECTED`. The UDP protocol does not establish virtual connections between applications; any messages sent are datagrams, one-off messages that may or may not reach their destinations. It does, however, support the connect BSD socket operation. A connection operation on a UDP INET BSD socket simply sets up the addresses of the remote application: its IP address and its IP port number. Additionally, it sets up a cache of the routing table entry, so that UDP packets sent on this BSD socket do not need to check the routing database again (unless this route becomes invalid). The cached routing information is pointed at from the `ip_route_cache` pointer in the INET `sock` data structure. If no addressing information is given, this cached routing and IP addressing information will automatically be used for messages sent using this BSD socket. UDP moves the `sock`'s state to `TCP_ESTABLISHED`.

For a connect operation on a TCP BSD socket, TCP must build a TCP message containing the connection information, and send it to the IP destination given. The TCP message contains information about the connection, a unique starting message sequence number, the maximum sized message that can be managed by the initiating host, the transmit and receive window size, and so on. Within TCP, all messages are numbered and the initial sequence number is used as the first message number. Linux chooses a reasonably random value to avoid malicious protocol attacks. Every message transmitted by one end of the TCP connection and successfully received by the other is acknowledged to say that it arrived successfully and uncorrupted. Unacknowledged messages will be retransmitted.

The transmit and receive window size is the number of outstanding messages that there can be without an acknowledgment being sent. The maximum message size is based on the network device that is being used at the initiating end of the request. If the receiving end's network device supports smaller maximum message sizes, then the connection will use the minimum of the two. The application making the outbound TCP connection request must now wait for a response from the target application to accept or reject the connection request. As the TCP `sock` is now expecting incoming messages, it is added to the `tcp_listening_hash`, so that incoming TCP messages can be directed to this `sock` data structure. TCP also starts timers, so that the outbound connection request can be timed out if the target application does not respond to the request.

10.4.4 Listening On An INET BSD Socket

Once a socket has had an address bound to it, it may listen for incoming connection requests specifying the bound addresses. A network application can listen on a socket without first binding an address to it; in this case, the INET socket layer finds an unused port number (for this protocol) and automatically binds it to the socket. The listen socket function moves the socket into state `TCP_LISTEN` and does any network specific work needed to allow incoming connections.

For UDP sockets, changing the socket's state is enough, but TCP now adds the socket's `sock` data structure into two hash tables as it is now active. These are the `tcp_bound_hash` table and the `tcp_listening_hash`. Both are indexed via a hash function based on the IP port number.

Whenever an incoming TCP connection request is received for an active listening socket, TCP builds a new `sock` data structure to represent it. This `sock` data structure will become the bottom half of the TCP connection when it is eventually accepted. It also clones the incoming `sk_buff` containing the connection request, and queues it onto the `receive_queue` for the listening `sock` data structure. The clone `sk_buff` contains a pointer to the newly created `sock` data structure.

10.4.5   Accepting Connection Requests

UDP does not support the concept of connections; accepting INET socket connection requests only applies to the TCP protocol as an accept operation on a listening socket causes a new `socket` data structure to be cloned from the original listening `socket`. The accept operation is then passed to the supporting protocol layer, in this case INET, to accept any incoming connection requests. The INET protocol layer will fail the accept operation if the underlying protocol, say UDP, does not support connections. Otherwise, the accept operation is passed through to the real protocol, in this case TCP. The accept operation can be either blocking or nonblocking. In the nonblocking case, if there are no incoming connections to accept, the accept operation will fail and the newly created `socket` data structure will be thrown away. In the blocking case, the network application performing the accept operation will be added to a wait queue and then suspended until a TCP connection request is received. Once a connection request has been received, the `sk_buff` containing the request is discarded, and the `sock` data structure is returned to the INET socket layer where it is linked to the new `socket` data structure, created earlier. The file descriptor (`fd`) number of the new `socket` is returned to the network application, and the application can then use that file descriptor in socket operations on the newly created INET BSD socket.

10.5   The IP Layer
10.5.1   Socket Buffers

One of the problems of having many layers of network protocols, each one using the services of another, is that each protocol needs to add protocol headers and tails to data as it is transmitted, and to remove them as it processes received data. This make passing data buffers between the protocols difficult, as each layer needs to find where its particular protocol headers and tails are. One solution is to copy buffers at each layer, but that would be inefficient. Instead, Linux uses socket buffers, or `sk_buffs`, to pass data between the protocol layers and the network device drivers. `sk_buffs` contain pointer and length fields that allow each protocol layer to manipulate the application data via standard functions or "methods."

Figure 10.4 shows the sk_buff data structure; each sk_buff has a block of data associated with it. The sk_buff has four data pointers, which are used to manipulate and manage the socket buffer's data:

♦ head—points to the start of the data area in memory. This is fixed when the sk_buff and its associated data block is allocated.

♦ data—points at the current start of the protocol data. This pointer varies depending on the protocol layer that currently owns the sk_buff.

♦ tail—points at the current end of the protocol data. Again, this pointer varies depending on the owning protocol layer.

♦ end—points at the end of the data area in memory. This is fixed when the sk_buff is allocated.

There are two length fields, len and truesize, which describe the length of the current protocol packet and the total size of the data buffer, respectively. The sk_buff handling code provides standard mechanisms for adding and removing protocol headers and tails to the application data. These safely manipulate the data, tail, and len fields in the sk_buff:

♦ push—This moves the data pointer toward the start of the data area and increments the len field. This is used when adding data or protocol headers to the start of the data to be transmitted.

♦ pull—This moves the data pointer away from the start, toward the end of the data area and decrements the len field. This is used when removing data or protocol headers from the start of the data that has been received.

♦ put—This moves the tail pointer toward the end of the data area and increments the len field. This is used when adding data or protocol information to the end of the data to be transmitted.

♦ trim—This moves the tail pointer toward the start of the data area and decrements the len field. This is used when removing data or protocol tails from the received packet.

The sk_buff data structure also contains pointers that are used as it is stored in doubly linked circular lists of sk_buff's during processing. There are generic sk_buff routines for adding sk_buffs to the front and back of these lists and for removing them.

10.5.2 Receiving IP Packets

Chapter 9 described how Linux's network drivers are built into the kernel and initialized. This results in a series of device data structures linked together in the dev_base list. Each device data structure describes its device, and provides a set of callback routines that the network protocol layers call when they need the network driver to perform work. These functions are mostly concerned with transmitting data and with the network device's addresses. When a network device receives packets from its network, it must convert the

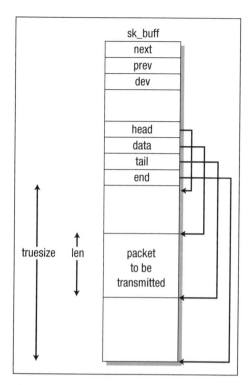

Figure 10.4
The socket buffer (sk_buff).

received data into sk_buff data structures. These received sk_buffs are added onto the backlog queue by the network drivers as they are received.

If the backlog queue grows too large, then the received sk_buffs are discarded. The network bottom half is flagged as ready to run as there is work to do. When the network bottom half handler is run by the scheduler, it processes any network packets waiting to be transmitted before processing the backlog queue of sk_buffs determining which protocol layer to pass the received packets to. As the Linux networking layers were initialized, each protocol registered itself by adding a packet_type data structure onto either the ptype_all list or into the ptype_base hash table. The packet_type data structure contains the protocol type, a pointer to a network device, a pointer to the protocol's receive data processing routine and, finally, a pointer to the next packet_type data structure in the list or hash chain. The ptype_all chain is used to snoop all packets being received from any network device, and is not normally used. The ptype_base hash table is hashed by protocol identifier and is used to decide which protocol should receive the incoming network packet. The network bottom half matches the protocol types of incoming sk_buffs against one or more of the packet_type entries in either table. The protocol may match more than one entry, for example, when snooping all network traffic, and in this case the sk_buff will be cloned. The sk_buff is passed to the matching protocol's handling routine.

10.5.3   Sending IP Packets

Packets are transmitted by applications exchanging data, or else they are generated by the network protocols as they support established connections or connections being established. Whichever way the data is generated, an `sk_buff` is built to contain the data and various headers are added by the protocol layers as it passes through them.

The `sk_buff` needs to be passed to a network device to be transmitted. First though, the protocol, for example, IP, needs to decide which network device to use. This depends on the best route for the packet. For computers connected by modem to a single network, say, via the PPP protocol, the routing choice is easy. The packet should either be sent to the local host via the loopback device, or to the gateway at the end of the PPP modem connection. For computers connected to an Ethernet the choices are harder, as there are many computers connected to the network.

For every IP packet transmitted, IP uses the routing tables to resolve the route for the destination IP address. Each IP destination successfully looked up in the routing tables returns a `rtable` data structure describing the route to use. This includes the source IP address to use, the address of the network `device` data structure and, sometimes, a prebuilt hardware header. This hardware header is network device-specific, and contains the source and destination physical addresses and other media-specific information. If the network device is an Ethernet device, the hardware header would be as shown in Figure 10.1, and the source and destination addresses would be physical Ethernet addresses. The hardware header is cached with the route because it must be appended to each IP packet transmitted on this route, and constructing it takes time. The hardware header may contain physical addresses that have to be resolved using the ARP protocol. In this case, the outgoing packet is stalled until the address has been resolved. Once it has been resolved and the hardware header built, the hardware header is cached, so that future IP packets sent using this interface do not have to ARP.

10.5.4   Data Fragmentation

Every network device has a maximum packet size, and it cannot transmit or receive a data packet bigger than this. The IP protocol allows for this and will fragment data into smaller units to fit into the packet size that the network device can handle. The IP protocol header includes a fragment field which contains a flag and the fragment offset.

When an IP packet is ready to be transmitted, IP finds the network device to send the IP packet out on. This device is found from the IP routing tables. Each `device` has a field describing its maximum transfer unit (in bytes), this is the `mtu` field. If the device's mtu is smaller than the packet size of the IP packet that is waiting to be transmitted, then the IP packet must be broken down into smaller (mtu-sized) fragments. Each fragment is represented by an `sk_buff`; its IP header marked to show that it is a fragment and what offset into the data this IP packet contains. The last packet is marked as being the last IP fragment. If, during the fragmentation, IP cannot allocate an `sk_buff`, the transmit will fail.

Receiving IP fragments is a little more difficult than sending them, because the IP fragments can be received in any order and they must all be received before they can be reassembled. Each time an IP packet is received, it is checked to see if it is an IP fragment. The first time that the fragment of a message is received, IP creates a new `ipq` data structure, and this is linked into the `ipqueue` list of IP fragments awaiting recombination. As more IP fragments are received, the correct `ipq` data structure is found, and a new `ipfrag` data structure is created to describe this fragment. Each `ipq` data structure uniquely describes a fragmented IP receive frame with its source and destination IP addresses, the upper-layer protocol identifier, and the identifier for this IP frame. When all of the fragments have been received, they are combined into a single `sk_buff` and passed up to the next protocol level to be processed. Each `ipq` contains a timer that is restarted each time a valid fragment is received. If this timer expires, the `ipq` data structure and its `ipfrags` are dismantled, and the message is presumed to have been lost in transit. It is then up to the higher-level protocols to retransmit the message.

10.6   The Address Resolution Protocol (ARP)

The Address Resolution Protocol's role is to provide translations of IP addresses into physical hardware addresses, such as Ethernet addresses. IP needs this translation just before it passes the data (in the form of an `sk_buff`) to the device driver for transmission.

It performs various checks to see if this device needs a hardware header and, if it does, if the hardware header for the packet needs to be rebuilt. Linux caches hardware headers to avoid frequent rebuilding of them. If the hardware header needs rebuilding, it calls the device specific hardware header rebuilding routine. All Ethernet devices use the same generic header rebuilding routine, which in turn uses the ARP services to translate the destination IP address into a physical address.

The ARP protocol itself is very simple, and consists of two message types: an ARP request and an ARP reply. The ARP *request* contains the IP address that needs translating, and the reply (hopefully) contains the translated IP address, the hardware address. The ARP request is broadcast to all hosts connected to the network, so, for an Ethernet network, all of the machines connected to the Ethernet will see the ARP request. The machine that owns the IP address in the request will respond to the ARP request with an ARP *reply*, containing its own physical address.

The ARP protocol layer in Linux is built around a table of `arp_table` data structures which each describe an IP-to-physical-address translation. These entries are created as IP addresses need to be translated and removed as they become stale over time. Each `arp_table` data structure has the following fields:

last used	The time that this ARP entry was last used
last updated	The time that this ARP entry was last updated
flags	These describe this entry's state, if it is complete, and so on

IP address	The IP address that this entry describes
hardware address	The translated hardware address
hardware header	This is a pointer to a cached hardware header
timer	This is a `timer_list` entry used to time out ARP requests that do not get a response
retries	The number of times that this ARP request has been retried
`sk_buff` queue	List of `sk_buff` entries waiting for this IP address to be resolved

The ARP table consists of a table of pointers (the `arp_tables` vector) to chains of `arp_table` entries. The entries are cached to speed up access to them; each entry is found by taking the last two bytes of its IP address to generate an index into the table and then following the chain of entries until the correct one is found. Linux also caches prebuilt hardware headers off the `arp_table` entries in the form of `hh_cache` data structures.

When an IP address translation is requested and there is no corresponding `arp_table` entry, ARP must send an ARP request message. It creates a new `arp_table` entry in the table, and queues the `sk_buff` containing the network packet that needs the address translation on the `sk_buff` queue of the new entry. It sends out an ARP request and sets the ARP expiry timer running. If there is no response, then ARP will retry the request a number of times; and if there is still no response, ARP will remove the `arp_table` entry. Any `sk_buff` data structures queued waiting for the IP address to be translated will be notified, and it is up to the protocol layer that is transmitting them to cope with this failure. UDP does not care about lost packets, but TCP will attempt to retransmit on an established TCP link. If the owner of the IP address responds with its hardware address, the `arp_table` entry is marked as complete, and any queued `sk_buff`s will be removed from the queue and will go on to be transmitted. The hardware address is written into the hardware header of each `sk_buff`.

The ARP protocol layer must also respond to ARP requests that specify its IP address. It registers its protocol type (`ETH_P_ARP`), generating a `packet_type` data structure. This means that it will be passed all ARP packets that are received by the network devices. As well as ARP replies, this includes ARP requests. It generates an ARP reply using the hardware address kept in the receiving device's `device` data structure.

Network topologies can change over time, and IP addresses can be reassigned to different hardware addresses. For example, some dial-up services assign an IP address as each connection is established. In order that the ARP table contains up-to-date entries, ARP runs a periodic timer, which looks through all of the `arp_table` entries to see which have timed out. It is very careful not to remove entries that contain one or more cached hardware headers. Removing these entries is dangerous, as other data structures rely on them. Some `arp_table` entries are permanent and these are marked so that they will not be deallocated. The ARP table cannot be allowed to grow too large; each `arp_table` entry consumes some kernel memory. Whenever the a new entry needs to be allocated and the ARP table has reached its maximum size, the table is pruned by searching out the oldest entries and removing them.

10.7 IP Routing

The IP routing function determines where to send IP packets destined for a particular IP address. There are many choices to be made when transmitting IP packets. Can the destination be reached at all? If it can be reached, which network device should be used to transmit it? If there is more than one network device that could be used to reach the destination, which is the better one? The IP routing database maintains information that gives answers to these questions. There are two databases, the most important being the Forwarding Information Database. This is an exhaustive list of known IP destinations and their best routes. A smaller and much faster database, the *route cache*, is used for quick lookups of routes for IP destinations. Like all caches, it must contain only the frequently accessed routes; its contents are derived from the Forwarding Information Database.

Routes are added and deleted via IOCTL requests to the BSD socket interface. These are passed on to the protocol to process. The INET protocol layer only allows processes with superuser privileges to add and delete IP routes. These routes can be fixed, or they can be dynamic and change over time. Most systems use fixed routes, unless they themselves are routers. Routers run routing protocols, which constantly check on the availability of routes to all known IP destinations. Systems that are not routers are known as *end systems*. The routing protocols are implemented as daemons, for example, GATED, and they also add and delete routes via the IOCTL BSD socket interface.

10.7.1 The Route Cache

Whenever an IP route is looked up, the route cache is first checked for a matching route. If there is no matching route in the route cache, the Forwarding Information Database is searched for a route. If no route can be found there, the IP packet will fail to be sent and the application notified. If a route is in the Forwarding Information Database and not in the route cache, then a new entry is generated and added into the route cache for this route. The route cache is a table (`ip_rt_hash_table`) that contains pointers to chains of `rtable` data structures. The index into the route table is a hash function based on the least significant two bytes of the IP address. These are the two bytes most likely to be different between destinations, and provide the best spread of hash values. Each `rtable` entry contains information about the route: the destination IP address, the network `device` to use to reach that IP address, the maximum size of message that can be used, and so on. It also has a reference count, a usage count, and a timestamp of the last time that they were used (in `jiffies`). The reference count is incremented each time the route is used to show the number of network connections using this route. It is decremented as applications stop using the route. The usage count is incremented each time the route is looked up, and is used to order the `rtable` entry in its chain of hash entries. The last-used timestamp for all of the entries in the route cache is periodically checked to see if the `rtable` is too old. If the route has not been recently used, it is discarded from the route cache. If routes are kept in the route cache, they are ordered so that the most used entries are at the front of the hash chains. This means that finding them will be quicker when routes are looked up.

10.7.2   The Forwarding Information Database

The Forwarding Information Database shown in Figure 10.5 contains IP's view of the routes available to this system at this time. It is quite a complicated data structure and, although it is reasonably efficiently arranged, it is not a quick database to consult. In particular, it would be very slow to look up destinations in this database for every IP packet transmitted. This is the reason that the route cache exists: to speed up IP packet transmission using known good routes. The route cache is derived from the forwarding database and represents its commonly used entries.

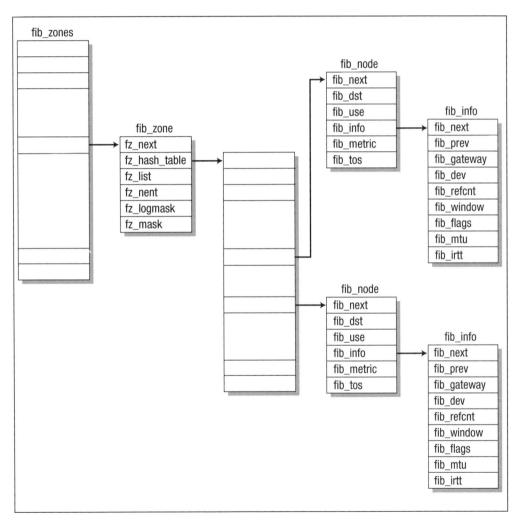

Figure 10.5
The Forwarding Information Database.

Each IP subnet is represented by a `fib_zone` data structure. All of these are pointed at from the `fib_zones` hash table. The hash index is derived from the IP subnet mask. All routes to the same subnet are described by pairs of `fib_node` and `fib_info` data structures queued onto the `fz_list` of each `fib_zone` data structure. If the number of routes in this subnet grows large, a hash table is generated to make finding the `fib_node` data structures easier.

Several routes may exist to the same IP subnet, and these routes can go through one of several gateways. The IP routing layer does not allow more than one route to a subnet using the same gateway. In other words, if there are several routes to a subnet, then each route is guaranteed to use a different gateway. Associated with each route is its metric. This is a measure of how advantageous this route is. A route's metric is, essentially, the number of IP subnets that it must hop across before it reaches the destination subnet. The higher the metric, the worse the route.

Chapter 11
Kernel Mechanisms

This chapter describes some of the general tasks and mechanisms that the Linux kernel needs to supply, so that other parts of the kernel work effectively together.

11.1   Bottom Half Handling

There are often times in a kernel when you do not want to do work at this moment. A good example of this is during interrupt processing. When the interrupt was asserted, the processor stopped what it was doing, and the operating system delivered the interrupt to the appropriate device driver. Device drivers should not spend too much time handling interrupts as, during this time, nothing else in the system can run. There is often some work that could just as well be done later on. Linux's *bottom half handlers* were invented so that device drivers and other parts of the Linux kernel could queue work to be done later on. Figure 11.1 shows the kernel data structures associated with bottom half handling.

There can be up to 32 different bottom half handlers; bh_base is a vector of pointers to each of the kernel's bottom half handling routines. bh_active and bh_mask have their bits set according to what handlers have been installed and are active. If bit N of bh_mask is set, then the Nth element of bh_base contains the address of a bottom half routine. If bit N of bh_active is set, then the Nth bottom half handler routine should be called as soon as the scheduler deems reasonable. These indices are statically defined; the timer bottom half handler is the highest priority (index 0), the console bottom half handler is next in priority (index 1), and so on. Typically, the bottom half handling routines have

161

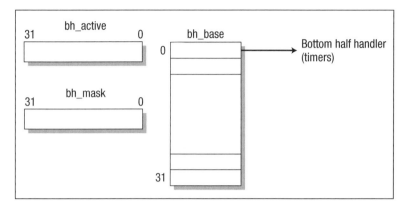

Figure 11.1
Bottom half handling data structures.

lists of tasks associated with them. For example, the immediate bottom half handler works its way through the immediate tasks queue (`tq_immediate`), which contains tasks that need to be performed immediately.

Some of the kernel's bottom half handers are device-specific, but others are more generic:

◆ TIMER—This handler is marked as active each time the system's periodic timer interrupts, and is used to drive the kernel's timer queue mechanisms.

◆ CONSOLE—This handler is used to process console messages.

◆ TQUEUE—This handler is used to process `tty` messages.

◆ NET—This handler handles general network processing.

◆ IMMEDIATE—This is a generic handler used by several device drivers to queue work to be done later.

Whenever a device driver or some other part of the kernel needs to schedule work to be done later, it adds work to the appropriate system queue, for example, the timer queue, and then signals the kernel that some bottom half handling needs to be done. It does this by setting the appropriate bit in `bh_active`. Bit 8 is set if the driver has queued something on the immediate queue and wishes the immediate bottom half handler to run and process it. The `bh_active` bitmask is checked at the end of each system call, just before control is returned to the calling process. If it has any bits set, the bottom half handler routines that are active are called. Bit 0 is checked first, then 1, and so on, until bit 31.

The bit in `bh_active` is cleared as each bottom half handling routine is called. `bh_active` is transient; it only has meaning between calls to the scheduler, and is a way of not calling bottom half handling routines when there is no work for them to do.

11.2   Task Queues

Task queues are the kernel's way of deferring work until later. Linux has a generic mechanism for queuing work on queues and for processing them later.

Task queues are often used in conjunction with bottom half handlers; the timer task queue is processed when the timer queue bottom half handler runs. A task queue is a simple data structure; see Figure 11.2, which consists of a singly linked list of `tq_struct` data structures, each of which contains the address of a routine and a pointer to some data.

The routine will be called when the element on the task queue is processed, and it will be passed a pointer to the data.

Anything in the kernel, for example, a device driver, can create and use task queues, but there are three task queues created and managed by the kernel:

◆ timer—This queue is used to queue work that will be done as soon after the next system clock tick as is possible. Each clock tick, this queue is checked to see if it contains any entries; if it does, the timer queue bottom half handler is made active. The timer queue bottom half handler is processed, along with all the other bottom half handlers, when the scheduler next runs. This queue should not be confused with system timers, which are a much more sophisticated mechanism.

◆ immediate—This queue is also processed when the scheduler processes the active bottom half handlers. The immediate bottom half handler is not as high in priority as the timer queue bottom half handler, and so these tasks will be run later.

◆ scheduler—This task queue is processed directly by the scheduler. It is used to support other task queues in the system and, in this case, the task to be run will be a routine that processes a task queue, say, for a device driver.

When task queues are processed, the pointer to the first element in the queue is removed from the queue and replaced with a null pointer. In fact, this removal is an atomic operation, one that cannot be interrupted. Then each element in the queue has its handling routine called, in turn. The elements in the queue are often statically allocated data. However, there is no inherent mechanism for discarding allocated memory. The task queue processing routine simply moves onto the next element in the list. It is the job of the task itself to ensure that it properly cleans up any allocated kernel memory.

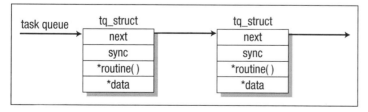

Figure 11.2
A task queue.

11.3 Timers

An operating system needs to be able to schedule an activity sometime in the future. A mechanism is needed whereby activities can be scheduled to run at some relatively precise time. Any microprocessor that wishes to support an operating system must have a programmable interval timer that periodically interrupts the processor. This periodic interrupt is known as a *system clock tick* and it acts like a metronome, orchestrating the system's activities.

Linux has a very simple view of what time it is; it measures time in clock ticks since the system booted. All system times are based on this measurement, which is known as `jiffies`, after the globally available variable of the same name.

Linux has two types of system timers; both queue routines to be called at some system time, but they are slightly different in their implementations. Figure 11.3 shows both mechanisms.

The first, the old timer mechanism, has a static array of 32 pointers to `timer_struct` data structures and a mask of active timers, `timer_active`.

Where the timers go in the timer table is statically defined (rather like the bottom half handler table `bh_base`). Entries are added into this table mostly at system initialization time. The second, newer, mechanism uses a linked list of `timer_list` data structures held in ascending expiry time order.

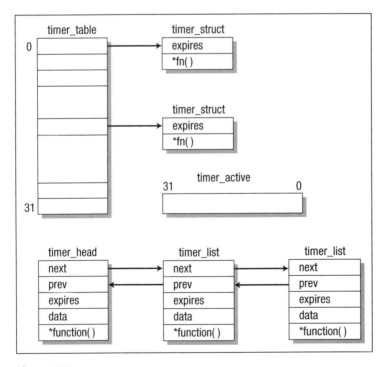

Figure 11.3
System timers.

Both methods use the time in jiffies as an expiry time, so that a timer that wished to run in fives would have to convert fives to units of jiffies, and add that to the current system time to get the system time, in jiffies, when the timer should expire. Every system clock tick, the timer bottom half handler is marked as active, so that the when the scheduler next runs, the timer queues will be processed. The timer bottom half handler processes both types of system timer. For the old system timers, the timer_active bit mask is checked for bits that are set.

If the expiry time for an active timer has expired (expiry time is less than the current system jiffies), its timer routine is called, and its active bit is cleared. For new system timers, the entries in the linked list of timer_list data structures are checked.

Every expired timer is removed from the list and its routine is called. The new timer mechanism has the advantage of being able to pass an argument to the timer routine.

11.4   Wait Queues

There are many times when a process must wait for a system resource. For example, a process may need the VFS inode describing a directory in the file system, and that inode may not be in the buffer cache. In this case, the process must wait for that inode to be fetched from the physical media containing the file system before it can carry on.

The Linux kernel uses a simple data structure, a *wait queue* (see Figure 11.4), which consists of a pointer to the processes task_struct and a pointer to the next element in the wait queue.

When processes are added to the end of a wait queue, they can either be interruptible or uninterruptible. Interruptible processes may be interrupted by events, such as timers expiring or signals being delivered while they are waiting on a wait queue. The waiting processes state will reflect this and either be INTERRUPTIBLE or UNINTERRUPTIBLE. As this process cannot now continue to run, the scheduler is run and, when it selects a new process to run, the waiting process will be suspended.

When the wait queue is processed, the state of every process in the wait queue is set to RUNNING. If the process has been removed from the run queue, it is put back onto the run

Figure 11.4
Wait queue.

queue. The next time the scheduler runs, the processes that are on the wait queue are now candidates to be run, as they are now no longer waiting. When a process on the wait queue is scheduled, the first thing that it will do is remove itself from the wait queue. Wait queues can be used to synchronize access to system resources, and they are used by Linux in its implementation of semaphores (see below).

11.5   Buzz Locks

These are better known as spin locks, and they are a primitive way of protecting a data structure or piece of code. They allow only one process at a time to be within a critical region of code. They are used in Linux to restrict access to fields in data structures, using a single integer field as a lock. Each process wishing to enter the region attempts to change the lock's initial value from zero to one. If its current value is one, the process tries again, spinning in a tight loop of code. The access to the memory location holding the lock must be atomic, the action of reading its value, checking that it is zero, and then changing it to one cannot be interrupted by any other process. Most CPU architectures provide support for this via special instructions, but you can also implement buzz locks using uncached main memory.

When the owning process leaves the critical region of code, it decrements the buzz lock, returning its value to zero. Any processes spinning on the lock will now read it as zero; the first one to do this will increment it to one and enter the critical region.

11.6   Semaphores

Semaphores are used to protect critical regions of code or data structures. Remember that each access of a critical piece of data, such as a VFS inode describing a directory, is made by kernel code running on behalf of a process. It would be very dangerous to allow one process to alter a critical data structure that is being used by another process. One way to achieve this would be to use a buzz lock around the critical piece of data is being accessed, but this is a simplistic approach that would not give very good system performance. Instead, Linux uses semaphores to allow just one process at a time to access critical regions of code and data; all other processes wishing to access this resource will be made to wait until it becomes free. The waiting processes are suspended; other processes in the system can continue to run as normal.

A Linux `semaphore` data structure contains the following information:

♦ count—This field keeps track of the count of processes wishing to use this resource. A positive value means that the resource is available. A negative or zero value means that processes are waiting for it. An initial value of one means that one and only one process at a time can use this resource. When processes want this resource, they decrement the count, and when they have finished with this resource they increment the count.

♦ waking—This is the count of processes waiting for this resource, which is also the number of processes waiting to be woken up when this resource becomes free.

♦ wait queue—When processes are waiting for this resource, they are put onto this wait queue.

♦ lock—A buzz lock used when accessing the `waking` field.

Suppose the initial count for a semaphore is one. The first process to come along will see that the count is positive and decrement it by one, making it zero. The process now "owns" the critical piece of code or resource that is being protected by the semaphore. When the process leaves the critical region, it increments the semaphore's count. The most optimal case is where there are no other processes contending for ownership of the critical region. Linux has implemented semaphores to work efficiently for this, the most common case.

If another process wishes to enter the critical region while it is owned by a process, it too will decrement the count. As the count is now negative (–1) the process cannot enter the critical region. Instead, it must wait until the owning process exits it. Linux makes the waiting process sleep until the owning process wakes it on exiting the critical region. The waiting process adds itself to the semaphore's wait queue and sits in a loop, checking the value of the `waking` field and calling the scheduler until `waking` is nonzero.

The owner of the critical region increments the semaphore's count, and if it is less than or equal to zero, then there are processes sleeping, waiting for this resource. In the optimal case, the semaphore's count would have been returned to its initial value of one and no further work would be necessary. The owning process increments the waking counter and wakes up the process sleeping on the semaphore's wait queue. When the waiting process wakes up, the waking counter is now one, and it knows that it may now enter the critical region. It decrements the waking counter, returning it to a value of zero, and continues. All access to the waking field of semaphore are protected by a buzz lock using the semaphore's lock.

Chapter 12
Modules

This chapter describes how the Linux kernel can dynamically load functions, for example, file systems, only when they are needed.

Linux is a *monolithic kernel*; that is, it is one single, large program where all the functional components of the kernel have access to all of its internal data structures and routines.

The alternative is to have a *micro-kernel structure*, where the functional pieces of the kernel are broken out into separate units with strict communication mechanisms between them. This makes adding new components into the kernel via the configuration process rather time-consuming. Say you wanted to use a SCSI driver for an NCR 810 SCSI, and you had not built it into the kernel. You would have to configure and then build a new kernel before you could use the NCR 810.

There is an alternative; Linux allows you to dynamically load and unload components of the operating system as you need them. Linux modules are lumps of code that can be dynamically linked into the kernel at any point after the system has booted. They can be unlinked from the kernel and removed when they are no longer needed. Mostly, Linux kernel modules are device drivers, pseudo-device drivers such as network drivers, or file systems.

You can either load and unload Linux kernel modules explicitly using the **insmod** and **rmmod** commands, or the kernel itself can demand that the kernel daemon (`kerneld`) loads and unloads the modules as they are needed.

Dynamically loading code as it is needed is attractive, as it keeps the kernel size to a minimum and makes the kernel very flexible. My current Intel kernel uses modules extensively and is only 406KB long. I only occasionally use VFAT file systems, and so I build my Linux kernel to automatically load the VFAT file system module as I mount a VFAT partition. When I have unmounted the VFAT partition, the system detects that I no longer need the VFAT file system module and removes it from the system. Modules can also be useful for trying out new kernel code without having to rebuild and reboot the kernel every time you try it out.

Nothing, though, is for free, and there is a slight performance and memory penalty associated with kernel modules. There is a little more code that a loadable module must provide, and this and the extra data structures take a little more memory. There is also a level of indirection introduced that makes accesses of kernel resources slightly less efficient for modules.

Once a Linux module has been loaded, it is as much a part of the kernel as any normal kernel code. It has the same rights and responsibilities as any kernel code; in other words, Linux kernel modules can crash the kernel just like all kernel code or device drivers can.

So that modules can use the kernel resources that they need, they must be able to find them. Say a module needs to call `kmalloc()`, the kernel memory allocation routine. At the time that it is built, a module does not know where in memory `kmalloc()` is, so when the module is loaded, the kernel must fix up all of the module's references to `kmalloc()` before the module can work. The kernel keeps a list of all of the kernel's resources in the kernel symbol table, so that it can resolve references to those resources from the modules as they are loaded.

Linux allows module stacking; this is where one module requires the services of another module. For example, the VFAT file system module requires the services of the FAT file system module, as the VFAT file system is more or less a set of extensions to the FAT file system. One module requiring services or resources from another module is very similar to the situation where a module requires services and resources from the kernel itself. Only here the required services are in another, previously loaded module. As each module is loaded, the kernel modifies the kernel symbol table, adding to it all of the resources or symbols exported by the newly loaded module. This means that when the next module is loaded, it has access to the services of the already loaded modules.

When an attempt is made to unload a module, the kernel needs to know that the module is unused, and it needs some way of notifying the module that it is about to be unloaded. That way, the module will be able to free up any system resources that it has allocated, for example kernel memory or interrupts, before it is removed from the kernel. When the module is unloaded, the kernel removes any symbols that that module exported into the kernel symbol table.

Apart from the ability of a loaded module to crash the operating system by being badly written, it presents another danger. What happens if you load a module built for an earlier or later kernel than the one that you are now running? This may cause a problem if, say, the module makes a call to a kernel routine and supplies the wrong arguments. The kernel can, optionally, protect against this by making rigorous version checks on the module as it is loaded.

12.1   Loading A Module

There are two ways that a kernel module can be loaded. The first way is to use the **insmod** command to manually insert it into the kernel. The second and much more clever way is to load the module as it is needed; this is known as *demand loading*.

When the kernel discovers the need for a module, for example, when the user mounts a file system that is not in the kernel, the kernel will request that the kernel daemon (`kerneld`) attempt to load the appropriate module.

The kernel daemon is a normal user process, albeit with super-user privileges. When it is started up, usually at system boot time, it opens up an interprocess communication (IPC) channel to the kernel. This link is used by the kernel to send messages to the `kerneld`, asking for various tasks to be performed.

`kerneld`'s major function is to load and unload kernel modules, but it is also capable of other tasks, such as starting up the PPP link over serial line when it is needed, and closing it down when it is not. `kerneld` does not perform these tasks itself; it runs the necessary programs, such as **insmod**, to do the work. `kerneld` is just an agent of the kernel, scheduling work on its behalf.

The **insmod** utility must find the requested kernel module that it is to load. Demand-loaded kernel modules are normally kept in `/lib/modules/kernel-version`. The kernel modules are linked object files just like other programs in the system except that they are linked as *relocatable images*, that is, images that are not linked to run from a particular address. They can be either `a.out` or `elf` format object files.

insmod makes a privileged system call to find the kernel's exported symbols. These are kept in pairs, containing the symbol's name and its value, for example, its address. The kernel's exported symbol table is held in the first `module` data structure in the list of modules maintained by the kernel, and pointed at by the `module_list` pointer.

Only specifically entered symbols are added into the table, which is built when the kernel is compiled and linked; not *every* symbol in the kernel is exported to its modules. An example symbol is "`request_irq`," which is the kernel routine that must be called when a driver wishes to take control of a particular system interrupt. In my current kernel, this has a value of 0x0010cd30. You can easily see the exported kernel symbols and their values by looking at `/proc/ksyms`, or by using the **ksyms** utility. The **ksyms** utility can either show you all of the exported kernel symbols, or only those symbols exported by loaded modules. **insmod** reads the module into its virtual memory, and fixes up its unresolved references to kernel routines and resources using the exported symbols from the kernel. This fixing up takes the form of patching the module image in memory. **insmod** physically writes the address of the symbol into the appropriate place in the module.

When **insmod** has fixed up the module's references to exported kernel symbols, it asks the kernel for enough space to hold the new kernel, again using a privileged system call. The kernel allocates a new `module` data structure and enough kernel memory to hold the new module, and puts it at the end of the kernel modules list. The new module is marked as `UNINITIALIZED`.

Figure 12.1 shows the list of kernel modules after two modules, VFAT and VFAT, have been loaded into the kernel. Not shown in the diagram is the first module on the list, which is a pseudo-module that is only there to hold the kernel's exported symbol table. You can use the command **lsmod** to list all of the loaded kernel modules and their interdependencies. **lsmod** simply reformats `/proc/modules`, which is built from the list of kernel `module` data structures. The memory that the kernel allocates for it is mapped into the **insmod** process's address space, so that it can access it. **insmod** copies the module into the allocated space, and relocates it so that it will run from the kernel address that it has been allocated. This must happen, as the module cannot expect to be loaded at the same address twice, let alone into the same address in two different Linux systems. Again, this relocation involves patching the module image with the appropriate addresses.

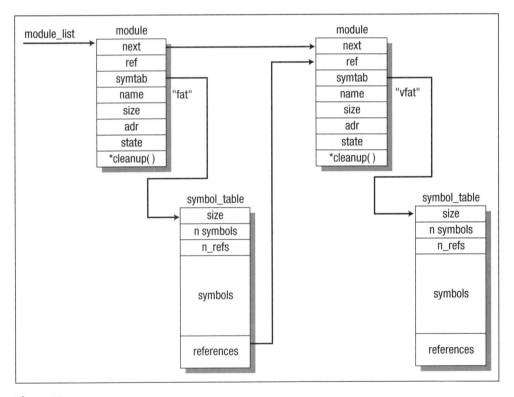

Figure 12.1
The list of kernel modules.

The new module also exports symbols to the kernel, and **insmod** builds a table of these exported images. Every kernel module must contain module initialization and module cleanup routines, and these symbols are deliberately not exported; but **insmod** must know the addresses of them, so that it can pass them to the kernel. All being well, **insmod** is now ready to initialize the module, and it makes a privileged system call passing the kernel the addresses of the module's initialization and cleanup routines.

When a new module is added into the kernel, it must update the kernel's set of symbols and modify the modules that are being used by the new module. Modules that have other modules dependent on them must maintain a list of references at the end of their symbol table, pointed at by their `module` data structure. Figure 12.1 shows that the VFAT file system module is dependent on the FAT file system module. So, the FAT module contains a reference to the VFAT module; the reference was added when the VFAT module was loaded. The kernel calls the modules initialization routine and, if it is successful, it carries on installing the module. The module's cleanup routine address is stored in its `module` data structure, and it will be called by the kernel when that module is unloaded. Finally, the module's state is set to `RUNNING`.

12.2   Unloading A Module

Modules can be removed using the **rmmod** command, but demand-loaded modules are automatically removed from the system by `kerneld` when they are no longer being used. Every time its idle timer expires, `kerneld` makes a system call, requesting that all unused demand loaded modules be removed from the system. The timer's value is set when you start `kerneld`; my `kerneld` checks every 180 seconds. So, for example, if you mount an `iso9660` CD-ROM and your `iso9660` file system is a loadable module, then shortly after the CD-ROM is unmounted, the `iso9660` module will be removed from the kernel.

A module cannot be unloaded so long as other components of the kernel are depending on it. For example, you cannot unload the VFAT module if you have one or more VFAT file systems mounted. If you look at the output of **lsmod**, you will see that each module has a count associated with it. For example:

```
Module:        #pages:  Used by:
msdos             5                  1
vfat              4                  1 (autoclean)
fat               6      [vfat msdos] 2 (autoclean)
```

The count is the number of kernel entities that are dependent on this module. In the above example, the `vfat` and `msdos` modules are both dependent on the `fat` module, and so it has a count of 2. Both the `vfat` and `msdos` modules have one dependent, which is a mounted file system. If I were to load another VFAT file system, then the `vfat` module's count would become two. A module's count is held in the first long word of its image.

This field is slightly overloaded, as it also holds the AUTOCLEAN and VISITED flags. Both of these flags are used for demand-loaded modules. These modules are marked as AUTOCLEAN, so that the system can recognize which ones it may automatically unload. The VISITED flag marks the module as in use by one or more other system components; it is set whenever another component makes use of the module. Each time the system is asked by kerneld to remove unused demand-loaded modules, it looks through all of the modules in the system for likely candidates. It only looks at modules marked as AUTOCLEAN and in the state RUNNING. If the candidate has its VISITED flag cleared, then it will remove the module; otherwise, it will clear the VISITED flag and go on to look at the next module in the system.

Assuming that a module can be unloaded, its cleanup routine is called to allow it to free up the kernel resources that it has allocated. The module data structure is marked as DE-LETED, and it is unlinked from the list of kernel modules. Any other modules that it is dependent on have their reference lists modified, so that they no longer have it as a dependent. All of the kernel memory that the module needed is deallocated.

Chapter 13

Processors

Linux runs on a number of processors. This chapter gives a brief outline of each of them.

13.1 X86

TBD

13.2 ARM

The ARM processor implements a low-power, high-performance 32-bit RISC architecture. It is being widely used in embedded devices such as mobile phones and PDAs (personal digital assistants). It has 31 32-bit registers with 16 visible in any mode. Its instructions are simple load-and-store instructions (load a value from memory, perform an operation, and store the result back into memory). One interesting feature it has is that every instruction is conditional. For example, you can test the value of a register and, until you next test for the same condition, you can conditionally execute instructions as and when you like. Another interesting feature is that you can perform arithmetic and shift operations on values as you load them. It operates in several modes, including a system mode that can be entered from user mode via a SWI (software interrupt).

It is a synthesizable core. ARM (the company) does not itself manufacture processors. Instead, the ARM partners (companies such as Intel or LSI, for example) implement the ARM architecture in silicon. It allows other processors to be tightly coupled via a co-processor interface, and it has several memory management unit variations. These range from simple memory protection schemes to complex page hierarchies.

13.3   Alpha AXP Processor

The Alpha AXP architecture is a 64-bit load/store RISC architecture designed with speed in mind. All registers are 64 bits in length: 32 integer registers and 32 floating point registers. Integer register 31 and floating point register 31 are used for null operations. A read from them generates a zero value, and a write to them has no effect. All instructions are 32 bits long, and memory operations are either reads or writes. The architecture allows different implementations, so long as the implementations follow the architecture.

There are no instructions that operate directly on values stored in memory; all data manipulation is done between registers. So, if you want to increment a counter in memory, you first read it into a register, then modify it and write it out. The instructions only interact with each other by one instruction writing to a register or memory location, and another register reading that register or memory location. One interesting feature of Alpha AXP is that there are instructions that can generate flags, such as testing if two registers are equal; the result is not stored in a processor status register, but is instead stored in a third register. This may seem strange at first, but removing this dependency from a status register means that it is much easier to build a CPU which can issue multiple instructions every cycle. Instructions on unrelated registers do not have to wait for each other to execute as they would if there were a single status register. The lack of direct operations on memory and the large number of registers also help issue multiple instructions.

The Alpha AXP architecture uses a set of subroutines, called privileged architecture library code (PALcode). PALcode is specific to the operating system, the CPU implementation of the Alpha AXP architecture, and to the system hardware. These subroutines provide operating system primitives for context switching, interrupts, exceptions, and memory management. These subroutines can be invoked by hardware or by CALL_PAL instructions. PALcode is written in standard Alpha AXP assembler with some implementation specific extensions to provide direct access to low-level hardware functions, for example, internal processor registers. PALcode is executed in PALmode, a privileged mode that stops some system events happening and allows the PALcode complete control of the physical system hardware.

Chapter 14
The Linux Kernel Sources

This chapter describes where, in the Linux kernel sources, you should start looking for particular kernel functions.

This book does not depend on a knowledge of the C programming language, or require that you have the Linux kernel sources available, in order to understand how the Linux kernel works. That said, it is a fruitful exercise to look at the kernel sources to get an in-depth understanding of the Linux operating system. This chapter gives an overview of the kernel sources, how they are arranged, and where you might start to look for particular code.

14.1   Where To Get The Linux Kernel Sources

All of the major Linux distributions (Craftworks, Debian, Slackware, Red Hat, and so forth) include the kernel sources in them. Usually, the Linux kernel that got installed on your Linux system was built from those sources. By their very nature, these sources tend to be a little out of date, so you may want to get the latest sources from one of the Web sites mentioned in Appendix A. They are kept on **ftp://ftp.kernel.org/**, and all of the other Web sites shadow them. This makes the Helsinki Web site the most up to date, but sites like MIT and Sunsite are never very far behind.

If you do not have access to the Web, there are many CD-ROM vendors who offer snapshots of the world's major Web sites at a very reasonable cost. Some even offer a subscription service, with quarterly or even monthly updates. Your local Linux User Group is also a good source of sources.

The Linux kernel sources have a very simple numbering system. Any even number kernel (for example 2.0.30) is a stable, released kernel, and any odd numbered kernel (for example 2.1.42) is a development kernel. This book is based on the stable 2.0.30 source tree. Development kernels have all of the latest features and support all of the latest devices. Although they can be unstable, which may not be exactly what you want, it is important that the Linux community tries the latest kernels. That way they are tested for the whole community. Remember that it is *always* worth backing up your system thoroughly, if you do try out nonproduction kernels.

Changes to the kernel sources are distributed as **patch** files. The **patch** utility is used to apply a series of edits to a set of source files. So, for example, if you have the 2.0.29 kernel source tree and you wanted to move to the 2.0.30 source tree, you would obtain the 2.0.30 patch file and apply the patches (edits) to that source tree:

```
$ cd /usr/src/linux
$ patch -p1 < patch-2.0.30
```

This saves copying whole source trees, perhaps over slow serial connections. A good source of kernel patches (official and unofficial) is the **http://www.linuxhq.com** Web site.

14.2   How The Kernel Sources Are Arranged

At the very top level of the source tree /usr/src/linux you will see a number of directories:

♦ arch—The arch subdirectory contains all of the architecture specific kernel code. It has further subdirectories, one per supported architecture, for example, i386 and alpha.

♦ include—The include subdirectory contains most of the include files needed to build the kernel code. It, too, has further subdirectories, including one for every architecture supported. The include/asm subdirectory is a soft link to the real include directory needed for this architecture, for example include/asm-i386. To change architectures, you need to edit the kernel makefile and rerun the Linux kernel configuration program.

♦ init—This directory contains the initialization code for the kernel, and it is a very good place to start looking at how the kernel works.

♦ mm—This directory contains all of the memory management code. The architecture specific memory management code lives down in arch/*/mm/, for example arch/i386/mm/fault.c.

♦ drivers—All of the system's device drivers live in this directory. They are further sub-divided into classes of device driver, for example block.

♦ ipc—This directory contains the kernels interprocess communications code.

♦ modules—This is simply a directory used to hold built modules.

- fs—All of the file system code. This is further subdivided into directories, one per supported file system, for example `vfat` and `ext2`.

- kernel—The main kernel code. Again, the architecture specific kernel code is in `arch/*/kernel`.

- net—The kernel's networking code.

- lib—This directory contains the kernel's library code. The architecture-specific library code can be found in `arch/*/lib/`.

- scripts—This directory contains the scripts (for example `awk` and `tk` scripts) that are used when the kernel is configured.

14.3   Where To Start Looking

A large complex program like the Linux kernel can be rather daunting to look at. It is rather like a large ball of string, with no end showing. Looking at one part of the kernel often leads to looking at several other related files, and before long you have forgotten what you were looking for. The next subsections give you a hint as to where in the source tree the best place to look is, for a given subject.

14.3.1   System Startup And Initialization

On an Intel-based system, the kernel starts when either loadlin.exe or LILO has loaded the kernel into memory and passed control to it. Look in `arch/i386/kernel/head.S` for this part. `head.S` does some architecture-specific setup, and then jumps to the `main()` routine in `init/main.c`.

14.3.2   Memory Management

This code is mostly in `mm`, but the architecture specific code is in `arch/*/mm`. The page fault handling code is in `mm/memory.c`. The memory mapping and page cache code is in `mm/filemap.c`. The buffer cache is implemented in `mm/buffer.c`, and the swap cache in `mm/swap_state.c` and `mm/swapfile.c`.

14.3.3   Kernel

Most of the relevant generic code is in `kernel`, with the architecture-specific code in `arch/*/kernel`. The scheduler is in `kernel/sched.c`, and the fork code is in `kernel/fork.c`. The bottom half handling code is in `include/linux/interrupt.h`. The `task_struct` data structure can be found in `include/linux/sched.h`.

14.3.4   PCI

The PCI pseudo driver is in `drivers/pci/pci.c`, with the system-wide definitions in `include/linux/pci.h`. Each architecture has some specific PCI BIOS code; Alpha AXPs is in `arch/alpha/kernel/bios32.c`.

14.3.5 Interprocess Communication

This is all in `ipc`. All System V IPC objects include an `ipc_perm` data structure; this can be found in `include/linux/ipc.h`. System V messages are implemented in `ipc/msg.c`, shared memory in `ipc/shm.c`, and semaphores in `ipc/sem.c`. Pipes are implemented in `ipc/pipe.c`.

14.3.6 Interrupt Handling

The kernel's interrupt handling code is almost all microprocessor (and often platform) specific. The Intel interrupt handling code is in `arch/i386/kernel/irq.c`, and its definitions in `include/asm-i386/irq.h`.

14.3.7 Device Drivers

Most of the lines of the Linux kernel's source code are in its device drivers. All of Linux's device driver sources are held in `drivers`, but these are further broken out by type:

♦ /block—block device drivers such as ide (in `ide.c`). If you want to look at how all of the devices that could possibly contain file systems are initialized, then you should look at `device_setup()` in `drivers/block/genhd.c`. It initializes not only the hard disks but also the network, as you need a network to mount nfs file systems. Block devices include both IDE- and SCSI-based devices.

♦ /char—This the place to look for character-based devices such as `ttys`, serial ports, and mice.

♦ /cdrom—All of the CD-ROM code for Linux. It is here that the special CD-ROM devices (such as Soundblaster CD-ROM) can be found. Note that the IDE CD driver is `ide-cd.c` in `drivers/block,` and that the SCSI CD driver is in `scsi.c` in `drivers/scsi`.

♦ /pci—This are the sources for the PCI pseudo-driver, a good place to look at how the PCI subsystem is mapped and initialized. The Alpha AXP PCI fixup code is also worth looking at, in `arch/alpha/kernel/bios32.c`.

♦ /scsi—This is where to find all of the SCSI code, as well as all of the drivers for the SCSI devices supported by Linux.

♦ /net—This is where to look to find the network device drivers, such as the DECChip 21040 PCI Ethernet driver, which is in `tulip.c`.

♦ /sound—This is where all of the sound card drivers are.

14.3.8 File Systems

The sources for the EXT2 file system are all in the `fs/ext2/` directory, with data structure definitions in `include/linux/ext2_fs.h, ext2_fs_i.h` and `ext2_fs_sb.h`. The Virtual File System data structures are described in `include/linux/fs.h`, and the code is in `fs/*`. The buffer cache is implemented in `fs/buffer.c`, along with the `update` kernel daemon.

14.3.9 Network

The networking code is kept in `net`, with most of the include files in `include/net`. The BSD socket code is in `net/socket.c` and the IP version 4 INET socket code is in `net/ipv4/af_inet.c`. The generic protocol support code (including the `sk_buff` handling routines) is in `net/core`, with the TCP/IP networking code in `net/ipv4`. The network device drivers are in `drivers/net`.

14.3.10 Modules

The kernel module code is partially in the kernel, and partially in the `modules` package. The kernel code is all in `kernel/modules.c`, with the data structures and kernel demon `kerneld` messages in `include/linux/module.h` and `include/linux/kerneld.h`, respectively. You may want to look at the structure of an ELF object file in `include/linux/elf.h`.

Chapter 15
Linux Data Structures

This chapter lists the major data structures that Linux uses, which are described in this book. They have been edited slightly to fit the paper.

15.1 block_dev_struct

`block_dev_struct` data structures are used to register block devices as available for use by the buffer cache. They are held together in the `blk_dev` vector.

```
struct blk_dev_struct {
    void (*request_fn)(void);
    struct request * current_request;
    struct request   plug;
    struct tq_struct plug_tq;
};
```

15.2 buffer_head

The `buffer_head` data structure holds information about a block buffer in the buffer cache.

```
/* bh state bits */
#define BH_Uptodate  0   /* 1 if the buffer contains
valid data       */
#define BH_Dirty     1   /* 1 if the buffer is dirty
*/
#define BH_Lock      2   /* 1 if the buffer is locked
*/
```

```
#define BH_Req       3    /* 0 if the buffer has been invalidated  */
#define BH_Touched   4    /* 1 if the buffer has been touched (aging) */
#define BH_Has_aged  5    /* 1 if the buffer has been aged (aging)   */
#define BH_Protected 6    /* 1 if the buffer is protected            */
#define BH_FreeOnIO  7    /* 1 to discard the buffer_head after IO   */

struct buffer_head {
  /* First cache line: */
  unsigned long      b_blocknr;     /* block number                  */
  kdev_t             b_dev;         /* device (B_FREE = free)        */
  kdev_t             b_rdev;        /* Real device                   */
  unsigned long      b_rsector;     /* Real buffer location on disk  */
  struct buffer_head *b_next;       /* Hash queue list               */
  struct buffer_head *b_this_page;  /* circular list of buffers in one
                                       page                          */


  /* Second cache line: */
  unsigned long      b_state;       /* buffer state bitmap (above)   */
  struct buffer_head *b_next_free;
  unsigned int       b_count;       /* users using this block        */
  unsigned long      b_size;        /* block size                    */

  /* Non-performance-critical data follows. */
  char               *b_data;       /* pointer to data block         */
  unsigned int       b_list;        /* List that this buffer appears */
  unsigned long      b_flushtime;   /* Time when this (dirty) buffer
                                     * should be written             */
  unsigned long      b_lru_time;    /* Time when this buffer was
                                     * last used.                    */
  struct wait_queue  *b_wait;
  struct buffer_head *b_prev;       /* doubly linked hash list       */
  struct buffer_head *b_prev_free;  /* doubly linked list of buffers */
  struct buffer_head *b_reqnext;    /* request queue                 */
};
```

15.3   device

Every network device in the system is represented by a `device` data structure.

```
struct device
{

  /*
   * This is the first field of the "visible" part of this structure
   * (i.e. as seen by users in the "Space.c" file).  It is the name
```

```
 * the interface.
 */
char                    *name;

/* I/O specific fields                                              */
unsigned long           rmem_end;       /* shmem "recv" end     */
unsigned long           rmem_start;     /* shmem "recv" start   */
unsigned long           mem_end;        /* shared mem end       */
unsigned long           mem_start;      /* shared mem start     */
unsigned long           base_addr;      /* device I/O address   */
unsigned char           irq;            /* device IRQ number    */

/* Low-level status flags. */
volatile unsigned char  start,          /* start an operation   */
                        interrupt;      /* interrupt arrived    */
unsigned long           tbusy;          /* transmitter busy     */
struct device           *next;

/* The device initialization function. Called only once.        */
int                     (*init)(struct device *dev);

/* Some hardware also needs these fields, but they are not part of
   the usual set specified in Space.c. */
unsigned char           if_port;        /* Selectable AUI,TP,   */
unsigned char           dma;            /* DMA channel          */

struct enet_statistics* (*get_stats)(struct device *dev);

/*
 * This marks the end of the "visible" part of the structure. All
 * fields hereafter are internal to the system, and may change at
 * will (read: may be cleaned up at will).
 */

/* These may be needed for future network-power-down code.      */
unsigned long           trans_start;    /* Time (jiffies) of
                                            last transmit     */
unsigned long           last_rx;        /* Time of last Rx      */
unsigned short          flags;          /* interface flags (BSD)*/
unsigned short          family;         /* address family ID    */
unsigned short          metric;         /* routing metric       */
unsigned short          mtu;            /* MTU value            */
unsigned short          type;           /* hardware type        */
unsigned short          hard_header_len; /* hardware hdr len    */
void                    *priv;          /* private data         */
```

```
/* Interface address info. */
unsigned char           broadcast[MAX_ADDR_LEN];
unsigned char           pad;
unsigned char           dev_addr[MAX_ADDR_LEN];
unsigned char           addr_len;        /* hardware addr len    */
unsigned long           pa_addr;         /* protocol address     */
unsigned long           pa_brdaddr;      /* protocol broadcast addr*/
unsigned long           pa_dstaddr;      /* protocol P-P other addr*/
unsigned long           pa_mask;         /* protocol netmask     */
unsigned short          pa_alen;         /* protocol address len */

struct dev_mc_list      *mc_list;        /* M'cast mac addrs     */
int                     mc_count;        /* No installed mcasts  */

struct ip_mc_list       *ip_mc_list;     /* IP m'cast filter chain */
__u32                   tx_queue_len;    /* Max frames per queue    */

/* For load balancing driver pair support */
unsigned long           pkt_queue;       /* Packets queued       */
struct device           *slave;          /* Slave device         */
struct net_alias_info   *alias_info;     /* main dev alias info  */
struct net_alias        *my_alias;       /* alias devs           */

/* Pointer to the interface buffers. */
struct sk_buff_head     buffs[DEV_NUMBUFFS];

/* Pointers to interface service routines. */
int                     (*open)(struct device *dev);
int                     (*stop)(struct device *dev);
int                     (*hard_start_xmit) (struct sk_buff *skb,
                                            struct device *dev);
int                     (*hard_header) (struct sk_buff *skb,
                                        struct device *dev,
                                        unsigned short type,
                                        void *daddr,
                                        void *saddr,
                                        unsigned len);
int                     (*rebuild_header)(void *eth,
                                        struct device *dev,
                                        unsigned long raddr,
                                        struct sk_buff *skb);
void                    (*set_multicast_list)(struct device *dev);
int                     (*set_mac_address)(struct device *dev,
                                        void *addr);
int                     (*do_ioctl)(struct device *dev,
                                        struct ifreq *ifr,
```

```
                                           int cmd);
     int                 (*set_config)(struct device *dev,
                                           struct ifmap *map);
     void                (*header_cache_bind)(struct hh_cache **hhp,
                                           struct device *dev,
                                           unsigned short htype,
                                           __u32 daddr);
     void                (*header_cache_update)(struct hh_cache *hh,
                                           struct device *dev,
                                           unsigned char *  haddr);
     int                 (*change_mtu)(struct device *dev,
                                           int new_mtu);
     struct iw_statistics*  (*get_wireless_stats)(struct device *dev);
};
```

15.4   device_struct

device_struct data structures are used to register character and block devices; they hold its name and the set of file operations that can be used for this device. Each valid member of the chrdevs and blkdevs vectors represents a character or block device, respectively.

```
struct device_struct {
    const char * name;
    struct file_operations * fops;
};
```

15.5   file

Each open file, socket, etc. is represented by a file data structure.

```
struct file {
  mode_t f_mode;
  loff_t f_pos;
  unsigned short f_flags;
  unsigned short f_count;
  unsigned long f_reada, f_ramax, f_raend, f_ralen, f_rawin;
  struct file *f_next, *f_prev;
  int f_owner;         /* pid or -pgrp where SIGIO should be sent */
  struct inode * f_inode;
  struct file_operations * f_op;
  unsigned long f_version;
  void *private_data;  /* needed for tty driver, and maybe others */
};
```

15.6 files_struct

The `files_struct` data structure describes the files that a process has open.

```
struct files_struct {
  int count;
  fd_set close_on_exec;
  fd_set open_fds;
  struct file * fd[NR_OPEN];
};
```

15.7 fs_struct

```
struct fs_struct {
  int count;
  unsigned short umask;
  struct inode * root, * pwd;
};
```

15.8 gendisk

The `gendisk` data structure holds information about a hard disk. It is used during initialization, when the disks are found and then probed for partitions.

```
struct hd_struct {
    long start_sect;
    long nr_sects;
};

struct gendisk {
    int major;                /* major number of driver */
    const char *major_name;   /* name of major driver */
    int minor_shift;          /* number of times minor is shifted to
                                 get real minor */
    int max_p;                /* maximum partitions per device */
    int max_nr;               /* maximum number of real devices */

    void (*init)(struct gendisk *);
                              /* Initialization called before we
                                 do our thing */
    struct hd_struct *part;   /* partition table */
    int *sizes;               /* device size in blocks, copied to
                                 blk_size[] */
```

```
    int nr_real;                /* number of real devices */

    void *real_devices;         /* internal use */
    struct gendisk *next;
};
```

15.9 inode

The VFS inode data structure holds information about a file or directory on disk.

```
struct inode {
    kdev_t                      i_dev;
    unsigned long               i_ino;
    umode_t                     i_mode;
    nlink_t                     i_nlink;
    uid_t                       i_uid;
    gid_t                       i_gid;
    kdev_t                      i_rdev;
    off_t                       i_size;
    time_t                      i_atime;
    time_t                      i_mtime;
    time_t                      i_ctime;
    unsigned long               i_blksize;
    unsigned long               i_blocks;
    unsigned long               i_version;
    unsigned long               i_nrpages;
    struct semaphore            i_sem;
    struct inode_operations     *i_op;
    struct super_block          *i_sb;
    struct wait_queue           *i_wait;
    struct file_lock            *i_flock;
    struct vm_area_struct       *i_mmap;
    struct page                 *i_pages;
    struct dquot                *i_dquot[MAXQUOTAS];
    struct inode                *i_next, *i_prev;
    struct inode                *i_hash_next, *i_hash_prev;
    struct inode                *i_bound_to, *i_bound_by;
    struct inode                *i_mount;
    unsigned short              i_count;
    unsigned short              i_flags;
    unsigned char               i_lock;
    unsigned char               i_dirt;
    unsigned char               i_pipe;
    unsigned char               i_sock;
    unsigned char               i_seek;
```

```
      unsigned char                i_update;
      unsigned short               i_writecount;
      union {
          struct pipe_inode_info   pipe_i;
          struct minix_inode_info  minix_i;
          struct ext_inode_info    ext_i;
          struct ext2_inode_info   ext2_i;
          struct hpfs_inode_info   hpfs_i;
          struct msdos_inode_info  msdos_i;
          struct umsdos_inode_info umsdos_i;
          struct iso_inode_info    isofs_i;
          struct nfs_inode_info    nfs_i;
          struct xiafs_inode_info  xiafs_i;
          struct sysv_inode_info   sysv_i;
          struct affs_inode_info   affs_i;
          struct ufs_inode_info    ufs_i;
          struct socket            socket_i;
          void                     *generic_ip;
      } u;
};
```

15.10   ipc_perm

The ipc_perm data structure describes the access permissions of a System V IPC object.

```
struct ipc_perm
{
  key_t  key;
  ushort uid;    /* owner euid and egid */
  ushort gid;
  ushort cuid;   /* creator euid and egid */
  ushort cgid;
  ushort mode;   /* access modes see mode flags below */
  ushort seq;    /* sequence number */
};
```

15.11   irqaction

The irqaction data structure is used to describe the system's interrupt handlers.

```
struct irqaction {
  void (*handler)(int, void *, struct pt_regs *);
  unsigned long flags;
```

```
  unsigned long mask;
  const char *name;
  void *dev_id;
  struct irqaction *next;
};
```

15.12   linux_binfmt

Each binary file format that Linux understands is represented by a `linux_binfmt` data structure.

```
struct linux_binfmt {
  struct linux_binfmt * next;
  long *use_count;
  int (*load_binary)(struct linux_binprm *, struct  pt_regs * regs);
  int (*load_shlib)(int fd);
  int (*core_dump)(long signr, struct pt_regs * regs);
};
```

15.13   mem_map_t

The `mem_map_t` data structure (also known as `page`) is used to hold information about each page of physical memory.

```
typedef struct page {
  /* these must be first (free area handling) */
  struct page          *next;
  struct page          *prev;
  struct inode         *inode;
  unsigned long        offset;
  struct page          *next_hash;
  atomic_t             count;
  unsigned             flags;      /* atomic flags, some possibly
                                      updated asynchronously */
  unsigned             dirty:16,
                       age:8;
  struct wait_queue    *wait;
  struct page          *prev_hash;
  struct buffer_head   *buffers;
  unsigned long        swap_unlock_entry;
  unsigned long        map_nr;     /* page->map_nr == page - mem_map */
} mem_map_t;
```

15.14   mm_struct

The `mm_struct` data structure is used to describe the virtual memory of a task or process.

```
struct mm_struct {
  int count;
  pgd_t * pgd;
  unsigned long context;
  unsigned long start_code, end_code, start_data, end_data;
  unsigned long start_brk, brk, start_stack, start_mmap;
  unsigned long arg_start, arg_end, env_start, env_end;
  unsigned long rss, total_vm, locked_vm;
  unsigned long def_flags;
  struct vm_area_struct * mmap;
  struct vm_area_struct * mmap_avl;
  struct semaphore mmap_sem;
};
```

15.15   pci_bus

Every PCI bus in the system is represented by a `pci_bus` data structure.

```
struct pci_bus {
  struct pci_bus  *parent;      /* parent bus this bridge is on */
  struct pci_bus  *children;    /* chain of P2P bridges on this bus */
  struct pci_bus  *next;        /* chain of all PCI buses */

  struct pci_dev  *self;        /* bridge device as seen by parent */
  struct pci_dev  *devices;     /* devices behind this bridge */

  void    *sysdata;             /* hook for sys-specific extension */

  unsigned char  number;        /* bus number */
  unsigned char  primary;       /* number of primary bridge */
  unsigned char  secondary;     /* number of secondary bridge */
  unsigned char  subordinate;   /* max number of subordinate buses */
};
```

15.16   pci_dev

Every PCI device in the system, including PCI-PCI and PCI-ISA bridge devices, is represented by a `pci_dev` data structure.

```
/*
 * There is one pci_dev structure for each slot-number/function-number
 * combination:
 */
struct pci_dev {
  struct pci_bus  *bus;        /* bus this device is on */
  struct pci_dev  *sibling;    /* next device on this bus */
  struct pci_dev  *next;       /* chain of all devices */

  void    *sysdata;            /* hook for sys-specific extension */

  unsigned int  devfn;         /* encoded device & function index */
  unsigned short  vendor;
  unsigned short  device;
  unsigned int  class;         /* 3 bytes: (base,sub,prog-if) */
  unsigned int  master : 1;    /* set if device is master capable */
  /*
   * In theory, the irq level can be read from configuration
   * space and all would be fine.  However, old PCI chips don't
   * support these registers and return 0 instead.  For example,
   * the Vision864-P rev 0 chip can uses INTA, but returns 0 in
   * the interrupt line and pin registers.  pci_init()
   * initializes this field with the value at PCI_INTERRUPT_LINE
   * and it is the job of pcibios_fixup() to change it if
   * necessary.  The field must not be 0 unless the device
   * cannot generate interrupts at all.
   */
  unsigned char  irq;          /* irq generated by this device */
};
```

15.17   request

request data structures are used to make requests to the block devices in the system. The requests are always to read or write blocks of data to or from the buffer cache.

```
struct request {
    volatile int rq_status;
#define RQ_INACTIVE            (-1)
#define RQ_ACTIVE             1
#define RQ_SCSI_BUSY          0xffff
#define RQ_SCSI_DONE          0xfffe
#define RQ_SCSI_DISCONNECTING 0xffe0
```

```
        kdev_t rq_dev;
        int cmd;            /* READ or WRITE */
        int errors;
        unsigned long sector;
        unsigned long nr_sectors;
        unsigned long current_nr_sectors;
        char * buffer;
        struct semaphore * sem;
        struct buffer_head * bh;
        struct buffer_head * bhtail;
        struct request * next;
    };
```

15.18   rtable

Each `rtable` data structure holds information about the route to take in order to send packets to an IP host. `rtable` data structures are used within the IP route cache.

```
struct rtable
{
    struct rtable       *rt_next;
    __u32               rt_dst;
    __u32               rt_src;
    __u32               rt_gateway;
    atomic_t            rt_refcnt;
    atomic_t            rt_use;
    unsigned long       rt_window;
    atomic_t            rt_lastuse;
    struct hh_cache     *rt_hh;
    struct device       *rt_dev;
    unsigned short      rt_flags;
    unsigned short      rt_mtu;
    unsigned short      rt_irtt;
    unsigned char       rt_tos;
};
```

15.19   semaphore

Semaphores are used to protect critical data structures and regions of code.

```
struct semaphore {
    int count;
    int waking;
```

```
        int lock ;                      /* to make waking testing atomic */
        struct wait_queue *wait;
};
```

15.20 sk_buff

The sk_buff data structure is used to describe network data as it moves between the layers of protocol.

```
struct sk_buff
{
  struct sk_buff      *next;        /* Next buffer in list                */
  struct sk_buff      *prev;        /* Previous buffer in list            */
  struct sk_buff_head *list;        /* List we are on                     */
  int                 magic_debug_cookie;
  struct sk_buff      *link3;       /* Link for IP protocol level buffer chains
*/
  struct sock         *sk;          /* Socket we are owned by             */
  unsigned long       when;         /* used to compute rtt's              */
  struct timeval      stamp;        /* Time we arrived                    */
  struct device       *dev;         /* Device we arrived on/are leaving by */
  union
  {
      struct tcphdr   *th;
      struct ethhdr   *eth;
      struct iphdr    *iph;
      struct udphdr   *uh;
      unsigned char   *raw;
      /* for passing file handles in a unix domain socket */
      void            *filp;
  } h;

  union
  {
      /* As yet incomplete physical layer views */
      unsigned char   *raw;
      struct ethhdr   *ethernet;
  } mac;

  struct iphdr        *ip_hdr;      /* For IPPROTO_RAW                    */
  unsigned long       len;          /* Length of actual data             */
  unsigned long       csum;         /* Checksum                          */
  __u32               saddr;        /* IP source address                 */
  __u32               daddr;        /* IP target address                 */
```

```
        __u32               raddr;      /* IP next hop address              */
        __u32               seq;        /* TCP sequence number              */
        __u32               end_seq;    /* seq [+ fin] [+ syn] + datalen    */
        __u32               ack_seq;    /* TCP ack sequence number          */
        unsigned char       proto_priv[16];
        volatile char       acked,      /* Are we acked ?                   */
                            used,       /* Are we in use ?                  */
                            free,       /* How to free this buffer          */
                            arp;        /* Has IP/ARP resolution finished   */
        unsigned char       tries,      /* Times tried                      */
                            lock,       /* Are we locked ?                  */
                            localroute, /* Local routing asserted for this frame */
                            pkt_type,   /* Packet class                     */
                            pkt_bridged, /* Tracker for bridging            */
                            ip_summed;  /* Driver fed us an IP checksum     */
#define PACKET_HOST         0           /* To us
*/
#define PACKET_BROADCAST    1           /* To all
*/
#define PACKET_MULTICAST    2           /* To group
*/
#define PACKET_OTHERHOST    3           /* To someone else
*/
        unsigned short      users;      /* User count - see datagram.c,tcp.c  */
        unsigned short      protocol;   /* Packet protocol from driver.     */
        unsigned int        truesize;   /* Buffer size                      */
        atomic_t            count;      /* reference count                  */
        struct sk_buff      *data_skb;  /* Link to the actual data skb      */
        unsigned char       *head;      /* Head of buffer                   */
        unsigned char       *data;      /* Data head pointer                */
        unsigned char       *tail;      /* Tail pointer                     */
        unsigned char       *end;       /* End pointer                      */
        void                (*destructor)(struct sk_buff *); /* Destruct function */
        __u16               redirport;  /* Redirect port                    */
};
```

15.21   sock

Each `sock` data structure holds protocol-specific information about a BSD socket. For example, for an INET (Internet Address Domain) socket, this data structure would hold all of the TCP/IP- and UDP/IP-specific information.

```
struct sock
{
```

```
          /* This must be first. */
          struct sock               *sklist_next;
          struct sock               *sklist_prev;

          struct options            *opt;
          atomic_t                  wmem_alloc;
          atomic_t                  rmem_alloc;
          unsigned long             allocation;       /* Allocation mode */
          __u32                     write_seq;
          __u32                     sent_seq;
          __u32                     acked_seq;
          __u32                     copied_seq;
          __u32                     rcv_ack_seq;
          unsigned short            rcv_ack_cnt;      /* count of same ack */
          __u32                     window_seq;
          __u32                     fin_seq;
          __u32                     urg_seq;
          __u32                     urg_data;
          __u32                     syn_seq;
          int                       users;            /* user count */
  /*
   *      Not all are volatile, but some are, so we
   *      might as well say they all are.
   */
          volatile char             dead,
                                    urginline,
                                    intr,
                                    blog,
                                    done,
                                    reuse,
                                    keepopen,
                                    linger,
                                    delay_acks,
                                    destroy,
                                    ack_timed,
                                    no_check,
                                    zapped,
                                    broadcast,
                                    nonagle,
                                    bsdism;
          unsigned long             lingertime;
          int                       proc;

          struct sock               *next;
          struct sock               **pprev;
          struct sock               *bind_next;
```

```
    struct sock              **bind_pprev;
    struct sock              *pair;
    int                      hashent;
    struct sock              *prev;
    struct sk_buff           *volatile send_head;
    struct sk_buff           *volatile send_next;
    struct sk_buff           *volatile send_tail;
    struct sk_buff_head      back_log;
    struct sk_buff           *partial;
    struct timer_list        partial_timer;
    long                     retransmits;
    struct sk_buff_head      write_queue,
                             receive_queue;
    struct proto             *prot;
    struct wait_queue        **sleep;
    __u32                    daddr;
    __u32                    saddr;            /* Sending source */
    __u32                    rcv_saddr;        /* Bound address */
    unsigned short           max_unacked;
    unsigned short           window;
    __u32                    lastwin_seq;      /* sequence number when we last
                                                  updated the window we offer */
    __u32                    high_seq;         /* sequence number when we did
                                                  current fast retransmit */
    volatile unsigned long   ato;             /* ack timeout */
    volatile unsigned long   lrcvtime;        /* jiffies at last data rcv */
    volatile unsigned long   idletime;        /* jiffies at last rcv */
    unsigned int             bytes_rcv;
/*
 *   mss is min(mtu, max_window)
 */
    unsigned short           mtu;             /* mss negotiated in the syn's */
    volatile unsigned short mss;              /* current eff. mss - can change
*/
    volatile unsigned short user_mss;         /* mss requested by user in ioctl
*/
    volatile unsigned short max_window;
    unsigned long            window_clamp;
    unsigned int             ssthresh;
    unsigned short           num;
    volatile unsigned short cong_window;
    volatile unsigned short cong_count;
    volatile unsigned short packets_out;
    volatile unsigned short shutdown;
    volatile unsigned long   rtt;
    volatile unsigned long   mdev;
    volatile unsigned long   rto;
```

```
    volatile unsigned short backoff;
    int                     err, err_soft;   /* Soft holds errors that don't
                                                cause failure but are the
cause
                                                of a persistent failure not
                                                just 'timed out' */
    unsigned char           protocol;
    volatile unsigned char  state;
    unsigned char           ack_backlog;
    unsigned char           max_ack_backlog;
    unsigned char           priority;
    unsigned char           debug;
    int                     rcvbuf;
    int                     sndbuf;
    unsigned short          type;
    unsigned char           localroute;      /* Route locally only */
/*
 *    This is where all the private (optional) areas that don't
 *    overlap will eventually live.
 */
    union
    {
          struct unix_opt   af_unix;
#if defined(CONFIG_ATALK) || defined(CONFIG_ATALK_MODULE)
          struct atalk_sock af_at;
#endif
#if defined(CONFIG_IPX) || defined(CONFIG_IPX_MODULE)
          struct ipx_opt    af_ipx;
#endif
#ifdef CONFIG_INET
          struct inet_packet_opt  af_packet;
#ifdef CONFIG_NUTCP
          struct tcp_opt    af_tcp;
#endif
#endif
    } protinfo;
/*
 *    IP 'private area'
 */
    int                     ip_ttl;          /* TTL setting */
    int                     ip_tos;          /* TOS */
    struct tcphdr           dummy_th;
    struct timer_list       keepalive_timer; /* TCP keepalive hack */
    struct timer_list       retransmit_timer; /* TCP retransmit timer */
    struct timer_list       delack_timer;    /* TCP delayed ack timer */
    int                     ip_xmit_timeout; /* Why the timeout is running */
```

```
        struct rtable              *ip_route_cache; /* Cached output route */
        unsigned char              ip_hdrincl;      /* Include headers ? */
#ifdef CONFIG_IP_MULTICAST
        int                        ip_mc_ttl;       /* Multicasting TTL */
        int                        ip_mc_loop;      /* Loopback */
        char                       ip_mc_name[MAX_ADDR_LEN]; /* Multicast device name
*/
        struct ip_mc_socklist      *ip_mc_list;     /* Group array */
#endif

    /*
     *   This part is used for the timeout functions (timer.c).
     */
        int                        timeout;         /* What are we waiting for? */
        struct timer_list          timer;           /* This is the TIME_WAIT/receive
                                                      * timer when we are doing IP
                                                      */
        struct timeval             stamp;
    /*
     *   Identd
     */
        struct socket              *socket;
    /*
     *   Callbacks
     */
      void                         (*state_change)(struct sock *sk);
      void                         (*data_ready)(struct sock *sk,int bytes);
      void                         (*write_space)(struct sock *sk);
      void                         (*error_report)(struct sock *sk);

    };
```

15.22   socket

Each socket data structure holds information about a BSD socket. It does not exist independently; it is, instead, part of the VFS inode data structure.

```
struct socket {
  short               type;       /* SOCK_STREAM, ...               */
  socket_state        state;
  long                flags;
  struct proto_ops    *ops;       /* protocols do most everything */
  void                *data;      /* protocol data                  */
  struct socket       *conn;      /* server socket connected to    */
  struct socket       *iconn;     /* incomplete client conn.s      */
```

```
struct socket        *next;
struct wait_queue    **wait;       /* ptr to place to wait on    */
struct inode         *inode;
struct fasync_struct *fasync_list; /* Asynchronous wake up list  */
struct file          *file;        /* File back pointer for gc   */
};
```

15.23   task_struct

Each `task_struct` data structure describes a process or task in the system.

```
struct task_struct {
/* these are hardcoded - don't touch */
  volatile long      state;         /* -1 unrunnable, 0 runnable, >0 stopped
*/
  long               counter;
  long               priority;
  unsigned           long signal;
  unsigned           long blocked;  /* bitmap of masked signals */
  unsigned           long flags;    /* per process flags, defined below */
  int errno;
  long               debugreg[8];   /* Hardware debugging registers */
  struct exec_domain *exec_domain;
/* various fields */
  struct linux_binfmt *binfmt;
  struct task_struct *next_task, *prev_task;
  struct task_struct *next_run,  *prev_run;
  unsigned long      saved_kernel_stack;
  unsigned long      kernel_stack_page;
  int                exit_code, exit_signal;
  /* ??? */
  unsigned long      personality;
  int                dumpable:1;
  int                did_exec:1;
  int                pid;
  int                pgrp;
  int                tty_old_pgrp;
  int                session;
  /* boolean value for session group leader */
  int                leader;
  int                groups[NGROUPS];
  /*
   * pointers to (original) parent process, youngest child, younger sibling,
   * older sibling, respectively.  (p->father can be replaced with
   * p->p_pptr->pid)
   */
```

```
    struct task_struct    *p_opptr, *p_pptr, *p_cptr,
                          *p_ysptr, *p_osptr;
  struct wait_queue       *wait_chldexit;
  unsigned short          uid,euid,suid,fsuid;
  unsigned short          gid,egid,sgid,fsgid;
  unsigned long           timeout, policy, rt_priority;
  unsigned long           it_real_value, it_prof_value, it_virt_value;
  unsigned long           it_real_incr, it_prof_incr, it_virt_incr;
  struct timer_list       real_timer;
  long                    utime, stime, cutime, cstime, start_time;
/* mm fault and swap info: this can arguably be seen as either
   mm-specific or thread-specific */
  unsigned long           min_flt, maj_flt, nswap, cmin_flt, cmaj_flt, cnswap;
  int swappable:1;
  unsigned long           swap_address;
  unsigned long           old_maj_flt;    /* old value of maj_flt */
  unsigned long           dec_flt;        /* page fault count of the last time */
  unsigned long           swap_cnt;       /* number of pages to swap on next pass
*/
/* limits */
  struct rlimit           rlim[RLIM_NLIMITS];
  unsigned short          used_math;
  char                    comm[16];
/* file system info */
  int                     link_count;
  struct tty_struct       *tty;           /* NULL if no tty */
/* ipc stuff */
  struct sem_undo         *semundo;
  struct sem_queue        *semsleeping;
/* ldt for this task - used by Wine.  If NULL, default_ldt is used */
  struct desc_struct *ldt;
/* tss for this task */
  struct thread_struct tss;
/* filesystem information */
  struct fs_struct        *fs;
/* open file information */
  struct files_struct  *files;
/* memory management info */
  struct mm_struct        *mm;
/* signal handlers */
  struct signal_struct *sig;
#ifdef __SMP__
  int                     processor;
  int                     last_processor;
  int                     lock_depth;    /* Lock depth.
```

```
                                          We can context switch in and out
                                          of holding a syscall kernel lock...
*/
#endif
};
```

15.24   timer_list

`timer_list` data structures are used to implement real-time timers for processes.

```
struct timer_list {
  struct timer_list *next;
  struct timer_list *prev;
  unsigned long expires;
  unsigned long data;
  void (*function)(unsigned long);
};
```

15.25   tq_struct

Each task queue (`tq_struct`) data structure holds information about work that has been queued. This is usually a task needed by a device driver, but which does not have to be done immediately.

```
struct tq_struct {
    struct tq_struct *next;    /* linked list of active bh's */
    int sync;                  /* must be initialized to zero */
    void (*routine)(void *);   /* function to call */
    void *data;                /* argument to function */
};
```

15.26   vm_area_struct

Each `vm_area_struct` data structure describes an area of virtual memory for a process.

```
struct vm_area_struct {
  struct mm_struct * vm_mm;  /* VM area parameters */
  unsigned long vm_start;
  unsigned long vm_end;
  pgprot_t vm_page_prot;
  unsigned short vm_flags;
/* AVL tree of VM areas per task, sorted by address */
```

```
    short vm_avl_height;
    struct vm_area_struct * vm_avl_left;
    struct vm_area_struct * vm_avl_right;
/* linked list of VM areas per task, sorted by address */
    struct vm_area_struct * vm_next;
/* for areas with inode, the circular list inode->i_mmap */
/* for shm areas, the circular list of attaches */
/* otherwise unused */
    struct vm_area_struct * vm_next_share;
    struct vm_area_struct * vm_prev_share;
/* more */
    struct vm_operations_struct * vm_ops;
    unsigned long vm_offset;
    struct inode * vm_inode;
    unsigned long vm_pte;        /* shared mem */
};
```

Appendix A
Useful Web And FTP Sites

The following World Wide Web and FTP sites are useful:

Note
Note from publisher: We have revised these URLs to be the most current ones.

www.azstarnet.com/!axplinux

Note
Note from publisher: The above URL works, but see also http://www.alphalinux.org/.

This is David Mosberger-Tang's Alpha AXP Linux Web site, and it is the place to go for all of the Alpha AXP HOWTOs. It also has a large number of pointers to Linux and Alpha AXP specific information such as CPU data sheets.

http://www.redhat.com
Red Hat's Web site. This has a lot of useful pointers.

ftp://sunsite.unc.edu/pub/linux/
This is the major site for a lot of free software. The Linux-specific software is held in *pub/Linux*.

http://www.intel.com
Intel's Web site and a good place to look for Intel chip information.

http://linuxjournal.com/

The Linux Journal is a very good Linux magazine and well worth the yearly subscription for its excellent articles.

http://www.blackdown.org/java-linux.html

This is the primary site for information on Java on Linux.

ftp://tsx-11.mit.edu/pub/linux/

MIT's Linux FTP site.

http://ftp.kernel.org/ and ftp://ftp.kernel.org/

Linus's kernel sources.

http://www.linux.org.uk

The UK Linux User Group.

http://metalab.unc.edu/LDP/

Home page for the Linux Documentation Project.

http://www.digital.com

Digital Equipment Corporation's main Web page.

http://altavista.digital.com

Digital's AltaVista search engine. A very good place to search for information within the Web and news groups.

http://www.linuxhq.com

The Linux HQ Web site holds up-to-date official and unofficial patches, as well as advice and Web pointers that help you get the best set of kernel sources possible for your system.

http://www.amd.com

The AMD Web site.

http://www.cyrix.com

Cyrix's Web site.

http://www.arm.com

ARM's Web site.

Appendix B
Glossary

Argument

Functions and routines are passed arguments to process.

ARP

Address Resolution Protocol. Used to translate IP addresses into physical hardware addresses.

ASCII

American Standard Code for Information Interchange. Each letter of the alphabet is represented by an 8-bit code. ASCII is most often used to store written characters.

Bit

A single bit of data that represents either 1 or 0 (on or off).

Bottom Half Handler

Handlers for work queued within the kernel.

Byte

8 bits of data.

C

A high-level programming language. Most of the Linux kernel is written in C.

CISC

Complex Instruction Set Computer. The opposite of RISC, a processor which supports a large number of often complex assembly instructions. The X86 architecture is a CISC architecture.

CPU

Central processing unit. The main engine of the computer. See also *microprocessor* and *processor*.

Data Structure

This is a set of data in memory comprised of fields.

Device Driver

The software controlling a particular device; for example, the NCR 810 device driver controls the NCR 810 SCSI device.

DMA

Direct Memory Access.

ELF

Executable and Linkable Format. This object file format designed by the Unix System Laboratories is now firmly established as the most commonly used format in Linux.

EIDE

Extended IDE.

Executable image

A structured file containing machine instructions and data. This file can be loaded into a process's virtual memory and executed. See also *program*.

Function

A piece of software that performs an action. For example, returning the bigger of two numbers.

IDE

Integrated Disk Electronics.

Image

See *executable image*.

IP

Internet Protocol.

IPC

Interprocess communication.

Interface

A standard way of calling routines and passing data structures. For example, the interface between two layers of code might be expressed in terms of routines that pass and return a particular data structure. Linux's VFS is a good example of an interface.

IRQ

Interrupt request queue.

ISA

Industry Standard Architecture. This is a standard, although now rather dated, data bus interface for system components such as floppy disk drivers.

Kernel module

A dynamically loaded kernel function such as a file system or a device driver.

Kilobyte

A thousand bytes of data, often written as K or KB.

Megabyte

A million bytes of data, often written as Mbyte or MB.

Microprocessor

A very integrated CPU. Most modern CPUs are microprocessors.

Module

A file containing CPU instructions in the form of either assembly language instructions or a high-level language like C.

Object file

A file containing machine code and data that has not yet been linked with other object files or libraries to become an executable image.

Page

Physical memory is divided up into equal-sized pages.

Pointer

A location in memory that contains the address of another location in memory.

Process

This is an entity which can execute programs. A process could be thought of as a program in action.

Processor

Short for microprocessor, equivalent to CPU.

PCI

Peripheral Component Interconnect. A standard describing how the peripheral components of a computer system may be connected together.

Peripheral

An intelligent processor that does work on behalf of the system's CPU. For example, an IDE controller chip.

Program

A coherent set of CPU instructions that performs a task, such as printing "hello world." See also *executable image*.

Protocol

A protocol is a networking language used to transfer application data between two cooperating processes or network layers.

Register

A location within a chip, used to store information or instructions.

Register file

The set of registers in a processor.

RISC

Reduced Instruction Set Computer. The opposite of CISC, that is, a processor with a small number of assembly instructions, each of which performs simple operations. The ARM and Alpha processors are both RISC architectures.

Routine

Similar to a function except that, strictly speaking, routines do not return values.

SCSI

Small Computer Systems Interface.

Shell

This is a program which acts as an interface between the operating system and a human user. Also called a command shell, the most commonly used shell in Linux is the **bash** shell.

SMP

Symmetrical multiprocessing. Systems with more than one processor which fairly share the work among those processors.

Socket

A socket represents one end of a network connection. Linux supports the BSD Socket interface.

Software

CPU instructions (both assembler and high-level languages like C) and data. Mostly interchangeable with *program*.

System V

A variant of Unix produced in 1983, which included, amongst other things, System V IPC mechanisms.

TCP

Transmission Control Protocol.

Task Queue

A mechanism for deferring work in the Linux kernel.

UDP

User Datagram Protocol.

Virtual memory

A hardware and software mechanism for making the physical memory in a system appear larger than it actually is.

Part II

The Linux Kernel Module Programming Guide

by Ori Pomerantz

Ori Pomerantz
Apt. #1032
2355 N Hwy 360
Grand Prairie, TX 75050
USA
Email: **mpg@simple-tech.com**

Linux Kernel Module Programming Guide

This document was generated using the LaTeX2HTML translator Version 98.1 release (February 19th, 1998)

Copyright © 1993, 1994, 1995, 1996, 1997, Nikos Drakos, Computer Based Learning Unit, University of Leeds.

The command line arguments were:
latex2html -dir html mpg.tex.

The translation was initiated on 1999-05-19

About The Author

Ori Pomerantz was born in 1974 in Israel. He first learned to program in Basic in 1983 on a Sinclair ZX 81, which had 16K of RAM. He went to Handesaim High School, where he learned about Linux in 1992 but couldn't get it to work.

Being fit for military duty (or at least appearing fit to the Israeli military, which proves they're not very perceptive), Ori was inducted into the IDF in 1992 and served as a programmer for three years. He was discharged in 1995 and went to work for Check Point, where he is still working as a senior trainer. In 1998, he left Israel for Dallas, Texas. He is now putting the finishing touches on his B.A. degree from the Open University of Israel.

Ori started using Linux in 1994. He wrote this book after he decided to learn how to write kernel modules and couldn't find any documentation to get him started.

Acknowledgments

I'd like to thank Yoav Weiss for many helpful ideas and discussions, as well as for finding mistakes within this document before its publication. Of course, any remaining mistakes are purely my fault.

The TEX skeleton for this book was shamelessly stolen from the Linux Installation And Getting Started guide, where the TeX work was done by Matt Welsh.

My gratitude to Linus Torvalds, Richard Stallman, and all the other people who made it possible for me to run a high-quality operating system on my computer and get the source code goes without saying (yeah, right—then why did I say it?).

For Version 1.0.1

I couldn't list everybody who emailed me here, and if I've left you out, I apologize in advance. The following people were specially helpful:

♦ **Frodo Looijaard from the Netherlands** For a host of useful suggestions, and information about the 2.1.x kernels.

♦ **Stephen Judd from New Zealand** Spelling corrections.

♦ **Magnus Ahltorp from Sweden** Correcting a mistake of mine about the difference between character and block devices.

For Version 1.1.0

♦ **Emmanuel Papirakis from Quebec, Canada** For porting all of the examples to version 2.2 of the kernel.

♦ **Frodo Looijaard from the Netherlands** For telling me how to create a multiple file kernel module (1.2).

Of course, any remaining mistakes are my own, and if you think they make the book unusable, you're welcome to apply for a full refund of the money you paid me for it.

217

Introduction

So, you want to write a kernel module. You know C, you've written a number of normal programs to run as processes, and now you want to get to where the real action is, to where a single wild pointer can wipe out your file system and a core dump means a reboot.

Well, welcome to the club. I once had a wild pointer wipe an important directory under DOS (thankfully, now it stands for the Dead Operating System), and I don't see why living under Linux should be any safer.

Warning: I wrote this and checked the program under versions 2.0.35 and 2.2.3 of the kernel running on a Pentium. For the most part, it should work on other CPUs and on other versions of the kernel, as long as they are 2.0.x or 2.2.x, but I can't promise anything. One exception is Chapter 11, which should not work on any architecture except for x86.

Who Should Read This

This document is for people who want to write kernel modules. Although I will touch on how things are done in the kernel in several places, that is not my purpose. There are enough good sources which do a better job than I could have done.

This document is also for people who know how to write kernel modules, but have not yet adapted to version 2.2 of the kernel. If you are such a person, I suggest you look at Appendix A to see all the differences I encountered while updating the examples. The list is nowhere near comprehensive, but I think it covers most of the basic functionality and will be enough to get you started.

The kernel is a great piece of programming, and I believe that programmers should read at least some kernel source files and understand them. Having said that, I also believe in the value of playing with the system first and asking questions later. When I learn a new programming language, I don't start with reading the library code, but by writing a small "hello, world" program. I don't see why playing with the kernel should be any different.

Note On The Style

I like to put as many jokes as possible into my documentation. I'm writing this because I enjoy it, and I assume most of you are reading this for the same reason. If you just want to get to the point, ignore all the normal text and read the source code. I promise to put all the important details in remarks.

Chapter 1
Hello, World

W hen the first caveman programmer chiseled the first program on the walls of the first cave computer, it was a program to paint the string "Hello, world" in antelope pictures. Roman programming textbooks began with the "Salut, Mundi" program. I don't know what happens to people who break with this tradition, and I think it's safer not to find out.

A kernel module has to have at least two functions: `init_module` which is called when the module is inserted into the kernel, and `cleanup_module` which is called just before it is removed. Typically, `init_module` either registers a handler for something with the kernel, or it replaces one of the kernel function with its own code (usually code to do something and then call the original function). The `cleanup_module` function is supposed to undo whatever `init_module` did, so the module can be unloaded safely.

```
ex hello.c

/* hello.c
 * Copyright (C) 1998 by Ori Pomerantz
 *
 * "Hello, world" - the kernel module version.
 */

/* The necessary header files */

/* Standard in kernel modules */
#include <linux/kernel.h>    /* We're doing kernel work
*/
#include <linux/module.h>    /* Specifically, a module */
```

221

```
/* Deal with CONFIG_MODVERSIONS */
#if CONFIG_MODVERSIONS==1
#define MODVERSIONS
#include <linux/modversions.h>
#endif




/* Initialize the module */
int init_module()
{
  printk("Hello, world - this is the kernel speaking\n");

  /* If we return a non zero value, it means that
   * init_module failed and the kernel module
   * can't be loaded */
  return 0;
}


/* Cleanup - undid whatever init_module did */
void cleanup_module()
{
  printk("Short is the life of a kernel module\n");
}
```

Makefiles For Kernel Modules

A kernel module is not an independent executable, but an object file which will be linked into the kernel in runtime. As a result, they should be compiled with the -c flag. Also, all kernel modules have to be compiled with certain symbols defined.

- ♦ _ _KERNEL_ _—This tells the header files that this code will be run in kernel mode, not as part of a user process.

- ♦ MODULE—This tells the header files to give the appropriate definitions for a kernel module.

- ♦ LINUX—Technically speaking, this is not necessary. However, if you ever want to write a serious kernel module which will compile on more than one operating system, you'll be happy you did. This will allow you to do conditional compilation on the parts which are OS-dependent.

There are other symbols which have to be included, or not, depending on the flags the kernel was compiled with. If you're not sure how the kernel was compiled, look it up in /usr/include/linux/config.h

♦ _ _SMP_ _—Symmetrical Multiprocessing. This has to be defined if the kernel was compiled to support symmetrical multiprocessing (even if it's running just on one CPU). If you use Symmetrical Multiprocessing, there are other things you need to do (see Chapter 12).

♦ CONFIG_MODVERSIONS—If CONFIG_MODVERSIONS was enabled, you need to have it defined when compiling the kernel module and to include /usr/include/linux/modversions.h. This can also be done by the code itself.

```
ex Makefile

# Makefile for a basic kernel module

CC=gcc
MODCFLAGS := -Wall -DMODULE -D__KERNEL__ -DLINUX

hello.o: hello.c /usr/include/linux/version.h
        $(CC) $(MODCFLAGS) -c hello.c
        echo insmod hello.o to turn it on
        echo rmmod hello to turn if off
        echo
        echo X and kernel programming do not mix.
        echo Do the insmod and rmmod from outside X.
```

So, now the only thing left is to su to root (you didn't compile this as root, did you? Living on the edge…), and then insmod hello and rmmod hello to your heart's content. While you do it, notice your new kernel module in /proc/modules.

By the way, the reason why the Makefile recommends against doing insmod from X is because when the kernel has a message to print with printk, it sends it to the console. When you don't use X, it just goes to the virtual terminal you're using (the one you chose with Alt-F<n>) and you see it. When you do use X, on the other hand, there are two possibilities. Either you have a console open with xterm -C, in which case the output will be sent there, or you don't, in which case the output will go to virtual terminal 7—the one "covered" by X.

If your kernel becomes unstable you're likelier to get the debug messages without X. Outside of X, printk goes directly from the kernel to the console. In X, on the other hand, printk's go to a user mode process (xterm -C). When that process receives CPU time, it is supposed to send it to the X server process. Then, when the X server receives the CPU, it is supposed to display it—but an unstable kernel usually means that the system is about to crash or reboot, so you don't want to delay the error messages, which might explain to you what went wrong, for longer than you have to.

Multiple File Kernel Modules

Sometimes it makes sense to divide a kernel module between several source files. In this case, you need to do the following:

1. In all the source files but one, add the line #define _ _NO_VERSION_ _. This is important because module.h normally includes the definition of kernel_version, a global variable with the kernel version the module is compiled for. If you need version.h, you need to include it yourself, because module.h won't do it for you with _ _NO_VERSION_ _.

2. Compile all the source files as usual.

3. Combine all the object files into a single one. Under x86, do it with ld -m elf_i386 -r -o <name of module>.o <1st source file>.o <2nd source file>.o.

Here's an example of such a kernel module.

```
ex start.c

/* start.c
 * Copyright (C) 1999 by Ori Pomerantz
 *
 * "Hello, world" - the kernel module version.
 * This file includes just the start routine
 */


/* The necessary header files */

/* Standard in kernel modules */
#include <linux/kernel.h>   /* We're doing kernel work */
#include <linux/module.h>   /* Specifically, a module */



/* Deal with CONFIG_MODVERSIONS */
#if CONFIG_MODVERSIONS==1
#define MODVERSIONS
#include <linux/modversions.h>
#endif



/* Initialize the module */
int init_module()
{
  printk("Hello, world - this is the kernel speaking\n");
```

```
  /* If we return a non zero value, it means that
   * init_module failed and the kernel module
   * can't be loaded */
  return 0;
}
ex stop.c

/* stop.c
 * Copyright (C) 1999 by Ori Pomerantz
 *
 * "Hello, world" - the kernel module version. This
 * file includes just the stop routine.
 */

/* The necessary header files */

/* Standard in kernel modules */
#include <linux/kernel.h>   /* We're doing kernel work */

#define __NO_VERSION__       /* This isn't "the" file
                             * of the kernel module */
#include <linux/module.h>   /* Specifically, a module */

#include <linux/version.h>   /* Not included by
                              * module.h because
                              * of the __NO_VERSION__ */



/* Deal with CONFIG_MODVERSIONS */
#if CONFIG_MODVERSIONS==1
#define MODVERSIONS
#include <linux/modversions.h>
#endif



/* Cleanup - undid whatever init_module did */
void cleanup_module()
{
  printk("Short is the life of a kernel module\n");
}
ex Makefile

# Makefile for a multifile kernel module
```

```
CC=gcc
MODCFLAGS := -Wall -DMODULE -D__KERNEL__ -DLINUX

hello.o:    start.o stop.o
            ld -m elf_i386 -r -o hello.o start.o stop.o

start.o:    start.c /usr/include/linux/version.h
            $(CC) $(MODCFLAGS) -c start.c

stop.o:            stop.c /usr/include/linux/version.h
            $(CC) $(MODCFLAGS) -c stop.c
```

Chapter 2
Character Device Files

So, now we're bold kernel programmers and we know how to write kernel modules to do nothing. We feel proud of ourselves and we hold our heads up high. But somehow we get the feeling that something is missing. Catatonic modules are not much fun.

There are two major ways for a kernel module to talk to processes. One is through device files (like the files in the /dev directory), the other is to use the proc file system. Since one of the major reasons to write something in the kernel is to support some kind of hardware device, we'll begin with device files.

The original purpose of device files is to allow processes to communicate with device drivers in the kernel, and through them with physical devices (modems, terminals, and so on). The way this is implemented is the following.

Each device driver, which is responsible for some type of hardware, is assigned its own major number. The list of drivers and their major numbers is available in /proc/devices. Each physical device managed by a device driver is assigned a minor number. The /dev directory is supposed to include a special file, called a device file, for each of those devices, whether or not it's really installed on the system.

For example, if you do **ls -l** /dev/hd[ab]*, you'll see all of the IDE hard disk partitions which might be connected to a machine. Notice that all of them use the same major number, 3, but the minor number changes from one to the other. *Disclaimer: This assumes you're using a PC architecture. I don't know about devices on Linux running on other architectures.*

When the system was installed, all of those device files were created by the `mknod` command. There's no technical reason why they have to be in the /dev directory, it's just a useful convention. When creating a device file for testing purposes, as with the exercise here, it would probably make more sense to place it in the directory where you compile the kernel module.

Devices are divided into two types: character devices and block devices. The difference is that block devices have a buffer for requests, so they can choose by which order to respond to them. This is important in the case of storage devices, where it's faster to read or write sectors which are close to each other, rather than those which are further apart. Another difference is that block devices can only accept input and return output in blocks (whose size can vary according to the device), whereas character devices are allowed to use as many or as few bytes as they like. Most devices in the world are character, because they don't need this type of buffering, and they don't operate with a fixed block size. You can tell whether a device file is for a block device or a character device by looking at the first character in the output of ls -l. If it's "b" then it's a block device, and if it's "c" then it's a character device.

This module is divided into two separate parts: The module part which registers the device and the device driver part. The `init_module` function calls `module_register_chrdev` to add the device driver to the kernel's character device driver table. It also returns the major number to be used for the driver. The `cleanup_module` function deregisters the device.

This (registering something and unregistering it) is the general functionality of those two functions. Things in the kernel don't run on their own initiative, like processes, but are called, by processes via system calls, or by hardware devices via interrupts, or by other parts of the kernel (simply by calling specific functions). As a result, when you add code to the kernel, you're supposed to register it as the handler for a certain type of event and when you remove it, you're supposed to unregister it.

The device driver proper is composed of the four `device_<action>` functions, which are called when somebody tries to do something with a device file which has our major number. The way the kernel knows to call them is via the `file_operations` structure, Fops, which was given when the device was registered, which includes pointers to those four functions.

Another point we need to remember here is that we can't allow the kernel module to be rmmoded whenever root feels like it. The reason is that if the device file is opened by a process and then we remove the kernel module, using the file would cause a call to the memory location where the appropriate function (read/write) used to be. If we're lucky, no other code was loaded there, and we'll get an ugly error message. If we're unlucky, another kernel module was loaded into the same location, which means a jump into the middle of another function within the kernel. The results of this would be impossible to predict, but they can't be positive.

Normally, when you don't want to allow something, you return an error code (a negative number) from the function which is supposed to do it. With `cleanup_module` that is impossible because it's a void function. Once `cleanup_module` is called, the module is dead. However, there is a use counter which counts how many other kernel modules are using this kernel module, called the reference count (that's the last number of the line in /proc/modules). If this number isn't zero, rmmod will fail. The module's reference count is available in the variable mod_use_count_. Because there are macros defined for handling this variable (MOD_INC_USE_COUNT and MOD_DEC_USE_COUNT), we prefer to use them, rather than mod_use_count_ directly, so we'll be safe if the implementation changes in the future.

```
ex chardev.c

/* chardev.c
 * Copyright (C) 1998-1999 by Ori Pomerantz
 *
 * Create a character device (read only)
 */

/* The necessary header files */

/* Standard in kernel modules */
#include <linux/kernel.h>   /* We're doing kernel work */
#include <linux/module.h>   /* Specifically, a module */

/* Deal with CONFIG_MODVERSIONS */
#if CONFIG_MODVERSIONS==1
#define MODVERSIONS
#include <linux/modversions.h>
#endif

/* For character devices */
#include <linux/fs.h>       /* The character device
                             * definitions are here */
#include <linux/wrapper.h>  /* A wrapper which does
                             * next to nothing at
                             * at present, but may
                             * help for compatibility
                             * with future versions
                             * of Linux */


/* In 2.2.3 /usr/include/linux/version.h includes
 * a macro for this, but 2.0.35 doesn't - so I add
 * it here if necessary. */
#ifndef KERNEL_VERSION
#define KERNEL_VERSION(a,b,c) ((a)*65536+(b)*256+(c))
#endif
```

```
/* Conditional compilation. LINUX_VERSION_CODE is
 * the code (as per KERNEL_VERSION) of this version. */
#if LINUX_VERSION_CODE > KERNEL_VERSION(2,2,0)
#include <asm/uaccess.h>  /* for put_user */
#endif



#define SUCCESS 0


/* Device Declarations **************************** */

/* The name for our device, as it will appear
 * in /proc/devices */
#define DEVICE_NAME "char_dev"


/* The maximum length of the message from the device */
#define BUF_LEN 80

/* Is the device open right now? Used to prevent
 * concurrent access into the same device */
static int Device_Open = 0;

/* The message the device will give when asked */
static char Message[BUF_LEN];

/* How far did the process reading the message
 * get? Useful if the message is larger than the size
 * of the buffer we get to fill in device_read. */
static char *Message_Ptr;


/* This function is called whenever a process
 * attempts to open the device file */
static int device_open(struct inode *inode,
                   struct file *file)
{
  static int counter = 0;

#ifdef DEBUG
  printk ("device_open(%p,%p)\n", inode, file);
#endif

  /* This is how you get the minor device number in
```

```
 * case you have more than one physical device using
 * the driver. */
printk("Device: %d.%d\n",
   inode->i_rdev >> 8, inode->i_rdev & 0xFF);


/* We don't want to talk to two processes at the
 * same time */
if (Device_Open)
  return -EBUSY;


/* If this was a process, we would have had to be
 * more careful here.
 *
 * In the case of processes, the danger would be
 * that one process might have check Device_Open
 * and then be replaced by the schedualer by another
 * process which runs this function. Then, when the
 * first process was back on the CPU, it would assume
 * the device is still not open.
 *
 * However, Linux guarantees that a process won't be
 * replaced while it is running in kernel context.
 *
 * In the case of SMP, one CPU might increment
 * Device_Open while another CPU is here, right after
 * the check. However, in version 2.0 of the
 * kernel this is not a problem because there's a lock
 * to guarantee only one CPU will be kernel module at
 * the same time. This is bad in  terms of
 * performance, so version 2.2 changed it.
 * Unfortunately, I don't have access to an SMP box
 * to check how it works with SMP.
 */


Device_Open++;

/* Initialize the message. */
sprintf(Message,
  "If I told you once, I told you %d times - %s",
  counter++,
  "Hello, world\n");
/* The only reason we're allowed to do this sprintf
 * is because the maximum length of the message
 * (assuming 32 bit integers - up to 10 digits
 * with the minus sign) is less than BUF_LEN, which
 * is 80. BE CAREFUL NOT TO OVERFLOW BUFFERS,
```

```
     * ESPECIALLY IN THE KERNEL!!!
     */

  Message_Ptr = Message;

  /* Make sure that the module isn't removed while
   * the file is open by incrementing the usage count
   * (the number of opened references to the module, if
   * it's not zero rmmod will fail)
   */
  MOD_INC_USE_COUNT;

  return SUCCESS;
}


/* This function is called when a process closes the
 * device file. It doesn't have a return value in
 * version 2.0.x because it can't fail (you must ALWAYS
 * be able to close a device). In version 2.2.x it is
 * allowed to fail - but we won't let it.
 */
#if LINUX_VERSION_CODE >= KERNEL_VERSION(2,2,0)
static int device_release(struct inode *inode,
                      struct file *file)
#else
static void device_release(struct inode *inode,
                      struct file *file)
#endif
{
#ifdef DEBUG
  printk ("device_release(%p,%p)\n", inode, file);
#endif

  /* We're now ready for our next caller */
  Device_Open -;

  /* Decrement the usage count, otherwise once you
   * opened the file you'll never get rid of the module.
   */
  MOD_DEC_USE_COUNT;

#if LINUX_VERSION_CODE >= KERNEL_VERSION(2,2,0)
  return 0;
#endif
}
```

```
/* This function is called whenever a process which
 * have already opened the device file attempts to
 * read from it. */


#if LINUX_VERSION_CODE >= KERNEL_VERSION(2,2,0)
static ssize_t device_read(struct file *file,
    char *buffer,    /* The buffer to fill with data */
    size_t length,   /* The length of the buffer */
    loff_t *offset)  /* Our offset in the file */
#else
static int device_read(struct inode *inode,
                        struct file *file,
    char *buffer,    /* The buffer to fill with
                  * the data */
    int length)      /* The length of the buffer
                      * (mustn't write beyond that!) */
#endif
{
  /* Number of bytes actually written to the buffer */
  int bytes_read = 0;

  /* If we're at the end of the message, return 0
   * (which signifies end of file) */
  if (*Message_Ptr == 0)
    return 0;

  /* Actually put the data into the buffer */
  while (length && *Message_Ptr) {

    /* Because the buffer is in the user data segment,
     * not the kernel data segment, assignment wouldn't
     * work. Instead, we have to use put_user which
     * copies data from the kernel data segment to the
     * user data segment. */
    put_user(*(Message_Ptr++), buffer++);


    length -;
    bytes_read ++;
  }

#ifdef DEBUG
   printk ("Read %d bytes, %d left\n",
     bytes_read, length);
#endif
```

```
     /* Read functions are supposed to return the number
      * of bytes actually inserted into the buffer */
    return bytes_read;
}




/* This function is called when somebody tries to write
 * into our device file - unsupported in this example. */
#if LINUX_VERSION_CODE >= KERNEL_VERSION(2,2,0)
static ssize_t device_write(struct file *file,
    const char *buffer,    /* The buffer */
    size_t length,    /* The length of the buffer */
    loff_t *offset)  /* Our offset in the file */
#else
static int device_write(struct inode *inode,
                        struct file *file,
                        const char *buffer,
                        int length)
#endif
{
  return -EINVAL;
}




/* Module Declarations ***************************** */

/* The major device number for the device. This is
 * global (well, static, which in this context is global
 * within this file) because it has to be accessible
 * both for registration and for release. */
static int Major;

/* This structure will hold the functions to be
 * called when a process does something to the device
 * we created. Since a pointer to this structure is
 * kept in the devices table, it can't be local to
 * init_module. NULL is for unimplemented functions. */


struct file_operations Fops = {
  NULL,    /* seek */
  device_read,
```

```
    device_write,
    NULL,    /* readdir */
    NULL,    /* select */
    NULL,    /* ioctl */
    NULL,    /* mmap */
    device_open,
#if LINUX_VERSION_CODE >= KERNEL_VERSION(2,2,0)
    NULL,    /* flush */
#endif
    device_release  /* a.k.a. close */
};


/* Initialize the module - Register the character device */
int init_module()
{
    /* Register the character device (atleast try) */
    Major = module_register_chrdev(0,
                                   DEVICE_NAME,
                                   &Fops);

    /* Negative values signify an error */
    if (Major < 0) {
        printk ("%s device failed with %d\n",
            "Sorry, registering the character",
            Major);
        return Major;
    }

    printk ("%s The major device number is %d.\n",
            "Registeration is a success.",
            Major);
    printk ("If you want to talk to the device driver,\n");
    printk ("you'll have to create a device file. \n");
    printk ("We suggest you use:\n");
    printk ("mknod <name> c %d <minor>\n", Major);
    printk ("You can try different minor numbers %s",
            "and see what happens.\n");

    return 0;
}


/* Cleanup - unregister the appropriate file from /proc */
void cleanup_module()
{
    int ret;
```

```
  /* Unregister the device */
  ret = module_unregister_chrdev(Major, DEVICE_NAME);

  /* If there's an error, report it */
  if (ret < 0)
    printk("Error in unregister_chrdev: %d\n", ret);
}
```

Multiple Kernel Versions Source Files

The system calls, which are the major interface the kernel shows to the processes, generally stay the same across versions. A new system call may be added, but usually the old ones will behave exactly like they used to. This is necessary for backward compatibility—a new kernel version is *not* supposed to break regular processes. In most cases, the device files will also remain the same. On the other hand, the internal interfaces within the kernel can and do change between versions.

The Linux kernel versions are divided between the stable versions (n.<even number>.m) and the development versions (n.<odd number>.m). The development versions include all the cool new ideas, including those which will be considered a mistake, or reimplemented, in the next version. As a result, you can't trust the interface to remain the same in those versions (which is why I don't bother to support them in this book; it's too much work and it would become dated too quickly). In the stable versions, on the other hand, we can expect the interface to remain the same regardless of the bug fix version (the m number).

This version of the MPG includes support for both version 2.0.x and version 2.2.x of the Linux kernel. Because there are differences between the two, this requires conditional compilation depending on the kernel version. The way to do this to use the macro `LINUX_VERSION_CODE`. In version a.b.c of the kernel, the value of this macro would be $2^{16}a+2^{8}b+c$. To get the value for a specific kernel version, we can use the `KERNEL_VERSION` macro. Because it's not defined in 2.0.35, we define it ourselves if necessary.

Chapter 3
The /proc File System

In Linux, there is an additional mechanism for the kernel and kernel modules to send information to processes—the /proc file system. Originally designed to allow easy access to information about processes (hence the name), it is now used by every bit of the kernel that has something interesting to report, such as /proc/ modules which has the list of modules and /proc/meminfo which has memory usage statistics.

The method to use the /proc file system is very similar to the one used with device drivers—you create a structure with all the information needed for the /proc file, including pointers to any handler functions (in our case there is only one, the one called when somebody attempts to read from the /proc file). Then, init_module registers the structure with the kernel and cleanup_module unregisters it.

The reason we use proc_register_dynamic is because we don't want to determine the inode number used for our file in advance, but to allow the kernel to determine it to prevent clashes. Normal file systems are located on a disk, rather than just in memory (which is where /proc is), and in that case the inode number is a pointer to a disk location where the file's index node (inode for short) is located. The inode contains information about the file, for example the file's permissions, together with a pointer to the disk location or locations where the file's data can be found.

Because we don't get called when the file is opened or closed, there's no where for us to put MOD_INC_USE_COUNT and MOD_DEC_USE_COUNT in this module, and if the file is opened and then the module is removed, there's no way to avoid the consequences. In the next chapter, we'll see a harder to implement, but more flexible, way of dealing with /proc files which will allow us to protect against this problem as well.

```
ex procfs.c

/* procfs.c -  create a "file" in /proc
 * Copyright (C) 1998-1999 by Ori Pomerantz
 */


/* The necessary header files */

/* Standard in kernel modules */
#include <linux/kernel.h>   /* We're doing kernel work */
#include <linux/module.h>   /* Specifically, a module */

/* Deal with CONFIG_MODVERSIONS */
#if CONFIG_MODVERSIONS==1
#define MODVERSIONS
#include <linux/modversions.h>
#endif


/* Necessary because we use the proc fs */
#include <linux/proc_fs.h>



/* In 2.2.3 /usr/include/linux/version.h includes a
 * macro for this, but 2.0.35 doesn't - so I add it
 * here if necessary. */
#ifndef KERNEL_VERSION
#define KERNEL_VERSION(a,b,c) ((a)*65536+(b)*256+(c))
#endif



/* Put data into the proc fs file.

   Arguments
   =========
   1. The buffer where the data is to be inserted, if
      you decide to use it.
   2. A pointer to a pointer to characters. This is
      useful if you don't want to use the buffer
      allocated by the kernel.
```

3. The current position in the file.
4. The size of the buffer in the first argument.
5. Zero (for future use?).

Usage and Return Value
========================

If you use your own buffer, like I do, put its
location in the second argument and return the
number of bytes used in the buffer.

A return value of zero means you have no further
information at this time (end of file). A negative
return value is an error condition.

For More Information
======================

The way I discovered what to do with this function
wasn't by reading documentation, but by reading the
code which used it. I just looked to see what uses
the get_info field of proc_dir_entry struct (I used a
combination of find and grep, if you're interested),
and I saw that it is used in <kernel source
directory>/fs/proc/array.c.

If something is unknown about the kernel, this is
usually the way to go. In Linux we have the great
advantage of having the kernel source code for
free - use it.
 */
int procfile_read(char *buffer,
            char **buffer_location,
            off_t offset,
            int buffer_length,
            int zero)
{
  int len; /* The number of bytes actually used */

  /* This is static so it will still be in memory
   * when we leave this function */
  static char my_buffer[80];

  static int count = 1;

```
    /* We give all of our information in one go, so if the
     * user asks us if we have more information the
     * answer should always be no.
     *
     * This is important because the standard read
     * function from the library would continue to issue
     * the read system call until the kernel replies
     * that it has no more information, or until its
     * buffer is filled.
     */
    if (offset > 0)
      return 0;

    /* Fill the buffer and get its length */
    len = sprintf(my_buffer,
      "For the %d%s time, go away!\n", count,
      (count % 100 > 10 && count % 100 < 14) ? "th" :
        (count % 10 == 1) ? "st" :
          (count % 10 == 2) ? "nd" :
            (count % 10 == 3) ? "rd" : "th" );
    count++;

    /* Tell the function which called us where the
     * buffer is */
    *buffer_location = my_buffer;

    /* Return the length */
    return len;
  }


struct proc_dir_entry Our_Proc_File =
  {
    0, /* Inode number - ignore, it will be filled by
         * proc_register[_dynamic] */
    4, /* Length of the file name */
    "test", /* The file name */
    S_IFREG | S_IRUGO, /* File mode - this is a regular
                        * file which can be read by its
                        * owner, its group, and everybody
                        * else */
    1,      /* Number of links (directories where the
          * file is referenced) */
    0, 0,  /* The uid and gid for the file - we give it
            * to root */
    80, /* The size of the file reported by ls. */
```

```
      NULL, /* functions which can be done on the inode
              * (linking, removing, etc.) - we don't
              * support any. */
      procfile_read, /* The read function for this file,
                       * the function called when somebody
                       * tries to read something from it. */
      NULL /* We could have here a function to fill the
            * file's inode, to enable us to play with
            * permissions, ownership, etc. */
    };



/* Initialize the module - register the proc file */
int init_module()
{
  /* Success if proc_register[_dynamic] is a success,
   * failure otherwise. */
#if LINUX_VERSION_CODE > KERNEL_VERSION(2,2,0)
  /* In version 2.2, proc_register assign a dynamic
   * inode number automatically if it is zero in the
   * structure, so there's no more need for
   * proc_register_dynamic
   */
  return proc_register(&proc_root, &Our_Proc_File);
#else
  return proc_register_dynamic(&proc_root, &Our_Proc_File);
#endif

  /* proc_root is the root directory for the proc
   * fs (/proc). This is where we want our file to be
   * located.
   */
}



/* Cleanup - unregister our file from /proc */
void cleanup_module()
{
  proc_unregister(&proc_root, Our_Proc_File.low_ino);
}
```

Chapter 4
Using /proc For Input

So far we have two ways to generate output from kernel modules: we can register a device driver and `mknod` a device file, or we can create a `/proc` file. This allows the kernel module to tell us anything it likes. The only problem is that there is no way for us to talk back. The first way we'll send input to kernel modules will be by writing back to the `/proc` file.

Because the proc file system was written mainly to allow the kernel to report its situation to processes, there are no special provisions for input. The `proc_dir_entry` struct doesn't include a pointer to an input function, the way it includes a pointer to an output function. Instead, to write into a `/proc` file, we need to use the standard file system mechanism.

In Linux there is a standard mechanism for file system registration. Since every file system has to have its own functions to handle inode and file operations, there is a special structure to hold pointers to all those functions, `struct inode_operations`, which includes a pointer to `struct file_operations`. In /proc, whenever we register a new file, we're allowed to specify which `struct inode_operations` will be used for access to it. This is the mechanism we use, a `struct inode_operations` which includes a pointer to a `struct file_operations` which includes pointers to our `module_input` and `module_output` functions.

It's important to note that the standard roles of read and write are reversed in the kernel. Read functions are used for output, whereas write functions are used for input. The reason for that is that read and write refer to the user's point of view—if a process reads something from the kernel, then the kernel needs to output it, and if a process writes something to the kernel, then the kernel receives it as input.

Another interesting point here is the `module_permission` function. This function is called whenever a process tries to do something with the `/proc` file, and it can decide whether to allow access or not. Right now it is only based on the operation and the uid of the current used (as available in `current`, a pointer to a structure which includes information on the currently running process), but it could be based on anything we like, such as what other processes are doing with the same file, the time of day, or the last input we received.

The reason for `put_user` and `get_user` is that Linux memory (under Intel architecture; it may be different under some other processors) is segmented. This means that a pointer, by itself, does not reference a unique location in memory, only a location in a memory segment, and you need to know which memory segment it is to be able to use it. There is one memory segment for the kernel, and one of each of the processes.

The only memory segment accessible to a process is its own, so when writing regular programs to run as processes, there's no need to worry about segments. When you write a kernel module, normally you want to access the kernel memory segment, which is handled automatically by the system. However, when the content of a memory buffer needs to be passed between the currently running process and the kernel, the kernel function receives a pointer to the memory buffer which is in the process segment. The `put_user` and `get_user` macros allow you to access that memory.

```
ex procfs.c

/* procfs.c -  create a "file" in /proc, which allows
 * both input and output. */

/* Copyright (C) 1998-1999 by Ori Pomerantz */


/* The necessary header files */

/* Standard in kernel modules */
#include <linux/kernel.h>   /* We're doing kernel work */
#include <linux/module.h>   /* Specifically, a module */

/* Deal with CONFIG_MODVERSIONS */
#if CONFIG_MODVERSIONS==1
#define MODVERSIONS
#include <linux/modversions.h>
#endif
```

```
/* Necessary because we use proc fs */
#include <linux/proc_fs.h>



/* In 2.2.3 /usr/include/linux/version.h includes a
 * macro for this, but 2.0.35 doesn't - so I add it
 * here if necessary. */
#ifndef KERNEL_VERSION
#define KERNEL_VERSION(a,b,c) ((a)*65536+(b)*256+(c))
#endif




#if LINUX_VERSION_CODE >= KERNEL_VERSION(2,2,0)
#include <asm/uaccess.h>   /* for get_user and put_user */
#endif

/* The module's file functions ********************** */



/* Here we keep the last message received, to prove
 * that we can process our input */
#define MESSAGE_LENGTH 80
static char Message[MESSAGE_LENGTH];



/* Since we use the file operations struct, we can't
 * use the special proc output provisions - we have to
 * use a standard read function, which is this function */
#if LINUX_VERSION_CODE >= KERNEL_VERSION(2,2,0)
static ssize_t module_output(
    struct file *file,   /* The file read */
    char *buf, /* The buffer to put data to (in the
                * user segment) */
    size_t len,   /* The length of the buffer */
    loff_t *offset) /* Offset in the file - ignore */
#else
static int module_output(
    struct inode *inode, /* The inode read */
    struct file *file,   /* The file read */
    char *buf, /* The buffer to put data to (in the
                * user segment) */
    int len)   /* The length of the buffer */
#endif
{
```

```
static int finished = 0;
int i;
char message[MESSAGE_LENGTH+30];

/* We return 0 to indicate end of file, that we have
 * no more information. Otherwise, processes will
 * continue to read from us in an endless loop. */
if (finished) {
  finished = 0;
  return 0;
}

/* We use put_user to copy the string from the kernel's
 * memory segment to the memory segment of the process
 * that called us. get_user, BTW, is
 * used for the reverse. */
sprintf(message, "Last input:%s", Message);
for(i=0; i<len && message[i]; i++)
  put_user(message[i], buf+i);

/* Notice, we assume here that the size of the message
 * is below len, or it will be received cut. In a real
 * life situation, if the size of the message is less
 * than len, then we'd return len and on the second call
 * start filling the buffer with the len+1'th byte of
 * the message. */
finished = 1;

return i;  /* Return the number of bytes "read" */
}


/* This function receives input from the user when the
 * user writes to the /proc file. */
#if LINUX_VERSION_CODE >= KERNEL_VERSION(2,2,0)
static ssize_t module_input(
    struct file *file,   /* The file itself */
    const char *buf,     /* The buffer with input */
    size_t length,       /* The buffer's length */
    loff_t *offset)      /* offset to file - ignore */
#else
static int module_input(
    struct inode *inode, /* The file's inode */
    struct file *file,   /* The file itself */
    const char *buf,     /* The buffer with the input */
    int length)          /* The buffer's length */
```

```
#endif
{
  int i;

  /* Put the input into Message, where module_output
   * will later be able to use it */
  for(i=0; i<MESSAGE_LENGTH-1 && i<length; i++)
#if LINUX_VERSION_CODE >= KERNEL_VERSION(2,2,0)
    get_user(Message[i], buf+i);
  /* In version 2.2 the semantics of get_user changed,
   * it not longer returns a character, but expects a
   * variable to fill up as its first argument and a
   * user segment pointer to fill it from as the its
   * second.
   *
   * The reason for this change is that the version 2.2
   * get_user can also read an short or an int. The way
   * it knows the type of the variable it should read
   * is by using sizeof, and for that it needs the
   * variable itself.
   */
#else
    Message[i] = get_user(buf+i);
#endif
  Message[i] = '\0';  /* we want a standard, zero
                       * terminated string */

  /* We need to return the number of input characters
   * used */
  return i;
}




/* This function decides whether to allow an operation
 * (return zero) or not allow it (return a non-zero
 * which indicates why it is not allowed).
 *
 * The operation can be one of the following values:
 * 0 - Execute (run the "file" - meaningless in our case)
 * 2 - Write (input to the kernel module)
 * 4 - Read (output from the kernel module)
 *
 * This is the real function that checks file
 * permissions. The permissions returned by ls -l are
 * for referece only, and can be overridden here.
 */
```

```
static int module_permission(struct inode *inode, int op)
{
  /* We allow everybody to read from our module, but
   * only root (uid 0) may write to it */
  if (op == 4 || (op == 2 && current->euid == 0))
    return 0;

  /* If it's anything else, access is denied */
  return -EACCES;
}




/* The file is opened - we don't really care about
 * that, but it does mean we need to increment the
 * module's reference count. */
int module_open(struct inode *inode, struct file *file)
{
  MOD_INC_USE_COUNT;

  return 0;
}



/* The file is closed - again, interesting only because
 * of the reference count. */
#if LINUX_VERSION_CODE >= KERNEL_VERSION(2,2,0)
int module_close(struct inode *inode, struct file *file)
#else
void module_close(struct inode *inode, struct file *file)
#endif
{
  MOD_DEC_USE_COUNT;

#if LINUX_VERSION_CODE >= KERNEL_VERSION(2,2,0)
  return 0;  /* success */
#endif
}


/* Structures to register as the /proc file, with
 * pointers to all the relevant functions. ********** */
```

```c
/* File operations for our proc file. This is where we
 * place pointers to all the functions called when
 * somebody tries to do something to our file. NULL
 * means we don't want to deal with something. */
static struct file_operations File_Ops_4_Our_Proc_File =
  {
    NULL,  /* lseek */
    module_output,  /* "read" from the file */
    module_input,   /* "write" to the file */
    NULL,  /* readdir */
    NULL,  /* select */
    NULL,  /* ioctl */
    NULL,  /* mmap */
    module_open,    /* Somebody opened the file */
#if LINUX_VERSION_CODE >= KERNEL_VERSION(2,2,0)
    NULL,   /* flush, added here in version 2.2 */
#endif
    module_close,   /* Somebody closed the file */
    /* etc. etc. etc. (they are all given in
     * /usr/include/linux/fs.h). Since we don't put
     * anything here, the system will keep the default
     * data, which in Unix is zeros (NULLs when taken as
     * pointers). */
  };



/* Inode operations for our proc file. We need it so
 * we'll have some place to specify the file operations
 * structure we want to use, and the function we use for
 * permissions. It's also possible to specify functions
 * to be called for anything else which could be done to
 * an inode (although we don't bother, we just put
 * NULL). */
static struct inode_operations Inode_Ops_4_Our_Proc_File =
  {
    &File_Ops_4_Our_Proc_File,
    NULL, /* create */
    NULL, /* lookup */
    NULL, /* link */
    NULL, /* unlink */
    NULL, /* symlink */
    NULL, /* mkdir */
    NULL, /* rmdir */
    NULL, /* mknod */
    NULL, /* rename */
```

```
        NULL, /* readlink */
        NULL, /* follow_link */
        NULL, /* readpage */
        NULL, /* writepage */
        NULL, /* bmap */
        NULL, /* truncate */
        module_permission /* check for permissions */
    };



    /* Directory entry */
    static struct proc_dir_entry Our_Proc_File =
      {
        0, /* Inode number - ignore, it will be filled by
            * proc_register[_dynamic] */
        7, /* Length of the file name */
        "rw_test", /* The file name */
        S_IFREG | S_IRUGO | S_IWUSR,
        /* File mode - this is a regular file which
         * can be read by its owner, its group, and everybody
         * else. Also, its owner can write to it.
         *
         * Actually, this field is just for reference, it's
         * module_permission that does the actual check. It
         * could use this field, but in our implementation it
         * doesn't, for simplicity. */
        1,   /* Number of links (directories where the
              * file is referenced) */
        0, 0,   /* The uid and gid for the file -
                 * we give it to root */
        80, /* The size of the file reported by ls. */
        &Inode_Ops_4_Our_Proc_File,
        /* A pointer to the inode structure for
         * the file, if we need it. In our case we
         * do, because we need a write function. */
        NULL
        /* The read function for the file. Irrelevant,
         * because we put it in the inode structure above */
      };




    /* Module initialization and cleanup ****************** */

    /* Initialize the module - register the proc file */
    int init_module()
```

```
{
  /* Success if proc_register[_dynamic] is a success,
   * failure otherwise */
#if LINUX_VERSION_CODE >= KERNEL_VERSION(2,2,0)
  /* In version 2.2, proc_register assign a dynamic
   * inode number automatically if it is zero in the
   * structure, so there's no more need for
   * proc_register_dynamic
   */
  return proc_register(&proc_root, &Our_Proc_File);
#else
  return proc_register_dynamic(&proc_root, &Our_Proc_File);
#endif
}


/* Cleanup - unregister our file from /proc */
void cleanup_module()
{
  proc_unregister(&proc_root, Our_Proc_File.low_ino);
}
```

Chapter 5
Talking To Device Files (writes And ioctls)

D evice files are supposed to represent physical devices. Most physical devices are used for output as well as input, so there has to be some mechanism for device drivers in the kernel to get the output to send to the device from processes. This is done by opening the device file for output and writing to it, just like writing to a file. In the following example, this is implemented by `device_write`.

This is not always enough. Imagine you had a serial port connected to a modem (even if you have an internal modem, it is still implemented from the CPU's perspective as a serial port connected to a modem, so you don't have to tax your imagination too hard). The natural thing to do would be to use the device file to write things to the modem (either modem commands or data to be sent through the phone line) and read things from the modem (either responses for commands or the data received through the phone line). However, this leaves open the question of what to do when you need to talk to the serial port itself, for example to send the rate at which data is sent and received.

The answer in Unix is to use a special function called `ioctl` (short for input output control). Every device can have its own `ioctl` commands, which can be read `ioctl`s (to send information from a process to the kernel), write `ioctl`s (to return information to a process), both, or neither. The `ioctl` function is called with three parameters: the file descriptor of the appropriate device file, the ioctl number, and a parameter, which is of type long so you can use a cast to use it to pass anything.

The ioctl number encodes the major device number, the type of the ioctl, the command, and the type of the parameter. This ioctl number is usually created by a macro call (`_IO`, `_IOR`, `_IOW`, or `_IOWR`—depending on the type) in a header file. This header file should then be `#include`'d both by the programs which will use `ioctl` (so they can generate the appropriate `ioctls`) and by the kernel module (so it can understand it). In the example below, the header file is `chardev.h` and the program which uses it is `ioctl.c`.

If you want to use `ioctls` in your own kernel modules, it is best to receive an official `ioctl` assignment, so if you accidentally get somebody else's `ioctls`, or if they get yours, you'll know something is wrong. For more information, consult the kernel source tree at '`Documentation/ioctl-number.txt`'.

```
ex chardev.c

/* chardev.c
 *
 * Create an input/output character device
 */


/* Copyright (C) 1998-99 by Ori Pomerantz */



/* The necessary header files */

/* Standard in kernel modules */
#include <linux/kernel.h>   /* We're doing kernel work */
#include <linux/module.h>   /* Specifically, a module */

/* Deal with CONFIG_MODVERSIONS */
#if CONFIG_MODVERSIONS==1
#define MODVERSIONS
#include <linux/modversions.h>
#endif

/* For character devices */

/* The character device definitions are here */
#include <linux/fs.h>

/* A wrapper which does next to nothing at
 * at present, but may help for compatibility
 * with future versions of Linux */
#include <linux/wrapper.h>
```

```
/* Our own ioctl numbers */
#include "chardev.h"


/* In 2.2.3 /usr/include/linux/version.h includes a
 * macro for this, but 2.0.35 doesn't - so I add it
 * here if necessary. */
#ifndef KERNEL_VERSION
#define KERNEL_VERSION(a,b,c) ((a)*65536+(b)*256+(c))
#endif



#if LINUX_VERSION_CODE >= KERNEL_VERSION(2,2,0)
#include <asm/uaccess.h>   /* for get_user and put_user */
#endif



#define SUCCESS 0


/* Device Declarations ****************************** */


/* The name for our device, as it will appear in
 * /proc/devices */
#define DEVICE_NAME "char_dev"


/* The maximum length of the message for the device */
#define BUF_LEN 80

/* Is the device open right now? Used to prevent
 * concurent access into the same device */
static int Device_Open = 0;

/* The message the device will give when asked */
static char Message[BUF_LEN];

/* How far did the process reading the message get?
 * Useful if the message is larger than the size of the
 * buffer we get to fill in device_read. */
static char *Message_Ptr;
```

```
/* This function is called whenever a process attempts
 * to open the device file */
static int device_open(struct inode *inode,
                       struct file *file)
{
#ifdef DEBUG
  printk ("device_open(%p)\n", file);
#endif

  /* We don't want to talk to two processes at the
   * same time */
  if (Device_Open)
    return -EBUSY;

  /* If this was a process, we would have had to be
   * more careful here, because one process might have
   * checked Device_Open right before the other one
   * tried to increment it. However, we're in the
   * kernel, so we're protected against context switches.
   *
   * This is NOT the right attitude to take, because we
   * might be running on an SMP box, but we'll deal with
   * SMP in a later chapter.
   */

  Device_Open++;

  /* Initialize the message */
  Message_Ptr = Message;

  MOD_INC_USE_COUNT;

  return SUCCESS;
}


/* This function is called when a process closes the
 * device file. It doesn't have a return value because
 * it cannot fail. Regardless of what else happens, you
 * should always be able to close a device (in 2.0, a 2.2
 * device file could be impossible to close). */
#if LINUX_VERSION_CODE >= KERNEL_VERSION(2,2,0)
static int device_release(struct inode *inode,
                          struct file *file)
#else
```

```
static void device_release(struct inode *inode,
                           struct file *file)
#endif
{
#ifdef DEBUG
  printk ("device_release(%p,%p)\n", inode, file);
#endif

  /* We're now ready for our next caller */
  Device_Open -;

  MOD_DEC_USE_COUNT;

#if LINUX_VERSION_CODE >= KERNEL_VERSION(2,2,0)
  return 0;
#endif
}




/* This function is called whenever a process which
 * has already opened the device file attempts to
 * read from it. */
#if LINUX_VERSION_CODE >= KERNEL_VERSION(2,2,0)
static ssize_t device_read(
    struct file *file,
    char *buffer, /* The buffer to fill with the data */
    size_t length,    /* The length of the buffer */
    loff_t *offset) /* offset to the file */
#else
static int device_read(
    struct inode *inode,
    struct file *file,
    char *buffer,   /* The buffer to fill with the data */
    int length)     /* The length of the buffer
                     * (mustn't write beyond that!) */
#endif
{
  /* Number of bytes actually written to the buffer */
  int bytes_read = 0;

#ifdef DEBUG
  printk("device_read(%p,%p,%d)\n",
    file, buffer, length);
#endif
```

```
    /* If we're at the end of the message, return 0
     * (which signifies end of file) */
    if (*Message_Ptr == 0)
      return 0;

    /* Actually put the data into the buffer */
    while (length && *Message_Ptr) {

      /* Because the buffer is in the user data segment,
       * not the kernel data segment, assignment wouldn't
       * work. Instead, we have to use put_user which
       * copies data from the kernel data segment to the
       * user data segment. */
      put_user(*(Message_Ptr++), buffer++);
      length -;
      bytes_read ++;
    }

#ifdef DEBUG
    printk ("Read %d bytes, %d left\n",
      bytes_read, length);
#endif

    /* Read functions are supposed to return the number
     * of bytes actually inserted into the buffer */
    return bytes_read;
}


/* This function is called when somebody tries to
 * write into our device file. */
#if LINUX_VERSION_CODE >= KERNEL_VERSION(2,2,0)
static ssize_t device_write(struct file *file,
                            const char *buffer,
                            size_t length,
                            loff_t *offset)
#else
static int device_write(struct inode *inode,
                        struct file *file,
                        const char *buffer,
                        int length)
#endif
{
  int i;
```

```
#ifdef DEBUG
  printk ("device_write(%p,%s,%d)",
    file, buffer, length);
#endif


  for(i=0; i<length && i<BUF_LEN; i++)
#if LINUX_VERSION_CODE >= KERNEL_VERSION(2,2,0)
    get_user(Message[i], buffer+i);
#else
    Message[i] = get_user(buffer+i);
#endif

  Message_Ptr = Message;

  /* Again, return the number of input characters used */
  return i;
}



/* This function is called whenever a process tries to
 * do an ioctl on our device file. We get two extra
 * parameters (additional to the inode and file
 * structures, which all device functions get): the number
 * of the ioctl called and the parameter given to the
 * ioctl function.
 *
 * If the ioctl is write or read/write (meaning output
 * is returned to the calling process), the ioctl call
 * returns the output of this function.
 */
int device_ioctl(
    struct inode *inode,
    struct file *file,
    unsigned int ioctl_num,/* The number of the ioctl */
    unsigned long ioctl_param) /* The parameter to it */
{
  int i;
  char *temp;
#if LINUX_VERSION_CODE >= KERNEL_VERSION(2,2,0)
  char ch;
#endif

  /* Switch according to the ioctl called */
  switch (ioctl_num) {
    case IOCTL_SET_MSG:
```

```
            /* Receive a pointer to a message (in user space)
             * and set that to be the device's message. */

            /* Get the parameter given to ioctl by the process */
            temp = (char *) ioctl_param;

            /* Find the length of the message */
#if LINUX_VERSION_CODE >= KERNEL_VERSION(2,2,0)
            get_user(ch, temp);
            for (i=0; ch && i<BUF_LEN; i++, temp++)
              get_user(ch, temp);
#else
            for (i=0; get_user(temp) && i<BUF_LEN; i++, temp++)
          ;
#endif

            /* Don't reinvent the wheel - call device_write */
#if LINUX_VERSION_CODE >= KERNEL_VERSION(2,2,0)
            device_write(file, (char *) ioctl_param, i, 0);
#else
            device_write(inode, file, (char *) ioctl_param, i);
#endif
            break;

        case IOCTL_GET_MSG:
          /* Give the current message to the calling
           * process - the parameter we got is a pointer,
           * fill it. */
#if LINUX_VERSION_CODE >= KERNEL_VERSION(2,2,0)
            i = device_read(file, (char *) ioctl_param, 99, 0);
#else
            i = device_read(inode, file, (char *) ioctl_param,
                            99);
#endif
            /* Warning - we assume here the buffer length is
             * 100. If it's less than that we might overflow
             * the buffer, causing the process to core dump.
             *
             * The reason we only allow up to 99 characters is
             * that the NULL which terminates the string also
             * needs room. */

            /* Put a zero at the end of the buffer, so it
             * will be properly terminated */
            put_user('\0', (char *) ioctl_param+i);
            break;
```

```
    case IOCTL_GET_NTH_BYTE:
      /* This ioctl is both input (ioctl_param) and
       * output (the return value of this function) */
      return Message[ioctl_param];
      break;
  }

  return SUCCESS;
}


/* Module Declarations *************************** */


/* This structure will hold the functions to be called
 * when a process does something to the device we
 * created. Since a pointer to this structure is kept in
 * the devices table, it can't be local to
 * init_module. NULL is for unimplemented functions. */
struct file_operations Fops = {
  NULL,   /* seek */
  device_read,
  device_write,
  NULL,   /* readdir */
  NULL,   /* select */
  device_ioctl,   /* ioctl */
  NULL,   /* mmap */
  device_open,
#if LINUX_VERSION_CODE >= KERNEL_VERSION(2,2,0)
  NULL,   /* flush */
#endif
  device_release  /* a.k.a. close */
};


/* Initialize the module - Register the character device */
int init_module()
{
  int ret_val;

  /* Register the character device (atleast try) */
  ret_val = module_register_chrdev(MAJOR_NUM,
                                   DEVICE_NAME,
                                   &Fops);

  /* Negative values signify an error */
```

```
    if (ret_val < 0) {
      printk ("%s failed with %d\n",
              "Sorry, registering the character device ",
              ret_val);
      return ret_val;
    }

    printk ("%s The major device number is %d.\n",
            "Registeration is a success",
            MAJOR_NUM);
    printk ("If you want to talk to the device driver,\n");
    printk ("you'll have to create a device file. \n");
    printk ("We suggest you use:\n");
    printk ("mknod %s c %d 0\n", DEVICE_FILE_NAME,
            MAJOR_NUM);
    printk ("The device file name is important, because\n");
    printk ("the ioctl program assumes that's the\n");
    printk ("file you'll use.\n");

    return 0;
}


/* Cleanup - unregister the appropriate file from /proc */
void cleanup_module()
{
    int ret;

    /* Unregister the device */
    ret = module_unregister_chrdev(MAJOR_NUM, DEVICE_NAME);

    /* If there's an error, report it */
    if (ret < 0)
      printk("Error in module_unregister_chrdev: %d\n", ret);
}
ex chardev.h

/* chardev.h - the header file with the ioctl definitions.
 *
 * The declarations here have to be in a header file,
 * because they need to be known both to the kernel
 * module (in chardev.c) and the process calling ioctl
 * (ioctl.c)
 */
```

```
#ifndef CHARDEV_H
#define CHARDEV_H

#include <linux/ioctl.h>



/* The major device number. We can't rely on dynamic
 * registration any more, because ioctls need to know
 * it. */
#define MAJOR_NUM 100



/* Set the message of the device driver */
#define IOCTL_SET_MSG _IOR(MAJOR_NUM, 0, char *)
/* _IOR means that we're creating an ioctl command
 * number for passing information from a user process
 * to the kernel module.
 *
 * The first arguments, MAJOR_NUM, is the major device
 * number we're using.
 *
 * The second argument is the number of the command
 * (there could be several with different meanings).
 *
 * The third argument is the type we want to get from
 * the process to the kernel.
 */

/* Get the message of the device driver */
#define IOCTL_GET_MSG _IOR(MAJOR_NUM, 1, char *)
 /* This IOCTL is used for output, to get the message
  * of the device driver. However, we still need the
  * buffer to place the message in to be input,
  * as it is allocated by the process.
  */



/* Get the n'th byte of the message */
#define IOCTL_GET_NTH_BYTE _IOWR(MAJOR_NUM, 2, int)
 /* The IOCTL is used for both input and output. It
  * receives from the user a number, n, and returns
  * Message[n]. */
```

```
/* The name of the device file */
#define DEVICE_FILE_NAME "char_dev"


#endif
ex ioctl.c

/* ioctl.c - the process to use ioctl's to control the
 * kernel module
 *
 * Until now we could have used cat for input and
 * output. But now we need to do ioctl's, which require
 * writing our own process.
 */

/* Copyright (C) 1998 by Ori Pomerantz */


/* device specifics, such as ioctl numbers and the
 * major device file. */
#include "chardev.h"


#include <fcntl.h>      /* open */
#include <unistd.h>     /* exit */
#include <sys/ioctl.h>  /* ioctl */



/* Functions for the ioctl calls */

ioctl_set_msg(int file_desc, char *message)
{
  int ret_val;

  ret_val = ioctl(file_desc, IOCTL_SET_MSG, message);

  if (ret_val < 0) {
    printf ("ioctl_set_msg failed:%d\n", ret_val);
    exit(-1);
  }
}
```

```
ioctl_get_msg(int file_desc)
{
  int ret_val;
  char message[100];

  /* Warning - this is dangerous because we don't tell
   * the kernel how far it's allowed to write, so it
   * might overflow the buffer. In a real production
   * program, we would have used two ioctls - one to tell
   * the kernel the buffer length and another to give
   * it the buffer to fill
   */
  ret_val = ioctl(file_desc, IOCTL_GET_MSG, message);

  if (ret_val < 0) {
    printf ("ioctl_get_msg failed:%d\n", ret_val);
    exit(-1);
  }

  printf("get_msg message:%s\n", message);
}




ioctl_get_nth_byte(int file_desc)
{
  int i;
  char c;

  printf("get_nth_byte message:");

  i = 0;
  while (c != 0) {
    c = ioctl(file_desc, IOCTL_GET_NTH_BYTE, i++);

    if (c < 0) {
      printf(
      "ioctl_get_nth_byte failed at the %d'th byte:\n", i);
      exit(-1);
    }

    putchar(c);
  }
  putchar('\n');
}
```

```
/* Main - Call the ioctl functions */
main()
{
  int file_desc, ret_val;
  char *msg = "Message passed by ioctl\n";

  file_desc = open(DEVICE_FILE_NAME, 0);
  if (file_desc < 0) {
    printf ("Can't open device file: %s\n",
            DEVICE_FILE_NAME);
    exit(-1);
  }

  ioctl_get_nth_byte(file_desc);
  ioctl_get_msg(file_desc);
  ioctl_set_msg(file_desc, msg);

  close(file_desc);
}
```

Chapter 6
Startup Parameters

In many of the previous examples, we had to hard-wire some thing into the kernel module, such as the file name for /proc files or the major device number for the device so we can have ioctls to it. This goes against the grain of the Unix and Linux philosophy, which is to write flexible programs the user can customize.

The way to tell a program, or a kernel module, something it needs before it can start working is by command line parameters. In the case of kernel modules, we don't get argc and argv—instead, we get something better. We can define global variables in the kernel module and insmod will fill them for us.

In this kernel module, we define two of them: str1 and str2. All you need to do is compile the kernel module and then run insmod str1=xxx str2=yyy. When init_module is called, str1 will point to the string 'xxx' and str2 to the string 'yyy'.

In version 2 there is no type checking on these arguments. If the first character of str1 or str2 is a digit the kernel will fill the variable with the value of the integer, rather than a pointer to the string. If a real life situation you have to check for this.

On the other hand, in version 2.2 you use the macro MACRO_PARM to tell insmod that you expect parameters, its name *and its type*. This solves the type problem and allows kernel modules to receive strings which begin with a digit, for example.

```
ex param.c
```

```
/* param.c
 *
 * Receive command line parameters at module installation
 */

/* Copyright (C) 1998-99 by Ori Pomerantz */




/* The necessary header files */

/* Standard in kernel modules */
#include <linux/kernel.h>   /* We're doing kernel work */
#include <linux/module.h>   /* Specifically, a module */

/* Deal with CONFIG_MODVERSIONS */
#if CONFIG_MODVERSIONS==1
#define MODVERSIONS
#include <linux/modversions.h>
#endif


#include <stdio.h>  /* I need NULL */



/* In 2.2.3 /usr/include/linux/version.h includes a
 * macro for this, but 2.0.35 doesn't - so I add it
 * here if necessary. */
#ifndef KERNEL_VERSION
#define KERNEL_VERSION(a,b,c) ((a)*65536+(b)*256+(c))
#endif



/* Emmanuel Papirakis:
 *
 * Parameter names are now (2.2) handled in a macro.
 * The kernel doesn't resolve the symbol names
 * like it seems to have once did.
 *
 * To pass parameters to a module, you have to use a macro
 * defined in include/linux/modules.h (line 176).
 * The macro takes two parameters. The parameter's name and
 * it's type. The type is a letter in double quotes.
```

```
 * For example, "i" should be an integer and "s" should
 * be a string.
 */


char *str1, *str2;


#if LINUX_VERSION_CODE >= KERNEL_VERSION(2,2,0)
MODULE_PARM(str1, "s");
MODULE_PARM(str2, "s");
#endif


/* Initialize the module - show the parameters */
int init_module()
{
  if (str1 == NULL || str2 == NULL) {
    printk("Next time, do insmod param str1=<something>");
    printk("str2=<something>\n");
  } else
    printk("Strings:%s and %s\n", str1, str2);

#if LINUX_VERSION_CODE >= KERNEL_VERSION(2,2,0)
  printk("If you try to insmod this module twice,");
  printk("(without rmmod'ing\n");
  printk("it first), you might get the wrong");
  printk("error message:\n");
  printk("'symbol for parameters str1 not found'.\n");
#endif

  return 0;
}


/* Cleanup */
void cleanup_module()
{
}
```

Chapter 7
System Calls

S o far, the only thing we've done was to use well-defined kernel mechanisms to register /proc files and device handlers. This is fine if you want to do something the kernel programmers thought you'd want, such as write a device driver. But what if you want to do something unusual, to change the behavior of the system in some way? Then, you're mostly on your own.

This is where kernel programming gets dangerous. While writing the example below, I killed the open system call. This meant I couldn't open any files, I couldn't run any programs, and I couldn't shutdown the computer. I had to pull the power switch. Luckily, no files died. To ensure you won't lose any files either, please run sync right before you do the insmod and the rmmod.

Forget about /proc files, forget about device files. They're just minor details. The *real* process to kernel communication mechanism, the one used by all processes, is *system calls*. When a process requests a service from the kernel (such as opening a file, forking to a new process, or requesting more memory), this is the mechanism used. If you want to change the behavior of the kernel in interesting ways, this is the place to do it. By the way, if you want to see which system calls a program uses, run strace <command> <arguments>.

In general, a process is not supposed to be able to access the kernel. It can't access kernel memory and it can't call kernel functions. The hardware of the CPU enforces this (that's the reason why it's called "protected mode"). System calls are an exception to this general rule. What happens is that the process fills the registers with the appropriate values and then calls a special instruction which jumps to a previously defined location in the kernel (of course, that location is readable by user processes, it is not writable by them). Under Intel CPUs, this is done by means of interrupt 0x80. The hardware knows that once you jump to this location, you are no longer running in restricted user mode, but as the operating system kernel—and therefore you're allowed to do whatever you want.

The location in the kernel a process can jump to is called `system_call`. The procedure at that location checks the system call number, which tells the kernel what service the process requested. Then, it looks at the table of system calls (`sys_call_table`) to see the address of the kernel function to call. Then it calls the function, and after it returns, does a few system checks and then returns back to the process (or to a different process, if the process time ran out). If you want to read this code, it's at the source file `arch/<architecture>/kernel/entry.S`, after the line `ENTRY(system_call)`.

So, if we want to change the way a certain system call works, what we need to do is to write our own function to implement it (usually by adding a bit of our own code, and then calling the original function) and then change the pointer at `sys_call_table` to point to our function. Because we might be removed later and we don't want to leave the system in an unstable state, it's important for `cleanup_module` to restore the table to its original state.

The source code here is an example of such a kernel module. We want to "spy" on a certain user, and to `printk` a message whenever that user opens a file. Toward this end, we replace the system call to open a file with our own function, called `our_sys_open`. This function checks the uid (user's ID) of the current process, and if it's equal to the uid we spy on, it calls `printk` to display the name of the file to be opened. Then, either way, it calls the original `open` function with the same parameters, to actually open the file.

The `init_module` function replaces the appropriate location in `sys_call_table` and keeps the original pointer in a variable. The `cleanup_module` function uses that variable to restore everything back to normal. This approach is dangerous, because of the possibility of two kernel modules changing the same system call. Imagine we have two kernel modules, A and B. A's open system call will be A_open and B's will be B_open. Now, when A is inserted into the kernel, the system call is replaced with A_open, which will call the original sys_open when it's done. Next, B is inserted into the kernel, which replaces the system call with B_open, which will call what it thinks is the original system call, A_open, when it's done.

Now, if B is removed first, everything will be well—it will simply restore the system call to A_open, which calls the original. However, if A is removed and then B is removed, the system will crash. A's removal will restore the system call to the original, sys_open, cutting B out of the loop. Then, when B is removed, it will restore the system call to what *it* thinks is the original, A_open, which is no longer in memory. At first glance, it appears we could solve this particular problem by checking if the system call is equal to our open function and if so not changing it at all (so that B won't change the system call when it's removed), but that will cause an even worse problem. When A is removed, it sees that the system call was changed to B_open so that it is no longer pointing to A_open, so it won't restore it to sys_open before it is removed from memory. Unfortunately, B_open will still try to call A_open, which is no longer there, so that even without removing B the system would crash.

I can think of two ways to prevent this problem. The first is to restore the call to the original value, sys_open. Unfortunately, sys_open is not part of the kernel system table in /proc/ ksyms, so we can't access it. The other solution is to use the reference count to prevent root from rmmod'ing the module once it is loaded. This is good for production modules, but bad for an educational sample—which is why I didn't do it here.

```
ex syscall.c

/* syscall.c
 *
 * System call "stealing" sample
 */


/* Copyright (C) 1998-99 by Ori Pomerantz */


/* The necessary header files */

/* Standard in kernel modules */
#include <linux/kernel.h>   /* We're doing kernel work */
#include <linux/module.h>   /* Specifically, a module */

/* Deal with CONFIG_MODVERSIONS */
#if CONFIG_MODVERSIONS==1
#define MODVERSIONS
#include <linux/modversions.h>
#endif

#include <sys/syscall.h>  /* The list of system calls */

/* For the current (process) structure, we need
 * this to know who the current user is. */
#include <linux/sched.h>




/* In 2.2.3 /usr/include/linux/version.h includes a
 * macro for this, but 2.0.35 doesn't - so I add it
 * here if necessary. */
#ifndef KERNEL_VERSION
#define KERNEL_VERSION(a,b,c) ((a)*65536+(b)*256+(c))
#endif
```

```
#if LINUX_VERSION_CODE >= KERNEL_VERSION(2,2,0)
#include <asm/uaccess.h>
#endif




/* The system call table (a table of functions). We
 * just define this as external, and the kernel will
 * fill it up for us when we are insmod'ed
 */
extern void *sys_call_table[];




/* UID we want to spy on - will be filled from the
 * command line */
int uid;

#if LINUX_VERSION_CODE >= KERNEL_VERSION(2,2,0)
MODULE_PARM(uid, "i");
#endif

/* A pointer to the original system call. The reason
 * we keep this, rather than call the original function
 * (sys_open), is because somebody else might have
 * replaced the system call before us. Note that this
 * is not 100% safe, because if another module
 * replaced sys_open before us, then when we're inserted
 * we'll call the function in that module--and it
 * might be removed before we are.
 *
 * Another reason for this is that we can't get sys_open.
 * It's a static variable, so it is not exported. */
asmlinkage int (*original_call)(const char *, int, int);




/* For some reason, in 2.2.3 current->uid gave me
 * zero, not the real user ID. I tried to find what went
 * wrong, but I couldn't do it in a short time, and
 * I'm lazy - so I'll just use the system call to get the
 * uid, the way a process would.
 *
 * For some reason, after I recompiled the kernel this
 * problem went away.
 */
asmlinkage int (*getuid_call)();
```

```
/* The function we'll replace sys_open (the function
 * called when you call the open system call) with. To
 * find the exact prototype, with the number and type
 * of arguments, we find the original function first
 * (it's at fs/open.c).
 *
 * In theory, this means that we're tied to the
 * current version of the kernel. In practice, the
 * system calls almost never change (it would wreck havoc
 * and require programs to be recompiled, since the system
 * calls are the interface between the kernel and the
 * processes).
 */
asmlinkage int our_sys_open(const char *filename,
                            int flags,
                            int mode)
{
  int i = 0;
  char ch;

  /* Check if this is the user we're spying on */
  if (uid == getuid_call()) {
   /* getuid_call is the getuid system call,
    * which gives the uid of the user who
    * ran the process which called the system
    * call we got */

    /* Report the file, if relevant */
    printk("Opened file by %d: ", uid);
    do {
#if LINUX_VERSION_CODE >= KERNEL_VERSION(2,2,0)
      get_user(ch, filename+i);
#else
      ch = get_user(filename+i);
#endif
      i++;
      printk("%c", ch);
    } while (ch != 0);
    printk("\n");
  }

  /* Call the original sys_open - otherwise, we lose
   * the ability to open files */
  return original_call(filename, flags, mode);
}
```

```
/* Initialize the module - replace the system call */
int init_module()
{
  /* Warning - too late for it now, but maybe for
   * next time... */
  printk("I'm dangerous. I hope you did a ");
  printk("sync before you insmod'ed me.\n");
  printk("My counterpart, cleanup_module(), is even");
  printk("more dangerous. If\n");
  printk("you value your file system, it will ");
  printk("be \"sync; rmmod\" \n");
  printk("when you remove this module.\n");

  /* Keep a pointer to the original function in
   * original_call, and then replace the system call
   * in the system call table with our_sys_open */
  original_call = sys_call_table[__NR_open];
  sys_call_table[__NR_open] = our_sys_open;

  /* To get the address of the function for system
   * call foo, go to sys_call_table[__NR_foo]. */

  printk("Spying on UID:%d\n", uid);

  /* Get the system call for getuid */
  getuid_call = sys_call_table[__NR_getuid];

  return 0;
}


/* Cleanup - unregister the appropriate file from /proc */
void cleanup_module()
{
  /* Return the system call back to normal */
  if (sys_call_table[__NR_open] != our_sys_open) {
    printk("Somebody else also played with the ");
    printk("open system call\n");
    printk("The system may be left in ");
    printk("an unstable state.\n");
  }

  sys_call_table[__NR_open] = original_call;
}
```

Chapter 8
Blocking Processes

What do you do when somebody asks you for something you can't do right away? If you're a human being and you're bothered by a human being, the only thing you can say is: "Not right now, I'm busy. *Go away!*" But if you're a kernel module and you're bothered by a process, you have another possibility. You can put the process to sleep until you can service it. After all, processes are being put to sleep by the kernel and woken up all the time (that's the way multiple processes appear to run on the same time on a single CPU).

This kernel module is an example of this. The file (called /proc /sleep) can only be opened by a single process at a time. If the file is already open, the kernel module calls module_inter-ruptible_sleep_on. This function changes the status of the task (a task is the kernel data structure which holds information about a process and the system call it's in, if any) to TASK_INTERRUPTIBLE, which means that the task will not run until it is woken up somehow, and adds it to WaitQ, the queue of tasks waiting to access the file. Then, the function calls the scheduler to context switch to a different process, one which has some use for the CPU.

When a process is done with the file, it closes it, and module_close is called. That function wakes up all the processes in the queue (there's no mechanism to only wake up one of them). It then returns and the process which just closed the file can continue to run. In time, the scheduler decides that that process has had enough and gives control of the CPU to another process. Eventually, one of the processes which was in the queue will be given control of the CPU by the scheduler. It starts at the point right after the call to `module_interruptible_sleep_on`. It can then proceed to set a global variable to tell all the other processes that the file is still open and go on with its life. When the other processes get a piece of the CPU, they'll see that global variable and go back to sleep.

To make our life more interesting, `module_close` doesn't have a monopoly on waking up the processes which wait to access the file. A signal, such as Ctrl+C (`SIGINT`) can also wake up a process. In that case, we want to return with `-EINTR` immediately. This is important so users can, for example, kill the process before it receives the file.

There is one more point to remember. Some times processes don't want to sleep; they want either to get what they want immediately, or to be told it cannot be done. Such processes use the `O_NONBLOCK` flag when opening the file. The kernel is supposed to respond by returning with the error code `-EAGAIN` from operations, which would otherwise block, such as opening the file in this example. The program cat_noblock, available in the source directory for this chapter, can be used to open a file with `O_NONBLOCK`.

```
ex sleep.c

/* sleep.c - create a /proc file, and if several
 * processes try to open it at the same time, put all
 * but one to sleep */


/* Copyright (C) 1998-99 by Ori Pomerantz */


/* The necessary header files */

/* Standard in kernel modules */
#include <linux/kernel.h>   /* We're doing kernel work */
#include <linux/module.h>   /* Specifically, a module */

/* Deal with CONFIG_MODVERSIONS */
#if CONFIG_MODVERSIONS==1
#define MODVERSIONS
#include <linux/modversions.h>
#endif

/* Necessary because we use proc fs */
#include <linux/proc_fs.h>

/* For putting processes to sleep and waking them up */
#include <linux/sched.h>
#include <linux/wrapper.h>
```

```
/* In 2.2.3 /usr/include/linux/version.h includes a
 * macro for this, but 2.0.35 doesn't - so I add it
 * here if necessary. */
#ifndef KERNEL_VERSION
#define KERNEL_VERSION(a,b,c) ((a)*65536+(b)*256+(c))
#endif


#if LINUX_VERSION_CODE >= KERNEL_VERSION(2,2,0)
#include <asm/uaccess.h>  /* for get_user and put_user */
#endif


/* The module's file functions ********************** */


/* Here we keep the last message received, to prove
 * that we can process our input */
#define MESSAGE_LENGTH 80
static char Message[MESSAGE_LENGTH];


/* Since we use the file operations struct, we can't use
 * the special proc output provisions - we have to use
 * a standard read function, which is this function */
#if LINUX_VERSION_CODE >= KERNEL_VERSION(2,2,0)
static ssize_t module_output(
    struct file *file,   /* The file read */
    char *buf, /* The buffer to put data to (in the
                * user segment) */
    size_t len,  /* The length of the buffer */
    loff_t *offset) /* Offset in the file - ignore */
#else
static int module_output(
    struct inode *inode, /* The inode read */
    struct file *file,   /* The file read */
    char *buf, /* The buffer to put data to (in the
                * user segment) */
    int len)  /* The length of the buffer */
#endif
{
  static int finished = 0;
  int i;
  char message[MESSAGE_LENGTH+30];
```

```
    /* Return 0 to signify end of file - that we have
     * nothing more to say at this point. */
    if (finished) {
      finished = 0;
      return 0;
    }

    /* If you don't understand this by now, you're
     * hopeless as a kernel  programmer. */
    sprintf(message, "Last input:%s\n", Message);
    for(i=0; i<len && message[i]; i++)
      put_user(message[i], buf+i);

    finished = 1;
    return i;   /* Return the number of bytes "read" */
}


/* This function receives input from the user when
 * the user writes to the /proc file. */
#if LINUX_VERSION_CODE >= KERNEL_VERSION(2,2,0)
static ssize_t module_input(
    struct file *file,   /* The file itself */
    const char *buf,     /* The buffer with input */
    size_t length,       /* The buffer's length */
    loff_t *offset)      /* offset to file - ignore */
#else
static int module_input(
    struct inode *inode, /* The file's inode */
    struct file *file,   /* The file itself */
    const char *buf,     /* The buffer with the input */
    int length)          /* The buffer's length */
#endif
{
  int i;

  /* Put the input into Message, where module_output
   * will later be able to use it */
  for(i=0; i<MESSAGE_LENGTH-1 && i<length; i++)
#if LINUX_VERSION_CODE >= KERNEL_VERSION(2,2,0)
    get_user(Message[i], buf+i);
#else
  Message[i] = get_user(buf+i);
#endif
/* we want a standard, zero terminated string */
  Message[i] = '\0';
```

```
  /* We need to return the number of input
   * characters used */
  return i;
}

/* 1 if the file is currently open by somebody */
int Already_Open = 0;

/* Queue of processes who want our file */
static struct wait_queue *WaitQ = NULL;


/* Called when the /proc file is opened */
static int module_open(struct inode *inode,
                       struct file *file)
{
  /* If the file's flags include O_NONBLOCK, it means
   * the process doesn't want to wait for the file.
   * In this case, if the file is already open, we
   * should fail with -EAGAIN, meaning "you'll have to
   * try again", instead of blocking a process which
   * would rather stay awake. */
  if ((file->f_flags & O_NONBLOCK) && Already_Open)
    return -EAGAIN;

  /* This is the correct place for MOD_INC_USE_COUNT
   * because if a process is in the loop, which is
   * within the kernel module, the kernel module must
   * not be removed. */
  MOD_INC_USE_COUNT;

  /* If the file is already open, wait until it isn't */
  while (Already_Open)
  {
#if LINUX_VERSION_CODE >= KERNEL_VERSION(2,2,0)
    int i, is_sig=0;
#endif

    /* This function puts the current process,
     * including any system calls, such as us, to sleep.
     * Execution will be resumed right after the function
     * call, either because somebody called
     * wake_up(&WaitQ) (only module_close does that,
     * when the file is closed) or when a signal, such
     * as Ctrl-C, is sent to the process */
    module_interruptible_sleep_on(&WaitQ);
```

```
        /* If we woke up because we got a signal we're not
         * blocking, return  -EINTR (fail the system call).
         * This allows processes to be killed or stopped. */




   /*
    * Emmanuel Papirakis:
    *
    * This is a little update to work with 2.2.*. Signals
    * now are contained in two words (64 bits) and are
    * stored in a structure that contains an array of two
    * unsigned longs. We now have to make 2 checks in our if.
    *
    * Ori Pomerantz:
    *
    * Nobody promised me they'll never use more than 64
    * bits, or that this book won't be used for a version
    * of Linux with a word size of 16 bits. This code
    * would work in any case.
    */
#if LINUX_VERSION_CODE >= KERNEL_VERSION(2,2,0)

    for(i=0; i<_NSIG_WORDS && !is_sig; i++)
      is_sig = current->signal.sig[i] &
        ~current->blocked.sig[i];
    if (is_sig) {
#else
    if (current->signal & ~current->blocked) {
#endif
        /* It's important to put MOD_DEC_USE_COUNT here,
         * because for processes where the open is
         * interrupted there will never be a corresponding
         * close. If we don't decrement the usage count
         * here, we will be left with a positive usage
         * count which we'll have no way to bring down to
         * zero, giving us an immortal module, which can
         * only be killed by rebooting the machine. */
        MOD_DEC_USE_COUNT;
        return -EINTR;
    }
  }

  /* If we got here, Already_Open must be zero */
```

```
    /* Open the file */
    Already_Open = 1;
    return 0;   /* Allow the access */
}




/* Called when the /proc file is closed */
#if LINUX_VERSION_CODE >= KERNEL_VERSION(2,2,0)
int module_close(struct inode *inode, struct file *file)
#else
void module_close(struct inode *inode, struct file *file)
#endif
{
  /* Set Already_Open to zero, so one of the processes
   * in the WaitQ will be able to set Already_Open back
   * to one and to open the file. All the other processes
   * will be called when Already_Open is back to one, so
   * they'll go back to sleep. */
  Already_Open = 0;

  /* Wake up all the processes in WaitQ, so if anybody
   * is waiting for the file, they can have it. */
  module_wake_up(&WaitQ);

  MOD_DEC_USE_COUNT;

#if LINUX_VERSION_CODE >= KERNEL_VERSION(2,2,0)
  return 0;   /* success */
#endif
}




/* This function decides whether to allow an operation
 * (return zero) or not allow it (return a non-zero
 * which indicates why it is not allowed).
 *
 * The operation can be one of the following values:
 * 0 - Execute (run the "file" - meaningless in our case)
 * 2 - Write (input to the kernel module)
 * 4 - Read (output from the kernel module)
 *
 * This is the real function that checks file
 * permissions. The permissions returned by ls -l are
 * for reference only, and can be overridden here.
 */
```

```
static int module_permission(struct inode *inode, int op)
{
  /* We allow everybody to read from our module, but
   * only root (uid 0) may write to it */
  if (op == 4 || (op == 2 && current->euid == 0))
    return 0;

  /* If it's anything else, access is denied */
  return -EACCES;
}


/* Structures to register as the /proc file, with
 * pointers to all the relevant functions. *********** */


/* File operations for our proc file. This is where
 * we place pointers to all the functions called when
 * somebody tries to do something to our file. NULL
 * means we don't want to deal with something. */
static struct file_operations File_Ops_4_Our_Proc_File =
  {
    NULL,  /* lseek */
    module_output,  /* "read" from the file */
    module_input,   /* "write" to the file */
    NULL,  /* readdir */
    NULL,  /* select */
    NULL,  /* ioctl */
    NULL,  /* mmap */
    module_open,/* called when the /proc file is opened */
#if LINUX_VERSION_CODE >= KERNEL_VERSION(2,2,0)
    NULL,   /* flush */
#endif
    module_close      /* called when it's classed */
  };


/* Inode operations for our proc file. We need it so
 * we'll have somewhere to specify the file operations
 * structure we want to use, and the function we use for
 * permissions. It's also possible to specify functions
 * to be called for anything else which could be done to an
 * inode (although we don't bother, we just put NULL). */
static struct inode_operations Inode_Ops_4_Our_Proc_File =
  {
    &File_Ops_4_Our_Proc_File,
```

```
        NULL, /* create */
        NULL, /* lookup */
        NULL, /* link */
        NULL, /* unlink */
        NULL, /* symlink */
        NULL, /* mkdir */
        NULL, /* rmdir */
        NULL, /* mknod */
        NULL, /* rename */
        NULL, /* readlink */
        NULL, /* follow_link */
        NULL, /* readpage */
        NULL, /* writepage */
        NULL, /* bmap */
        NULL, /* truncate */
        module_permission /* check for permissions */
    };


/* Directory entry */
static struct proc_dir_entry Our_Proc_File =
    {
        0, /* Inode number - ignore, it will be filled by
             * proc_register[_dynamic] */
        5, /* Length of the file name */
        "sleep", /* The file name */
        S_IFREG | S_IRUGO | S_IWUSR,
        /* File mode - this is a regular file which
         * can be read by its owner, its group, and everybody
         * else. Also, its owner can write to it.
         *
         * Actually, this field is just for reference, it's
         * module_permission that does the actual check. It
         * could use this field, but in our implementation it
         * doesn't, for simplicity. */
        1,  /* Number of links (directories where the
               * file is referenced) */
        0, 0,  /* The uid and gid for the file - we give
                  * it to root */
        80, /* The size of the file reported by ls. */
        &Inode_Ops_4_Our_Proc_File,
        /* A pointer to the inode structure for
         * the file, if we need it. In our case we
         * do, because we need a write function. */
        NULL  /* The read function for the file.
                 * Irrelevant, because we put it
                 * in the inode structure above */
    };
```

```
/* Module initialization and cleanup **************** */


/* Initialize the module - register the proc file */
int init_module()
{
  /* Success if proc_register_dynamic is a success,
   * failure otherwise */
#if LINUX_VERSION_CODE >= KERNEL_VERSION(2,2,0)
  return proc_register(&proc_root, &Our_Proc_File);
#else
  return proc_register_dynamic(&proc_root, &Our_Proc_File);
#endif

  /* proc_root is the root directory for the proc
   * fs (/proc). This is where we want our file to be
   * located.
   */
}


/* Cleanup - unregister our file from /proc. This could
 * get dangerous if there are still processes waiting in
 * WaitQ, because they are inside our open function,
 * which will get unloaded. I'll explain how to avoid
 * removal of a kernel module in such a case in
 * chapter 10. */
void cleanup_module()
{
  proc_unregister(&proc_root, Our_Proc_File.low_ino);
}
```

Chapter 9
Replacing printks

In the beginning (Chapter 1), I said that X and kernel module programming don't mix. That's true while developing the kernel module, but in actual use you want to be able to send messages to whichever tty the command to the module came from. This is important for identifying errors after the kernel module is released, because it will be used through all of them.

The way this is done is by using `current`, a pointer to the currently running task, to get the current task's tty structure. Then, we look inside that tty structure to find a pointer to a string write function, which we use to write a string to the tty.

```
ex printk.c

/* printk.c - send textual output to the tty you're
 * running on, regardless of whether it's passed
 * through X11, telnet, etc. */


/* Copyright (C) 1998 by Ori Pomerantz */


/* The necessary header files */

/* Standard in kernel modules */
#include <linux/kernel.h>    /* We're doing kernel work
*/
#include <linux/module.h>    /* Specifically, a module */
```

```
/* Deal with CONFIG_MODVERSIONS */
#if CONFIG_MODVERSIONS==1
#define MODVERSIONS
#include <linux/modversions.h>
#endif


/* Necessary here */
#include <linux/sched.h>    /* For current */
#include <linux/tty.h>      /* For the tty declarations */


/* Print the string to the appropriate tty, the one
 * the current task uses */
void print_string(char *str)
{
  struct tty_struct *my_tty;

  /* The tty for the current task */
  my_tty = current->tty;

  /* If my_tty is NULL, it means that the current task
   * has no tty you can print to (this is possible, for
   * example, if it's a daemon). In this case, there's
   * nothing we can do. */
  if (my_tty != NULL) {

    /* my_tty->driver is a struct which holds the tty's
     * functions, one of which (write) is used to
     * write strings to the tty. It can be used to take
     * a string either from the user's memory segment
     * or the kernel's memory segment.
     *
     * The function's first parameter is the tty to
     * write to, because the  same function would
     * normally be used for all tty's of a certain type.
     * The second parameter controls whether the
     * function receives a string from kernel memory
     * (false, 0) or from user memory (true, non zero).
     * The third parameter is a pointer to a string,
     * and the fourth parameter is the length of
     * the string.
     */
    (*(my_tty->driver).write)(
        my_tty, /* The tty itself */
        0, /* We don't take the string from user space */
    str, /* String */
    strlen(str));  /* Length */
```

```
    /* ttys were originally hardware devices, which
     * (usually) adhered strictly to the ASCII standard.
     * According to ASCII, to move to a new line you
     * need two characters, a carriage return and a
     * line feed. In Unix, on the other hand, the
     * ASCII line feed is used for both purposes - so
     * we can't just use \n, because it wouldn't have
     * a carriage return and the next line will
     * start at the column right
     *                              after the line feed.
     *
     * BTW, this is the reason why the text file
     *  is different between Unix and Windows.
     * In CP/M and its derivatives, such as MS-DOS and
     * Windows, the ASCII standard was strictly
     * adhered to, and therefore a new line requires
     * both a line feed and a carriage return.
     */
    (*(my_tty->driver).write)(
      my_tty,
      0,
      "\015\012",
      2);
  }
}


/* Module initialization and cleanup ***************** */


/* Initialize the module - register the proc file */
int init_module()
{
  print_string("Module Inserted");

  return 0;
}


/* Cleanup - unregister our file from /proc */
void cleanup_module()
{
  print_string("Module Removed");
}
```

Chapter 10
Scheduling Tasks

Very often, we have "housekeeping" tasks which have to be done at a certain time, or every so often. If the task is to be done by a process, we do it by putting it in the `crontab` file. If the task is to be done by a kernel module, we have two possibilities. The first is to put a process in the `crontab` file, which will wake up the module by a system call when necessary, for example, by opening a file. This is terribly inefficient, however—we run a new process off of `crontab`, read a new executable to memory, and all this just to wake up a kernel module which is in memory anyway.

Instead of doing that, we can create a function that will be called once for every timer interrupt. The way we do this is we create a task, held in a `struct tq_struct`, which will hold a pointer to the function. Then, we use `queue_task` to put that task on a task list called `tq_timer`, which is the list of tasks to be executed on the next timer interrupt. Because we want the function to keep on being executed, we need to put it back on `tq_timer` whenever it is called, for the next timer interrupt.

There's one more point we need to remember here. When a module is removed by `rmmod`, first its reference count is checked. If it is zero, `module_cleanup` is called. Then, the module is removed from memory with all its functions. Nobody checks to see if the timer's task list happens to contain a pointer to one of those functions, which will no longer be available. Ages later (from the computer's perspective, from a human perspective it's nothing, less than a hundredth of a second), the kernel has a timer interrupt and tries to call the function on the task list. Unfortunately, the function is no longer there. In most cases, the memory page where it sat is unused, and you get an ugly error message. But if some other code is now sitting at the same memory location, things could get *very* ugly. Unfortunately, we don't have an easy way to unregister a task from a task list.

Since `cleanup_module` can't return with an error code (it's a void function), the solution is to not let it return at all. Instead, it calls `sleep_on` or `module_sleep_on` to put the `rmmod` process to sleep. Before that, it informs the function called on the timer interrupt to stop attaching itself by setting a global variable. Then, on the next timer interrupt, the `rmmod` process will be woken up, when our function is no longer in the queue and it's safe to remove the module.

```
ex sched.c

/* sched.c - scheduale a function to be called on
 * every timer interrupt. */



/* Copyright (C) 1998 by Ori Pomerantz */



/* The necessary header files */

/* Standard in kernel modules */
#include <linux/kernel.h>    /* We're doing kernel work */
#include <linux/module.h>    /* Specifically, a module */

/* Deal with CONFIG_MODVERSIONS */
#if CONFIG_MODVERSIONS==1
#define MODVERSIONS
#include <linux/modversions.h>
#endif

/* Necessary because we use the proc fs */
#include <linux/proc_fs.h>

/* We scheduale tasks here */
#include <linux/tqueue.h>

/* We also need the ability to put ourselves to sleep
 * and wake up later */
#include <linux/sched.h>

/* In 2.2.3 /usr/include/linux/version.h includes a
 * macro for this, but 2.0.35 doesn't - so I add it
 * here if necessary. */
#ifndef KERNEL_VERSION
```

```
#define KERNEL_VERSION(a,b,c) ((a)*65536+(b)*256+(c))
#endif




/* The number of times the timer interrupt has been
 * called so far */
static int TimerIntrpt = 0;


/* This is used by cleanup, to prevent the module from
 * being unloaded while intrpt_routine is still in
 * the task queue */
static struct wait_queue *WaitQ = NULL;

static void intrpt_routine(void *);


/* The task queue structure for this task, from tqueue.h */
static struct tq_struct Task = {
  NULL,   /* Next item in list - queue_task will do
           * this for us */
  0,      /* A flag meaning we haven't been inserted
           * into a task queue yet */
  intrpt_routine, /* The function to run */
  NULL    /* The void* parameter for that function */
};



/* This function will be called on every timer
 * interrupt. Notice the void* pointer - task functions
 * can be used for more than one purpose, each time
 * getting a different parameter. */
static void intrpt_routine(void *irrelevant)
{
  /* Increment the counter */
  TimerIntrpt++;

  /* If cleanup wants us to die */
  if (WaitQ != NULL)
    wake_up(&WaitQ);   /* Now cleanup_module can return */
  else
    /* Put ourselves back in the task queue */
    queue_task(&Task, &tq_timer);
}
```

```
/* Put data into the proc fs file. */
int procfile_read(char *buffer,
                  char **buffer_location, off_t offset,
                  int buffer_length, int zero)
{
  int len;  /* The number of bytes actually used */

  /* This is static so it will still be in memory
   * when we leave this function */
  static char my_buffer[80];

  static int count = 1;

  /* We give all of our information in one go, so if
   * the anybody asks us if we have more information
   * the answer should always be no.
   */
  if (offset > 0)
    return 0;

  /* Fill the buffer and get its length */
  len = sprintf(my_buffer,
                "Timer was called %d times so far\n",
                TimerIntrpt);
  count++;

  /* Tell the function which called us where the
   * buffer is */
  *buffer_location = my_buffer;

  /* Return the length */
  return len;
}


struct proc_dir_entry Our_Proc_File =
  {
    0, /* Inode number - ignore, it will be filled by
        * proc_register_dynamic */
    5, /* Length of the file name */
    "sched", /* The file name */
    S_IFREG | S_IRUGO,
    /* File mode - this is a regular file which can
     * be read by its owner, its group, and everybody
     * else */
    1,  /* Number of links (directories where
```

```
                * the file is referenced) */
        0, 0,  /* The uid and gid for the file - we give
                * it to root */
        80, /* The size of the file reported by ls. */
        NULL, /* functions which can be done on the
                * inode (linking, removing, etc.) - we don't
                * support any. */
        procfile_read,
        /* The read function for this file, the function called
         * when somebody tries to read something from it. */
        NULL
        /* We could have here a function to fill the
         * file's inode, to enable us to play with
         * permissions, ownership, etc. */
    };



/* Initialize the module - register the proc file */
int init_module()
{
    /* Put the task in the tq_timer task queue, so it
     * will be executed at next timer interrupt */
    queue_task(&Task, &tq_timer);

    /* Success if proc_register_dynamic is a success,
     * failure otherwise */
#if LINUX_VERSION_CODE > KERNEL_VERSION(2,2,0)
    return proc_register(&proc_root, &Our_Proc_File);
#else
    return proc_register_dynamic(&proc_root, &Our_Proc_File);
#endif
}



/* Cleanup */
void cleanup_module()
{
    /* Unregister our /proc file */
    proc_unregister(&proc_root, Our_Proc_File.low_ino);

    /* Sleep until intrpt_routine is called one last
     * time. This is necessary, because otherwise we'll
     * deallocate the memory holding intrpt_routine and
     * Task while tq_timer still references them.
     * Notice that here we don't allow signals to
     * interrupt us.
```

```
         *
         * Since WaitQ is now not NULL, this automatically
         * tells the interrupt routine it's time to die. */
     sleep_on(&WaitQ);
 }
```

Chapter 11
Interrupt Handlers

E xcept for the last chapter, everything we did in the kernel so
far we've done as a response to a process asking for it, either
by dealing with a special file, sending an `ioctl`, or issuing a system call. But the job of the kernel isn't just to respond to process
requests. Another job, which is every bit as important, is to speak
to the hardware connected to the machine.

There are two types of interaction between the CPU and the rest
of the computer's hardware. The first type is when the CPU gives
orders to the hardware, the other is when the hardware needs to
tell the CPU something. The second, called *interrupts*, is much
harder to implement because it has to be dealt with when conve-
nient for the hardware, not the CPU. Hardware devices typically
have a very small amount of RAM, and if you don't read their
information when available, it is lost.

Under Linux, hardware interrupts are called IRQs (short for Interrupt Requests). There are two types of IRQs, short and long. A
short IRQ is one which is expected to take a *very* short period of
time, during which the rest of the machine will be blocked and no
other interrupts will be handled. A *long IRQ* is one which can
take longer, and during which other interrupts may occur (but
not interrupts from the same device). If at all possible, it's better
to declare an interrupt handler to be long.

When the CPU receives an interrupt, it stops whatever it's doing
(unless it's processing a more important interrupt, in which case it
will deal with this one only when the more important one is done),
saves certain parameters on the stack, and calls the interrupt handler. This means that certain things are not allowed in the interrupt

handler itself, because the system is in an unknown state. The solution to this problem is for the interrupt handler to do what needs to be done immediately, usually read something from the hardware or send something to the hardware, and then schedule the handling of the new information at a later time (this is called the "bottom half") and return. The kernel is then guaranteed to call the bottom half as soon as possible—and when it does, everything allowed in kernel modules will be allowed.

The way to implement this is to call `request_irq` to get your interrupt handler called when the relevant IRQ is received (there are 16 of them on Intel platforms). This function receives the IRQ number, the name of the function, flags, a name for `/proc/interrupts`, and a parameter to pass to the interrupt handler. The flags can include `SA_SHIRQ` to indicate you're willing to share the IRQ with other interrupt handlers (usually because a number of hardware devices sit on the same IRQ) and `SA_INTERRUPT` to indicate this is a fast interrupt. This function will only succeed if there isn't already a handler on this IRQ, or if you're both willing to share.

Then, from within the interrupt handler, we communicate with the hardware and then use `queue_task_irq` with `tq_immediate` and `mark_bh(BH_IMMEDIATE)` to schedule the bottom half. The reason we can't use the standard `queue_task` in version 2 is that the interrupt might happen right in the middle of somebody else's `queue_task`. We need `mark_bh` because earlier versions of Linux only had an array of 32 bottom halves, and now one of them (`BH_IMMEDIATE`) is used for the linked list of bottom halves for drivers which didn't get a bottom half entry assigned to them.

Keyboards On The Intel Architecture

Warning: The rest of this chapter is completely Intel-specific. If you're not running on an Intel platform, it will not work. Don't even try to compile the code here.

I had a problem with writing the sample code for this chapter. On one hand, for an example to be useful, it has to run on everybody's computer with meaningful results. On the other hand, the kernel already includes device drivers for all of the common devices, and those device drivers won't coexist with what I'm going to write. The solution I've found was to write something for the keyboard interrupt, and disable the regular keyboard interrupt handler first. Since it is defined as a static symbol in the kernel source files (specifically, `drivers/char/keyboard.c`), there is no way to restore it. Before `insmod`'ing this code, do on another terminal `sleep 120 ; reboot` if you value your file system.

This code binds itself to IRQ 1, which is the IRQ of the keyboard controlled under Intel architectures. Then, when it receives a keyboard interrupt, it reads the keyboard's status (that's the purpose of the `inb(0x64)`) and the scan code, which is the value returned by the keyboard. Then, as soon as the kernel think it's feasible, it runs `got_char` which gives the code of the key used (the first seven bits of the scan code) and whether it has been pressed (if the eighth bit is zero) or released (if it's one).

```
ex intrpt.c

/* intrpt.c - An interrupt handler. */


/* Copyright (C) 1998 by Ori Pomerantz */



/* The necessary header files */

/* Standard in kernel modules */
#include <linux/kernel.h>   /* We're doing kernel work */
#include <linux/module.h>   /* Specifically, a module */

/* Deal with CONFIG_MODVERSIONS */
#if CONFIG_MODVERSIONS==1
#define MODVERSIONS
#include <linux/modversions.h>
#endif

#include <linux/sched.h>
#include <linux/tqueue.h>

/* We want an interrupt */
#include <linux/interrupt.h>

#include <asm/io.h>


/* In 2.2.3 /usr/include/linux/version.h includes a
 * macro for this, but 2.0.35 doesn't - so I add it
 * here if necessary. */
#ifndef KERNEL_VERSION
#define KERNEL_VERSION(a,b,c) ((a)*65536+(b)*256+(c))
#endif



/* Bottom Half - this will get called by the kernel
 * as soon as it's safe to do everything normally
 * allowed by kernel modules. */
static void got_char(void *scancode)
{
  printk("Scan Code %x %s.\n",
    (int) *((char *) scancode) & 0x7F,
    *((char *) scancode) & 0x80 ? "Released" : "Pressed");
}
```

```c
/* This function services keyboard interrupts. It reads
 * the relevant information from the keyboard and then
 * schedules the bottom half to run when the kernel
 * considers it safe. */
void irq_handler(int irq,
                 void *dev_id,
                 struct pt_regs *regs)
{
  /* This variables are static because they need to be
   * accessible (through pointers) to the bottom
   * half routine. */
  static unsigned char scancode;
  static struct tq_struct task =
        {NULL, 0, got_char, &scancode};
  unsigned char status;

  /* Read keyboard status */
  status = inb(0x64);
  scancode = inb(0x60);

  /* Scheduale bottom half to run */
#if LINUX_VERSION_CODE > KERNEL_VERSION(2,2,0)
  queue_task(&task, &tq_immediate);
#else
  queue_task_irq(&task, &tq_immediate);
#endif
  mark_bh(IMMEDIATE_BH);
}




/* Initialize the module - register the IRQ handler */
int init_module()
{
  /* Since the keyboard handler won't co-exist with
   * another handler, such as us, we have to disable
   * it (free its IRQ) before we do anything. Since we
   * don't know where it is, there's no way to
   * reinstate it later - so the computer will have to
   * be rebooted when we're done.
   */
  free_irq(1, NULL);

  /* Request IRQ 1, the keyboard IRQ, to go to our
   * irq_handler. */
  return request_irq(
```

```
    1,  /* The number of the keyboard IRQ on PCs */
    irq_handler,  /* our handler */
    SA_SHIRQ,
    /* SA_SHIRQ means we're willing to have other
     * handlers on this IRQ.
     *
     * SA_INTERRUPT can be used to make the
     * handler into a fast interrupt.
     */
    "test_keyboard_irq_handler", NULL);
}


/* Cleanup */
void cleanup_module()
{
  /* This is only here for completeness. It's totally
   * irrelevant, since we don't have a way to restore
   * the normal keyboard interrupt so the computer
   * is completely useless and has to be rebooted. */
  free_irq(1, NULL);
}
```

Chapter 12
Symmetrical Multiprocessing

One of the easiest (read: cheapest) ways to improve hardware performance is to put more than one CPU on the board. This can be done either making the different CPUs take on different jobs (asymmetrical multiprocessing) or by making them all run in parallel, doing the same job (symmetrical multiprocessing, a.k.a. SMP). Doing asymmetrical multiprocessing effectively requires specialized knowledge about the tasks the computer should do, which is unavailable in a general purpose operating system such as Linux. On the other hand, symmetrical multiprocessing is relatively easy to implement. By relatively easy, I mean exactly that—not that it's *really* easy. In a symmetrical multiprocessing environment, the CPUs share the same memory, and as a result code running in one CPU can affect the memory used by another. You can no longer be certain that a variable you've set to a certain value in the previous line still has that value—the other CPU might have played with it while you weren't looking. Obviously, it's impossible to program like this.

In the case of process programming this normally isn't an issue, because a process will normally only run on one CPU at a time. The kernel, on the other hand, could be called by different processes running on different CPUs.

In version 2.0.x, this isn't a problem because the entire kernel is in one big spinlock. This means that if one CPU is in the kernel and another CPU wants to get in, for example, because of a system call, it has to wait until the first CPU is done. This makes Linux SMP safe, but terribly inefficient.

In version 2.2.x, several CPUs can be in the kernel at the same time. This is something module writers need to be aware of. I got somebody to give me access to an SMP box, so hopefully the next version of this book will include more information.

Chapter 13
Common Pitfalls

Before I send you on your way to go out into the world and write kernel modules, there are a few things I need to warn you about. If I fail to warn you and something bad happens, please report the problem to me for a full refund of the amount I got paid for your copy of the book.

1. **Using standard libraries**   You can't do that. In a kernel module you can only use kernel functions, which are the functions you can see in /proc/ksyms.

2. **Disabling interrupts**   You might need to do this for a short time and that is OK, but if you don't enable them afterward, your system will be stuck and you'll have to power it off.

3. **Sticking your head inside a large carnivore**   I probably don't have to warn you about this, but I figured I will anyway, just in case.

Appendix A
Changes Between 2.0 And 2.2

I don't know the entire kernel well enough do document all of the changes. In the course of converting the examples (or actually, adapting Emmanuel Papirakis's changes), I came across the following differences. I listed all of them here together to help module programmers, especially those who learned from previous versions of this book and are most familiar with the techniques I use, convert to the new version.

An additional resource for people who wish to convert to 2.2 is in **http://www.atnf.csiro.au/~rgooch/linux/docs/porting-to-2.2.html**.

1. **asm/uaccess.h**   If you need `put_user` or `get_user` you have to #include it.

2. **get_user**   In version 2.2, `get_user` receives both the pointer into user memory and the variable in kernel memory to fill with the information. The reason for this is that `get_user` can now read two or four bytes at a time if the variable we read is two or four bytes long.

3. **file_operations**   This structure now has a flush function between the `open` and `close` functions.

4. **close in file_operations**   In version 2.2, the close function returns an integer, so it's allowed to fail.

5. **read and write in file_operations**   The headers for these functions changed. They now return `ssize_t` instead of an integer, and their parameter list is different. The inode is no longer a parameter, and on the other hand the offset into the file is.

6. **proc_register_dynamic**   This function no longer exists. Instead, you call the regular `proc_register` and put zero in the inode field of the structure.

7. **Signals**   The signals in the task structure are no longer a 32-bit integer, but an array of `_NSIG_WORDS` integers.

8. **queue_task_irq**   Even if you want to scheduale a task to happen from inside an interrupt handler, you use `queue_task`, not `queue_task_irq`.

9. **Module parameters**   You no longer just declare module parameters as global variables. In 2.2 you have to also use `MODULE_PARM` to declare their type. This is a big improvement, because it allows the module to receive string parameters which start with a digits, for example, without getting confused.

10. **Symmetrical multiprocessing**   The kernel is no longer inside one huge spinlock, which means that kernel modules have to be aware of SMP.

Appendix B
Where From Here?

I could easily have squeezed a few more chapters into this book. I could have added a chapter about creating new file systems, or about adding new protocols stacks (as if there's a need for that—you'd have to dig under ground to find a protocol stack not supported by Linux). I could have added explanations of the kernel mechanisms we haven't touched upon, such as bootstrapping or the disk interface.

However, I chose not to. My purpose in writing this book was to provide initiation into the mysteries of kernel module programming and to teach the common techniques for that purpose. For people seriously interested in kernel programming, I recommend the list of kernel resources in **http://jungla.dit.upm.es/~jmseyas/ linux/kernel/hackers-docs.html**. Also, as Linus said, the best way is to learn the kernel is to read the source code yourself.

If you're interested in more examples of short kernel modules, I recommend *Phrack* magazine. Even if you're not interested in security, and as a programmer you should be, the kernel modules there are good examples of what you can do inside the kernel, and they're short enough not to require too much effort to understand.

I hope I have helped you in your quest to become a better programmer, or at least to have fun through technology. And, if you do write useful kernel modules, I hope you publish them under the GPL, so I can use them, too.

Appendix C
Goods And Services

I hope nobody minds the shameless promotions here. They are all things which are likely to be of use to beginning Linux Kernel Module programmers.

Getting This Book In Print

The Coriolis Group is going to print this book sometime in the summer of 1999. If this is already summer, and you want this book in print, you can go easy on your printer and buy it in a nice, bound form.

Appendix D
Showing Your Appreciation

This is a free document. You have no obligations beyond those given in the GNU Public License. However, if you want to do something in return for getting this book, there are a few things you could do.

♦ Send me a postcard to:
Ori Pomerantz
Apt. #1032
2355 N Hwy 360
Grand Prairie, TX 75050
USA
If you want to receive a thank-you from me, include your email address.

♦ Contribute money, or better yet, time, to the free software community. Write a program or a document and publish it under the GPL. Teach other people how to use free software, such as Linux or Perl.

♦ Explain to people how being selfish is not incompatible with living in a society or with helping other people. I enjoyed writing this document, and I believe publishing it will contribute to me in the future. At the same time, I wrote a book which, if you got this far, helps you. Remember that happy people are usually more useful to oneself than unhappy people, and able people are *way* better than people of low ability.

♦ **Be happy**. If I get to meet you, it will make the encounter better for me; it will make you more useful for me ;-).

Part III

The Linux Programmer's Guide

by Sven Goldt, Sven van der Meer,
Scott Burkett, and Matt Welsh

Authors

Sven Goldt

Sven van der Meer

Scott Burkett

Matt Welsh

Version 0.4

March 1995

The Linux Programmer's Guide

Chapter 1
The Linux Operating System

In March 1991, Linus Benedict Torvalds bought the multitasking system Minix for his AT 386. He used it to develop his own multitasking system, which he called Linux. In September 1991 he released the first prototype by email to some other Minix users on the Internet, thus beginning the Linux project. Many programmers, from that point on, have supported Linux. They have added device drivers, developed applications, and aimed for POSIX compliance. Today Linux is very powerful, but what is best is that it's free (free as in free speech, not free beer). Work is being done to port Linux to other platforms.

Chapter 2
The Linux Kernel

The base of Linux is the *kernel*. You could replace each and every library, but as long as the Linux kernel remained, it would still be Linux. The kernel contains device drivers, memory management, process management, and communication management. The kernel hacker gurus follow POSIX guidelines, which sometimes makes programming easier and sometimes harder. If your program behaves differently on a new Linux kernel release, chances are that a new POSIX guideline has been implemented. For programming information about the Linux kernel, read the *Linux Kernel Hacker's Guide*.

Chapter 3
The Linux libc Package

libc: ISO 8859.1, *<linux/param.h>*, YP functions, crypt functions, some basic shadow routines (by default not included), ... old routines for compatibility in libcompat (by default not activated), English, French, or German error messages, bsd 4.4lite compatible screen handling routines in libcurses, bsd compatible routines in libbsd, screen handling routines in libtermcap, database management routines in libdbm, mathematic routines in libm, entry to execute programs in crt0.o ???, byte sex information in libieee ??? (could someone give some infos instead of laughing ?), user space profiling in libgmon.

I wish someone of the Linux libc developers would write this chapter. All I can say now that there is going to be a change (*Note from publisher: This has already happened*) from the a.out executable format to the elf (executable and linkable format) which also means a change in building shared libraries. Currently both formats (a.out and elf) are supported.

Most parts of the Linux libc package are under the Library GNU Public License, though some are under a special exception copyright, like crt0.o. For commercial binary distributions this means a restriction that forbids statically linked executables. Dynamically linked executables are again a special exception. Richard Stallman of the FSF said:

> But it seems to me that we should unambiguously permit distribution of a dynamically linked executable *without* accompanying libraries, provided that the object files that

make up the executable are themselves unrestricted according to section 5 [...] So I'll make the decision now to permit this. Actually updating the LGPL will have to wait for when I have time to make and check a new version.

Chapter 4
System Calls

A *system call* is usually a request to the operating system (kernel) to do a hardware/system-specific or privileged operation. As of Linux 1.2, 140 system calls have been defined. System calls like close() are implemented in the Linux libc. This implementation often involves calling a macro, which eventually calls syscall(). Parameters passed to syscall() are the number of the system call followed by the needed arguments. The actual system call numbers can be found in *<linux/unistd.h>* while *<sys/syscall.h>* gets updated with a new libc. If new calls appear that don't have a stub in libc yet, you can use syscall(). As an example, you can close a file using syscall() like this (not advised):

```
#include <syscall.h>

extern int syscall(int, ...);

int my_close(int filedescriptor)
{
    return syscall(SYS_close, filedescriptor);
}
```

On the i386 architecture, system calls are limited to five arguments besides the system call number, because of the number of hardware registers. If you use Linux on another architecture you can check *<asm/unistd.h>* for the _syscall macros to see how many arguments your hardware supports or how many the developers chose to support. These _syscall macros can be used instead of syscall(), but this is not recommended since such a macro expands to a full function which might already exist in a library.

Therefore, only kernel hackers should play with the _syscall macros. To demonstrate, here is the close() example using a _syscall macro.

```
#include <linux/unistd.h>

_syscall1(int, close, int, filedescriptor);
```

The _syscall1 macro expands, revealing the close() function. Thus we have close() twice — once in libc, and once in our program. The return value of syscall() or a _syscall macro is -1 if the system call failed and 0 or greater on success. Take a look at the global variable errno to see what happened if a system call failed.

The following system calls that are available on BSD and Sys V are not available on Linux 1.2:

audit(), auditon(), auditsvc(), fchroot(), getauid(), getdents(), getmsg(), mincore(), poll(), putmsg(), setaudit(), setauid().

Chapter 5
The "Swiss Army Knife": ioctl

i octl stands for input/output control and is used to manipulate a character device via a file descriptor. The format of `ioctl` is

```
ioctl(unsigned int fd, unsigned int request, unsigned
long argument).
```

The return value is -1 if an error occurred and a value greater or equal than 0 if the request succeeded, just like other system calls. The kernel distinguishes special and regular files. Special files are mainly found in `/dev` and `/proc`. They differ from regular files in that way that they hide an interface to a driver and not to a real (regular) file that contains text or binary data. This is the Unix philosophy, and allows you to use normal read/write operations on every file. But if you need to do more with a special file or a regular file you can do it with... yes, `ioctl`. You more often need `ioctl` for special files than for regular files, but it's possible to use `ioctl` on regular files as well.

Chapter 6
Linux Interprocess Communications

A detailed overview of the IPC (interprocess communication) facilities implemented in the Linux operating system.

Introduction

The Linux IPC (interprocess communication) facilities provide a method for multiple processes to communicate with one another. There are several methods of IPC available to Linux C programmers:

- Half-duplex Unix pipes
- FIFOs (named pipes)
- SYSV-style message queues
- SYSV-style semaphore sets
- SYSV-style shared memory segments
- Networking sockets (Berkeley style) (not covered in this paper)
- Full-duplex pipes (STREAMS pipes) (not covered in this paper)

These facilities, when used effectively, provide a solid framework for client/server development on any Unix system (including Linux).

Half-Duplex Unix Pipes
Basic Concepts

Simply put, a *pipe* is a method of connecting the *standard output* of one process to the *standard input* of another. Pipes are the eldest of the IPC tools, having been around since the earliest incarnations of the Unix operating system. They provide a method of one-way communication (hence the term half-duplex) between processes.

This feature is widely used, even on the Unix command line (in the shell).

Figure 6.1 shows the set-up a pipeline, taking the output of ls as the input of sort, and the output of sort as the input of lp. The data is running through a half duplex pipe, traveling (visually) left to right through the pipeline.

Although most of us use pipes quite religiously in shell script programming, we often do so without giving a second thought to what transpires at the kernel level.

When a process creates a pipe, the kernel sets up two file descriptors for use by the pipe. One descriptor is used to allow a path of input into the pipe (write), while the other is used to obtain data from the pipe (read). At this point, the pipe is of little practical use, as the creating process can only use the pipe to communicate with itself. Consider this representation of a process and the kernel after a pipe has been created:

Note

Note from publisher: This diagram is not yet available.

From the above diagram, it is easy to see how the descriptors are connected together. If the process sends data through the pipe (fd0), it has the ability to obtain (read) that information from fd1. However, there is a much larger objective of the simplistic sketch above. While a pipe initially connects a process to itself, data traveling through the pipe moves through the kernel. Under Linux, in particular, pipes are actually represented internally with a valid inode. Of course, this inode resides within the kernel itself, and not within the bounds of any physical file system. This particular point will open up some pretty handy I/O doors for us, as we will see a bit later on.

At this point, the pipe is fairly useless. After all, why go to the trouble of creating a pipe if we are only going to talk to ourselves? At this point, the creating process typically forks a child process. Because a child process will inherit any open file descriptors from the parent, we now have the basis for multiprocess communication (between parent and child). Consider this updated version of our simple sketch in Figure 6.2.

Above, we see that both processes now have access to the file descriptors which constitute the pipeline. It is at this stage, that a critical decision must be made. In which direction do we desire data to travel? Does the child process send information to the parent, or vice versa? The two processes mutually agree on this issue, and proceed to "close" the end of the pipe that they are not concerned with. For discussion purposes, let's say the child performs some processing, and sends information back through the pipe to the parent. Our newly revised sketch appears in Figure 6.3.

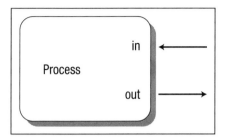

Figure 6.2

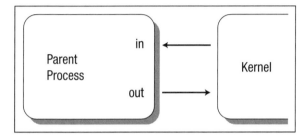

Figure 6.3

Construction of the pipeline is now complete! The only thing left to do is make use of the pipe. To access a pipe directly, the same system calls that are used for low-level file I/O can be used (recall that pipes are actually represented internally as a valid inode).

To send data to the pipe, we use the write() system call, and to retrieve data from the pipe, we use the read() system call. Remember, low-level file I/O system calls work with file descriptors! However, keep in mind that certain system calls, such as lseek(), do not work with descriptors to pipes.

Creating Pipes In C

Creating pipelines with the C programming language can be a bit more involved than our simple shell example. To create a simple pipe with C, we make use of the pipe() system call. It takes a single argument, which is an array of two integers, and if successful, the array will contain two new file descriptors to be used for the pipeline. After creating a pipe, the process typically spawns a new process (remember the child inherits open file descriptors).

```
SYSTEM CALL: pipe();

  PROTOTYPE: int pipe( int fd[2] );
    RETURNS: 0 on success
             -1 on error: errno = EMFILE (no free descriptors)
                                  EMFILE (system file table is full)
                                  EFAULT (fd array is not valid)
```

```
NOTES: fd[0] is set up for reading, fd[1] is set up for writing
```

The first integer in the array (element 0) is set up and opened for reading, while the second integer (element 1) is set up and opened for writing. Visually speaking, the output of fd1 becomes the input for fd0. Once again, all data traveling through the pipe moves through the kernel.

```
#include <stdio.h>
#include <unistd.h>
#include <sys/types.h>

main()
{
        int     fd[2];

        pipe(fd);
        .
        .
}
```

Remember that an array name in C decays into a pointer to its first member. Above, fd is equivalent to &fd[0]. Once we have established the pipeline, we then fork our new child process:

```
#include <stdio.h>
#include <unistd.h>
#include <sys/types.h>

main()
{
        int     fd[2];
        pid_t   childpid;

        pipe(fd);

        if((childpid = fork()) == -1)
        {
                perror("fork");
                exit(1);
        }
        .
        .
}
```

If the parent wants to receive data from the child, it should close fd1, and the child should close fd0. If the parent wants to send data to the child, it should close fd0, and the child should close fd1. Since descriptors are shared between the parent and child, we should always be sure to close the end of pipe we aren't concerned with. On a technical note, the EOF will never be returned if the unnecessary ends of the pipe are not explicitly closed.

```c
#include <stdio.h>
#include <unistd.h>
#include <sys/types.h>

main()
{
        int     fd[2];
        pid_t   childpid;

        pipe(fd);

        if((childpid = fork()) == -1)
        {
                perror("fork");
                exit(1);
        }

        if(childpid == 0)
        {
                /* Child process closes up input side of pipe */
                close(fd[0]);
        }
        else
        {
                /* Parent process closes up output side of pipe */
                close(fd[1]);
        }
        .
        .
        .
}
```

As mentioned previously, once the pipeline has been established, the file descriptors may be treated like descriptors to normal files.

```
/*****************************************************************************
Excerpt from "Linux Programmer's Guide - Chapter 6"
(C)opyright 1994-1995, Scott Burkett
*****************************************************************************
MODULE: pipe.c
*****************************************************************************/
```

```
#include <stdio.h>
#include <unistd.h>
#include <sys/types.h>

int main(void)
{
        int     fd[2], nbytes;
        pid_t   childpid;
        char    string[] = "Hello, world!\n";
        char    readbuffer[80];

        pipe(fd);

        if((childpid = fork()) == -1)
        {
                perror("fork");
                exit(1);
        }

        if(childpid == 0)
        {
                /* Child process closes up input side of pipe */
                close(fd[0]);

                /* Send "string" through the output side of pipe */
                write(fd[1], string, strlen(string));
                exit(0);
        }
        else
        {
                /* Parent process closes up output side of pipe */
                close(fd[1]);

                /* Read in a string from the pipe */
                nbytes = read(fd[0], readbuffer, sizeof(readbuffer));
                printf("Received string: %s", readbuffer);
        }

        return(0);
}
```

Often, the descriptors in the child are duplicated onto standard input or output. The child can then exec() another program, which inherits the standard streams. Let's look at the dup() system call:

SYSTEM CALL: dup();

```
    PROTOTYPE: int dup( int oldfd );
     RETURNS: new descriptor on success
             -1 on error: errno = EBADF (oldfd is not a valid descriptor)
                                  EBADF (newfd is out of range)
                                  EMFILE (too many descriptors for the process)
  Notes: The old descriptor is not closed! Both may be used interchangeably
```

Although the old descriptor and the newly created descriptor can be used interchangeably, we will typically close one of the standard streams first. The dup() system call uses the lowest-numbered, unused descriptor for the new one.

Consider:

```
        .

        .

        childpid = fork();

        if(childpid == 0)
        {
                /* Close up standard input of the child */
                close(0);

                /* Duplicate the input side of pipe to stdin */
                dup(fd[0]);
                execlp("sort", "sort", NULL);
                .
        }
```

Since file descriptor 0 (stdin) was closed, the call to dup() duplicated the input descriptor of the pipe (fd0) onto its standard input. We then make a call to execlp(), to overlay the child's text segment (code) with that of the sort program. Since newly exec'd programs inherit standard streams from their spawners, it actually inherits the input side of the pipe as its standard input! Now, anything that the original parent process sends to the pipe, goes into the sort facility.

There is another system call, dup2(), which can be used as well. This particular call originated with version 7 of Unix, and was carried on through the BSD releases and is now required by the POSIX standard.

```
  SYSTEM CALL: dup2();

  PROTOTYPE: int dup2( int oldfd, int newfd );
     RETURNS: new descriptor on success
             -1 on error: errno = EBADF (oldfd is not a valid descriptor)
                                  EBADF (newfd is out of range)
                                  EMFILE (too many descriptors for the process)
```

Notes: The old descriptor is closed with dup2()!

With this particular call, we have the close operation, and the actual descriptor duplication, wrapped up in one system call. In addition, it is guaranteed to be atomic, which essentially means that it will never be interrupted by an arriving signal. The entire operation will transpire before returning control to the kernel for signal dispatching. With the original dup() system call, programmers had to perform a close() operation before calling it. That resulted in two system calls, with a small degree of vulnerability in the brief amount of time which elapsed between them. If a signal arrived during that brief instance, the descriptor duplication would fail. Of course, dup2() solves this problem for us.

Consider:

```
        .
        .
        .
childpid = fork();

if(childpid == 0)
{
        /* Close stdin, duplicate the input side of pipe to stdin */
        dup2(0, fd[0]);
        execlp("sort", "sort", NULL);
        .
        .
        .
}
```

Pipes The Easy Way!

If all of the above ramblings seem like a very round-about way of creating and utilizing pipes, there is an alternative.

```
  LIBRARY FUNCTION: popen();

 PROTOTYPE: FILE *popen ( char *command, char *type);
   RETURNS: new file stream on success
           NULL on unsuccessful fork() or pipe() call
Notes: creates a pipe, and performs fork/exec operations using "command."
```

This standard library function creates a half-duplex pipeline by calling pipe() internally. It then forks a child process, execs the Bourne shell, and executes the "command" argument within the shell. Direction of data flow is determined by the second argument, "type." It can be "r" or "w", for "read" or "write." It cannot be both! Under Linux, the pipe will be opened up in the mode specified by the first character of the "type" argument. So, if you try to pass "rw," it will only open it up in "read" mode.

While this library function performs quite a bit of the dirty work for you, there is a substantial trade-off. You lose the fine control you once had by using the pipe() system call, and handling the fork/exec yourself. However, since the Bourne shell is used directly, shell metacharacter expansion (including wildcards) is permissible within the "command" argument.

Pipes which are created with popen() must be closed with pclose(). By now, you have probably realized that popen/pclose share a striking resemblance to the standard file stream I/O functions fopen() and fclose().

```
  LIBRARY FUNCTION: pclose();

  PROTOTYPE: int pclose( FILE *stream );
    RETURNS: exit status of wait4() call
             -1 if "stream" is not valid, or if wait4() fails
Notes: waits on the pipe process to terminate, then closes the stream.
```

The pclose() function performs a wait4() on the process forked by popen(). When it returns, it destroys the pipe and the file stream. Once again, it is synonymous with the fclose() function for normal stream-based file I/O.

Consider this example, which opens up a pipe to the sort command, and proceeds to sort an array of strings:

```
/****************************************************************************
 Excerpt from "Linux Programmer's Guide - Chapter 6"
 (C)opyright 1994-1995, Scott Burkett
 ****************************************************************************
 MODULE: popen1.c
 ****************************************************************************/

#include <stdio.h>

#define MAXSTRS 5

int main(void)
{
        int  cntr;
        FILE *pipe_fp;
        char *strings[MAXSTRS] = { "echo", "bravo", "alpha",
                                   "charlie", "delta"};

        /* Create one way pipe line with call to popen() */
        if (( pipe_fp = popen("sort", "w")) == NULL)
        {
                perror("popen");
```

```
                exit(1);
        }

        /* Processing loop */
        for(cntr=0; cntr<MAXSTRS; cntr++) {
                fputs(strings[cntr], pipe_fp);
                fputc('\n', pipe_fp);
        }

        /* Close the pipe */
        pclose(pipe_fp);

        return(0);
}
```

Because popen() uses the shell to do its bidding, all shell expansion characters and metacharacters are available for use! In addition, more advanced techniques such as redirection, and even output piping, can be utilized with popen(). Consider the following sample calls:

```
popen("ls ~scottb", "r");
popen("sort > /tmp/foo", "w");
popen("sort | uniq | more", "w");
```

As another example of popen(), consider this small program, which opens up two pipes (one to the ls command, the other to sort):

```
/****************************************************************************
 Excerpt from "Linux Programmer's Guide - Chapter 6"
 (C)opyright 1994-1995, Scott Burkett
 ****************************************************************************
 MODULE: popen2.c
 ****************************************************************************/

#include <stdio.h>

int main(void)
{
        FILE *pipein_fp, *pipeout_fp;
        char readbuf[80];

        /* Create one way pipe line with call to popen() */
        if (( pipein_fp = popen("ls", "r")) == NULL)
        {
                perror("popen");
                exit(1);
        }
```

```
/* Create one way pipe line with call to popen() */
if (( pipeout_fp = popen("sort", "w")) == NULL)
{
        perror("popen");
        exit(1);
}

/* Processing loop */
while(fgets(readbuf, 80, pipein_fp))
        fputs(readbuf, pipeout_fp);

/* Close the pipes */
pclose(pipein_fp);
pclose(pipeout_fp);

return(0);
}
```

For our final demonstration of popen(), let's create a generic program that opens up a pipe-line between a passed command and file name:

```
/**************************************************************************
 Excerpt from "Linux Programmer's Guide - Chapter 6"
 (C)opyright 1994-1995, Scott Burkett
 **************************************************************************
 MODULE: popen3.c
 **************************************************************************/

#include <stdio.h>

int main(int argc, char *argv[])
{
        FILE *pipe_fp, *infile;
        char readbuf[80];

        if( argc != 3) {
                fprintf(stderr, "USAGE:  popen3 [command] [filename]\n");
                exit(1);
        }

        /* Open up input file */
        if (( infile = fopen(argv[2], "rt")) == NULL)
        {
                perror("fopen");
                exit(1);
        }
```

```
        /* Create one way pipe line with call to popen() */
        if (( pipe_fp = popen(argv[1], "w")) == NULL)
        {
                perror("popen");
                exit(1);
        }

        /* Processing loop */
        do {
                fgets(readbuf, 80, infile);
                if(feof(infile)) break;

                fputs(readbuf, pipe_fp);
        } while(!feof(infile));

        fclose(infile);
        pclose(pipe_fp);

        return(0);
}
```

Try this program out, with the following invocations:

```
popen3 sort popen3.c
popen3 cat popen3.c
popen3 more popen3.c
popen3 cat popen3.c | grep main
```

Atomic Operations With Pipes

In order for an operation to be considered "atomic," it must not be interrupted for any reason at all. The entire operation occurs at once. The POSIX standard dictates in /usr/include/posix1_lim.h that the maximum buffer size for an atomic operation on a pipe is:

```
#define _POSIX_PIPE_BUF          512
```

Up to 512 bytes can be written or retrieved from a pipe atomically. Anything that crosses this threshold will be split, and not atomic. Under Linux, however, the atomic operational limit is defined in "linux/limits.h" as:

```
#define PIPE_BUF          4096
```

As you can see, Linux accommodates the minimum number of bytes required by POSIX, quite considerably I might add. The atomicity of a pipe operation becomes important when more than one process is involved (FIFOs). For example, if the number of bytes written to a pipe exceeds the atomic limit for a single operation, and multiple processes are writing to the pipe, the data will be "interleaved" or "chunked." In other words, one process may insert data into the pipeline between the writes of another.

Notes On Half-Duplex Pipes

◆ Two-way pipes can be created by opening up two pipes, and properly reassigning the file descriptors in the child process.

◆ The pipe( ) call must be made *before* a call to fork( ), or the descriptors will not be inherited by the child! (Same for popen( ).)

◆ With half-duplex pipes, any connected processes must share a related ancestry. Since the pipe resides within the confines of the kernel, any process that is not in the ancestry for the creator of the pipe has no way of addressing it. This is not the case with named pipes (FIFOs).

Named Pipes (FIFOs: First In First Out)
Basic Concepts

A named pipe works much like a regular pipe, but does have some noticeable differences.

◆ Named pipes exist as a device special file in the file system.

◆ Processes of different ancestry can share data through a named pipe.

◆ When all I/O is done by sharing processes, the named pipe remains in the file system for later use.

Creating A FIFO

There are several ways of creating a named pipe. The first two can be done directly from the shell.

```
mknod MYFIFO p
mkfifo a=rw MYFIFO
```

The above two commands perform identical operations, with one exception. The mkfifo command provides a hook for altering the permissions on the FIFO file directly after creation. With mknod, a quick call to the chmod command will be necessary.

FIFO files can be quickly identified in a physical file system by the "p" indicator seen here in a long directory listing:

```
$ ls -l MYFIFO
prw-r--r--   1 root     root              0 Dec 14 22:15 MYFIFO|
```

Also notice the vertical bar ("pipe sign") located directly after the file name. Another great reason to run Linux, eh?

To create a FIFO in C, we can make use of the mknod() system call:

```
LIBRARY FUNCTION: mknod();

PROTOTYPE: int mknod( char *pathname, mode_t mode, dev_t dev);
  RETURNS: 0 on success,
           -1 on error: errno = EFAULT (pathname invalid)
                                EACCES (permission denied)
                                ENAMETOOLONG (pathname too long)
                                ENOENT (invalid pathname)
                                ENOTDIR (invalid pathname)
                                (see man page for mknod for others)
Notes: Creates a filesystem node (file, device file, or FIFO)
```

I will leave a more detailed discussion of mknod() to the man page, but let's consider a simple example of FIFO creation from C:

```
mknod("/tmp/MYFIFO", S_IFIFO|0666, 0);
```

In this case, the file "/tmp/MYFIFO" is created as a FIFO file. The requested permissions are "0666," although they are affected by the umask setting as follows:

```
final_umask = requested_permissions & ~original_umask
```

A common trick is to use the umask() system call to temporarily zap the umask value:

```
umask(0);
mknod("/tmp/MYFIFO", S_IFIFO|0666, 0);
```

In addition, the third argument to mknod() is ignored unless we are creating a device file. In that instance, it should specify the major and minor numbers of the device file.

FIFO Operations

I/O operations on a FIFO are essentially the same as for normal pipes, with one major exception. An "open" system call or library function should be used to physically open up a channel to the pipe. With half-duplex pipes, this is unnecessary, since the pipe resides in the kernel and not on a physical file system. In our examples, we will treat the pipe as a stream, opening it up with fopen(), and closing it with fclose().

Consider a simple server process:

```
/***************************************************************************
  Excerpt from "Linux Programmer's Guide - Chapter 6"
  (C)opyright 1994-1995, Scott Burkett
  ***************************************************************************
  MODULE: fifoserver.c
  ***************************************************************************/

#include <stdio.h>
#include <stdlib.h>
#include <sys/stat.h>
#include <unistd.h>

#include <linux/stat.h>

#define FIFO_FILE        "MYFIFO"

int main(void)
{
        FILE *fp;
        char readbuf[80];

        /* Create the FIFO if it does not exist */
        umask(0);
        mknod(FIFO_FILE, S_IFIFO|0666, 0);

        while(1)
        {
                fp = fopen(FIFO_FILE, "r");
                fgets(readbuf, 80, fp);
                printf("Received string: %s\n", readbuf);
                fclose(fp);
        }

        return(0);
}
```

Since a FIFO blocks by default, run the server in the background after you compile it:

```
$ fifoserver&
```

We will discuss a FIFO's blocking action in a moment. First, consider the following simple client front end to our server:

```
/***************************************************************************
  Excerpt from "Linux Programmer's Guide - Chapter 6"
  (C)opyright 1994-1995, Scott Burkett
```

```
/*********************************************************************
MODULE: fifoclient.c
*********************************************************************/

#include <stdio.h>
#include <stdlib.h>

#define FIFO_FILE       "MYFIFO"

int main(int argc, char *argv[])
{
        FILE *fp;

        if ( argc != 2 ) {
                printf("USAGE: fifoclient [string]\n");
                exit(1);
        }

        if((fp = fopen(FIFO_FILE, "w")) == NULL) {
                perror("fopen");
                exit(1);
        }

        fputs(argv[1], fp);

        fclose(fp);
        return(0);
}
```

Blocking Actions On A FIFO

Normally, blocking occurs on a FIFO. In other words, if the FIFO is opened for reading, the process will "block" until some other process opens it for writing. This action works vice versa as well. If this behavior is undesirable, the O_NONBLOCK flag can be used in an open() call to disable the default blocking action.

In the case with our simple server, we just shoved it into the background, and let it do its blocking there. The alternative would be to jump to another virtual console and run the client end, switching back and forth to see the resulting action.

The Infamous SIGPIPE Signal

On a last note, pipes must have a reader and a writer. If a process tries to write to a pipe that has no reader, it will be sent the SIGPIPE signal from the kernel. This is imperative when more than two processes are involved in a pipeline.

System V IPC

Fundamental Concepts

With System V, AT&T introduced three new forms of IPC facilities (message queues, semaphores, and shared memory). While the POSIX committee has not yet completed its standardization of these facilities, most implementations do support these. In addition, Berkeley (BSD) uses sockets as its primary form of IPC, rather than the System V elements. Linux has the ability to use both forms of IPC (BSD and System V), although we will not discuss sockets until a later chapter.

The Linux implementation of System V IPC was authored by Krishna Balasubramanian, at **balasub@cis.ohio-state.edu**.

IPC Identifiers

Each IPC object has a unique IPC identifier associated with it. When we say "IPC object," we are speaking of a single message queue, semaphore set, or shared memory segment. This identifier is used within the kernel to uniquely identify an IPC object. For example, to access a particular shared memory segment, the only item you need is the unique ID value which has been assigned to that segment.

The uniqueness of an identifier is relevant to the type of object in question. To illustrate this, assume a numeric identifier of "12345." While there can never be two message queues with this same identifier, there exists the distinct possibility of a message queue and, say, a shared memory segment, which have the same numeric identifier.

IPC Keys

To obtain a unique ID, a key must be used. The key must be mutually agreed upon by both client and server processes. This represents the first step in constructing a client/server framework for an application.

When you use a telephone to call someone, you must know their number. In addition, the phone company must know how to relay your outgoing call to its final destination. Once the other party responds by answering the telephone call, the connection is made.

In the case of System V IPC facilities, the "telephone" correlates directly with the type of object being used. The "phone company," or routing method, can be directly associated with an IPC key.

The key can be the same value every time, by hard-coding a key value into an application. This has the disadvantage of the key possibly being in use already. Often, the ftok() function is used to generate key values for both the client and the server.

```
LIBRARY FUNCTION: ftok();
```

```
PROTOTYPE: key_t ftok ( char *pathname, char proj );
  RETURNS: new IPC key value if successful
           -1 if unsuccessful, errno set to return of stat() call
```

The returned key value from ftok() is generated by combining the inode number and minor device number from the file in argument one, with the one-character project identifier in the second argument. This doesn't guarantee uniqueness, but an application can check for collisions and retry the key generation.

```
key_t   mykey;
mykey = ftok("/tmp/myapp", 'a');
```

In the above snippet, the directory /tmp/myapp is combined with the one-letter identifier of a. Another common example is to use the current directory:

```
key_t   mykey;
mykey = ftok(".", 'a');
```

The key generation algorithm used is completely up to the discretion of the application programmer. As long as measures are in place to prevent race conditions, deadlocks, etc., any method is viable. For our demonstration purposes, we will use the ftok() approach. If we assume that each client process will be running from a unique "home" directory, the keys generated should suffice for our needs.

The key value, however it is obtained, is used in subsequent IPC system calls to create or gain access to IPC objects.

The ipcs Command

The ipcs command can be used to obtain the status of all System V IPC objects. The Linux version of this tool was also authored by Krishna Balasubramanian.

```
ipcs      -q:   Show only message queues
ipcs      -s:   Show only semaphores
ipcs      -m:   Show only shared memory
ipcs --help:   Additional arguments
```

By default, all three categories of objects are shown. Consider the following sample output of ipcs:

```
------ Shared Memory Segments --------
shmid     owner     perms     bytes     nattch     status

------ Semaphore Arrays --------
semid     owner     perms     nsems     status
```

```
------ Message Queues --------
msqid      owner       perms      used-bytes   messages
0          root        660        5            1
```

Here we see a single message queue which has an identifier of "0." It is owned by the user *root*, and has octal permissions of 660, or -rw-rw--. There is one message in the queue, and that message has a total size of five bytes.

The ipcs command is a very powerful tool which provides a peek into the kernel's storage mechanisms for IPC objects. Learn it, use it, revere it.

The ipcrm *Command*

The ipcrm command can be used to remove an IPC object from the kernel. While IPC objects can be removed via system calls in user code (we'll see how in a moment), the need often arises, especially under development environments, to remove IPC objects manually. Its usage is simple:

```
ipcrm <msg | sem | shm>  <IPC ID>
```

Simply specify whether the object to be deleted is a message queue (msg), a semaphore set (sem), or a shared memory segment (shm). The IPC ID can be obtained by the ipcs command. You have to specify the type of object, since identifiers are unique among the same type (recall our discussion of this earlier).

Message Queues

Basic Concepts

Message queues can be best described as an internal linked list within the kernel's addressing space. Messages can be sent to the queue in order and retrieved from the queue in several different ways. Each message queue (of course) is uniquely identified by an IPC identifier.

Internal And User Data Structures

The key to fully understanding such complex topics as System V IPC is to become intimately familiar with the various internal data structures that reside within the confines of the kernel itself. Direct access to some of these structures is necessary for even the most primitive operations, while others reside at a much lower level.

Message Buffer

The first structure we'll visit is the msgbuf structure. This particular data structure can be thought of as a *template* for message data. While it is up to the programmer to define structures of this type, it is imperative that you understand that there *is* actually a structure of type msgbuf. It is declared in linux/msg.h as follows:

```
/* message buffer for msgsnd and msgrcv calls */
struct msgbuf {
    long mtype;         /* type of message */
    char mtext[1];      /* message text */
};
```

There are two members in the `msgbuf` structure:

♦ `mtype`—The message type, represented in a positive number. This *must* be a positive number!

♦ `mtext`—The message data itself.

The ability to assign a given message a type, essentially gives you the capability to *multiplex* messages on a single queue. For instance, client processes could be assigned a magic number, which could be used as the message type for messages sent from a server process. The server itself could use some other number, which clients could use to send messages to it. In another scenario, an application could mark error messages as having a message type of 1, request messages could be type 2, and so on. The possibilities are endless.

On another note, do not be misled by the almost too-descriptive name assigned to the message data element (`mtext`). This field is not restricted to holding only arrays of characters, but any data, in any form. The field itself is actually completely arbitrary, since this structure gets redefined by the application programmer. Consider this redefinition:

```
struct my_msgbuf {
        long    mtype;        /* Message type */
        long    request_id;   /* Request identifier */
        struct  client info;  /* Client information structure */
};
```

Here we see the message type, as before, but the remainder of the structure has been replaced by two other elements, one of which is another structure! This is the beauty of message queues. The kernel makes no translations of data whatsoever. Any information can be sent.

There does exist an internal limit, however, of the maximum size of a given message. In Linux, this is defined in `linux/msg.h` as follows:

```
#define MSGMAX  4056    /* <= 4056 */   /* max size of message (bytes) */
```

Messages can be no larger than 4,056 bytes in total size, including the `mtype` member, which is 4 bytes in length (`long`).

Kernel msg *Structure*

The kernel stores each message in the queue within the framework of the `msg` structure. It is defined for us in `linux/msg.h` as follows:

```
/* one msg structure for each message */
struct msg {
    struct msg *msg_next;    /* next message on queue */
    long  msg_type;
    char *msg_spot;          /* message text address */
    short msg_ts;            /* message text size */
};
```

- ◆ msg_next—This is a pointer to the next message in the queue. They are stored as a singly linked list within kernel addressing space.

- ◆ msg_type—This is the message type, as assigned in the user structure msgbuf.

- ◆ msg_spot—A pointer to the beginning of the message body.

- ◆ msg_ts—The length of the message text, or body.

- ◆ Kernel msqid_ds structure—Each of the three types of IPC objects has an internal data structure which is maintained by the kernel. For message queues, this is the msqid_ds structure. The kernel creates, stores, and maintains an instance of this structure for every message queue created on the system. It is defined in linux/msg.h as follows:

```
/* one msqid structure for each queue on the system */
struct msqid_ds {
    struct ipc_perm msg_perm;
    struct msg *msg_first;  /* first message on queue */
    struct msg *msg_last;   /* last message in queue */
    time_t msg_stime;       /* last msgsnd time */
    time_t msg_rtime;       /* last msgrcv time */
    time_t msg_ctime;       /* last change time */
    struct wait_queue *wwait;
    struct wait_queue *rwait;
    ushort msg_cbytes;
    ushort msg_qnum;
    ushort msg_qbytes;      /* max number of bytes on queue */
    ushort msg_lspid;       /* pid of last msgsnd */
    ushort msg_lrpid;       /* last receive pid */
};
```

While you will rarely have to concern yourself with most of the members of this structure, a brief description of each is in order to complete our tour:

- ◆ msg_perm—An instance of the ipc_perm structure, which is defined for us in linux/ipc.h. This holds the permission information for the message queue, including the access permissions, and information about the creator of the queue (uid and so on).

- ◆ msg_first—Link to the first message in the queue (the head of the list).

- ◆ msg_last—Link to the last message in the queue (the tail of the list).

- ♦ msg_stime—Timestamp (time_t) of the last message that was sent to the queue.

- ♦ msg_rtime—Timestamp of the last message retrieved from the queue.

- ♦ msg_ctime—Timestamp of the last "change" made to the queue (more on this later).

- ♦ wwait and rwait—Pointers into the kernel's wait queue. They are used when an operation on a message queue deems the process go into a sleep state (i.e., queue is full and the process is waiting for an opening).

- ♦ msg_cbytes—Total number of bytes residing on the queue (sum of the sizes of all messages).

- ♦ msg_qnum—Number of messages currently in the queue.

- ♦ msg_qbytes—Maximum number of bytes on the queue.

- ♦ msg_lspid—The PID of the process who sent the last message.

- ♦ msg_lrpid—The PID of the process who retrieved the last message.

Kernel ipc_perm Structure

The kernel stores permission information for IPC objects in a structure of type ipc_perm. For example, in the internal structure for a message queue described above, the msg_perm member is of this type. It is declared for us in linux/ipc.h as follows:

```
struct ipc_perm
{
  key_t  key;
  ushort uid;    /* owner euid and egid */
  ushort gid;
  ushort cuid;   /* creator euid and egid */
  ushort cgid;
  ushort mode;   /* access modes see mode flags below */
  ushort seq;    /* slot usage sequence number */
};
```

All of the above are fairly self-explanatory. Stored along with the IPC key of the object is information about both the creator and owner of the object (they may be different). The octal access modes are also stored here, as an unsigned short. Finally, the *slot usage sequence number* is stored at the end. Each time an IPC object is closed via a system call (destroyed), this value gets incremented by the maximum number of IPC objects that can reside in a system. Will you have to concern yourself with this value? No.

There is an excellent discussion on this topic, and the security reasons as to its existence and behavior, in Richard Stevens's *UNIX Network Programming* book, p. 125.

System Call: msgget()

In order to create a new message queue, or access an existing queue, the msgget() system call is used.

```
SYSTEM CALL: msgget();

PROTOTYPE: int msgget ( key_t key, int msgflg );
  RETURNS: message queue identifier on success
           -1 on error: errno = EACCESS (permission denied)
                                EEXIST (Queue exists, cannot create)
                                EIDRM (Queue is marked for deletion)
                                ENOENT (Queue does not exist)
                                ENOMEM (Not enough memory to create queue)
                                ENOSPC (Maximum queue limit exceeded)
```

The first argument to `msgget()` is the key value (in our case returned by a call to `ftok()`). This key value is then compared to existing key values that exist within the kernel for other message queues. At that point, the open or access operation is dependent on the contents of the `msgflg` argument.

◆ IPC_CREAT—Create the queue if it doesn't already exist in the kernel.

◆ IPC_EXCL—When used with IPC_CREAT, fail if queue already exists.

If `IPC_CREAT` is used alone, `msgget()` either returns the message queue identifier for a newly created message queue, or returns the identifier for a queue which exists with the same key value. If `IPC_EXCL` is used along with `IPC_CREAT`, then either a new queue is created, or if the queue exists, the call fails with -1. `IPC_EXCL` is useless by itself, but when combined with `IPC_CREAT`, it can be used as a facility to guarantee that no existing queue is opened for access.

An optional octal mode may be OR'd into the mask, since each IPC object has permissions that are similar in functionality to file permissions on a Unix file system!

Let's create a quick wrapper function for opening or creating message queue:

```
int open_queue( key_t keyval )
{
        int     qid;

        if((qid = msgget( keyval, IPC_CREAT | 0660 )) == -1)
        {
                return(-1);
        }

        return(qid);
}
```

Note the use of the explicit permissions of 0660. This small function either returns a message queue identifier (int), or -1 on error. The key value must be passed to it as its only argument.

System Call: msgsnd()

Once we have the queue identifier, we can begin performing operations on it. To deliver a message to a queue, you use the `msgsnd` system call:

```
SYSTEM CALL: msgsnd();

PROTOTYPE: int msgsnd ( int msqid, struct msgbuf *msgp, int msgsz, int msgflg
);
  RETURNS: 0 on success
           -1 on error: errno = EAGAIN (queue is full, and IPC_NOWAIT was
asserted)
                        EACCES (permission denied, no write permis-
sion)
                        EFAULT (msgp address isn't accessable -
invalid)
                        EIDRM  (The message queue has been removed)
                        EINTR  (Received a signal while waiting to
write)
                        EINVAL (Invalid message queue identifier,
nonpositive
                                message type, or invalid message
size)
                        ENOMEM (Not enough memory to copy message
buffer)
```

The first argument to `msgsnd` is our queue identifier, returned by a previous call to `msgget`. The second argument, `msgp`, is a pointer to our redeclared and loaded message buffer. The `msgsz` argument contains the size of the message in bytes, excluding the length of the message type (four bytes long).

The msgflg argument can be set to 0 (ignored), or:

```
IPC_NOWAIT
```

If the message queue is full, then the message is not written to the queue, and control is returned to the calling process. If not specified, then the calling process will suspend (block) until the message can be written.

Let's create another wrapper function for sending messages:

```
int send_message( int qid, struct mymsgbuf *qbuf )
{
        int     result, length;

        /* The length is essentially the size of the structure minus
sizeof(mtype) */
        length = sizeof(struct mymsgbuf) - sizeof(long);
```

```
        if((result = msgsnd( qid, qbuf, length, 0)) == -1)
        {
                return(-1);
        }

        return(result);
}
```

This small function attempts to send the message residing at the passed address (qbuf) to the message queue designated by the passed queue identifier (qid). Here is a sample code snippet utilizing the two wrapper functions we have developed so far:

```
#include <stdio.h>
#include <stdlib.h>
#include <linux/ipc.h>
#include <linux/msg.h>

main()
{
        int    qid;
        key_t  msgkey;
        struct mymsgbuf {
                long    mtype;          /* Message type */
                int     request;        /* Work request number */
                double  salary;         /* Employee's salary */
        } msg;

        /* Generate our IPC key value */
        msgkey = ftok(".", 'm');

        /* Open/create the queue */
        if(( qid = open_queue( msgkey)) == -1) {
                perror("open_queue");
                exit(1);
        }

        /* Load up the message with arbitrary test data */
        msg.mtype   = 1;         /* Message type must be a positive number! */
        msg.request = 1;         /* Data element #1 */
        msg.salary  = 1000.00;   /* Data element #2 (my yearly salary!) */

        /* Bombs away! */
        if((send_message( qid, &msg )) == -1) {
                perror("send_message");
                exit(1);
        }
}
```

After creating/opening our message queue, we proceed to load up the message buffer with test data (note the lack of character data to illustrate our point about sending binary information). A quick call to send_message merrily distributes our message out to the message queue.

Now that we have a message on our queue, try the ipcs command to view the status of your queue. Now let's turn the discussion to actually retrieving the message from the queue. To do this, you use the msgrcv() system call:

```
  SYSTEM CALL: msgrcv();
  PROTOTYPE: int msgrcv ( int msqid, struct msgbuf *msgp, int msgsz, long
mtype, int msgflg );
    RETURNS: Number of bytes copied into message buffer
              -1 on error: errno = E2BIG  (Message length is greater than msgsz,
no MSG_NOERROR)
                            EACCES (No read permission)
                            EFAULT (Address pointed to by msgp is in-
valid)
                            EIDRM  (Queue was removed during retrieval)
                            EINTR  (Interrupted by arriving signal)
                            EINVAL (msgqid invalid, or msgsz less than 0)
                            ENOMSG (IPC_NOWAIT asserted, and no message
exists
                                in the queue to satisfy the request)
```

Obviously, the first argument is used to specify the queue to be used during the message retrieval process (should have been returned by an earlier call to msgget). The second argument (msgp) represents the address of a message buffer variable to store the retrieved message at. The third argument (msgsz) represents the size of the message buffer structure, excluding the length of the mtype member. Once again, this can easily be calculated as:

```
msgsz = sizeof(struct mymsgbuf) - sizeof(long);
```

The fourth argument (mtype) specifies the *type* of message to retrieve from the queue. The kernel will search the queue for the oldest message having a matching type, and will return a copy of it in the address pointed to by the msgp argument. One special case exists. If the mtype argument is passed with a value of zero, then the oldest message on the queue is returned, regardless of type.

If IPC_NOWAIT is passed as a flag, and no messages are available, the call returns ENOMSG to the calling process. Otherwise, the calling process blocks until a message arrives in the queue that satisfies the msgrcv() parameters. If the queue is deleted while a client is waiting on a message, EIDRM is returned. EINTR is returned if a signal is caught while the process is in the middle of blocking, and waiting for a message to arrive.

Let's examine a quick wrapper function for retrieving a message from our queue:

```
int read_message( int qid, long type, struct mymsgbuf *qbuf )
{
        int     result, length;

        /* The length is essentially the size of the structure minus
sizeof(mtype) */
        length = sizeof(struct mymsgbuf) - sizeof(long);

        if((result = msgrcv( qid, qbuf, length, type,  0)) == -1)
        {
                return(-1);
        }

        return(result);
}
```

After successfully retrieving a message from the queue, the message entry within the queue is destroyed.

The **MSG_NOERROR** bit in the `msgflg` argument provides some additional capabilities. If the size of the physical message data is greater than `msgsz`, and **MSG_NOERROR** is asserted, then the message is truncated, and only `msgsz` bytes are returned. Normally, the `msgrcv()` system call returns -1 (**E2BIG**), and the message will remain on the queue for later retrieval. This behavior can used to create another wrapper function, which will allow us to "peek" inside the queue, to see if a message has arrived that satisfies our request:

```
int peek_message( int qid, long type )
{
        int     result, length;

        if((result = msgrcv( qid, NULL, 0, type,  IPC_NOWAIT)) == -1)
        {
                if(errno == E2BIG)
                        return(TRUE);
        }

        return(FALSE);
}
```

Above, you will notice the lack of a buffer address and a length. In this particular case, we want the call to fail. However, we check for the return of E2BIG which indicates that a message does exist which matches our requested type. The wrapper function returns TRUE on success, FALSE otherwise. Also note the use of the IPC_NOWAIT flag, which prevents the blocking behavior described earlier.

System Call: msgctl()

Through the development of the wrapper functions presented earlier, you now have a simple, somewhat elegant approach to creating and utilizing message queues in your applications. Now, we will turn the discussion to directly manipulating the internal structures associated with a given message queue.

To perform control operations on a message queue, you use the msgctl() system call.

```
SYSTEM CALL: msgctl();
PROTOTYPE: int msgctl ( int msgqid, int cmd, struct msqid_ds *buf );
  RETURNS: 0 on success
           -1 on error: errno = EACCES (No read permission and cmd is
IPC_STAT)
                        EFAULT (Address pointed to by buf is invalid
with IPC_SET and
                        IPC_STAT commands)
                        EIDRM  (Queue was removed during retrieval)
                        EINVAL (msgqid invalid, or msgsz less than 0)
                        EPERM  (IPC_SET or IPC_RMID command was
issued, but
                        calling process does not have write
(alter)
                        access to the queue)
  NOTES:
```

Now, common sense dictates that direct manipulation of the internal kernel data structures could lead to some late-night fun. Unfortunately, the resulting duties on the part of the programmer could only be classified as fun if you like trashing the IPC subsystem. By using msgctl() with a selective set of commands, you have the ability to manipulate those items which are less likely to cause grief. Let's look at these commands:

IPC_STAT

Retrieves the msqid_ds structure for a queue, and stores it in the address of the buf argument.

IPC_SET

Sets the value of the ipc_perm member of the msqid_ds structure for a queue. Takes the values from the buf argument.

IPC_RMID

Removes the queue from the kernel.

Recall our discussion about the internal data structure for message queues (msqid_ds).

The kernel maintains an instance of this structure for each queue which exists in the system. By using the IPC_STAT command, we can retrieve a copy of this structure for examination. Let's look at a quick wrapper function that will retrieve the internal structure and copy it into a passed address:

```
int get_queue_ds( int qid, struct msgqid_ds *qbuf )
{
        if( msgctl( qid, IPC_STAT, qbuf) == -1)
        {
                return(-1);
        }

        return(0);
}
```

If we are unable to copy the internal buffer, -1 is returned to the calling function. If all went well, a value of 0 (zero) is returned, and the passed buffer should contain a copy of the internal data structure for the message queue represented by the passed queue identifier (qid).

Now that we have a copy of the internal data structure for a queue, what attributes can be manipulated, and how can we alter them? The only modifiable item in the data structure is the ipc_perm member. This contains the permissions for the queue, as well as information about the owner and creator. However, the only members of the ipc_perm structure that are modifiable are mode, uid, and gid. You can change the owner's user ID, the owner's group ID, and the access permissions for the queue.

Let's create a wrapper function designed to change the mode of a queue. The mode must be passed in as a character array (i.e., "660").

```
int change_queue_mode( int qid, char *mode )
{
        struct msqid_ds tmpbuf;

        /* Retrieve a current copy of the internal data structure */
        get_queue_ds( qid, &tmpbuf);

        /* Change the permissions using an old trick */
        sscanf(mode, "%ho", &tmpbuf.msg_perm.mode);

        /* Update the internal data structure */
        if( msgctl( qid, IPC_SET, &tmpbuf) == -1)
        {
                return(-1);
        }

        return(0);
}
```

We retrieve a current copy of the internal data structure by a quick call to our `get_queue_ds` wrapper function. We then make a call to `sscanf()` to alter the mode member of the associated `msg_perm` structure. No changes take place, however, until the new copy is used to update the internal version. This duty is performed by a call to `msgctl()` using the IPC_SET command.

Be careful! It is possible to alter the permissions on a queue, and in doing so, inadvertently lock yourself out! Remember, these IPC objects don't go away unless they are properly removed, or the system is rebooted. So, even if you can't see a queue with ipcs doesn't mean that it isn't there.

To illustrate this point, a somewhat humorous anecdote seems to be in order. While teaching a class on Unix internals at the University of South Florida, I ran into a rather embarrassing stumbling block. I had dialed into their lab server the night before, in order to compile and test the labwork to be used in the week-long class. In the process of my testing, I realized that I had made a typo in the code used to alter the permissions on a message queue. I created a simple message queue, and tested the sending and receiving capabilities with no incident. However, when I attempted to change the mode of the queue from "660" to "600," the resulting action was that I was locked out of my own queue! As a result, I could not test the message queue labwork in the same area of my source directory. Since I used the ftok() function to create the IPC key, I was trying to access a queue that I did not have proper permissions for. I ended up contacting the local system administrator on the morning of the class, only to spend an hour explaining to him what a message queue was, and why I needed him to run the ipcrm command for me. Grrrr.

After successfully retrieving a message from a queue, the message is removed. However, as mentioned earlier, IPC objects remain in the system unless explicitly removed, or the system is rebooted. Therefore, our message queue still exists within the kernel, available for use long after a single message disappears. To complete the life cycle of a message queue, they should be removed with a call to `msgctl()`, using the IPC_RMID command:

```
int remove_queue( int qid )
{
        if( msgctl( qid, IPC_RMID, 0) == -1)
        {
                return(-1);
        }

        return(0);
}
```

This wrapper function returns 0 if the queue was removed without incident, else a value of -1. The removal of the queue is atomic in nature, and any subsequent accesses to the queue for whatever purpose will fail miserably.

msgtool: An Interactive Message Queue Manipulator

Few can deny the immediate benefit of having accurate technical information readily available. Such materials provide a tremendous mechanism for learning and exploring new areas. On the same note, having real-world examples to accompany any technical information will speed up and reinforce the learning process.

Until now, the only useful examples which have been presented were the wrapper functions for manipulating message queues. While they are extremely useful, they have not been presented in a manner which would warrant further study and experimentation. To remedy this, you will be presented with *msgtool*, an interactive command line utility for manipulating IPC message queues. While it certainly functions as an adequate tool for education reinforcement, it can be applied directly into real world assignments, by providing message queue functionality via standard shell scripts.

Background

The `msgtool` program relies on command line arguments to determine its behavior. This is what makes it especially useful when called from a shell script. All of the capabilities are provided, from creating, sending, and retrieving, to changing the permissions and finally removing a queue. Currently, it uses a character array for data, allowing you to send textual messages. Changing it to facilitate additional data types is left as an exercise to the reader.

Command Line Syntax

Sending Messages

```
msgtool s (type) "text"
```

Retrieving Messages

```
msgtool r (type)
```

Changing the Permissions (mode)

```
msgtool m (mode)
```

Deleting A Queue

```
msgtool d
```

Examples

```
msgtool  s    1 test
msgtool  s    5 test
```

```
msgtool   s   1 "This is a test"
msgtool   r   1
msgtool   d
msgtool   m   660
```

The Source

The following is the source code for the `msgtool` facility. It should compile clean on any recent (decent) kernel revision that supports System V IPC. Be sure to enable System V IPC in your kernel when doing a rebuild!

On a side note, this utility will *create* a message queue if it does not exist, no matter what type of action is requested.

Since this tool uses the ftok() function to generate IPC key values, you may encounter directory conflicts. If you change directories at any point in your script, it probably won't work. Another solution would be to hardcode a more complete path into msgtool, such as "/tmp/msgtool," or possibly even allow the path to be passed on the command line, along with the operational arguments.

```c
/*****************************************************************************
 Excerpt from "Linux Programmer's Guide - Chapter 6"
 (C)opyright 1994-1995, Scott Burkett
 *****************************************************************************
 MODULE: msgtool.c
 *****************************************************************************
 A command line tool for tinkering with SysV style Message Queues
 *****************************************************************************/

#include <stdio.h>
#include <stdlib.h>
#include <ctype.h>
#include <sys/types.h>
#include <sys/ipc.h>
#include <sys/msg.h>

#define MAX_SEND_SIZE 80

struct mymsgbuf {
        long mtype;
        char mtext[MAX_SEND_SIZE];
};

void send_message(int qid, struct mymsgbuf *qbuf, long type, char *text);
void read_message(int qid, struct mymsgbuf *qbuf, long type);
void remove_queue(int qid);
void change_queue_mode(int qid, char *mode);
void usage(void);
```

```
int main(int argc, char *argv[])
{
        key_t key;
        int   msgqueue_id;
        struct mymsgbuf qbuf;

        if(argc == 1)
                usage();

        /* Create unique key via call to ftok() */
        key = ftok(".", 'm');

        /* Open the queue - create if necessary */
        if((msgqueue_id = msgget(key, IPC_CREAT|0660)) == -1) {
                perror("msgget");
                exit(1);
        }

        switch(tolower(argv[1][0]))
        {
                case 's': send_message(msgqueue_id, (struct mymsgbuf *)&qbuf,
                                        atol(argv[2]), argv[3]);
                        break;
                case 'r': read_message(msgqueue_id, &qbuf, atol(argv[2]));
                        break;
                case 'd': remove_queue(msgqueue_id);
                        break;
                case 'm': change_queue_mode(msgqueue_id, argv[2]);
                        break;

                 default: usage();

        }

        return(0);
}

void send_message(int qid, struct mymsgbuf *qbuf, long type, char *text)
{
        /* Send a message to the queue */
        printf("Sending a message ...\n");
        qbuf->mtype = type;
        strcpy(qbuf->mtext, text);

        if((msgsnd(qid, (struct msgbuf *)qbuf,
                strlen(qbuf->mtext)+1, 0)) ==-1)
```

```
                {
                        perror("msgsnd");
                        exit(1);
                }
        }


        void read_message(int qid, struct mymsgbuf *qbuf, long type)
        {
                /* Read a message from the queue */
                printf("Reading a message ...\n");
                qbuf->mtype = type;
                msgrcv(qid, (struct msgbuf *)qbuf, MAX_SEND_SIZE, type, 0);

                printf("Type: %ld Text: %s\n", qbuf->mtype, qbuf->mtext);
        }


        void remove_queue(int qid)
        {
                /* Remove the queue */
                msgctl(qid, IPC_RMID, 0);
        }


        void change_queue_mode(int qid, char *mode)
        {
                struct msqid_ds myqueue_ds;

                /* Get current info */
                msgctl(qid, IPC_STAT, &myqueue_ds);

                /* Convert and load the mode */
                sscanf(mode, "%ho", &myqueue_ds.msg_perm.mode);

                /* Update the mode */
                msgctl(qid, IPC_SET, &myqueue_ds);
        }


        void usage(void)
        {
                fprintf(stderr, "msgtool - A utility for tinkering with msg queues\n");
                fprintf(stderr, "\nUSAGE: msgtool (s)end <type> <messagetext>\n");
                fprintf(stderr, "                      (r)ecv <type>\n");
                fprintf(stderr, "                      (d)elete\n");
                fprintf(stderr, "                      (m)ode <octal mode>\n");
                exit(1);
        }
```

Semaphores

Basic Concepts

Semaphores can best be described as counters used to control access to shared resources by multiple processes. They are most often used as a locking mechanism to prevent processes from accessing a particular resource while another process is performing operations on it. Semaphores are often dubbed the most difficult to grasp of the three types of System V IPC objects. In order to fully understand semaphores, we'll discuss them briefly before engaging any system calls and operational theory.

The name *semaphore* is actually an old railroad term, referring to the crossroads "arms" that prevent cars from crossing the tracks at intersections. The same can be said about a simple semaphore set. If the semaphore is on (the arms are up), then a resource is available (cars may cross the tracks). However, if the semaphore is off (the arms are down), then resources are not available (the cars must wait).

While this simple example may stand to introduce the concept, it is important to realize that semaphores are actually implemented as *sets*, rather than as single entities. Of course, a given semaphore set might only have one semaphore, as in our railroad example.

Perhaps another approach to the concept of semaphores, is to think of them as *resource counters*. Let's apply this concept to another real-world scenario. Consider a print spooler, capable of handling multiple printers, with each printer handling multiple print requests. A hypothetical print spool manager will utilize semaphore sets to monitor access to each printer.

Assume that in our corporate print room, we have five printers online. Our print spool manager allocates a semaphore set with five semaphores in it, one for each printer on the system. Since each printer is only physically capable of printing one job at a time, each of our five semaphores in our set will be initialized to a value of 1 (one), meaning that they are all online, and accepting requests.

John sends a print request to the spooler. The print manager looks at the semaphore set, and finds the first semaphore which has a value of 1. Before sending John's request to the physical device, the print manager decrements the semaphore for the corresponding printer by a value of negative one (-1). Now, that semaphore's value is 0. In the world of System V semaphores, a value of zero represents 100 percent resource utilization on that semaphore. In our example, no other request can be sent to that printer until it is no longer equal to zero.

When John's print job has completed, the print manager increments the value of the semaphore which corresponds to the printer. Its value is now back up to one (1), which means it is available again. Naturally, if all five semaphores had a value of zero, that would indicate that they are all busy printing requests, and that no printers are available.

Although this was a simple example, please do not be confused by the initial value of one (1) which was assigned to each semaphore in the set. Semaphores, when thought of as resource counters, may be initialized to *any positive* integer value, and are not limited to either being zero or one. If it were possible for each of our five printers to handle 10 print jobs at a time, we could initialize each of our semaphores to 10, decrementing by one for every new job, and incrementing by one whenever a print job was finished. As you will discover in the next chapter, semaphores have a close working relationship with shared memory segments, acting as a watchdog to prevent multiple writes to the same memory segment.

Before delving into the associated system calls, lets take a brief tour through the various internal data structures utilized during semaphore operations.

Internal Data Structures

Let's briefly look at data structures maintained by the kernel for semaphore sets.

Kernel semid_ds Structure

As with message queues, the kernel maintains a special internal data structure for each semaphore set which exists within its addressing space. This structure is of type semid_ds, and is defined in linux/sem.h as follows:

```
        /* One semid data structure for each set of semaphores in the system.
*/
        struct semid_ds {
                struct ipc_perm sem_perm;       /* permissions .. see ipc.h */
                time_t          sem_otime;      /* last semop time */
                time_t          sem_ctime;      /* last change time */
                struct sem      *sem_base;      /* ptr to first semaphore in
array */
                struct wait_queue *eventn;
                struct wait_queue *eventz;
                struct sem_undo  *undo;         /* undo requests on this array
*/
                ushort          sem_nsems;      /* no. of semaphores in array
*/
        };
```

As with message queues, operations on this structure are performed by a special system call, and should not be tinkered with directly. Here are descriptions of the more pertinent fields:

sem_perm

This is an instance of the ipc_perm structure, which is defined for us in linux/ipc.h. This holds the permission information for the semaphore set, including the access permissions, and information about the creator of the set (uid and so forth).

sem_otime

Time of the last semop() operation (more on this in a moment).

sem_ctime

Time of the last change to this structure (mode change and so forth).

sem_base

Pointer to the first semaphore in the array (see next structure).

sem_undo

Number of undo requests in this array (more on this in a moment).

sem_nsems

Number of semaphores in the semaphore set (the array).

Kernel sem *Structure*

In the semid_ds structure, there exists a pointer to the base of the semaphore array itself. Each array member is of the sem structure type. It is also defined in linux/sem.h:

```
/* One semaphore structure for each semaphore in the system. */
struct sem {
        short   sempid;         /* pid of last operation */
        ushort  semval;         /* current value */
        ushort  semncnt;        /* num procs awaiting increase in
semval */
        ushort  semzcnt;        /* num procs awaiting semval = 0 */
};
```

sem_pid

The PID (process ID) that performed the last operation.

sem_semval

The current value of the semaphore.

sem_semncnt

Number of processes waiting for resources to become available.

sem_semzcnt

Number of processes waiting for 100 percent resource utilization.

System Call: semget()

In order to create a new semaphore set, or access an existing set, the semget() system call is used.

```
SYSTEM CALL: semget();
```

```
PROTOTYPE: int semget ( key_t key, int nsems, int semflg );
  RETURNS: semaphore set IPC identifier on success
           -1 on error: errno = EACCESS (permission denied)
                                EEXIST (set exists, cannot create (IPC_EXCL))
                                EIDRM (set is marked for deletion)
                                ENOENT (set does not exist, no IPC_CREAT was
used)
                                ENOMEM (Not enough memory to create new set)
                                ENOSPC (Maximum set limit exceeded)
  NOTES:
```

The first argument to semget() is the key value (in our case returned by a call to ftok()). This key value is then compared to existing key values that exist within the kernel for other semaphore sets. At that point, the open or access operation is dependent upon the contents of the semflg argument.

IPC_CREAT
Create the semaphore set if it doesn't already exist in the kernel.

IPC_EXCL
When used with IPC_CREAT, fail if semaphore set already exists.

If IPC_CREAT is used alone, semget() either returns the semaphore set identifier for a newly created set, or returns the identifier for a set which exists with the same key value. If IPC_EXCL is used along with IPC_CREAT, then either a new set is created, or if the set exists, the call fails with -1. IPC_EXCL is useless by itself, but when combined with IPC_CREAT, it can be used as a facility to guarantee that no existing semaphore set is opened for access.

As with the other forms of System V IPC, an optional octal mode may be OR'd into the mask to form the permissions on the semaphore set.

The nsems argument specifies the number of semaphores that should be created in a new set. This represents the number of printers in our fictional print room described earlier. The maximum number of semaphores in a set is defined in linux/sem.h as:

```
#define SEMMSL  32        /* <=512 max num of semaphores per id */
```

Note that the nsems argument is ignored if you are explicitly opening an existing set.

Let's create a wrapper function for opening or creating semaphore sets:

```
int open_semaphore_set( key_t keyval, int numsems )
{
        int     sid;
```

```
        if ( ! numsems )
                return(-1);

        if((sid = semget( mykey, numsems, IPC_CREAT | 0660 )) == -1)
        {
                return(-1);
        }


        return(sid);
}
```

Note the use of the explicit permissions of 0660. This small function either returns a semaphore set identifier (int), or -1 on error. The key value must be passed to it, as well as the number of semaphores to allocate space for if creating a new set. In the example presented at the end of this section, notice the use of the IPC_EXCL flag to determine whether or not the semaphore set exists or not.

System Call: semop()

```
   SYSTEM CALL: semop();
   PROTOTYPE: int semop ( int semid, struct sembuf *sops, unsigned nsops);
     RETURNS: 0 on success (all operations performed)
              -1 on error: errno = E2BIG (nsops greater than max number of ops
allowed atomically)
                                      EACCESS (permission denied)
                                      EAGAIN (IPC_NOWAIT asserted, operation could
not go through)
                                      EFAULT (invalid address pointed to by sops
argument)
                                      EIDRM (semaphore set was removed)
                                      EINTR (Signal received while sleeping)
                                      EINVAL (set doesn't exist, or semid is
invalid)
                                      ENOMEM (SEM_UNDO asserted, not enough memory
to create the
                                             undo structure necessary)
                                      ERANGE (semaphore value out of range)
   NOTES:
```

The first argument to semget() is the key value (in our case returned by a call to semget). The second argument (sops) is a pointer to an array of *operations* to be performed on the semaphore set, while the third argument (nsops) is the number of operations in that array.

The sops argument points to an array of type sembuf. This structure is declared in linux/sem.h as follows:

```
/* semop system call takes an array of these */
struct sembuf {
        ushort  sem_num;        /* semaphore index in array */
        short   sem_op;         /* semaphore operation */
        short   sem_flg;        /* operation flags */
};
```

sem_num
The number of the semaphore you wish to deal with.

sem_op
The operation to perform (positive, negative, or zero).

sem_flg
Operational flags.

If sem_op is negative, then its value is subtracted from the semaphore. This correlates with obtaining resources that the semaphore controls or monitors access of. If IPC_NOWAIT is not specified, then the calling process sleeps until the requested amount of resources are available in the semaphore (another process has released some).

If sem_op is positive, then its value is added to the semaphore. This correlates with returning resources back to the application's semaphore set. Resources should always be returned to a semaphore set when they are no longer needed!

Finally, if sem_op is zero (0), then the calling process will sleep() until the semaphore's value is 0. This correlates to waiting for a semaphore to reach 100 percent utilization. A good example of this would be a daemon running with super-user permissions that could dynamically adjust the size of the semaphore set if it reaches full utilization.

In order to explain the semop call, let's revisit our print room scenario. Let's assume only one printer, capable of only one job at a time. We create a semaphore set with only one semaphore in it (only one printer), and initialize that one semaphore to a value of one (only one job at a time).

Each time we desire to send a job to this printer, we need to first make sure that the resource is available. We do this by attempting to obtain one unit from the semaphore. Let's load up a sembuf array to perform the operation:

```
struct sembuf sem_lock = { 0, -1, IPC_NOWAIT };
```

Translation of the above initialized structure dictates that a value of -1 will be added to semaphore number 0 in the semaphore set. In other words, one unit of resources will be obtained from the only semaphore in our set (0th member). IPC_NOWAIT is specified, so the call will either go through immediately, or fail if another print job is currently printing. Here is an example of using this initialized `sembuf` structure with the `semop` system call:

```
if((semop(sid, &sem_lock, 1) == -1)
        perror("semop");
```

The third argument (`nsops`) says that we are only performing one (1) operation (there is only one `sembuf` structure in our array of operations). The `sid` argument is the IPC identifier for our semaphore set.

When our print job has completed, we must return the resources back to the semaphore set, so that others may use the printer.

```
struct sembuf sem_unlock = { 0, 1, IPC_NOWAIT };
```

Translation of the above initialized structure dictates that a value of 1 will be added to semaphore number 0 in the semaphore set. In other words, one unit of resources will be returned to the set.

System Call: semctl()

```
SYSTEM CALL: semctl();
PROTOTYPE: int semctl ( int semid, int semnum, int cmd, union semun arg );
  RETURNS: positive integer on success
           -1 on error: errno = EACCESS (permission denied)
                                EFAULT (invalid address pointed to by arg
argument)
                                EIDRM (semaphore set was removed)
                                EINVAL (set doesn't exist, or semid is
invalid)
                                EPERM (EUID has no privileges for cmd in arg)
                                ERANGE (semaphore value out of range)
  NOTES: Performs control operations on a semaphore set
```

The semctl system call is used to perform control operations on a semaphore set. This call is analogous to the msgctl system call which is used for operations on message queues. If you compare the argument lists of the two system calls, you will notice that the list for semctl varies slightly from that of msgctl. Recall that semaphores are actually implemented as sets, rather than as single entities. With semaphore operations, not only does the IPC key need to be passed, but the target semaphore within the set as well.

Both system calls utilize a cmd argument, for specification of the command to be performed on the IPC object. The remaining difference lies in the final argument to both calls. In msgctl, the final argument represents a copy of the internal data structure used by the kernel. Recall that we used this structure to retrieve internal information about a message queue, as well as to set or change permissions and ownership of the queue. With semaphores, additional operational commands are supported, thus requiring a more complex data type as the final argument. The use of a union confuses many neophyte semaphore programmers to a substantial degree. We will dissect this structure carefully, in an effort to prevent any confusion.

The first argument to semctl() is the key value (in our case returned by a call to semget). The second argument (semun) is the semaphore number that an operation is targeted towards. In essence, this can be thought of as an *index* into the semaphore set, with the first semaphore (or only one) in the set being represented by a value of zero (0).

The cmd argument represents the command to be performed against the set. As you can see, the familiar IPC_STAT/IPC_SET commands are present, along with a wealth of additional commands specific to semaphore sets:

IPC_STAT
Retrieves the semid_ds structure for a set, and stores it in the address of the buf argument in the semun union.

IPC_SET
Sets the value of the ipc_perm member of the semid_ds structure for a set. Takes the values from the buf argument of the semun union.

IPC_RMID
Removes the set from the kernel.

GETALL
Used to obtain the values of all semaphores in a set. The integer values are stored in an array of unsigned short integers pointed to by the *array* member of the union.

GETNCNT
Returns the number of processes currently waiting for resources.

GETPID
Returns the PID of the process which performed the last *semop* call.

GETVAL
Returns the value of a single semaphore within the set.

GETZCNT
Returns the number of processes currently waiting for 100 percent resource utilization.

SETALL

Sets all semaphore values with a set to the matching values contained in the *array* member of the union.

SETVAL

Sets the value of an individual semaphore within the set to the *val* member of the union.

The `arg` argument represents an instance of type `semun`. This particular union is declared in `linux/sem.h` as follows:

```
/* arg for semctl system calls. */
union semun {
        int val;                  /* value for SETVAL */
        struct semid_ds *buf;   /* buffer for IPC_STAT & IPC_SET */
        ushort *array;          /* array for GETALL & SETALL */
        struct seminfo *__buf;  /* buffer for IPC_INFO */
        void *__pad;
};
```

val

Used when the SETVAL command is performed. Specifies the value to set the semaphore to.

buf

Used in the IPC_STAT/IPC_SET commands. Represents a copy of the internal semaphore data structure used in the kernel.

array

A pointer used in the GETALL/SETALL commands. Should point to an array of integer values to be used in setting or retrieving all semaphore values in a set.

The remaining arguments __*buf* and __*pad* are used internally in the semaphore code within the kernel, and are of little or no use to the application developer. As a matter of fact, these two arguments are specific to the Linux operating system, and are not found in other Unix implementations.

Because this particular system call is arguably the most difficult to grasp of all the System V IPC calls, we'll examine multiple examples of it in action.

The following snippet returns the value of the passed semaphore. The final argument (the union) is ignored when the GETVAL command is used:

```
int get_sem_val( int sid, int semnum )
{
        return( semctl(sid, semnum, GETVAL, 0));
}
```

To revisit the printer example, let's say the status of all five printers was required:

```
#define MAX_PRINTERS 5

printer_usage()
{
        int x;

        for(x=0; x<MAX_PRINTERS; x++)
                printf("Printer %d: %d\n\r", x, get_sem_val( sid, x ));
}
```

Consider the following function, which could be used to initialize a new semaphore value:

```
void init_semaphore( int sid, int semnum, int initval)
{
        union semun semopts;

        semopts.val = initval;
        semctl( sid, semnum, SETVAL, semopts);
}
```

Note that the final argument of semctl is a copy of the union, rather than a pointer to it. While we're on the subject of the union as an argument, allow me to demonstrate a rather common mistake when using this system call.

Recall from the msgtool project that the IPC_STAT and IPC_SET commands were used to alter permissions on the queue. While these commands are supported in the semaphore implementation, their usage is a bit different, as the internal data structure is retrieved and copied from a member of the union, rather than as a single entity. Can you locate the bug in this code?

```
/* Required permissions should be passed in as text (ex: "660") */

void changemode(int sid, char *mode)
{
        int rc;
        struct semid_ds mysemds;

        /* Get current values for internal data structure */
        if((rc = semctl(sid, 0, IPC_STAT, semopts)) == -1)
        {
                perror("semctl");
                exit(1);
        }
```

```
        printf("Old permissions were %o\n", semopts.buf->sem_perm.mode);

        /* Change the permissions on the semaphore */
        sscanf(mode, "%o", &semopts.buf->sem_perm.mode);

        /* Update the internal data structure */
        semctl(sid, 0, IPC_SET, semopts);

        printf("Updated...\n");
}
```

The code is attempting to make a local copy of the internal data structure for the set, modify the permissions, and IPC_SET them back to the kernel. However, the first call to semctl promptly returns EFAULT, or bad address for the last argument (the union!). In addition, if we hadn't checked for errors from that call, we would have gotten a memory fault. Why?

Recall that the IPC_SET/IPC_STAT commands use the buf member of the union, which is a *pointer* to a type semid_ds. Pointers are pointers are pointers are pointers! The buf member must point to some valid storage location in order for our function to work properly. Consider this revamped version:

```
void changemode(int sid, char *mode)
{
        int rc;
        struct semid_ds mysemds;

        /* Get current values for internal data structure */

        /* Point to our local copy first! */
        semopts.buf = &mysemds;

        /* Let's try this again! */
        if((rc = semctl(sid, 0, IPC_STAT, semopts)) == -1)
        {
                perror("semctl");
                exit(1);
        }

        printf("Old permissions were %o\n", semopts.buf->sem_perm.mode);

        /* Change the permissions on the semaphore */
        sscanf(mode, "%o", &semopts.buf->sem_perm.mode);

        /* Update the internal data structure */
        semctl(sid, 0, IPC_SET, semopts);
```

```
            printf("Updated...\n");
    }
```

semtool: An Interactive Semaphore Manipulator

Background

The semtool program relies on command line arguments to determine its behavior. This is what makes it especially useful when called from a shell script. All of the capabilities are provided, from creating and manipulating, to changing the permissions and finally removing a semaphore set. It can be used to control shared resources via standard shell scripts.

Command Line Syntax

Creating A Semaphore Set

```
semtool c (number of semaphores in set)
```

Locking A Semaphore

```
semtool l (semaphore number to lock)
```

Unlocking A Semaphore

```
semtool u (semaphore number to unlock)
```

Changing The Permissions (mode)

```
semtool m (mode)
```

Deleting A Semaphore Set

```
semtool d
```

Examples

```
semtool  c 5
semtool  l
semtool  u
semtool  m 660
semtool  d
```

The Source

```
/**********************************************************************
  Excerpt from "Linux Programmer's Guide - Chapter 6"
```

```
(C)opyright 1994-1995, Scott Burkett
*************************************************************************
MODULE: semtool.c
*************************************************************************
A command line tool for tinkering with SysV style Semaphore Sets


*************************************************************************/

#include <stdio.h>
#include <ctype.h>
#include <stdlib.h>
#include <sys/types.h>
#include <sys/ipc.h>
#include <sys/sem.h>

#define SEM_RESOURCE_MAX        1       /* Initial value of all semaphores */

void opensem(int *sid, key_t key);
void createsem(int *sid, key_t key, int members);
void locksem(int sid, int member);
void unlocksem(int sid, int member);
void removesem(int sid);
unsigned short get_member_count(int sid);
int getval(int sid, int member);
void dispval(int sid, int member);
void changemode(int sid, char *mode);
void usage(void);

int main(int argc, char *argv[])
{
        key_t key;
        int    semset_id;

        if(argc == 1)
                usage();

        /* Create unique key via call to ftok() */
        key = ftok(".", 's');

        switch(tolower(argv[1][0]))
        {
                case 'c': if(argc != 3)
                                usage();
                          createsem(&semset_id, key,  atoi(argv[2]));
                          break;
                case 'l': if(argc != 3)
                                usage();
```

```
                            opensem(&semset_id, key);
                            locksem(semset_id, atoi(argv[2]));
                            break;
                case 'u': if(argc != 3)
                                usage();
                            opensem(&semset_id, key);
                            unlocksem(semset_id, atoi(argv[2]));
                            break;
                case 'd': opensem(&semset_id, key);
                            removesem(semset_id);
                            break;
                case 'm': opensem(&semset_id, key);
                            changemode(semset_id, argv[2]);
                            break;
                 default: usage();

        }

        return(0);
}


void opensem(int *sid, key_t key)
{
        /* Open the semaphore set - do not create! */

        if((*sid = semget(key, 0, 0666)) == -1)
        {
                printf("Semaphore set does not exist!\n");
                exit(1);
        }

}


void createsem(int *sid, key_t key, int members)
{
        int cntr;
        union semun semopts;

        if(members > SEMMSL) {
                printf("Sorry, max number of semaphores in a set is %d\n",
                        SEMMSL);
                exit(1);
        }

        printf("Attempting to create new semaphore set with %d members\n",
                            members);
```

```
        if((*sid = semget(key, members, IPC_CREAT|IPC_EXCL|0666))
                        == -1)
        {
                fprintf(stderr, "Semaphore set already exists!\n");
                exit(1);
        }

        semopts.val = SEM_RESOURCE_MAX;

        /* Initialize all members (could be done with SETALL) */
        for(cntr=0; cntr<members; cntr++)
                semctl(*sid, cntr, SETVAL, semopts);
}

void locksem(int sid, int member)
{
        struct sembuf sem_lock={ 0, -1, IPC_NOWAIT};

        if( member<0 || member>(get_member_count(sid)-1))
        {
                fprintf(stderr, "semaphore member %d out of range\n", member);
                return;
        }

        /* Attempt to lock the semaphore set */
        if(!getval(sid, member))
        {
                fprintf(stderr, "Semaphore resources exhausted (no lock)!\n");
                exit(1);
        }

        sem_lock.sem_num = member;

        if((semop(sid, &sem_lock, 1)) == -1)
        {
                fprintf(stderr, "Lock failed\n");
                exit(1);
        }
        else
                printf("Semaphore resources decremented by one (locked)\n");

        dispval(sid, member);
}

void unlocksem(int sid, int member)
{
```

```
                struct sembuf sem_unlock={ member, 1, IPC_NOWAIT};
                int semval;

                if( member<0 || member>(get_member_count(sid)-1))
                {
                        fprintf(stderr, "semaphore member %d out of range\n", member);
                        return;
                }

                /* Is the semaphore set locked? */
                semval = getval(sid, member);
                if(semval == SEM_RESOURCE_MAX) {
                        fprintf(stderr, "Semaphore not locked!\n");
                        exit(1);
                }

                sem_unlock.sem_num = member;

                /* Attempt to lock the semaphore set */
                if((semop(sid, &sem_unlock, 1)) == -1)
                {
                        fprintf(stderr, "Unlock failed\n");
                        exit(1);
                }
                else
                        printf("Semaphore resources incremented by one (unlocked)\n");

                dispval(sid, member);
        }


void removesem(int sid)
{
        semctl(sid, 0, IPC_RMID, 0);
        printf("Semaphore removed\n");
}


unsigned short get_member_count(int sid)
{
        union semun semopts;
        struct semid_ds mysemds;

        semopts.buf = &mysemds;

        /* Return number of members in the semaphore set */
        return(semopts.buf->sem_nsems);
}
```

```
int getval(int sid, int member)
{
        int semval;

        semval = semctl(sid, member, GETVAL, 0);
        return(semval);
}

void changemode(int sid, char *mode)
{
        int rc;
        union semun semopts;
        struct semid_ds mysemds;

        /* Get current values for internal data structure */
        semopts.buf = &mysemds;

        rc = semctl(sid, 0, IPC_STAT, semopts);

        if (rc == -1) {
                perror("semctl");
                exit(1);
        }

        printf("Old permissions were %o\n", semopts.buf->sem_perm.mode);

        /* Change the permissions on the semaphore */
        sscanf(mode, "%ho", &semopts.buf->sem_perm.mode);

        /* Update the internal data structure */
        semctl(sid, 0, IPC_SET, semopts);

        printf("Updated...\n");

}

void dispval(int sid, int member)
{
        int semval;

        semval = semctl(sid, member, GETVAL, 0);
        printf("semval for member %d is %d\n", member, semval);
}

void usage(void)
{
```

```
                fprintf(stderr, "semtool - A utility for tinkering with semaphores\n");
                fprintf(stderr, "\nUSAGE:  semtool4 (c)reate <semcount>\n");
                fprintf(stderr, "                    (l)ock <sem #>\n");
                fprintf(stderr, "                    (u)nlock <sem #>\n");
                fprintf(stderr, "                    (d)elete\n");
                fprintf(stderr, "                    (m)ode <mode>\n");
                exit(1);
        }
```

semstat: A semtool Companion Program

As an added bonus, the source code to a companion program called semstat is provided
next. The `semstat` program displays the values of each of the semaphores in the set created by `semtool`.

```
/***********************************************************************
Excerpt from "Linux Programmer's Guide - Chapter 6"
(C)opyright 1994-1995, Scott Burkett
***********************************************************************
MODULE: semstat.c
***********************************************************************
A companion command line tool for the semtool package.  semstat displays
the current value of all semaphores in the set created by semtool.
***********************************************************************/

#include <stdio.h>
#include <stdlib.h>
#include <sys/types.h>
#include <sys/ipc.h>
#include <sys/sem.h>

int get_sem_count(int sid);
void show_sem_usage(int sid);
int get_sem_count(int sid);
void dispval(int sid);

int main(int argc, char *argv[])
{
        key_t key;
        int    semset_id;

        /* Create unique key via call to ftok() */
        key = ftok(".", 's');

        /* Open the semaphore set - do not create! */
        if((semset_id = semget(key, 1, 0666)) == -1)
```

```
        {
                printf("Semaphore set does not exist\n");
                exit(1);
        }

        show_sem_usage(semset_id);
        return(0);
}

void show_sem_usage(int sid)
{
        int cntr=0, maxsems, semval;

        maxsems = get_sem_count(sid);

        while(cntr < maxsems) {
                semval = semctl(sid, cntr, GETVAL, 0);
                printf("Semaphore #%d:  --> %d\n", cntr, semval);
                cntr++;
        }
}

int get_sem_count(int sid)
{
        int rc;
        struct semid_ds mysemds;
        union semun semopts;

        /* Get current values for internal data structure */
        semopts.buf = &mysemds;

        if((rc = semctl(sid, 0, IPC_STAT, semopts)) == -1) {
                perror("semctl");
                exit(1);
        }

        /* return number of semaphores in set */
        return(semopts.buf->sem_nsems);
}

void dispval(int sid)
{
        int semval;

        semval = semctl(sid, 0, GETVAL, 0);
        printf("semval is %d\n", semval);
}
```

Shared Memory

Basic Concepts

Shared memory can best be described as the mapping of an area (segment) of memory that will be mapped and shared by more than one process. This is by far the fastest form of IPC, because there is no intermediation (i.e., a pipe, a message queue, and so on). Instead, information is mapped directly from a memory segment, and into the addressing space of the calling process. A segment can be created by one process, and subsequently written to and read from by any number of processes.

Internal And User Data Structures

Let's briefly look at data structures maintained by the kernel for shared memory segments.

Kernel shmid_ds Structure

As with message queues and semaphore sets, the kernel maintains a special internal data structure for each shared memory segment which exists within its addressing space. This structure is of type shmid_ds, and is defined in linux/shm.h as follows:

```
        /* One shmid data structure for each shared memory segment in the
system. */
        struct shmid_ds {
                struct ipc_perm shm_perm;       /* operation perms */
                int     shm_segsz;              /* size of segment (bytes) */
                time_t  shm_atime;              /* last attach time */
                time_t  shm_dtime;              /* last detach time */
                time_t  shm_ctime;              /* last change time */
                unsigned short  shm_cpid;       /* pid of creator */
                unsigned short  shm_lpid;       /* pid of last operator */
                short   shm_nattch;             /* no. of current attaches */

                                                /* the following are private
*/

                unsigned short  shm_npages;     /* size of segment (pages) */
                unsigned long   *shm_pages;     /* array of ptrs to frames ->
SHMMAX */
                struct vm_area_struct *attaches; /* descriptors for attaches */
        };
```

Operations on this structure are performed by a special system call, and should not be tinkered with directly. Here are descriptions of the more pertinent fields:

shm_perm

This is an instance of the ipc_perm structure, which is defined for us in linux/ipc.h. This holds the permission information for the segment, including the access permissions, and information about the creator of the segment (uid and so forth).

shm_segsz
Size of the segment (measured in bytes).

shm_atime
Time the last process attached the segment.

shm_dtime
Time the last process detached the segment.

shm_ctime
Time of the last change to this structure (mode change, etc.).

shm_cpid
The PID of the creating process.

shm_lpid
The PID of the last process to operate on the segment.

shm_nattch
Number of processes currently attached to the segment.

System Call: shmget()

In order to create a new message queue, or access an existing queue, the shmget() system call is used.

```
SYSTEM CALL: shmget();

PROTOTYPE: int shmget ( key_t key, int size, int shmflg );
  RETURNS: shared memory segment identifier on success
           -1 on error: errno = EINVAL (Invalid segment size specified)
                                EEXIST (Segment exists, cannot create)
                                EIDRM (Segment is marked for deletion, or was
removed)
                                ENOENT (Segment does not exist)
                                EACCES (Permission denied)
                                ENOMEM (Not enough memory to create segment)
  NOTES:
```

This particular call should almost seem like old news at this point. It is strikingly similar to the corresponding get calls for message queues and semaphore sets.

The first argument to shmget() is the key value (in our case returned by a call to ftok()). This key value is then compared to existing key values that exist within the kernel for other shared memory segments. At that point, the open or access operation is dependent on the contents of the shmflg argument.

IPC_CREAT
Create the segment if it doesn't already exist in the kernel.

IPC_EXCL
When used with IPC_CREAT, fail if segment already exists.

If IPC_CREAT is used alone, shmget() either returns the segment identifier for a newly created segment, or returns the identifier for a segment which exists with the same key value. If IPC_EXCL is used along with IPC_CREAT, then either a new segment is created, or if the segment exists, the call fails with -1. IPC_EXCL is useless by itself, but when combined with IPC_CREAT, it can be used as a facility to guarantee that no existing segment is opened for access.

Once again, an optional octal mode may be OR'd into the mask.

Let's create a wrapper function for locating or creating a shared memory segment :

```
int open_segment( key_t keyval, int segsize )
{
        int     shmid;

        if((shmid = shmget( keyval, segsize, IPC_CREAT | 0660 )) == -1)
        {
                return(-1);
        }

        return(shmid);
}
```

Note the use of the explicit permissions of 0660. This small function either returns a shared memory segment identifier (int), or -1 on error. The key value and requested segment size (in bytes) are passed as arguments.

Once a process has a valid IPC identifier for a given segment, the next step is for the process to attach or map the segment into its own addressing space.

System Call: shmat()

```
SYSTEM CALL: shmat();

PROTOTYPE: int shmat ( int shmid, char *shmaddr, int shmflg);
   RETURNS: address at which segment was attached to the process, or
            -1 on error: errno = EINVAL (Invalid IPC ID value or attach
address passed)

                         ENOMEM (Not enough memory to attach segment)
```

NOTES:

If the addr argument is zero (0), the kernel tries to find an unmapped region. This is the recommended method. An address can be specified, but is typically only used to facilitate proprietary hardware or to resolve conflicts with other apps. The SHM_RND flag can be OR'd into the flag argument to force a passed address to be page aligned (rounds down to the nearest page size).

In addition, if the SHM_RDONLY flag is OR'd in with the flag argument, then the shared memory segment will be mapped in, but marked as read-only.

This call is perhaps the simplest to use. Consider this wrapper function, which is passed a valid IPC identifier for a segment, and returns the address that the segment was attached to:

```
char *attach_segment( int shmid )
{
        return(shmat(shmid, 0, 0));
}
```

Once a segment has been properly attached, and a process has a pointer to the start of that segment, reading and writing to the segment become as easy as simply referencing or dereferencing the pointer! Be careful not to lose the value of the original pointer! If this happens, you will have no way of accessing the base (start) of the segment.

System Call: shmctl()

```
  SYSTEM CALL: shmctl();
  PROTOTYPE: int shmctl ( int shmqid, int cmd, struct shmid_ds *buf );
    RETURNS: 0 on success
             -1 on error: errno = EACCES (No read permission and cmd is
IPC_STAT)
                             EFAULT (Address pointed to by buf is invalid
with IPC_SET and
                                 IPC_STAT commands)
                           EIDRM  (Segment was removed during retrieval)
                           EINVAL (shmqid invalid)
                           EPERM  (IPC_SET or IPC_RMID command was
issued, but
                                 calling process does not have write
(alter)
                                 access to the segment)
        NOTES:
```

This particular call is modeled directly after the msgctl call for message queues. In light of this fact, it won't be discussed in too much detail. Valid command values are:

IPC_STAT

Retrieves the shmid_ds structure for a segment, and stores it in the address of the buf argument.

IPC_SET

Sets the value of the ipc_perm member of the shmid_ds structure for a segment. Takes the values from the buf argument.

IPC_RMID

Marks a segment for removal.

The IPC_RMID command doesn't actually remove a segment from the kernel. Rather, it marks the segment for removal. The actual removal itself occurs when the last process currently attached to the segment has properly detached it. Of course, if no processes are currently attached to the segment, the removal seems immediate.

To properly detach a shared memory segment, a process calls the shmdt system call.

System Call: shmdt()

```
SYSTEM CALL: shmdt();

PROTOTYPE: int shmdt ( char *shmaddr );
  RETURNS: -1 on error: errno = EINVAL (Invalid attach address passed)
```

After a shared memory segment is no longer needed by a process, it should be detached by calling this system call. As mentioned earlier, this is not the same as removing the segment from the kernel! After a detach is successful, the shm_nattch member of the associates shmid_ds structure is decremented by one. When this value reaches zero (0), the kernel will physically remove the segment.

shmtool: An Interactive Shared Memory Manipulator

Background

Our final example of System V IPC objects will be shmtool, which is a command line tool for creating, reading, writing, and deleting shared memory segments. Once again, like the previous examples, the segment is created during any operation, if it did not previously exist.

Command Line Syntax

Writing Strings To The Segment

```
shmtool w "text"
```

Retrieving Strings From The Segment

```
shmtool r
```

Changing The Permissions (mode)

```
shmtool m (mode)
```

Deleting The Segment

```
shmtool d
```

Examples

```
shmtool  w    test
shmtool  w    "This is a test"
shmtool  r
shmtool  d
shmtool  m    660
```

The Source

```c
#include <stdio.h>
#include <sys/types.h>
#include <sys/ipc.h>
#include <sys/shm.h>

#define SEGSIZE 100

main(int argc, char *argv[])
{
        key_t key;
        int   shmid, cntr;
        char  *segptr;

        if(argc == 1)
                usage();

        /* Create unique key via call to ftok() */
        key = ftok(".", 'S');

        /* Open the shared memory segment - create if necessary */
        if((shmid = shmget(key, SEGSIZE, IPC_CREAT|IPC_EXCL|0666)) == -1)
```

```
        {
                printf("Shared memory segment exists - opening as client\n");

                /* Segment probably already exists - try as a client */
                if((shmid = shmget(key, SEGSIZE, 0)) == -1)
                {
                        perror("shmget");
                        exit(1);
                }
        }
        else
        {
                printf("Creating new shared memory segment\n");
        }

        /* Attach (map) the shared memory segment into the current process */
        if((segptr = shmat(shmid, 0, 0)) == -1)
        {
                perror("shmat");
                exit(1);
        }

        switch(tolower(argv[1][0]))
        {
                case 'w': writeshm(shmid, segptr, argv[2]);
                        break;
                case 'r': readshm(shmid, segptr);
                        break;
                case 'd': removeshm(shmid);
                        break;
                case 'm': changemode(shmid, argv[2]);
                        break;
                 default: usage();

        }
}

writeshm(int shmid, char *segptr, char *text)
{
        strcpy(segptr, text);
        printf("Done...\n");
}

readshm(int shmid, char *segptr)
```

```
{
        printf("segptr: %s\n", segptr);
}


removeshm(int shmid)
{
        shmctl(shmid, IPC_RMID, 0);
        printf("Shared memory segment marked for deletion\n");
}


changemode(int shmid, char *mode)
{
        struct shmid_ds myshmds;

        /* Get current values for internal data structure */
        shmctl(shmid, IPC_STAT, &myshmds);

        /* Display old permissions */
        printf("Old permissions were: %o\n", myshmds.shm_perm.mode);

        /* Convert and load the mode */
        sscanf(mode, "%o", &myshmds.shm_perm.mode);

        /* Update the mode */
        shmctl(shmid, IPC_SET, &myshmds);

        printf("New permissions are : %o\n", myshmds.shm_perm.mode);
}


usage()
{
        fprintf(stderr, "shmtool - A utility for tinkering with shared
memory\n");
        fprintf(stderr, "\nUSAGE:  shmtool (w)rite <text>\n");
        fprintf(stderr, "                        (r)ead\n");
        fprintf(stderr, "                        (d)elete\n");
        fprintf(stderr, "                        (m)ode change <octal mode>\n");
        exit(1);
}
```

Chapter 7
Sound Programming

A PC has at least one sound device: the internal speaker. But, you can also buy a sound card to plug into your PC to provide a more sophisticated sound device. Look at the Linux Sound User's Guide or the Sound HOWTO for supported sound cards.

Programming The Internal Speaker

Believe it or not, your PC speaker is part of the Linux console and thus a character device. Therefore, ioctl() requests exist to manipulate it. For the internal speaker the following two requests exist:

1. KDMKTONE

   Generates a beep for a specified time using the kernel timer.

   Example: `ioctl (fd, KDMKTONE,(long) argument)`.

2. KIOCSOUND

   Generates an endless beep or stops a currently sounding beep.

   Example: `ioctl(fd,KIOCSOUND,(int) tone)`.

The `argument` consists of the `tone` value in the low word and the duration in the high word. The `tone` value is not the frequency. The PC mainboard timer 8254 is clocked at 1.19 MHz and so it's 1190000/frequency. The duration is measured in timer ticks. Both ioctl calls return immediately, so you can this way produce beeps without blocking the program

KDMKTONE should be used for warning signals because you don't have to worry about stopping the tone.

KIOCSOUND can be used to play melodies as demonstrated in the example program splay. To stop the beep you have to use the `tone` value 0.

Programming A Sound Card

For you as a programmer, it is important to know if the current Linux system has a sound card plugged in. One way to check is to examine /dev/sndstat. If opening /dev/sndstat fails and errno=ENODEV, then no sound driver is activated which means you will get no help from the kernel sound driver. The same result might be achieved by trying to open /dev/dsp as long as it is not a link to the pcsnd driver in which case open() will not fail.

If you want to mess with a sound card at the hardware level you know that some combination of outb() and inb() calls will detect the sound card you are looking for.

By using the sound driver for your programs, chances are that they will work on other i386 systems as well, since some clever people decided to use the same driver for Linux, isc, FreeBSD, and most other i386-based systems. It will aid in porting programs if Linux on other architectures offers the same sound device interface. A sound card is not part of the Linux console, but is a special device. A sound card mostly offers three main features:

♦ Digital sample input/output

♦ Frequency modulation output

♦ A MIDI interface

Each of these features have their own device driver interface. For digital samples it is /dev/dsp, for the frequency modulation it is /dev/sequencer and for the MIDI interface it is /dev/midi. The sound settings (like volume, balance, or bass) can be controlled via the /dev/mixer interface. For compatibility reasons a /dev/audio device exists which can read SUN -law sound data, but it maps to the digital sample device.

You are right if you guessed that you use ioctl() to manipulate these devices. The ioctl() requests are defined in *<linux/soundcard.h>* and begin with SNDCTL_.

Since I don't own a sound card someone else has to continue here.

Chapter 8
Character Cell Graphics

This chapter deals with screen input and output that is not pixel-based, but character-based. When we say character, we mean a composition of pixels that can be changed depending on a charset. Your graphics card already offers one or more charsets and operates by default in text (charset) mode because text can be processed much faster than pixel graphics. There is more to do with terminals than to use them as simple (dumb) and boring text displays. I will describe how to use the special features that your Linux terminal, especially the Linux console, offers.

♦ **printf, sprintf, fprintf, scanf, sscanf, fscanf**—With these functions from Linux, you can output formatted strings to (standard output), (standard error), or other streams defined as `FILE *stream` (files, for example). **Scanf(...)** provides a similar way to read formatted input from Linux.

♦ **termcap**—The TERMinal CAPabilities database is a set of terminal description entries in the ASCII file /etc/termcap. Here you can find information about how to display special characters, how to perform operations (delete, insert characters or lines, etc.) and how to initialize a terminal. The database is used, for example, by the editor vi. There are view library functions to read and use the terminal capabilities (termcap(3x)). With this database, programs can work with a variety of terminals with the same code. Using the termcap database and library functions provides only low-level access to the terminal. Changing attributes or colors, parameterized output, and optimization must be done by the programmer himself.

♦ **terminfo database**—The TERMinal INFOrmation database is based on the termcap database and also describes terminal capabilities, but on a higher level than termcap. Using terminfo, the program can easily change screen attributes, use special keys such as function keys and more. The database can be found in /usr/lib/terminfo/[A-z,0-9]*. Every file describes one terminal.

♦ **curses**—Terminfo is a good base to use for terminal handling in a program. The (BSD-) CURSES library gives you high-level access to the terminal and is based on the terminfo database. Curses allows you to open and manipulate windows on the screen, provides a complete set of input and output functions, and can alter video attributes in a terminal independent manner on more than 150 terminals. The curses library can be found in /usr/lib/libcurses.a. This is the BSD version of curses.

♦ **ncurses**—Ncurses is the next improvement. In version 1.8.6 it should be compatible with AT&T curses as defined in SYSVR4 and has some extensions such as color manipulation, special optimization for output, terminal-specific optimizations, and more. It has been tested on a lot of systems such as Sun OS, HP, and Linux. I recommend using ncurses instead of the others. On SYSV Unix systems (such as Sun's Solaris) there should exist a curses library with the same functionality as ncurses (actually the solaris curses has some more functions and mouse support).

In the following sections, I will describe how to use the different packages to access a terminal. With Linux we have the GNU-version of termcap and we can use ncurses instead of curses.

I/O Function In libc
Formatted Output

The **printf(...)** functions in provide formatted output and allow transformations of the arguments.

```
int fprintf(FILE *stream, const char *format, ...),
```

will transform the output (arguments to fill in . . .) and write it to `stream`. The format defined in `format` will be written, too. The function will return the number of written characters or a negative value on error.

`format` contains two kinds of objects:

1. normal characters for the output, and

2. information how to transform or format the arguments.

Format information must begin with % followed by values for the format followed by a character for the translation (to print % by itself use %%). Possible values for the format are:

Flags

```
The formatted argument will be printed on the left margin (default is the right
margin in the argument field).
+
```

Every number will be printed with a sign, e.g., +12 or -2.32.

```
Blank
```

When the first character is not a sign, a blank will be inserted.

```
0
```

For numeric transformation the field width will be filled up with 0's on the left side.

```
#
```

Alternate output depending on the transformation for the argument

+ For *o* the first number is a *0*.
+ For *x* or *X* *0x* or *0X* will be printed in front of the argument.
+ For *e*, *E*, *f*, or *F* the output has a decimal point.
+ For *g* or *G* zeroes on the end of the argument are printed.

```
A number for the minimal field width.
```

The transformed argument is printed in a field which is at least as big as the argument itself. With a number you can make the field width bigger. If the formatted argument is smaller, then the field width will be filled with zeroes or blanks.

```
A point to separate the field width and the precision.
A number for the precision.
```

Possible values for the transformation are in Table 8.1.

```
int printf(const char *format, ...)
```

Same as fprintf(stdout, ...).

```
int sprintf(char *s, const char *format, ...)
```

Same as **printf(...)**, except that the output will be written to the the character pointer s (with a following \0).

You must allocate enough memory for s.

```
vprintf(const char *format, va_list arg)
vfprintf(FILE *stream, const char *format, va_list arg)
vsprintf(char *s, const char *format, va_list arg)
```

The same as the functions above, only the argument list is set to `arg`.

Table 8.1   Libc - printf transformations

Formatted Input

Just as **printf(...)** is used for formatted output you can use **scanf(...)** for formatted input.

```
int fscanf(FILE *stream, const char *format, ...)
```

fscanf(...) reads from `stream` and will transform the input with the rules defined in `format`. The results will be placed in the arguments given by `...`(**Note:** the arguments **must** be pointer.) The read ends, when no more transformation rules are in `format`. **fscanf(...)** will return EOF when the first transformation reached the file end or some error occured. Otherwise it will return the number of transformed arguments.

`format` can include rules on how to format the input arguments (see Table 8.2 below). It can also include:

♦ Spaces or tabs, which are ignored.

♦ any normal character (except %). The characters must be in the input on the corresponding position.

♦ transformation rules, which assembled with a %, the optional character * (this will permit **fscanf(...)** to assign to an argument), an optional number, an optional character *h*, *l*, or *L* (this is for the length of the target) and the transformation character.

```
int scanf(const char *format, ...)
```

The same as fscanf(stdin,...).

```
int sscanf(char *str, const char *format, ...)
```

As **scanf(...)**, but the input comes from `str`.

Table 8.2   Libc - scanf transformations

The termcap Library

Introduction

The termcap library is an API to the termcap database which can be found in /etc/termcap/. The library functions allow the following actions:

◆ Get a description of the current terminal: **tgetent(...)**.

◆ Search the description for information: **tgetnum(...)**, **tgetflag(...)**, **tgetstr(...)**.

◆ Encode numeric parameters in a terminal specific form: **tparam(...)**, **tgoto(...)**.

◆ Compute and perform padding **tputs(...)**.

Programs using the termcap library must include .h and should be linked with:

Note
Note from publisher: No table available.

Termcap functions are terminal independent routines, but only give the programmer low level access to the terminal. For a higher level package, curses or ncurses should be used.

Find A Terminal Description

```
int tgetent(void *buffer, const char *termtype)
```

On the Linux operating system the current terminal name is contained in the environment variable TERM. So, `termtype` is the result of a call to (3).

For `buffer`, no memory has to be allocated when using the GNU version of termcap. This is what we can assume under Linux! Otherwise, you'll have to allocate 2,048 bytes. (Formerly, `buffer` only needed to be 1,024 bytes, but the size has doubled).

tgetent(...) returns 1 on success and 0 when the database is found but has no entry for TERM. Other errors will return different values.

The following example should explain how to use **tgetent(...)**:

Note
Note from publisher: No example available.

By default, termcap uses /etc/termcap/ as the database. If the environment variable TERMCAP is set, with $HOME/mytermcap for instance, all functions will use instead of /etc/termcap. With no leading slash in TERMCAP, the defined value is used as a name for a terminal.

Look At A Terminal Description

Every piece of information is called a capability, every capability is a two letter code, and every two letter code is followed by the value for the capability. Possible types are:

♦ **Numeric**: For instance *co* - number of columns

♦ **Boolean** or **Flag**: For instance *hc* - hardcopy terminal

♦ **String**: For instance *st* - set tab stop

Each capability is associated with a single value type. (*co* is always numeric, *hc* is always a flag and *st* is always a string). There are three different types of values, so there are also three functions to interrogate them. `char *name` is the two-letter code for the capability.

```
int tgetnum(char *name)
```

Get a capability value that is numeric, such as *co*. **tgetnum(...)** returns the numeric value if the capability is available, otherwise 1. (Note: the returned value is not negative.)

```
int tgetflag(char *name)
```

Get a capability value that is Boolean (or flag). Returns 1 if the flag is present, 0 otherwise.

```
char *tgetstr(char *name, char **area)
```

Get a capability value that is a string. Returns a pointer to the string or NULL if not present. In the GNU version, if `area` is NULL, termcap will allocate memory by itself. termcap will never refer to this pointer again, so don't forget to free `name` before leaving the program. This method is preferred, because you don't know how much space is needed for the pointer, so let termcap do this for you.

termcap Capabilities

Boolean Capabilities

5I	Printer will not echo on screen
am	Automatic margins, which means automatic line wrap
bs	Control+H (8 dec.) performs a backspace
bw	Backspace on left margin wraps to previous line and right margin
da	Display retained above screen
db	Display retained below screen
eo	A space erases all characters at cursor position
es	Escape sequences and special characters work in status line
gn	Generic device
hc	This is a hard-copy terminal
HC	The cursor is hard to see when not on bottom line

(continued)

Table *(Continued)*

Boolean Capabilities	
hs	Has a status line
hz	Hazeltine bug, the terminal cannot print tilde characters
in	Terminal inserts nulls, not spaces, to fill white space
km	Terminal has a meta key
mi	Cursor movement works in insert mode
ms	Cursor movement works in standout/underline mode
NP	No pad character
NR	ti does not reverse te
nx	No padding, must use XON/XOFF
os	Terminal can overstrike
ul	Terminal underlines although it can not overstrike
xb	Beehive glitch, F1 sends ESCAPE, F2 sends ^C
xn	Newline/wraparound glitch
xo	Terminal uses XON/XOFF protocol
xs	Text typed over standout text will be displayed in standout
xt	Teleray glitch, destructive tabs and odd standout mode

Numeric Capabilities

String Capabilities

Ncurses: Introduction

The following terminology will be used in this chapter:

♦ window: is an internal representation containing an image of a part of the screen. WIN-DOW is defined in curses.h.

♦ screen: is a window with the size of the entire screen (from the upper left to the lower right) and are screens.

♦ terminal: is a special screen with information about what the screen currently looks like.

♦ variables: the following variables and constants defined in curses.h

WINDOW *curscr: current screen	
WINDOW *stdscr: standard screen	
int LINES: lines on the terminal	
int COLS: columns on the terminal	
bool TRUE: true flag, 1	
bool FALSE: false flag, 0	
int ERR: error flag, -1	
int OK: ok flag, 0	

♦ functions: in the function description the arguments are of the following type:

win: WINDOW*
bf: bool
ch: chtype
str: char*
chstr: chtype*
fmt: char*
otherwise int

Usually a program using the ncurses library looks like this:

Note

Note from publisher: No image available.

Including ncurses.h. will define variables and types for ncurses, such as WINDOW and function prototypes. It automatically includes stdio.h, ncurses/unctrl.h, stdarg.h, and stddef.h.

initscr() is used to initialize the ncurses data structures and to read the proper terminfo file. Memory for and will be allocated. If an error occurs, initscr will return ERR, otherwise a pointer to will be returned. Additionally, the screen will be erased and will be initialized.

endwin() will clean up all allocated resources from ncurses and restore the tty modes to the status they had before calling **initscr()**. It must be called before any other function from the ncurses library and **endwin()** must be called before your program exits. When you want to do output to more than one terminal, you can use **newterm(...)** instead of **initscr()**.

Compile the program with:

Note

Note from publisher: Missing text.

In flags you can include anything you like (gcc(1)). Since the path for ncurses.h has changed you have to include the following line:

Note

Note from publisher: Missing line.

Otherwise, ncurses.h, nterm.h, termcap.h, and unctrl.h will not be found. Possible other flags for Linux are:

♦ 2 tells gcc to do some optimization

♦ *-ansi* is for ansi conformant c-code

- *-Wall* will print out all warnings
- *-m486* will use optimized code for an Intel 486 (the binary can be used on an Intel 386, too).

The ncurses library can be found in /usr/lib/. There are three versions of the ncurses library:

- **libncurses.a**—the normal ncurses library.
- **libdcurses.a**—ncurses for debugging.
- **libpcurses.a**—ncurses for profiling (since 1.8.6 libpcurses.a exists no longer?).
- **libcurses.a**—No fourth version, but the original BSD curses (in my Slackware 2.1.0 it is the bsd package).

The data structures for the screen are called *windows* as defined in ncurses.h. A window is something like a character array in memory which the programmer can manipulate without output to the terminal. The default window is with the size of the terminal. You can create other windows with **newwin(...)**.

To update the physical terminal optimally, ncurses has another window declared. This is an image of how the terminal actually looks and is an image of how the terminal should look. The output will be done when you call **refresh()**. Ncurses will then update and the physical terminal with the information in Linux. The library functions will use internal optimization for the update process so you can change different windows and then update the screen at once in the most optimal way.

With the ncurses functions you can manipulate the data structure window. Functions beginning with w allow you to specify a window, while others will usually affect Linux. Functions beginning with *mv* will move the cursor to the position y,x first.

A character has the type *chtype* which is *long unsigned int* to store additional information about it (attributes etc.).

Ncurses use the database. Normally the database is located in /lib/terminfo/ and ncurses will look there for local terminal definitions. If you want to test some other definitions for a terminal without changing the original terminfo, set the environment variable. Ncurses will check this variable and use the definitions stored there instead of /usr/lib/terminfo/.

Current ncurses version is 1.8.6 ().

Note

Note from publisher: Current is 4.2, ***www.gnu.ai.mit.edu/software/ncurses/ncurses.html****.*

At the end of this chapter you can find a table with an overview for the BSD-Curses, ncurses and the curses from Sun OS 5.4. Refer to it when you want to look for a specific function and where it is implemented.

Initializing

- `WINDOW *initscr()`—This is the first function usually called from a program using ncurses. In some cases it is useful to call **slk_init(int)**, **filter()**, **ripoffline(...)** or **use_env(bf)** before **initscr()**. When using multiple terminals (or perhaps testing capabilities), you can use **newterm(...)** instead of **initscr()**.

- **initscr()** will read the proper terminfo file and initialize the ncurses data structures, allocate memory for and and set and to the values the terminal has. It will return a pointer to or ERR when an error has occured. You don't need to initialize the pointer with:

- **initscr()** will do this for you. If the return value is ERR, your program should exit because no ncurses function will work:

- `SCREEN *newterm(char *type, FILE *outfd, FILE *infd)`

- For multiple terminal output call **newterm(...)** for every terminal you would access with ncurses instead of **initscr()**. `type` is the name of the terminal as contained in $TERM (ansi, xterm, vt100, for example), `outfd` is the output pointer and `infd` is the pointer used for input. Call **endwin()** for every terminal opened with **newterm(...)**.

- `SCREEN *set_term(SCREEN *new)`

- With **set_term(SCREEN)** you can switch the current terminal. All functions will affect the current terminal which is set with **set_term(SCREEN)**.

- `int endwin()`

- **endwin()** will do the cleanup, restore the terminal modes in the state they had before calling **initscr()**, and move the cursor to the lower left corner. Don't forget to close all opened windows before you call **endwin()** to exit your program.

- An additional call to **refresh()** after **endwin()** will restore the terminal to the status it had before calling **initscr()** (visual-mode) otherwise it will be cleared (nonvisual-mode).

- `int isendwin()`

- Returns TRUE if **endwin()** was called with a following **refresh()**, otherwise FALSE.

- `void delscreen(SCREEN* sp)`

- After **endwin()** call **delscreen(SCREEN)** to free up all occupied resources, when SCREEN is no longer needed. (**Note:** not implemented yet.)

Windows

Windows can be created, deleted, moved, copied, touched, duplicated, and more.

- `WINDOW *newwin(nlines, ncols, begy, begx)`

- `begy` and `begx` are the window coordinates of the upper left corner. `nlines` is an integer with the number of lines and `ncols` is an integer with the number of columns.

Figure 8.1
Ncurses—scheme for newwin.

Note

Note from publisher: Figure missing.

The upper left corner of our window is in line 10 and column 10 and the window has 10 lines and 60 columns. If `nlines` is zero, the window will have *LINES-begy* rows. In the same way the, window will have *COLS-begx* columns when `ncols` is zero.

When you call **newwin(...)** with all argument zero:

the opened window will have the size of the screen.

With and we can open windows in the middle of the screen, whatever dimension it has:

This will open a window with 22 lines and 70 rows in the middle of the screen. Check the screen size before opening windows. In the Linux console we have 25 or more lines and 80 or more columns, but in xterms this may not be the case (they're resizable).

Alternatively, use and to adapt two windows to the screen size:

See .c in the example directory for more explanations.

♦ `int delwin(win)`

♦ Delete the window `win`. When there are subwindows delete them before `win`. It will free up all resources occupied by `win`. Delete all windows you have opened before calling **endwin()**.

♦ `int mvwin(win, by, bx)`

♦ Will move a window to the coordinates `by,bx`. If this means moving the window beyond the edges of the screen, nothing is done, and ERR is returned.

♦ `WINDOW *subwin(origwin, nlines, ncols, begy, begx)`

♦ Returns a subwindow in the middle of `origwin`. When you change one of the two windows (`origwin` or the new one) this change will be reflected in both windows. Call **touchwin(origwin)** before the next **refresh()**.

♦ `begx` and `begy` are relative to the screen, not to `origwin`.

♦ `WINDOW *derwin(origwin, nlines, ncols, begy, begx)`

♦ The same as **subwin(...)** except that `begx` and `begy` are relative to the window `origwin` than to the screen.

♦ `int mvderwin(win, y, x)`

♦ Will move `win` inside its parent window. (**Note:** not implemented yet.)

♦ `WINDOW *dupwin(win)`

- ◆ Duplicate the window `win`.
- ◆ `int syncok(win, bf)`
- ◆ `void wsyncup(win)`
- ◆ `void wcursyncup(win)`
- ◆ `void wsyncdown(win)` (Note: not implemented yet.)
- ◆ `int overlay(win1, win2)`
- ◆ `int overwrite(win1, win2)`
- ◆ **overlay(...)** will copy all text from `win1` to `win2` without copying blanks. **overwrite(...)** does the same, but copies blanks, too.
- ◆ `int copywin(win1, win2, sminrow, smincol, dminrow, dmincol, dmaxrow, dmaxcol, overlay)`
- ◆ Similar to **overlay(...)** and **overwrite(...)**, but provides control over what region of the window to copy.

Output

- ◆ `int addch(ch)`
- ◆ `int waddch(win, ch)`
- ◆ `int mvaddch(y, x, ch)`
- ◆ `int mvwaddch(win, y, x, ch)`
- ◆ These functions are used for character output to a window. They will manipulate the window and you will have to call **refresh()** to put it on screen. **addch(...)** and **waddch(...)** put the character `ch` in the window or `win`. **mvaddch(...)** and **mvwaddch(...)** do the same except that they move the cursor to position y,x first.
- ◆ `int addstr(str)`
- ◆ `int addnstr(str, n)`
- ◆ `int waddstr(win, str)`
- ◆ `int waddnstr(win, str, n)`
- ◆ `int mvaddstr(y, x, str)`
- ◆ `int mvaddnstr(y, x, str, n)`
- ◆ `int mvwaddstr(win, y, x, str)`
- ◆ `int mvwaddnstr(win, y, x, str, n)`
- ◆ These functions write a string to a window and are equivalent to series of calls to **addch(...)**. `str` is a null terminated string (*"blafoo\0"*). Functions with *w* write the string `str` to

the window `win`, while other funcions write to. Functions with `n` write n characters of `str`. If n is -1, the entire string `str` is written.

- ◆ `int addchstr(chstr)`
- ◆ `int addchnstr(chstr, n)`
- ◆ `int waddchstr(win, chstr)`
- ◆ `int waddchnstr(win, chstr, n)`
- ◆ `int mvaddchstr(y, x, chstr)`
- ◆ `int mvaddchnstr(y, x, chstr, n)`
- ◆ `int mvwaddchstr(win, y, x, chstr)`
- ◆ `int mvwaddchnstr(win, y, x, chstr, n)`
- ◆ These functions copy `chstr` to the window image (or `win`). The starting position is the current cursor position. Functions with `n` write n characters of `chstr`. If n is -1, the entire string `chstr` is written. The cursor is not moved and no control character check is done. These functions are faster than the **addstr(...)** routines. `chstr` is a pointer to an array of chtype.
- ◆ `int echochar(ch)`
- ◆ `int wechochar(win, ch)`
- ◆ The same as call **addch(...)** (**waddch(...)** followed by **refresh()** (**wrefresh(win)**.

Formatted Output

```
int printw(fmt, ...)
```

```
int wprintw(win, fmt, ...)
```

```
int mvprintw(y, x, fmt, ...)
```

```
int mvwprintw(win, y, x, fmt, ...)
```

```
int vwprintw(win, fmt, va_list)
```

These functions correspond to **printf(...)** and its counterparts from Linux.

In the package **printf(...)** is used for formatted output. You can define an output string and include variables of different types in it.

For the use of **vwprintw(...)** you have to include also .h.

Insert Characters/Lines

```
int insch(c)
```

```
int winsch(win, c)
```

```
int mvinsch(y,x,c)
```

```
int mvwinsch(win,y,x,c)
```

Character ch is inserted to the left of the cursor and all characters are moved one position to the right. The character on the right end of the line may be lost).

```
int insertln()
```

```
int winsertln(win)
```

Insert a blank line above the current one. (The bottom line will be lost.)

```
int insdelln(n)
```

```
int winsdelln(win, n)
```

For positive n, these functions will insert n lines above the cursor in the appropriate window (so the n bottom lines will be lost). When n is negative, n lines under the cursor will be deleted and the rest will moved up.

```
int insstr(str)
```

```
int insnstr(str, n)
```

```
int winsstr(win, str)
```

```
int winsnstr(win, str, n)
```

```
int mvinsstr(y, x, str)
```

```
int mvinsnstr(y, x, str, n)
int mvwinsstr(win, y, x, str)
int mvwinsnstr(win, y, x, str, n)
```

These functions will insert str in the current line left from the cursor (as many characters as fit to the line). The characters on the right of the cursor are moved right and will be lost when the end of the line is reached. The cursor position is not changed.

y and x are the coordinates to which the cursor is moved before str will be inserted, n is the number of characters to insert (with n=0 the entire string is inserted).

Delete Characters/Lines

```
int delch()
```

```
int wdelch(win)
```

```
int mvdelch(y, x)
```

```
int mvwdelch(win, y, x)
```

Delete the character under the cursor and move the remaining characters to the right of the cursor one position to the left.

y and x are the coordinates to which the cursor will be moved to before deleting.

```
int deleteln()
```

```
int wdeleteln(win)
```

Delete the line under the cursor and move all other lines below one position up. Additionally, the bottom line of the window will be erased.

Boxes And Lines

```
int border(ls, rs, ts, bs, tl, tr, bl, br)
```

```
int wborder(win, ls, rs, ts, bs, tl, tr, bl, br)
```

```
int box(win, vert, hor)
```

Draw a border around the edges of a window (or win). In the following table you see the characters and their default values when zero in a call to **box(...)**. In the picture you can see the position from the characters in a box.

Table 8.3   Ncurses: border characters.

Figure 8.2
Ncurses: box characters.

Note

Note from publisher: Table and figure missing.

```
int vline(ch, n)
```

```
int wvline(win, ch, n)
```

```
int hline(ch, n)
```

```
int whline(win, ch, n)
```

These functions draw a vertical or horizontal line starting at the current cursor position. `ch` is the character to use and `n` is the number of characters to draw. The cursor position is not advanced.

Background Character

```
void bkgdset(ch)
```

```
void wbkgdset(win, ch)
```

Set the background character and attribute for the screen or a window. The attribute in `ch` will be OR'd with every nonblank character in the window. The background is then part of the window and will not be changed with scrolling and in- or output.

```
int bkgd(ch)
int wbkgd(win, ch)
```

Will change the background character and attribute to `ch`.

Input

```
int getch()
```

```
int wgetch(win)
```

```
int mvgetch(y, x)
```

```
int mvwgetch(win, y, x)
```

getch() will read input from the terminal in a manner depending on whether delay mode is set or not. If delay is on, **getch()** will wait until a key is pressed, otherwise it will return the key in the input buffer or ERR if this buffer is empty. **mvgetch(...)** and **mvwgetch(...)** will move the cursor to position y , x first. The w functions read input from the terminal related to the window win, **getch()** and **mvgetch(...)** from the terminal related to.

With **keypad(...)** enabled, **getch()** will return a code defined in .h as KEY_* macros when a function key is pressed. When escape is pressed (which can be the beginning of a function key) ncurses will start a one-second timer. If the remainder of the keystroke is not finished in this second, the key is returned. Otherwise, the function key value is returned. (If necessary, use **notimeout()** to disable the second timer.)

```
int ungetch(ch)
```

Will put the character ch back to the input buffer.

```
int getstr(str)
int wgetstr(win, str)
int mvgetstr(y, x, str)
int mvwgetstr(win, y, x, str)
int wgetnstr(win, str, n)
```

These functions will do a series of calls to **getch()** until a newline is received. The characters are placed in str (so don't forget to allocate memory for your character pointer before calling **getstr(...)**). If echo is enabled the string is echoed (use **noecho()** to disable echo) and the user's kill and delete characters will be interpreted.

```
chtype inch()

chtype winch(win)
chtype mvinch(y, x)
chtype mvwinch(win, y, x)
```

These functions return a character from the screen or window. Because the type of the return value is chtype attribute information is included. This information can be extracted from the character using the A_* constants.

```
int instr(str)
int innstr(str, n)
int winstr(win, str)
int winnstr(win, str, n)
int mvinstr(y, x, str)
int mvinnstr(y, x, str, n)
int mvwinstr(win, y, x, str)
int mvwinnstr(win, y, x, str, n)
```

Return a character string from the screen or a window. (**Note:** not implemented yet.)

```
int inchstr(chstr)
int inchnstr(chstr, n)
int winchstr(win, chstr)
int winchnstr(win, chstr, n)
int mvinchstr(y, x, chstr)
int mvinchnstr(y, x, chstr, n)
int mvwinchstr(win, y, x, chstr)
int mvwinchnstr(win, y, x, chstr, n)
```

Return a chtype string from the screen or window. In the string, attribute information is included for every character. (**Note:** not implemented yet, lib_inchstr not included in the ncurses lib.)

Formatted Input

```
int scanw(fmt, ...)
int wscanw(win, fmt, ...)
int mvscanw(y, x, fmt, ...)
int mvwscanw(win, y, x, fmt, ...)
int vwscanw(win, fmt, va_list)
```

These are similar to **scanf(...)**. **wgetstr(...)** is called and the results will be used as input for the scan.

Options
Output Options

```
int idlok(win, bf)
void idcok(win, bf)
```

Enable or disable terminal's insert/delete features for the window (**idlok(...)** for lines and **idcok(...)** for characters). (**Note: idcok(...)** not implemented yet.)

```
void immedok(win, bf)
```

If set TRUE, every change to the window `win` will cause a refresh to the physical screen. This can decrease the performance of a program, so the default value is FALSE. (**Note:** not implemented yet.)

```
int clearok(win, bf)
```

If `bf` is TRUE the next call to **wrefresh(win)** will clear the screen and redraw it completely. (as in the editor vi when you press Ctrl+L).

```
int leaveok(win, bf)
```

The default behavior is for ncurses to leave the physical cursor in the same place it was on the last refresh of the window. Programs which don't use the cursor can set **leaveok(...)** TRUE and save the time normally required for cursor motion. In addition, ncurses will try to make the terminal cursor invisible.

```
int nl()
int nonl()
```

Control the translation for newline. Turned on with **nl()** will translate a newline in carriage return and line feed on output. **nonl()** will turn translation off. With disabled translation ncurses can do faster cursor motion.

Input Options

```
int keypad(win, bf)
```

If TRUE, it enables the keypad on the keyboard of the user's terminal when waiting for input. ncurses will then return a key code defined in .h as KEY_* for the function and arrow keys on the keypad. This is very useful for a PC keyboard because you can enable the numerical block and the cursor keys.

```
int meta(win, bf)
```

If TRUE, the key codes returned from **getch()** are 8-bit-clean (the highest bit will not be stripped).

```
int cbreak()
int nocbreak()
int crmode()
int nocrmode()
```

cbreak() and **nocbreak()** will turn the terminal CBREAK mode on or off. When CBREAK is on, input from a read will be immediately available to the program, when off the input will be buffered until newline occurs. (**Note: crmode()** and **nocrmode()** are for upward compatibility, don't use them.)

```
int raw()
int noraw()
```

Turn RAW mode on or off. RAW is the same as CBREAK, except that in RAW mode no special character processing will be done.

```
int echo()
int noecho()
```

Set **echo()** to echo input typed by the user and **noecho()** to be silent about it.

```
int halfdelay(t)
```

As **cbreak()** with a delay of **t** seconds.

```
int nodelay(win, bf)
```

Terminal will be set to no blocking mode. **cetch()** will return ERR if no input is ready. If set to FALSE, **getch()** will wait until a key is pressed.

```
int timeout(t)
int wtimeout(win, t)
```

It is recommended to use these functions instead of **halfdelay(t)** and **nodelay(win,bf)**. The result of **getch()** depends on the value of **t**. If **t** is positive, the read is blocked for **t** milliseconds, if **t** is zero, no blocking is done, and when **t** is negative the program blocks until input is available.

```
int notimeout(win, bf)
```

If **bf** is TRUE, **getch()** will use a special timer (of one second length) to interpret and input sequence beginning with keys as ESCAPE etc.

```
int typeahead(fd)
```

If **fd** is -1 no typeahead check will be done, else ncurses will use the file descriptor **fd** instead of for these checks.

```
int intrflush(win, bf)
```

When enabled with **bf** TRUE an interrupt key pressed on the terminal (quit, break ...) will flush all output in the tty driver queue.

```
void noqiflush()
void qiflush()
```

(**Note:** not implemented yet.)

Terminal Attributes

```
int baudrate()
```

Returns the terminal speed in bps.

```
char erasechar()
```

Returns the current erase character.

```
char killchar()
```

Returns the current kill character.

```
int has_ic()
int has_il()
```

has_ic() returns TRUE if the terminal has insert/delete character capability, **has_il()** returns TRUE when the terminal has insert/delete line capability. Otherwise the functions return ERR. (**Note:** not implemented yet.)

```
char *longname()
```

The returned pointer gives access to the description of the current terminal.

```
chtype termattrs()
```

(**Note:** not implemented yet.)

```
char *termname()
```

Returns the contents of TERM from the users environment. (**Note:** not implemented yet.)

Use Options

Now we have seen the window options and terminal modes it is time to describe their use.

First, on Linux you should enable the keypad. This will allow use of the cursor keys and the numeric block on the PC keyboard.

Now, there are two main types of input.

1. The program wants the user to enter a key and then will call a function depend on this key. (For example, something like "press 'q' for quit" and wait for *q*)

2. The program wants a string of characters typed by the user in a mask on the screen. For example: a directory or an address in a database.

For the first we use the following options and modes and the while loop will work correctly.

The program will hang until a key is pressed. If the key was *q* we call our quit function else we wait for other input.

The switch statement can be expanded until we have an input function that fits our wishes. Use the KEY_* macros to check special keys, for instance for the cursor keys on the keyboard. For a file viewer the loop can look like this:

For the second, we only need to set **echo()** and the characters typed by the user will be printed to the screen. To have the characters printed on the position you want, use **move(...)** or **wmove(...)**.

Or, we could open a window with a mask in it (some other colors than those of the window will do this) and ask the user to input a string:

Note
Note from publisher: Example missing.

See .c in the example directory for more explanation.

Updating The Terminal

As written in the overview, ncurses windows are images in memory. This means that any change to a window is not printed to the physical screen until a refresh is done. This optimizes the output to the screen because you can do a lot of manipulations and then, once, call refresh to print it to screen. Otherwise, every change would be printed to the terminal and decrease the performance of your programs.

```
int refresh()
int wrefresh(win)
```

refresh() copies to the terminal and **wrefresh(win)** copies the window image to and then makes looks like.

```
int wnoutrefresh(win)
int doupdate()
```

wnoutrefresh(win) copies the window **win** to only. This means that no output to the terminal is done but the virtual screen actually looks like the programmer wanted. **doupdate()**

will do the output to the terminal. A program can change various windows, call **wnoutrefresh(win)** for every window and then call **doupdate()** to update the physical screen only once.

For instance, we have the following program with two windows. We change both windows by altering some lines of text. We can write *changewin(win)* with **wrefresh(win)**.

This will cause ncurses to update the terminal twice and slow down our execution. With **doupdate()** we change *changewin(win)* and our main function and will get better a performance.

```
int redrawwin(win)
int wredrawln(win, bline, nlines)
```

Use these functions when some lines or the entire screen should thrown away before writing anything new in it (may be when the lines are trashed or so).

```
int touchwin(win)
int touchline(win, start, count)
int wtouchln(win, y, n, changed)
int untouchwin(win)
```

Tells ncurses that the whole window `win` or the lines from `start` up to `start+count` have been manipulated. For instance, when you have some overlapping windows (as in the example .c) a change to one window will not affect the image from the other.

wtouchln(...) will touch n lines starting at `y`. If `change` is TRUE the lines are touched, otherwise untouched (changed or unchanged).

untouchwin(win) will mark the window `win` as unchanged since the last call to **refresh()**.

```
int is_linetouched(win, line)
int is_wintouched(win)
```

With these functions you can check if the line `line` or the window `win` has been touched since the last call to **refresh()**.

Video Attributes And Color

Attributes are special terminal capabilities used when printing characters to the screen. Characters can be printed bold, underlined, blinking, and so on. In ncurses you have the ability to turn attributes on or off to get better looking output. Possible attributes are listed in the following table.

Table 8.4   Ncurses: attributes.

Note
Note from publisher: Table missing.

Ncurses defines eight colors you can use on a terminal with color support. First, initialize the color data structures with **start_color()**, then check the terminal capabilities with **has_colors()**. **start_color()** will initialize *COLORS*, the maximum colors the terminal supports, and *COLOR_PAIR*, the maximum number of color pairs you can define.

Table 8.5   Ncurses: colors.

Note
Note from publisher: Table missing.

The attributes can be combined with the OR operator '   COLORPAIRS-1 COLORS-1.

Note
Note from publisher: Code missing.

```
int color_content(color, r, g, b)
```

Get the color components r, g, and b for color.

And how to combine attributes and colors? Some terminals, as the console in Linux, have colors and some not (xterm, vs100, and so on). The following code should solve the problem:

Note
Note from publisher: Code missing.

First, the function *CheckColor* initializes the colors with **start_color()**, then the function **has_colors()** will return TRUE if the current terminal has colors. We check this and call **init_pair(…)** to combine foreground and background colors and **wattrset(…)** to set these pairs for the specified window. Alternatively, we can use **wattrset(…)** alone to set attributes if we have a black and white terminal.

To get colors in an xterm the best way I found out is to use the ansi_xterm with the patched terminfo entries from the Midnight Commander. Just get the sources of ansi_xterm and Midnight Commander (mc-x.x.tar.gz). Then compile the ansi_xterm and use tic with xterm.ti and vt100.ti from the mc-x.x.tar.gz archive. Execute ansi_xterm and test it out.

Cursor And Window Coordinates

```
int move(y, x)
int wmove(win, y, x)
```

move() moves the cursor from , **wmove(win)** the cursor from window `win`. For input/output functions, additional macros are defined which move the cursor before the specified function is called.

```
int curs_set(bf)
```

This will turn the cursor visibility on or off, if the terminal has this capability.

```
void getyx(win, y, x)
```

getyx(...) will return the current cursor position. (**Note:** this is a macro.)

```
void getparyx(win, y, x)
```

When `win` is a sub window, **getparyx(...)** will store the window coordinates relative to the parent window in `y` and `x`. Otherwise `y` and `x` are -1. (**Note:** not implemented yet.)

```
void getbegyx(win, y, x)
void getmaxyx(win, y, x)
int getmaxx(win)
int getmaxy(win)
```

Store the begin and size coordinates for `win` in `y` and `x`.

```
int getsyx(int y, int x)
int setsyx(int y, int x)
```

Store the virtual screen cursor in `y` and `x` or set this cursor. When `y` and `x` are -1 and you call **getsyx(...)** *leaveok* will be set.

Scrolling

```
int scrollok(win, bf)
```

If TRUE, the text in the window `win` will be scrolled up one line when the cursor is on the lower right corner and a character is typed (or newline). If FALSE, the cursor is left in the same position.

When turned on the contents of a window can be scrolled with the following functions. (**Note:** It would be also scrolled, if you print a new line in the last line of the window. So, be careful with **scrollok(...)** or you will get unreasonable results.)

```
int scroll(win)
```

This function will scroll up the window (and the lines in the data structure) one line.

```
int scrl(n)
int wscrl(win, n)
```

These functions will scroll the window or `win` up or down depending on the value of the integer `n`. If `n` is positive the window will be scrolled up `n` lines, otherwise if `n` is negative the window will be scrolled down `n` lines.

```
int setscrreg(t, b)
int wsetscrreg(win, t, b)
```

Set a software scrolling region.

The following code should explain how to get the effect of scrolling a text on the screen. Look also in .c in the example directory.

Note

Note from publisher: Code missing.

We have a window with 18 lines and 66 columns and want to scroll a text in it. *S[]* is a character array with the text. *Max_s* is the number of the last line in *s[]*. *Clear_line* will print blank characters from the current cursor position up to the end of the line using the current attributes from the window (not A_NORMAL as clrtoeol does). *Beg* is the last line from *s[]* currently shown on the screen. *Scroll* is an enumerate to tell the function what to do, show the NEXT or PREVious line from the text.

Pads

```
WINDOW *newpad(nlines, ncols)
WINDOW *subpad(orig, nlines, ncols, begy, begx)
int prefresh(pad, pminrow, pmincol, sminrow, smincol, smaxrow, smaxcol)
int pnoutrefresh(pad, pminrow, pmincol, sminrow, smincol, smaxrow, smaxcol)
int pechochar(pad, ch)
```

Soft-Labels

```
int slk_init(int fmt)
int slk_set(int labnum, char *label, int fmt)
int slk_refresh()
int slk_noutrefresh()
char *slk_label(int labnum)
int slk_clear()
int slk_restore()
int slk_touch()
int slk_attron(chtype attr)
int slk_attrset(chtype attr)
int slk_attroff(chtype attr)
```

These functions correspond to **attron(attr)**, **attrset(attr)**, and **attroff(attr)**. Not implemented yet.

Miscellaneous

```
int beep()
int flash()
char *unctrl(chtype c)
char *keyname(int c)
int filter()
```

(**Note:** not implemented yet.)

```
void use_env(bf)
int putwin(WINDOW *win, FILE *filep)
```

(**Note:** not implemented yet.)

```
WINDOW *getwin(FILE *filep)
```

(**Note:** not implemented yet.)

```
int delay_output(int ms)
int flushinp()
```

Low-Level Access

```
int def_prog_mode()
int def_shell_mode()
int reset_prog_mode()
int reset_shell_mode()
int resetty()
int savetty()
int ripoffline(int line, int (*init)(WINDOW *, int))
int napms(int ms)
```

Screen Dump

```
int scr_dump(char *filename)
```

(**Note:** not implemented yet.)

```
int scr_restore(char *filename)
```

(**Note:** not implemented yet.)

```
int scr_init(char *filename)
```

(**Note:** not implemented yet.)

```
int scr_set(char *filename)
```

(**Note:** not implemented yet.)

Termcap Emulation

```
int tgetent(char *bp, char *name)
int tgetflag(char id[2])
int tgetnum(char id[2])
char *tgetstr(char id[2], char **area)
char *tgoto(char *cap, int col, int row)
int tputs(char *str, int affcnt, int (*putc)())
```

Terminfo Functions

```
int setupterm(char *term, int fildes, int *errret)
int setterm(char *term)
int set_curterm(TERMINAL *nterm)
int del_curterm(TERMINAL *oterm)
int restartterm(char *term, int fildes, int *errret)
```

(**Note:** not implemented yet.)

```
char *tparm(char *str, p1, p2, p3, p4, p5, p6, p7, p8, p9)
p1 - p9 long int.
int tputs(char *str, int affcnt, int (*putc)(char))
int putp(char *str)
int vidputs(chtype attr, int (*putc)(char))
int vidattr(chtype attr)
int mvcur(int oldrow, int oldcol, int newrow, int newcol)
int tigetflag(char *capname)
int tigetnum(char *capname)
int tigetstr(char *capname)
```

Debug Function

- ◆ `void _init_trace()`
- ◆ `void _tracef(char *, ...)`
- ◆ `char *_traceattr(mode)`
- ◆ `void traceon()`
- ◆ `void traceoff()`

Terminfo Capabilities
Boolean Capabilities

Variable	Cap. Name	Int. Code	Description
auto_left_margin	bw	bw	cub1 wraps from column 0 to last column
auto_right_margin	am	am	Terminal has automatic margins
back_color_erase	bce	ut	screen erased with background color
can_change	ccc	cc	terminal can redefine exiting colors

(continued)

Table   Boolean Capabilities *(Continued)*

Variable	Cap. Name	Int. Code	Description
ceol_standout_glitch	xhp	xs	Standout not erased by overwriting (hp)
col_addr_glitch	xhpa	YA	only positive motion for hpa/mhpa caps
cpi_changes_res	cpix	YF	changing character pitch changes resolution
cr_cancels_micro_mode	crxm	YB	using cr turns off micro mode
eat_newline_glitch	xenl	xn	newline ignored after 80 cols (Concept)
erase_overstrike	eo	eo	Can erase overstrikes with a blank
generic_type	gn	gn	Generic line type (e.g., dialup, switch).
hard_copy	hc	hc	Hardcopy terminal
hard_cursor	chts	HC	cursor is hard to see
has_meta_key	km	km	Has a meta key (shift, sets parity bit)
has_print_wheel	daisy	YC	printer needs operator to change character set
has_status_line	hs	hs	Has extra "status line"
hue_lightness_saturation	hls	hl	terminal uses only HLS color notation (Tektronix)
insert_null_glitch	in	in	Insert mode distinguishes nulls
lpi_changes_res	lpix	YG	changing line pitch changes resolution
memory_above	da	da	Display may be retained above the screen
memory_below	db	db	Display may be retained below the screen
move_insert_mode	mir	mi	Safe to move while in insert mode
move_standout_mode	msgr	ms	Safe to move in standout modes
needs_xon_xoff	nxon	nx	padding won't work, xon/xoff required
no_esc_ctl_c	xsb	xb	Beehive (F1=escape, F2=ctrl C)
non_rev_rmcup	nrrmc	NR	smcup does not reverse rmcup
no_pad_char	npc	NP	pad character does not exist
non_dest_scroll_region	ndscr	ND	scrolling region is nondestructive
over_strike	os	os	Terminal overstrikes
prtr_silent	mc5i	5i	printer won't echo on screen
row_addr_glitch	xvpa	YD	only positive motion for vhp/mvpa caps
semi_auto_right_margin	sam	YE	printing in last column causes cr
status_line_esc_ok	eslok	es	Escape can be used on the status line
dest_tabs_magic_smso	xt	xt	Tabs ruin, magic so char (Teleray 1061)
tilde_glitch	hz	hz	Hazel-tine; can not print ~'s
transparent_underline	ul	ul	underline character overstrikes
xon_xoff	xon	xo	Terminal uses xon/xoff handshaking

Numbers

Variable	Cap. Name	Int. Code	Description
bit_image_entwining	bitwin	Yo	Undocumented in SYSV
buffer_capacity	bufsz	Ya	numbers of bytes buffered before printing
columns	cols	co	Number of columns in a line
dot_vert_spacing	spinv	Yb	spacing of dots horizontally in dots per inch
dot_horz_spacing	spinh	Yc	spacing of pins vertically in pins per inch
init_tabs	it	it	Tabs initially every # spaces
label_height	lh	lh	rows in each label
label_width	lw	lw	columns in each label
lines	lines	li	Number of lines on screen or page
lines_of_memory	lm	lm	Lines of memory if > lines. 0 means varies
magic_cookie_glitch	xmc	sg	Number of blank chars left by smso or rmso
max_colors	colors	Co	maximum numbers of colors on screen
max_micro_address	maddr	Yd	maximum value in micro_..._address
max_micro_jump	mjump	Ye	maximum value in parm_..._micro
max_pairs	pairs	pa	maximum number of color-pairs on the screen
micro_col_size	mcs	Yf	Character step size when in micro mode
micro_line_size	mls	Yg	Line step size when in micro mode
no_color_video	ncv	NC	video attributes that can't be used with colors
number_of_pins	npins	Yh	numbers of pins in print-head
num_labels	nlab	Nl	number of labels on screen
output_res_char	orc	Yi	horizontal resolution in units per line
output_res_line	orl	Yj	vertical resolution in units per line
output_res_horz_inch	orhi	Yk	horizontal resolution in units per inch
output_res_vert_inch	orvi	Yl	vertical resolution in units per inch
padding_baud_rate	pb	pb	Lowest baud where cr/nl padding is needed
virtual_terminal	vt	vt	Virtual terminal number (Unix system)
width_status_line	wsl	ws	No. columns in status line

(The following numeric capabilities are present in the SYSV term structure, but are not yet documented in the man page. Comments are from the term structure header.)

bit_image_type	bitype	Yp	Type of bit-image device
buttons	btns	BT	Number of mouse buttons
max_attributes	ma	ma	Max combined attributes terminal can handle
maximum_windows	wnum	MW	Max number of definable windows
print_rate	cps	Ym	Print rate in chars per second
wide_char_size	widcs	Yn	Char step size in double wide mode

Strings

Variable	Cap. Name	Int. Code	Description
acs_chars	acsc	ac	Graphics charset pairs - def=vt100
alt_scancode_esc is VT100)	scesa	S8	Alternate esc for scancode emulation (default
back_tab	cbt	bt	Back tab (P)
bell	bel	bl	Audible signal (bell) (P)
bit_image_repeat	birep	Xy	Repeat bit image cell #1 #2 times (use tparm)
bit_image_newline	binel	Zz	Move to next row of the bit image (use tparm)
bit_image_carriage_return	bicr	Yv	Move to beginning of same row (use tparm)
carriage_return	cr	cr	Carriage return (P*)
change_char_pitch	cpi	ZA	Change # chars per inch
change_line_pitch	lpi	ZB	Change # lines per inch
change_res_horz	chr	ZC	Change horizontal resolution
change_res_vert	cvr	ZD	Change vertical resolution
change_scroll_region	csr	cs	Change to lines #1 through #2 (VT100) (PG)
char_padding	rmp	rP	Like ip but when in insert mode
char_set_names	csnm	Zy	List of character set names
clear_all_tabs	tbc	ct	Clear all tab stops (P)
clear_margins	mgc	MC	Clear all margins (top, bottom, and sides)
clear_screen	clear	cl	Clear screen and home cursor (P*)
clr_bol	el1	cb	Clear to beginning of line
clr_eol	el	ce	Clear to end of line (P)
clr_eos	ed	cd	Clear to end of display (P*)
code_set_init	csin	ci	Init sequence for multiple code sets
color_names	colornm	Yw	Give name for color #1
column_address	hpa	ch	Set cursor column (PG)
command_character	cmdch	CC	Term. settable cmd char in prototype
cursor_address	cup	cm	Screen rel. cursor motion row #1 col #2 (PG)
cursor_down	cud1	do	Down one line
cursor_home	home	ho	Home cursor (if no cup)
cursor_invisible	civis	vi	Make cursor invisible
cursor_left	cub1	le	Move cursor left one space
cursor_mem_address	mrcup	CM	Memory relative cursor addressing
cursor_normal	cnorm	ve	Make cursor appear normal (undo vs/vi)
cursor_right	cuf1	nd	Nondestructive space (cursor right)
cursor_to_ll	ll	ll	Last line, first column (if no cup)
cursor_up	cuu1	up	Upline (cursor up)
cursor_visible	cvvis	vs	Make cursor very visible
define_bit_image_region	defbi	Yx	Define rectangular bit image region (use tparm)
define_char	defc	ZE	Define character in a character set
delete_character	dch1	dc	Delete character (P*)

(continued)

Table Strings *(Continued)*

Variable	Cap. Name	Int. Code	Description
delete_line	dl1	dl	Delete line (P*)
device_type	devt	dv	Indicate language/codeset support
dis_status_line	dsl	ds	Disable status line
display_pc_char	dispc	S1	Display PC character
down_half_line	hd	hd	Half-line down (forward 1/2 linefeed)
ena_acs	enacs	eA	enable alternate char set
end_bit_image_region	endbi	Yy	End bit image region (use tparm)
enter_alt_charset_mode	smacs	as	Start alternate character set (P)
enter_am_mode	smam	SA	turn on automatic margins
enter_blink_modeblink	mb		Turn on blinking
enter_bold_mode	bold	md	Turn on bold (extra bright) mode
enter_ca_mode	smcup	ti	String to begin programs that use cup
enter_delete_mode	smdc	dm	Delete mode (enter)
enter_dim_mode	dim	mh	Turn on half-bright mode
enter_doublewide_mode	swidm	ZF	Enable double-wide mode
enter_draft_quality	sdrfq	ZG	Set draft-quality printing
enter_insert_mode	smir	im	Insert mode (enter);
enter_italics_mode	sitm	ZH	Enable italics mode
enter_leftward_mode	slm	ZI	Enable leftward carriage motion
enter_micro_mode	smicm	ZJ	Enable micro-motion capabilities
enter_near_letter_quality	snlq	ZK	Set NLQ printing
enter_normal_quality	snrmq	ZL	Set normal quality printing
enter_pc_charset_mode	smpch	S2	Enter PC character display mode
enter_protected_mode	prot	mp	Turn on protected mode
enter_reverse_mode	rev	mr	Turn on reverse video mode
enter_scancode_mode	smsc	S4	Enter PC scancode mode
enter_secure_mode	invis	mk	Turn on blank mode (chars invisible)
enter_shadow_mode	sshm	ZM	Enable shadow-mode printing
nter_standout_mode	smso	so	Begin stand out mode
enter_subscript_mode	ssubm	ZN	Enable subscript printing
enter_superscript_mode	ssupm	ZO	Enable superscript printing
enter_underline_mode	smul	us	Start underscore mode
enter_upward_mode	sum	ZP	Enable upward carriage motion
enter_xon_mode	smxon	SX	Turn on xon/xoff handshaking
erase_chars	ech	ec	Erase #1 characters (PG)
exit_alt_charset_mode	rmacs	ae	End alternate character set (P)
exit_am_mode	rmam	RA	Turn off automatic margins
exit_attribute_mode	sgr0	me	Turn off all attributes
exit_ca_mode	rmcup	te	String to end programs that use cup
exit_delete_mode	rmdc	ed	End delete mode
exit_doublewide_mode	rwidm	ZQ	Disable doublewide printing

(continued)

Table Strings *(Continued)*

Variable	Cap. Name	Int. Code	Description
exit_insert_mode	rmir	ei	End insert mode
exit_italics_mode	ritm	ZR	Disable italic printing
exit_leftward_mode	rlm	ZS	Enable rightward (normal) carriage motion
exit_micro_mode	rmicm	ZT	Disable micro motion capabilities
exit_pc_charset_mode	rmpch	S3	Disable PC character display
exit_scancode_mode	rmsc	S5	Disable PC scancode mode
exit_shadow_mode	rshm	ZU	Disable shadow printing
exit_standout_mode	rmso	se	End stand out mode
exit_subscript_mode	rsubm	ZV	Disable subscript printing
exit_superscript_mode	rsupm	ZW	Disable superscript printing
exit_underline_mode	rmul	ue	End underscore mode
exit_upward_mode	rum	ZX	Enable downward (normal) carriage motion
exit_xon_mode	rmxon	RX	turn off xon/xoff handshaking
flash_screen	flash	vb	Visible bell (may not move cursor)
form_feed	ff	ff	Hardcopy terminal page eject (P*)
from_status_line	fsl	fs	Return from status line
init_1string	is1	i1	Terminal initialization string
init_2string	is2	i2	Terminal initialization string
init_3string	is3	i3	Terminal initialization string
init_file	if	if	Name of file containing is
init_prog	iprog	iP	Path name of program for init
initialize_color	initc	Ic	Initialize the definition of color
initialize_pair	initp	Ip	Initialize color-pair
insert_character	ich1	ic	Insert character (P)
insert_line	il1	al	Add new blank line (P*)
insert_padding	ip	ip	Insert pad after character inserted (p*)
key_a1	ka1	K1	Upper left of keypad
key_a3	ka3	K3	Upper right of keypad
key_b2	kb2	K2	Center of keypad
key_backspace	kbs	kb	Sent by backspace key
key_beg	kbeg	1	begin key
key_btab	kcbt	kB	back-tab key
key_c1	kc1	K4	Lower left of keypad
key_c3	kc3	K5	Lower right of keypad
key_cancel	kcan	2	cancel key
key_catab	ktbc	ka	Sent by clear-all-tabs key
key_clear	kclr	kC	Sent by clear screen or erase key
key_close	kclo	3	close key
key_command	kcmd	4	command key
key_copy	kcpy	5	copy key

(continued)

Table   Strings *(Continued)*

Variable	Cap. Name	Int. Code	Description
key_create	kcrt	6	create key
key_ctab	kctab	kt	Sent by clear-tab key
key_dc	kdch1	kD	Sent by delete character key
key_dl	kdl1	kL	Sent by delete line key
key_down	kcud1	kd	Sent by terminal down arrow key
key_eic	krmir	kM	Sent by rmir or smir in insert mode
key_end	kend	7	end key
key_enter	kent	8	enter/send key
key_eol	kel	kE	Sent by clear-to-end-of-line key
key_eos	ked	kS	Sent by clear-to-end-of-screen key
key_exit	kext	9	exit key
key_find	kfnd	0	find key
key_help	khlp	%1	help key
key_home	khome	kh	Sent by home key
key_ic	kich1	kI	Sent by ins char/enter ins mode key
key_il	kil1	kA	Sent by insert line
key_left	kcub1	kl	Sent by terminal left arrow key
key_ll	kll	kH	Sent by home-down key
key_mark	kmrk	%2	mark key
key_message	kmsg	%3	message key
key_move	kmov	%4	move key
key_next	knxt	%5	next key
key_npage	knp	kN	Sent by next-page key
key_open	kopn	%6	open key
key_options	kopt	%7	options key
key_ppage	kpp	kP	Sent by previous-page key
key_previous	kprv	%8	previous key
key_print	kprt	%9	print key
key_redo	krdo	%0	redo key
key_reference	kref	&1	reference key
key_refresh	krfr	&2	refresh key
key_replace	krpl	&3	replace key
key_restart	krst	&4	restart key
key_resume	kres	&5	resume key
key_right	kcuf1	kr	Sent by terminal right arrow key
key_save	ksav	&6	save key
key_sbeg	kBEG	&9	shifted begin key
key_scancel	kCAN	&0	shifted cancel key
key_scommand	kCMD	*1	shifted command key
key_scopy	kCPY	*2	shifted copy key

(continued)

Table   Strings *(Continued)*

Variable	Cap. Name	Int. Code	Description
key_screate	kCRT	*3	shifted create key
key_sdc	kDC	*4	shifted delete char key
key_sdl	kDL	*5	shifted delete line key
key_select	kslt	*6	select key
key_send	kEND	*7	shifted end key
key_seol	kEOL	*8	shifted end of line key
key_sexit	kEXT	*9	shifted exit key
key_sf	kind	kF	Sent by scroll-forward/down key
key_sfind	kFND	*0	shifted find key
key_shelp	kHLP	#1	shifted help key
key_shome	kHOM	#2	shifted home key
key_sic	kIC	#3	shifted insert char key
key_sleft	kLFT	#4	shifted left key
key_smessage	kMSG	%a	shifted message key
key_smove	kMOV	%b	shifted move key
key_snext	kNXT	%c	shifted next key
key_soptions	kOPT	%d	shifted options key
key_sprevious	kPRV	%e	shifted previous key
key_sprint	kPRT	%f	shifted print key
key_sr	kri	kR	Sent by scroll-backward/up key
key_sredo	kRDO	%g	shifted redo key
key_sreplace	kRPL	%h	shifted replace key
key_sright	kRIT	%l	shifted right key
key_srsume	kRES	%j	shifted resume key
key_ssave	kSAV	!1	shifted save key
key_ssuspend	kSPD	!2	shifted suspend key
key_stab	khts	kT	Sent by set-tab key
key_sundo	kUND	!3	shifted undo key
key_suspend	kspd	&7	suspend key
key_undo	kund	&8	undo key
key_up	kcuu1	ku	Sent by terminal up arrow key
keypad_local	rmkx	ke	Out of "keypad transmit" mode
keypad_xmit	smkx	ks	Put terminal in "keypad transmit" mode
lab_f0	lf0	l0	Labels on function key f0 if not f0
lab_f1	lf1	l1	Labels on function key f1 if not f1
lab_f2	lf2	l2	Labels on function key f2 if not f2
lab_f3	lf3	l3	Labels on function key f3 if not f3
lab_f4	lf4	l4	Labels on function key f4 if not f4
lab_f5	lf5	l5	Labels on function key f5 if not f5
lab_f6	lf6	l6	Labels on function key f6 if not f6

(continued)

Table   Strings *(Continued)*

Variable	Cap. Name	Int. Code	Description
lab_f7	lf7	l7	Labels on function key f7 if not f7
lab_f8	lf8	l8	Labels on function key f8 if not f8
lab_f9	lf9	l9	Labels on function key f9 if not f9
lab_f10	lf10	la	Labels on function key f10 if not f10
label_on	smln	LO	turn on soft labels
label_off	rmln	LF	turn off soft labels
meta_off	rmm	mo	Turn off "meta mode"
meta_on	smm	mm	Turn on "meta mode" (8th bit)
micro_column_address	mhpa	ZY	Like column_address for micro adjustment
micro_down	mcud1	ZZ	Like cursor_down for micro adjustment
micro_left	mcub1	Za	Like cursor_left for micro adjustment
micro_right	mcuf1	Zb	Like cursor_right for micro adjustment
micro_row_address	mvpa	Zc	Like row_address for micro adjustment
micro_up	mcuu1	Zd	Like cursor_up for micro adjustment
newline	nel	nw	Newline (behaves like cr followed by lf)
order_of_pins	porder	Ze	Matches software buts to print-head pins
orig_colors	oc	oc	Reset all color pairs
orig_pair	op	op	Set default color-pair to original one
pad_char	pad	pc	Pad character (rather than null)
parm_dch	dch	DC	Delete #1 chars (PG*)
parm_delete_line	dl	DL	Delete #1 lines (PG*)
parm_down_cursor	cud	DO	Move cursor down #1 lines (PG*)
parm_down_micro	mcud	Zf	Like cud for micro adjust
parm_ich	ich	IC	Insert #1 blank chars (PG*)
parm_index	indn	SF	Scroll forward #1 lines (PG)
parm_insert_line	il	AL	Add #1 new blank lines (PG*)
parm_left_cursor	cub	LE	Move cursor left #1 spaces (PG)
parm_left_micro	mcub	Zg	Like cul for micro adjust
parm_right_cursor	cuf	RI	Move cursor right #1 spaces (PG*)
parm_right_micro	mcuf	Zh	Like cuf for micro adjust
parm_rindex	rin	SR	Scroll backward #1 lines (PG)
parm_up_cursor	cuu	UP	Move cursor up #1 lines (PG*)
parm_up_micro	mcuu	Zi	Like cuu for micro adjust
pkey_key	pfkey	pk	Prog funct key #1 to type string #2
pkey_local	pfloc	pl	Prog funct key #1 to execute string #2
pkey_xmit	pfx	px	Prog funct key #1 to xmit string #2
pkey_plab	pfxl	xl	Program key #1 to xmit #2 and show #3
plab_norm	pln	pn	program label #1 to show string #2
print_screen	mc0	ps	Print contents of the screen
prtr_non	mc5p	pO	Turn on the printer for #1 bytes

(continued)

Table   Strings *(Continued)*

Variable	Cap. Name	Int. Code	Description
prtr_off	mc4	pf	Turn off the printer
prtr_on	mc5	po	Turn on the printer
repeat_char	rep	rp	Repeat char #1 #2 times. (PG*)
req_for_input	rfi	RF	request for input
reset_1string	rs1	r1	Reset terminal completely to sane modes.
reset_2string	rs2	r2	Reset terminal completely to sane modes.
reset_3string	rs3	r3	Reset terminal completely to sane modes.
reset_file	rf	rf	Name of file containing reset string
restore_cursor	rc	rc	Restore cursor to position of last sc
row_address	vpa	cv	Vertical position absolute (set row) (PG)
save_cursor	sc	sc	Save cursor position (P)
scancode_escape	scesc	S7	Escape for scancode emulation
scroll_forward	ind	sf	Scroll text up (P)
scroll_reverse	ri	sr	Scroll text down (P)
select_char_set	scs	Zj	Select character set
set0_des_seq	s0ds	s0	Shift to codeset 0 (EUC set 0, ASCII)
set1_des_seq	s1ds	s1	Shift to codeset 1
set2_des_seq	s2ds	s2	Shift to codeset 2
set3_des_seq	s3ds	s3	Shift to codeset 3
set_a_background	setab	AB	Set background color using ANSI escape
set_a_foreground	setaf	AF	Set foreground color using ANSI escape
set_attributes	sgr	sa	Define the video attributes (PG9)
set_background	setb	Sb	Set current background color
set_bottom_margin	smgb	Zk	Set bottom margin at current line
set_bottom_margin_parm	smgbp	Zl	Set bottom line at line #1 or #2 lines from bottomset_color_band
setcolor	Yz		Change to ribbon color #1
set_color_pair	scp	sp	Set current color pair
set_foreground	setf	Sf	Set current foreground color
set_left_margin	smgl	ML	Set left margin at current line
set_left_margin_parm	smglp	Zm	Set left (right) margin at #1 (#2)
set_lr_margin	smglr	ML	Set both left and right margins
set_page_length	slines	YZ	Set page length to #1 lines (use tparm)
set_right_margin	smgr	MR	Set right margin at current column
set_right_margin_parm	smgrp	Zn	Set right margin at column #1
set_tab	hts	st	Set a tab in all rows, current column
set_tb_margin	smgtb	MT	Sets both top and bottom margins
set_top_margin	smgt	Zo	Set top margin at current line
set_top_margin_parm	smgtp	Zp	Set top margin at line #1
set_window	wind	wi	Current window is lines #1-#2 cols #3-#4

(continued)

Table   Strings *(Continued)*

Variable	Cap. Name	Int. Code	Description
start_bit_image	sbim	Zq	Start printing bit image graphics
start_char_set_def	scsd	Zr	Start definition of a character set
stop_bit_image	rbim	Zs	End printing bit image graphics
stop_char_set_def	rcsd	Zt	End definition of character set
subscript_characters	subcs	Zu	List of subscriptable chars
superscript_characters	supcs	Zv	List of superscriptable chars
tab	ht	ta	Tab to next 8 space hardware tab stop
these_cause_cr	docr	Zw	These characters cause a CR
to_status_line	tsl	ts	Go to status line, column #1
underline_char	uc	uc	Underscore one char and move past it
up_half_line	hu	hu	Half-line up (reverse 1/2 linefeed)
xoff_character	xoffc	XF	XON character
xon_character	xonc	XN	XOFF character

(The following string capabilities are present in the SYSVr term structure, but are not documented in the man page. Comments are from the term structure header.)

label_format	fln	Lf	??
set_clock	sclk	SC	Set time-of-day clock
display_clock	dclk	DK	Display time-of-day clock
remove_clock	rmclk	RC	Remove time-of-day clock??
create_window	cwin	CW	Define win #1 to go from #2,#3 to #4,#5
goto_window	wingo	WG	Goto window #1
hangup	hup	HU	Hang up phone
dial_phone	dial	DI	Dial phone number #1
quick_dial	qdial	QD	Dial phone number #1, without progress detection
tone	tone	TO	Select touch tone dialing
pulse	pulse	PU	Select pulse dialing
flash_hook	hook	fh	Flash the switch hook
fixed_pause	pause	PA	Pause for 2-3 seconds
wait_tone	wait	WA	Wait for dial tone
user0	u0	u0	User string # 0
user1	u1	u1	User string # 1
user2	u2	u2	User string # 2
user3	u3	u3	User string # 3
user4	u4	u4	User string # 4
user5	u5	u5	User string # 5
user6	u6	u6	User string # 6
user7	u7	u7	User string # 7

(continued)

Table   Strings *(Continued)*

Variable	Cap. Name	Int. Code	Description
user8	u8	u8	User string # 8
user9	u9	u9	User string # 9
get_mouse	getm	Gm	Curses should get button events
key_mouse	kmous	Km	??
mouse_info	minfo	Mi	Mouse status information
pc_term_options	pctrm	S6	PC terminal options
req_mouse_pos	reqmp	RQ	Request mouse position report
zero_motion	zerom	Zx	No motion for the subsequent character

[N]Curses Function Overview

In the following text you will find an overview over the different (n)curses packages. In the first column is the bsd-curses (as it is in Slackware 2.1.0 and in Sun OS 4.x), in the second is the sysv-curses (in Sun OS 5.4 / Solaris 2) and in the third is the ncurses (version 1.8.6).

In the fourth column is a reference to the page in the text where the function is described (if it is actually described).

Note

Note from publisher: Missing text.

x

package has this function

n

function not yet implemented

To be continued...

Chapter 9
Programming I/O Ports

U sually a PC at least has two serial and one parallel interfaces. These interfaces are special devices and are mapped as follows:

♦ These are the RS232 serial devices 0-**n** where **n** depends on your hardware.

♦ These are the parallel devices 0-**n** where **n** depends on your hardware.

♦ These are the joystick devices 0-**n**.

The difference between the */dev/ttyS** and */dev/cua** devices is how a call to open( ) is handled. The */dev/cua** devices are supposed to be used as callout devices and thus get other default settings by a call to open( ) than the */dev/ttyS** devices which will be initialized for incoming and outgoing calls.

> **Note**
>
> *Note from publisher: /dev/cua* devices are officially depreciated.*

By default, the devices are controlling devices for the process that opened them. Normally ioctl( ) requests should handle all these special devices, but POSIX preferred to define new functions to handle asynchronous terminals heavily depending on the struct termios. Both methods require including <*termios.h*>.

1. method ioctl: TCSBRK, TCSBRKP, TCGETA (get attributes), TCSETA (set attributes)
   Terminal I/O control (TIOC) requests:
   TIOCGSOFTCAR (set soft carrier), TIOCSSOFTCAR

(get soft carrier), TIOCSCTTY (set controlling tty), TIOCMGET (get modemlines), TIOCMSET (set modemlines), TIOCGSERIAL, TIOCSSERIAL, TIOCSERCONFIG, TIOCSERGWILD, TIOCSERSWILD, TIOCSERGSTRUCT, TIOCMBIS, TIOCMBIC, ...

2. method POSIX: tcgetattr( ), tcsetattr( ), tcsendbreak( ), tcdrain( ), tcflush( ), tcflow( ), tcgetpgrp( ), tcsetpgrp( )
   cfsetispeed( ), cfgetispeed( ), cfsetospeed( ), cfgetospeed( )

3. other methods: outb, inb for hardware near programming like using the printer port not for a printer.

Mouse Programming

A mouse is either connected to a serial port or directly to the AT bus and different types of mouse send distinct kinds of data, which makes mouse programming a bit harder. But, Andrew Haylett was so kind as to put a generous copyright on his selection program which means you can use his mouse routines for your own programs. Included in this guide you can find the pre-release of selection 1.8 with the copyright notice. X11 already offers a comfortable mouse API, so Andrew's routines should be used for non-X11 applications only.

You only need the modules mouse.c and mouse.h from the selection package. To get mouse events you basically have to call ms_init( ) and get_ms_event( ). ms_init needs the following 10 arguments:

1. *int acceleration*   is the acceleration factor. If you move the mouse more than *delta* pixels, motion becomes faster depending on this value.

2. *int baud*   is the bps rate your mouse uses (normally 1,200).

3. *int delta*   this is the number of pixels that you have to move the mouse before the acceleration starts.

4. *char *device*   is the name of your mouse device (e.g., /dev/mouse).

5. *int toggle*   toggle the DTR, RTS, or both DTR and RTS mouse modem lines on initialization (normally 0).

6. *int sample*   the resolution (dpi) of your mouse (normally 100).

7. *mouse_type mouse*   the identifier of the connected mouse, like P_MSC (Mouse Systems Corp.) for my mouse ;).

8. *int slack*   amount of slack for wraparound which means if slack is -1 a try to move the mouse over the screen border will leave the mouse at the border. Values >= 0 mean that the mouse cursor will wrap to the other end after moving the mouse *slack* pixels against the border.

9. *int maxx*   the resolution of your current terminal in x direction. With the default font, a char is 10 pixels wide, and therefore the overall x screen resolution is 10*80-1.

10. *int maxy*   the resolution of your current terminal in y direction. With the default font, a char is 12 pixels high and therefore the overall y screen resolution is 12*25-1.

get_ms_event() just needs a pointer to a struct ms_event. If get_ms_event() returns -1, an error occurred. On success, it returns 0, and the struct ms_event will contain the actual mouse state.

Modem Programming

See example miniterm.c.

Use termios to control rs232 port.

Use Hayes commands to control modem.

Printer Programming

See example checklp.c.

Don't use termios to control printer port. Use ioctl and inb/outb if necessary.
Use Epson, Postscript, PCL, etc. commands to control printer.
<linux/lp.h>
ioctl calls: LPCHAR, LPTIME, LPABORT, LPSETIRQ, LPGETIRQ, LPWAIT
inb/outb for status and control port.

Joystick Programming

See example js.c in the joystick loadable kernel module package.

<linux/joystick.h>

ioctl calls: JS_SET_CAL, JS_GET_CAL, JS_SET_TIMEOUT, JS_GET_TIMEOUT, JS_SET_TIMELIMIT, JS_GET_TIMELIMIT, JS_GET_ALL, JS_SET_ALL. A read operation on /dev/jsn will return the struct JS_DATA_TYPE.

Chapter 10
Porting Applications To Linux

Introduction

Porting Unix applications to the Linux operating system is remarkably easy. Linux, and the GNU C library used by it, have been designed with applications portability in mind, meaning that many applications will compile simply by issuing `make`. Those which don't generally use some obscure feature of a particular implementation, or rely strongly on undocumented or undefined behavior of, say, a particular system call.

Linux is mostly compliant with IEEE Std 1003.1-1988 (POSIX.1), but has not actually been certified as such. Similarly, Linux also implements many features found in the SVID and BSD strains of Unix, but again does not necessarily adhere to them in all cases. In general, Linux has been designed to be compatible with other Unix implementations, to make applications porting easier, and in a number of instances has improved upon or corrected behavior found in those implementations.

As an example, the timeout argument passed to the select system call is actually decremented during the poll operation by Linux. Other implementations don't modify this value at all, and applications which aren't expecting this could break when compiled under Linux. The BSD and SunOS man pages for select warn that in a "future implementation," the system call may modify the timeout pointer. Unfortunately, many applications still assume that the value will be untouched.

The goal of this paper is to provide an overview of the major issues associated with porting applications to Linux, highlighting the differences between Linux, POSIX.1, SVID, and BSD in the following areas: signal handling, terminal I/O, process control and information gathering, and portable conditional compilation.

Signal Handling

Over the years, the definition and semantics of signals have been modified in various ways by different implementations of Unix. Today, there are two major classes of symbols: *unreliable* and *reliable*. Unreliable signals are those for which the signal handler does not remain installed once called. These "one-shot" signals must re-install the signal handler within the signal handler itself, if the program wishes the signal to remain installed. Because of this, there is a race condition in which the signal can arrive again before the handler is re-installed, which can cause either the signal to be lost or for the original behavior of the signal to be triggered (such as killing the process). Therefore, these signals are "unreliable" because the signal catching and handler reinstallation operations are nonatomic.

Under unreliable signal semantics, system calls are not restarted automatically when interrupted by a signal. Therefore, in order for a program to account for all cases, the program would need to check the value of *errno* after every system call, and reissue the system call if its value is *EINTR*.

Along similar lines, unreliable signal semantics don't provide an easy way to get an atomic pause operation (put the process to sleep until a signal arrives). Because of the unreliable nature of reinstalling signal handlers, there are cases in which a signal can arrive without the program realizing this.

Under reliable signal semantics, on the other hand, the signal handler remains installed when called, and the race condition for reinstallation is avoided. Also, certain system calls can be restarted, and an atomic pause operation is available via the POSIX *sigsuspend* function.

Signals Under SVR4, BSD, And POSIX.1

The SVR4 implementation of signals incorporates the functions *signal*, *sigset*, *sighold*, *sigrelse*, *sigignore*, and *sigpause*. The *signal* function under SVR4 is identical to the classic Unix V7 signals, providing only unreliable signals. The other functions do provide signals with automatic reinstallation of the signal handler, but no system call restarting is supported.

Under BSD, the functions *signal*, *sigvec*, *sigblock*, *sigsetmask*, and *sigpause* are supported. All of the functions provide reliable signals with system call restarting by default, but that behavior can be disabled if the programmer wishes.

Under POSIX.1, *sigaction*, *sigprocmask*, *sigpending*, and *sigsuspend* are provided. Note that there is no signal function, and according to POSIX.1 it is depreciated. These functions provide reliable signals, but system call restart behavior is not defined by POSIX. If *sigaction* is used under SVR4 and BSD, system call restarting is disabled by default, but it can be turned on if the signal flag SA_RESTART is specified.

Therefore, the "best" way to use signals in a program is to use *sigaction*, which allows you to explicitly specify the behavior of signal handlers. However, signal is still used in many applications, and as we can see above signal provides different semantics under SVR4 and BSD.

Linux Signal Options

The following values for the `sa_flags` member of the `sigaction` structure are defined for Linux.

 * `SA_NOCLDSTOP`: Don't send `SIGCHLD` when a child process is stopped.

 * `SA_RESTART`: Force restart of certain system calls when interrupted by a signal handler.

 * `SA_NOMASK`: Disable signal mask (which blocks signals during execution of a signal handler).

 * `SA_ONESHOT`: Clear signal handler after execution. Note that SVR4 uses `SA_RESETHAND` to mean the same thing.

 * `SA_INTERRUPT`: Defined under Linux, but unused. Under SunOS, system calls were automatically restarted, and this flag disabled that behavior.

 * `SA_STACK`: Currently a no-op, to be used for signal stacks.

Note that POSIX.1 defines only `SA_NOCLDSTOP`, and there are several other options defined by SVR4 not available under Linux. When porting applications which use `sigaction`, you may have to modify the values of `sa_flags` to get the appropriate behavior.

Signal Under Linux

Under Linux, the signal function is equivalent to using `sigaction` with the `SA_ONESHOT` and `SA_NOMASK` options; that is, it corresponds to the classic, unreliable signal semantics as used under SVR4.

If you wish signal to use BSD semantics, most Linux systems provide a BSD compatibility library which can be linked with. To use this library, you could add the options

```
-I/usr/include/bsd -lbsd
```

to the compilation command line. When porting applications using signal, pay close attention to what assumptions the program makes about use of signal handlers, and modify the code (or compile with the appropriate definitions) to get the right behavior.

Signals Supported By Linux

Linux supports nearly every signal provided by SVR4, BSD, and POSIX, with few exceptions:

 * `SIGEMT` is not supported; it corresponds to a hardware fault under SVR4 and BSD.

 * `SIGINFO` is not supported; it is used for keyboard information requests under SVR4.

- ◆ SIGSYS is not supported; it refers to an invalid system call in SVR4 and BSD. If you link with libbsd, this signal is redefined to SIGUNUSED.

- ◆ SIGABRT and SIGIOT are identical.

- ◆ SIGIO, SIGPOLL, and SIGURG are identical.

- ◆ SIGBUS is defined as SIGUNUSED. Technically there is no "bus error" in the Linux environment.

Terminal I/O

As with signals, terminal I/O control has three different implementations under SVR4, BSD, and POSIX.1.

SVR4 uses the termio structure, and various *ioctl* calls (such as TCSETA, TCGETA, and so forth) on a terminal device to obtain and set parameters with the termio structure. This structure looks like:

```
struct termio {
  unsigned short c_iflag;  /* Input modes */
  unsigned short c_oflag;  /* Output modes */
  unsigned short c_cflag;  /* Control modes */
  unsigned short c_lflag;  /* Line discipline modes */
  char c_line;             /* Line discipline */
  unsigned char c_cc[NCC]; /* Control characters */
};
```

Under BSD, the sgtty structure is used with various *ioctl* calls, such as TIOCGETP, TIOCSETP, and so forth.

Under POSIX, the termios struct is used, along with various functions defined by POSIX.1, such as tcsetattr and tcgetattr. The termios structure is identical to struct termio used by SVR4, but the types are renamed (such as tcflag_t instead of unsigned short), and NCCS is used for the size of the c_cc array.

Under Linux, both POSIX.1 termios and SVR4 termio are supported directly by the kernel. This means that if your program uses either of these methods for accessing terminal I/O, it should compile directly under Linux. If you're ever in doubt, it's easy to modify code using termio to use termios, using a bit of knowledge of both methods. Hopefully, this shouldn't ever be necessary. But, do pay attention if a program attempts to use the c_line field in the termio structure. For nearly all applications, this should be N_TTY, and if the program assumes that some other line discipline is available you might have trouble.

If your program uses the BSD *sgtty* implementation, you can link against libbsd.a as described above. This will provide a replacement for *ioctl* which will resubmit the terminal I/O requests in terms of the POSIX termios calls used by the kernel. When compiling such a program, if symbols such as TIOCGETP are undefined, you will need to link against libbsd.

Process Information And Control

Programs such as *ps*, *top*, and `free` must have some way to obtain information from the kernel about a processes and system resources. Similarly, debuggers and other like tools need the ability to control and inspect a running process. These features have been provided by a number of interfaces by different versions of Unix, and nearly all of them are either machine-specific or tied to a particular kernel design. So far, there has been no universally accepted interface for this kind of process-kernel interaction.

kvm Routines

Many systems use routines such as *kvm_open*, *kvm_nlist*, and *kvm_read* to access kernel data structures directly via the */dev/kmem* device. In general, these programs will open */dev/kmem*, read the kernel's symbol table, locate data in the running kernel with this table, and read the appropriate addresses in the kernel address space with these routines. Because this requires the user program and the kernel to agree on the size and format of data structures read in this fashion, such programs often have to be rebuilt for each kernel revision, CPU type, and so forth.

ptrace And The */proc* File System

The *ptrace* system call is used in 4.3BSD and SVID to control a process and read information from it. It is classically used by debuggers to, say, trap execution of a running process or examine its state. Under SVR4, *ptrace* is superseded by the */proc* file system, which appears as a directory containing a single file entry for each running process, named by process ID. The user program can open the file corresponding to the process of interest and issue various *ioctl* calls on it to control its execution or obtain information from the kernel on the process. Similarly, the program can read or write data directly in the process's address space through the file descriptor into the */proc* file system.

Process Control Under Linux

Under Linux, the *ptrace* system call is supported for process control, and it works as in 4.3BSD. To obtain process and system information, Linux also provides a */proc* file system, but with very different semantics. Under Linux, */proc* consists of a number of files providing general system information, such as memory usage, load average, loaded module statistics, and network statistics. These files are generally accessed using *read* and *write* and their contents can be parsed using *scanf*. The */proc* file system under Linux also provides a directory entry for each running process, named by process ID, which contains file entries for information such as the command line, links to the current working directory and executable file, open file descriptors, and so forth. The kernel provides all of this information on the fly in response to *read* requests. This implementation is not unlike the */proc* file system found in Plan 9, but it does have its drawbacks—for example, for a tool such as *ps* to list a table of information on all running processes, many directories must be traversed and many files opened and read. By comparison, the *kvm* routines used on other Unix systems read kernel data structures directly with only a few system calls.

Obviously, each implementation is so vastly different that porting applications which use them can prove to be a real task. It should be pointed out that the SVR4 */proc* file system is a very different beast than that found in Linux, and they may not be used in the same context. Arguably, any program which uses the *kvm* routines or SVR4 */proc* file system is not really portable, and those sections of code should be rewritten for each operating system.

The Linux *ptrace* call is nearly identical to that found in BSD, but there are a few differences:

♦ The requests `PTRACE_PEEKUSER` and `PTRACE_POKEUSER` under BSD are named `PTRACE_PEEKUSR` and `PTRACE_POKEUSR`, respectively, under Linux.

♦ Process registers can be set using the `PTRACE_POKEUSR` request with offsets found in `/usr/include/linux/ptrace.h`.

♦ The SunOS requests `PTRACE_{READ,WRITE}{TEXT,DATA}` are not supported, nor are `PTRACE_SETACBKPT`, `PTRACE_SETWRBKPT`, `PTRACE_CLRBKPT`, or `PTRACE_DUMPCORE`. These missing requests should only affect a small number of existing programs.

Linux does *not* provide the *kvm* routines for reading the kernel address space from a user program, but some programs (most notably *kmem_ps*) implement their own versions of these routines. In general, these are not portable, and any code which uses the *kvm* routines is probably depending on the availability of certain symbols or data structures in the kernel—not a safe assumption to make. Use of *kvm* routines should be considered architecture-specific.

Portable Conditional Compilation

If you need to make modifications to existing code in order to port it to Linux, you may need to use `ifdef…endif` pairs to surround parts of Linux-specific code—or, for that matter, code corresponding to other implementations. No real standard for selecting portions of code to be compiled based on the operating system exists, but many programs use a convention such as defining `SVR4` for System V code, `BSD` for BSD code, and `linux` for Linux-specific code.

The GNU C library used by Linux allows you to turn on various features of the library by defining various macros at compile time. These are:

♦ `__STRICT_ANSI__`: For ANSI C features only

♦ `_POSIX_SOURCE`: For POSIX.1 features

♦ `_POSIX_C_SOURCE`: If defined as 1, POSIX.1 features; if defined as 2, POSIX.2 features.

♦ `_BSD_SOURCE`: ANSI, POSIX, and BSD features.

♦ `_SVID_SOURCE`: ANSI, POSIX, and System V features.

♦ `_GNU_SOURCE`: ANSI, POSIX, BSD, SVID, and GNU extensions. This is the default if none of the above are defined.

If you define _BSD_SOURCE yourself, the additional definition _FAVOR_BSD will be defined for the library. This will cause BSD behavior for certain things to be selected over POSIX or SVR4. For example, if _FAVOR_BSD is defined, *setjmp* and *longjmp* will save and restore the signal mask, and *getpgrp* will accept a PID argument. Note that you must still link against libbsd to get BSD-like behavior for the features mentioned earlier in this paper.

Under Linux, gcc defines a number of macros automatically which you can use in your program. These are:

♦ _ _GNUC_ _ (major GNU C version, e.g., 2)

♦ _ _GNUC_MINOR_ _ (minor GNU C version, e.g., 5)

♦ unix

♦ i386

♦ linux

♦ _ _unix_ _

♦ _ _i386_ _

♦ _ _linux_ _

♦ _ _unix

♦ _ _i386

♦ _ _linux

Many programs use

```
#ifdef linux
```

to surround Linux-specific code. Using these compile-time macros you can easily adapt existing code to include or exclude changes necessary to port the program to Linux, Note that because Linux supports more System V-like features in general, the best code base to start from with a program written for both System V and BSD is probably the System V version. Alternately, you can start from the BSD base and link against libbsd.

Additional Comments

This chapter covers most of the porting issues except the missing system calls that are named in the system calls chapter and the yet missing streams (rumors say a loadable stream module should exist at **ftp.uni-stuttgart.de** in pub/systems/linux/isdn).

Appendix
System Calls In Alphabetical Order

Table A.1   System Calls In Alphabetical Order

System Call	Description
_exit	like exit but with fewer actions (m+c)
accept	accept a connection on a socket (m+c!)
access	check user's permissions for a file (m+c)
acct	not yet implemented (mc)
adjtimex	set/get kernel time variables (-c)
afs_syscall	reserved andrew file system call (-)
alarm	send SIGALRM at a specified time (m+c)
bdflush	flush dirty buffers to disk (-c)
bind	name a socket for interprocess communication (m!c)
break	not yet implemented (-)
brk	change data segment size (mc)
chdir	change working directory (m+c)
chmod	change file attributes (m+c)
chown	change ownership of a file (m+c)
chroot	set a new root directory (mc)
clone	see fork (m-)
close	close a file by reference (m+c)
connect	link two sockets (m!c)
creat	create a file (m+c)
create_module	allocate space for a loadable kernel module (-)
delete_module	unload a kernel module (-)
dup	create a file descriptor duplicate (m+c)
dup2	duplicate a file descriptor (m+c)
execl, execlp, execle,...	see execve (m+!c)
execve	execute a file (m+c)

(continued)

443

Table A.1   System Calls In Alphabetical Order *(Continued)*

System Call	Description
exit	terminate a program (m+c)
fchdir	change working directory by reference ()
fchmod	see chmod (mc)
fchown	change ownership of a file (mc)
fclose	close a file by reference (m+!c)
fcntl	file/filedescriptor control (m+c)
flock	change file locking (m!c)
fork	create a child process (m+c)
fpathconf	get info about a file by reference (m+!c)
fread	read array of binary data from stream (m+!c)
fstat	get file status (m+c)
fstatfs	get file system status by reference (mc)
fsync	write file cache to disk (mc)
ftime	get timezone+seconds since 1.1.1970 (m!c)
ftruncate	change file size (mc)
fwrite	write array of binary datas to stream (m+!c)
get_kernel_syms	get kernel symbol table or its size (-)
getdomainname	get system's domain name (m!c)
getdtablesize	get filedescriptor table size (m!c)
getegid	get effective group id (m+c)
geteuid	get effective user id (m+c)
getgid	get real group id (m+c)
getgroups	get supplemental groups (m+c)
gethostid	get unique host identifier (m!c)
gethostname	get system's hostname (m!c)
getitimer	get value of interval timer (mc)
getpagesize	get size of a system page (m-!c)
getpeername	get address of a connected peer socket (m!c)
getpgid	get parent group id of a process (+c)
getpgrp	get parent group id of current process (m+c)
getpid	get process id of current process (m+c)
getppid	get process id of the parent process (m+c)
getpriority	get a process/group/user priority (mc)
getrlimit	get resource limits (mc)
getrusage	get usage of resources (m)
getsockname	get the address of a socket (m!c)
getsockopt	get option settings of a socket (m!c)
gettimeofday	get timezone+seconds since 1.1.1970 (mc)
getuid	get real uid (m+c)
gtty	not yet implemented ()
idle	make a process a candidate for swap (mc)

(continued)

Table A.1   System Calls In Alphabetical Order *(Continued)*

System Call	Description
init_module	insert a loadable kernel module (-)
ioctl	manipulate a character device (mc)
ioperm	set some i/o port's permissions (m-c)
iopl	set all i/o ports' permissions (m-c)
ipc	interprocess communication (-c)
kill	send a signal to a process (m+c)
killpg	send a signal to a process group (mc!)
klog	see syslog (-!)
link	create a hardlink for an existing file (m+c)
listen	listen for socket connections (m!c)
llseek	lseek for large files (-)
lock	not implemented yet ()
lseek	change the position ptr of a file descriptor (m+c)
lstat	get file status (mc)
mkdir	create a directory (m+c)
mknod	create a device (mc)
mmap	map a file into memory (mc)
modify_ldt	read or write local descriptor table (-)
mount	mount a file system (mc)
mprotect	read, write, or execute protect memory (-)
mpx	not implemented yet ()
msgctl	ipc message control (m!c)
msgget	get an ipc message queue id (m!c)
msgrcv	receive an ipc message (m!c)
msgsnd	send an ipc message (m!c)
munmap	unmap a file from memory (mc)
nice	change process priority (mc)
oldfstat	no longer existing
oldlstat	no longer existing
oldolduname	no longer existing
oldstat	no longer existing
olduname	no longer existing
open	open a file (m+c)
pathconf	get information about a file (m+!c)
pause	sleep until signal (m+c)
personality	change current execution domain for ibcs (-)
phys	not implemented yet (m)
pipe	create a pipe (m+c)
prof	not yet implemented ()
profil	execution time profile (m!c)
ptrace	trace a child process (mc)

(continued)

Table A.1   System Calls In Alphabetical Order *(Continued)*

System Call	Description
quotactl	not implemented yet ()
read	read data from a file (m+c)
readv	read data blocks from a file (m!c)
readdir	read a directory (m+c)
readlink	get content of a symbolic link (mc)
reboot	reboot or toggle vulcan death grip (-mc)
recv	receive a message from a connected socket (m!c)
recvfrom	receive a message from a socket (m!c)
rename	move/rename a file (m+c)
rmdir	delete an empty directory (m+c)
sbrk	see brk (mc!)
select	sleep until action on a filedescriptor (mc)
semctl	ipc semaphore control (m!c)
semget	ipc get a semaphore set identifier (m!c)
semop	ipc operation on semaphore set members (m!c)
send	send a message to a connected socket (m!c)
sendto	send a message to a socket (m!c)
setdomainname	set system's domain name (mc)
setfsgid	set file system group id ()
setfsuid	set file system user id ()
setgid	set real group id (m+c)
setgroups	set supplemental groups (mc)
sethostid	set unique host identifier (mc)
sethostname	set the system's hostname (mc)
setitimer	set interval timer (mc)
setpgid	set process group id (m+c)
setpgrp	has no effect (mc!)
setpriority	set a process/group/user priority (mc)
setregid	set real and effective group id (mc)
setreuid	set real and effective user id (mc)
setrlimit	set resource limit (mc)
setsid	create a session (+c)
setsockopt	change options of a socket (mc)
settimeofday	set timezone+seconds since 1.1.1970 (mc)
setuid	set real user id (m+c)
setup	initialize devices and mount root (-)
sgetmask	see siggetmask (m)
shmat	attach shared memory to data segment (m!c)
shmctl	ipc manipulate shared memory (m!c)
shmdt	detach shared memory from data segment (m!c)
shmget	get/create shared memory segment (m!c)

(continued)

Table A.1   System Calls In Alphabetical Order *(Continued)*

System Call	Description
shutdown	shutdown a socket (m!c)
sigaction	set/get signal handler (m+c)
sigblock	block signals (m!c)
siggetmask	get signal blocking of current process (!c)
signal	set up a signal handler (mc)
sigpause	use a new signal mask until a signal (mc)
sigpending	get pending, but blocked signals (m+c)
sigprocmask	set/get signal blocking of current process (+c)
sigreturn	not yet used ()
sigsetmask	set signal blocking of current process (c!)
sigsuspend	replacement for sigpause (m+c)
sigvec	see sigaction (m!)
socket	create a socket communication endpoint (m!c)
socketcall	socket call multiplexer (-)
socketpair	create two connected sockets (m!c)
ssetmask	see sigsetmask (m)
stat	get file status (m+c)
statfs	get file system status (mc)
stime	set seconds since 1.1.1970 (mc)
stty	not yet implemented ()
swapoff	stop swapping to a file/device (m-c)
swapon	start swapping to a file/device (m-c)
symlink	create a symbolic link to a file (m+c)
sync	sync memory and disk buffers (mc)
syscall	execute a system call by number (-!c)
sysconf	get value of a system variable (m+!c)
sysfs	get infos about configured file systems ()
sysinfo	get Linux system infos (m-)
syslog	manipulate system logging (m-c)
system	execute a shell command (m!c)
time	get seconds since 1.1.1970 (m+c)
times	get process times (m+c)
truncate	change file size (mc)
ulimit	get/set file limits (c!)
umask	set file creation mask (m+c)
umount	unmount a file system (mc)
uname	get system information (m+c)
unlink	remove a file when not busy (m+c)
uselib	use a shared library (m-c)
ustat	not yet implemented (c)
utime	modify inode time entries (m+c)

(continued)

Table A.1   System Calls In Alphabetical Order *(Continued)*

System Call	Description
utimes	see utime (m!c)
vfork	see fork (m!c)
vhangup	virtually hang up current tty (m-c)
vm86	enter virtual 8086 mode (m-c)
wait	wait for process termination (m+!c)
wait3	bsd wait for a specified process (m!c)
wait4	bsd wait for a specified process (mc)
waitpid	wait for a specified process (m+c)
write	write data to a file (m+c)
writev	write datablocks to a file (m!c)

Legend

- ◆ (m) manual page exists.
- ◆ (+) POSIX compliant.
- ◆ (-) Linux specific.
- ◆ (c) in libc.
- ◆ (!) not a sole system call, uses a different system call.

Part IV

Conceptual Architecture
Of The Linux Kernel

by Ivan Bowman

Ivan Bowman
ID 90037932
itbowman@maestro.uwaterloo.ca
January 1998
For Ric Holt
CS746G Assignment One

Available at: **http://www.grad.math.uwaterloo.ca/~itbowman/CS746G/a1/**

Abstract

This paper describes the *abstract* or *conceptual* software architecture of the Linux kernel. This level of architecture is concerned with the large-scale subsystems within the kernel, but not
with particular procedures or variables. One of the purposes of such
an abstract architecture is to form a mental model for Linux developers and architects. The model may not reflect the as-built
architecture perfectly, but it provides a useful way to think about
the overall structure. This model is most useful for entry-level developers, but is also a good way for experienced developers to
maintain a consistent and accurate system vocabulary.

The architecture presented here is the result of reverse engineering an existing Linux implementation; the primary sources of
information used were the documentation and source code. Unfortunately, no developer interviews were used to extract the live
architecture of the system.

The Linux kernel is composed of five main subsystems that communicate using procedure calls. Four of these five subsystems are
discussed at the module interconnection level, and we discuss the
architectural style in the sense used by Garlan and Shaw. At all
times the relation of particular subsystems to the overall Linux
system is considered.

The architecture of the kernel is one of the reasons that Linux has
been successfully adopted by many users. In particular, the Linux
kernel architecture was designed to support a large number of volunteer developers. Further, the subsystems that are most likely to
need enhancements were architected to easily support extensibility. These two qualities are factors in the success of the overall
system.

Introduction

Purpose

The goal of this paper is to present the *abstract* architecture of the Linux kernel. This is described by Soni ([Soni 1995]) as being the *conceptual* architecture. By concentrating on high-level design, this architecture is useful to entry-level developers that need to see the high-level architecture before understanding where their changes fit in. In addition, the conceptual architecture is a good way to create a formal system vocabulary that is shared by experienced developers and system designers. This architectural description may not perfectly reflect the actual implementation architecture, but can provide a useful mental model for all developers to share. Ideally, the conceptual architecture should be created before the system is implemented, and should be updated to be an ongoing system conscience in the sense of [Monroe 1997], showing clearly the load-bearing walls as described in [Perry 1992].

Challenges Of This Paper

This presentation is somewhat unusual, in that the conceptual architecture is usually formed before the as-built architecture is complete. Since the author of this paper was not involved in either the design or implementation of the Linux system, this paper is the result of reverse engineering the Slackware 2.0.27 kernel source and documentation. A few architectural descriptions were used (in particular, [Rusling 1997] and [Wirzenius 1997] were quite helpful), but these descriptions were also based on the existing system implementation. By deriving the conceptual architecture from an existing implementation, this paper probably presents some implementation details as conceptual architecture.

In addition, the mechanisms used to derive the information in this paper omitted the best source of information—the live knowledge of the system architects and developers. For a proper abstraction of the system architecture, interviews with these individuals would be required. Only in this way can an accurate mental model of the system architecture be described.

Despite these problems, this paper offers a useful conceptualization of the Linux kernel software, although it cannot be taken as an accurate depiction of the system as implemented.

Organization

The next section describes the overall objective and architecture of the Linux kernel as a whole. Next, each individual subsystem is elaborated to the module level, with a discussion of the relations between modules in a subsystem and to other subsystems. Finally, we discuss how the architecture of the Linux kernel was useful in the implementation of the system and contributed to the overall success of the system.

Chapter 1
System Architecture

1.1 System Overview

The Linux kernel is useless in isolation; it participates as one part in a larger system that, as a whole, is useful. As such, it makes sense to discuss the kernel in the context of the entire system. Figure 1.1 shows a decomposition of the entire Linux operating system:

The Linux operating system is composed of four major subsystems:

♦ User applications—the set of applications in use on a particular Linux system will be different depending on what the computer system is used for, but typical examples include a word-processing application and a Web browser.

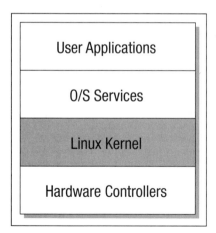

Figure 1.1
Decomposition of Linux system into major subsystems.

455

- O/S services—these are services that are typically considered part of the operating system (a windowing system, command shell, and so on); also, the programming interface to the kernel (compiler tool and library) is included in this subsystem.

- Linux kernel—this is the main area of interest in this paper; the kernel abstracts and mediates access to the hardware resources, including the CPU.

- Hardware controllers—this subsystem is comprised of all the possible physical devices in a Linux installation; for example, the CPU, memory hardware, hard disks, and network hardware are all members of this subsystem

This decomposition follows Garlan and Shaw's layered style discussed in [Garlan 1994]; each subsystem layer can only communicate with the subsystem layers that are immediately adjacent to it. In addition, the dependencies between subsystems are from the top down: layers pictured near the top depend on lower layers, but subsystems nearer the bottom do not depend on higher layers.

Since the primary interest of this paper is the Linux kernel, we will completely ignore the user applications subsystem, and only consider the hardware and O/S services subsystems to the extent that they interface with the Linux kernel subsystem.

1.2   Purpose Of The Kernel

The Linux kernel presents a virtual machine interface to user processes. Processes are written without needing any knowledge of what physical hardware is installed on a computer—the Linux kernel abstracts all hardware into a consistent virtual interface. In addition, Linux supports multitasking in a manner that is transparent to user processes: each process can act as though it is the only process on the computer, with exclusive use of main memory and other hardware resources. The kernel actually runs several processes concurrently, and is responsible for mediating access to hardware resources so that each process has fair access while interprocess security is maintained.

1.3   Overview Of The Kernel Structure

The Linux kernel is composed of five main subsystems:

1. The Process Scheduler (SCHED) is responsible for controlling process access to the CPU. The scheduler enforces a policy that ensures that processes will have fair access to the CPU, while ensuring that necessary hardware actions are performed by the kernel on time.

2. The Memory Manager (MM) permits multiple process to securely share the machine's main memory system. In addition, the memory manager supports virtual memory that allows Linux to support processes that use more memory than is available in the system. Unused memory is swapped out to persistent storage using the file system then swapped back in when it is needed.

3. The Virtual File System (VFS) abstracts the details of the variety of hardware devices by presenting a common file interface to all devices. In addition, the VFS supports several file system formats that are compatible with other operating systems.

4. The Network Interface (NET) provides access to several networking standards and a variety of network hardware.

5. The Interprocess Communication (IPC) subsystem supports several mechanisms for process-to-process communication on a single Linux system.

Figure 1.2 shows a high-level decomposition of the Linux kernel, where lines are drawn from dependent subsystems to the subsystems they depend on.

This diagram emphasizes that the most central subsystem is the process scheduler: all other subsystems depend on the process scheduler since all subsystems need to suspend and resume processes. Usually a subsystem will suspend a process that is waiting for a hardware operation to complete, and resume the process when the operation is finished. For example, when a process attempts to send a message across the network, the network interface may

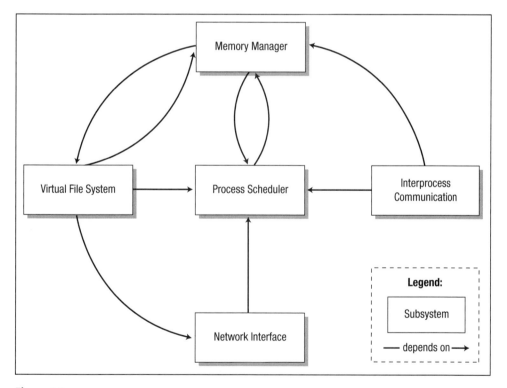

Figure 1.2
Kernel subsystem overview.

need to suspend the process until the hardware has completed sending the message success-fully. After the message has been sent (or the hardware returns a failure), the network interface then resumes the process with a return code indicating the success or failure of the operation. The other subsystems (memory manager, virtual file system, and interprocess communica-tion) all depend on the process scheduler for similar reasons.

The other dependencies are somewhat less obvious, but equally important:

♦ The process-scheduler subsystem uses the memory manager to adjust the hardware memory map for a specific process when that process is resumed.

♦ The interprocess communication subsystem depends on the memory manager to support a shared-memory communication mechanism. This mechanism allows two processes to access an area of common memory in addition to their usual private memory.

♦ The virtual file system uses the network interface to support a network file system (NFS), and also uses the memory manager to provide a ramdisk device.

♦ The memory manager uses the virtual file system to support swapping; this is the only reason that the memory manager depends on the process scheduler. When a process accesses memory that is currently swapped out, the memory manager makes a request to the file system to fetch the memory from persistent storage, and suspends the process.

In addition to the dependencies that are shown explicitly, all subsystems in the kernel rely on some common resources that are not shown in any subsystem. These include procedures that all kernel subsystems use to allocate and free memory for the kernel's use, procedures to print warning or error messages, and system debugging routines. These resources will not be referred to explicitly since they are assumed ubiquitously available and used within the kernel layer of Figure 1.1.

The architectural style at this level resembles the data abstraction style discussed by Garlan and Shaw in [Garlan 1994]. Each of the depicted subsystems contains state information that is accessed using a procedural interface, and the subsystems are each responsible for maintaining the integrity of their managed resources.

1.4   Supporting Multiple Developers

The Linux system was developed by a large number of volunteers (the current CREDITS file lists 196 developers that have worked on the Linux system). The large number of devel-opers and the fact that they are volunteers has an impact on how the system should be architected. With such a large number of geographically dispersed developers, a tightly coupled system would be quite difficult to develop—developers would be constantly tread-ing on each others' code. For this reason, the Linux system was architected to have the subsystems that were anticipated to need the most modification—the file systems, hard-ware interfaces, and network system—designed to be highly modular. For example, an implementation of Linux can be expected to support many hardware devices which each have distinct interfaces; a naive architecture would put the implementation of all hardware devices into one subsystem. An approach that better supports multiple developers is to separate the code for each hardware device into a device driver that is a distinct module in the file system. Analyzing the credits file gives Figure 1.3.

Figure 1.3 shows most of the developers who have worked on the Linux kernel, and the areas that they appeared to have implemented. A few developers modified many parts of the kernel; for clarity, these developers were not included. For example, Linus Torvalds was the original implementer of most of the kernel subsystems, although subsequent development was done by others. This diagram can't be considered accurate because developer signatures were not maintained consistently during the development of the kernel, but it gives a general idea of what systems developers spent most of their effort implementing.

This diagram confirms the large-scale structure of the kernel as outlined earlier. It is interesting to note that very few developers worked on more than one system; where this did occur, it occurred mainly where there is a subsystem dependency. The organization supports the well-known rule of thumb stated by Melvin Conway (see [Raymond 1993]) that system organization often reflects developer organization. Most of the developers worked on hardware device drivers, logical file system modules, network device drivers, and network protocol modules. It's not surprising that these four areas of the kernel have been architected to support extensibility the most.

1.5   System Data Structures

1.5.1   Task List

The process scheduler maintains a block of data for each process that is active. These blocks of data are stored in a linked list called the *task list*; the process scheduler always maintains a current pointer that indicates the current process that is active.

1.5.2   Memory Map

The memory manager stores a mapping of virtual to physical addresses on a per-process basis, and also stores additional information on how to fetch and replace particular pages. This information is stored in a memory-map data structure that is stored in the process scheduler's task list.

1.5.3   I-nodes

The Virtual File System uses index-nodes (i-nodes) to represent files on a logical file system. The i-node data structure stores the mapping of file block numbers to physical device addresses. I-node data structures can be shared across processes if two processes have the same file open. This sharing is accomplished by both task data blocks pointing to the same i-node.

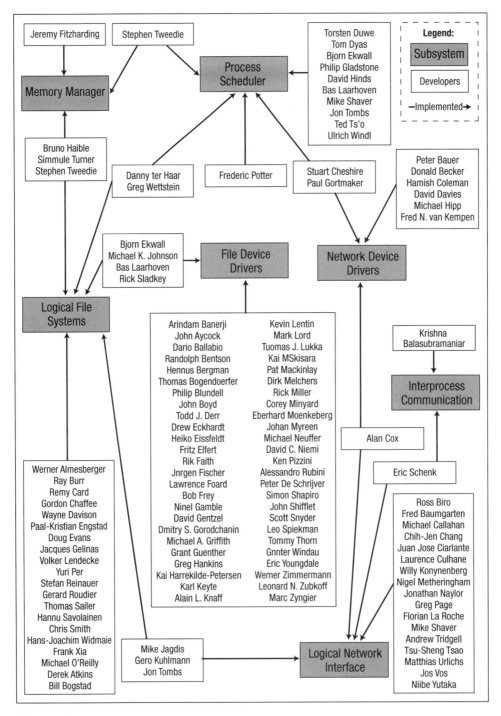

Figure 1.3
Division of developer responsibilities.

1.5.4   Data Connection

All of the data structures are rooted at the task list of the process scheduler. Each process on the system has a data structure containing a pointer to its memory mapping information, and also pointers to the i-nodes representing all of the opened files. Finally, the task data structure also contains pointers to data structures representing all of the opened network connections associated with each task.

Chapter 2
Subsystem Architectures

2.1 Process Scheduler Architecture

2.1.1 Goals

The process scheduler is the most important subsystem in the Linux kernel. Its purpose is to control access to the computer's CPU(s). This includes not only access by user processes but also access for other kernel subsystems.

2.1.2 Modules

The scheduler is divided into three main modules:

1. The scheduling policy module is responsible for judging which process will have access to the CPU; the policy is designed so that processes will have fair access to the CPU.

2. Architecture-specific modules are designed with a common interface to abstract the details of any particular computer architecture. These modules are responsible for communicating with a CPU to suspend and resume a process. These operations involve knowing what registers and state information need to be preserved for each process and executing the assembly code to effect a suspend or resume operation.

2. The architecture-independent module communicates with the policy module to determine which process will execute next, then calls the architecture-specific module to resume the appropriate process. In addition, this module calls the memory manager to ensure that the memory hardware is restored properly for the resumed process.

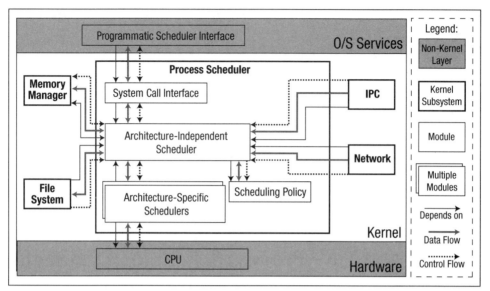

Figure 2.1
Process scheduler subsystem in context.

The system call interface module permits user processes access to only those resources that are explicitly exported by the kernel. This limits the dependency of user processes on the kernel to a well-defined interface that rarely changes, despite changes in the implementation of other kernel modules.

2.1.3   Data Representation

The scheduler maintains a data structure, the task list, with one entry for each active process. This data structure contains enough information to suspend and resume the processes, but also contains additional accounting and state information. This data structure is publicly available throughout the kernel layer.

2.1.4   Dependencies, Data Flow, And Control Flow

The process scheduler calls the memory manager subsystem as mentioned earlier; because of this, the process scheduler subsystem depends on the memory manager subsystem. In addition, all of the other kernel subsystems depend on the process scheduler to suspend and resume processes while waiting for hardware requests to complete. These dependencies are expressed through function calls and access to the shared task list data structure. All kernel subsystems read and write the data structure representing the current task, leading to bidirectional data flow throughout the system.

In addition to the data and control flow within the kernel layer, the O/S services layer provides an interface for user processes to register for timer notification. This corresponds to the implicit execution architectural style described in [Garlan 1994]. This leads to a flow of control from the scheduler to the user processes. The usual case of resuming a dormant process is not considered a flow of control in the normal sense because the user process cannot detect this operation. Finally, the scheduler communicates with the CPU to suspend and resume processes; this leads to a data flow, and a flow of control. The CPU is responsible for interrupting the currently executing process and allowing the kernel to schedule another process.

2.2 Memory Manager Architecture

2.2.1 Goals

The memory manager subsystem is responsible for controlling process access to the hardware memory resources. This is accomplished through a hardware memory-management system that provides a mapping between process memory references and the machine's physical memory. The memory manager subsystem maintains this mapping on a per-process basis, so that two processes can access the same virtual memory address and actually use different physical memory locations. In addition, the memory manager subsystem supports swapping; it moves unused memory pages to persistent storage to allow the computer to support more virtual memory than there is physical memory.

2.2.2 Modules

The memory manager subsystem is composed of three modules:

1. The architecture-specific module presents a virtual interface to the memory management hardware

2. The architecture-independent manager performs all of the per-process mapping and virtual memory swapping. This module is responsible for determining which memory pages will be evicted when there is a page fault—there is no separate policy module since it is not expected that this policy will need to change.

3. A system call interface is provided to provide restricted access to user processes. This interface allows user processes to allocate and free storage, and also to perform memory mapped file I/O.

2.2.3 Data Representation

The memory manager stores a per-process mapping of physical addresses to virtual addresses. This mapping is stored as a reference in the process scheduler's task list data structure. In addition to this mapping, additional details in the data block tell the memory manager how to fetch and store pages. For example, executable code can use the executable image as a backing store, but dynamically allocated data must be backed to the system paging file. Finally, the memory manager stores permissions and accounting information in this data structure to ensure system security.

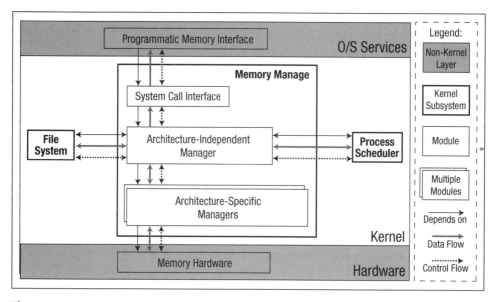

Figure 2.2
Memory manager subsystem in context.

2.2.4 Data Flow, Control Flow, And Dependencies

The memory manager controls the memory hardware, and receives a notification from the hardware when a page fault occurs—this means that there is bidirectional data and control flow between the memory manager modules and the memory manager hardware. Also, the memory manager uses the file system to support swapping and memory mapped I/O. This requirement means that the memory manager needs to make procedure calls to the file system to store and fetch memory pages from persistent storage. Because the file system requests cannot be completed immediately, the memory manager needs to suspend a process until the memory is swapped back in; this requirement causes the memory manager to make procedure calls into the process scheduler. Also, since the memory mapping for each process is stored in the process scheduler's data structures, there is a bidirectional data flow between the memory manager and the process scheduler. User processes can set up new memory mappings within the process address space, and can register themselves for notification of page faults within the newly mapped areas. This introduces a control flow from the memory manager, through the system call interface module, to the user processes. There is no data flow from user processes in the traditional sense, but user processes can retrieve some information from the memory manager using select system calls in the system call interface module.

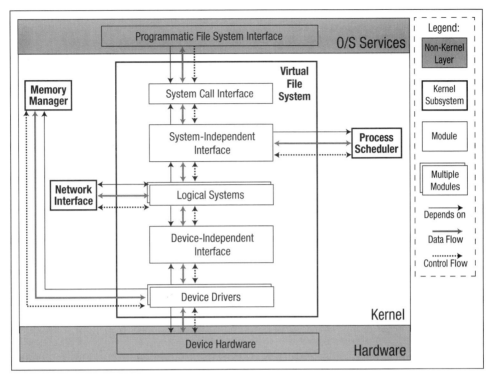

Figure 2.3
Virtual file system in context.

2.3   Virtual File System Architecture
2.3.1   Goals

The virtual file system is designed to present a consistent view of data as stored on hardware devices. Almost all hardware devices in a computer are represented using a generic device driver interface. The virtual file system goes further, and allows the system administrator to mount any of a set of logical file systems on any physical device. Logical file systems promote compatibility with other operating system standards, and permit developers to implement file systems with different policies. The virtual file system abstracts the details of both physical device and logical file system, and allows user processes to access files using a common interface, without necessarily knowing what physical or logical system the file resides on.

In addition to traditional file-system goals, the virtual file system is also responsible for loading new executable programs. This responsibility is accomplished by the logical file system module, and this allows Linux to support several executable formats.

2.3.2 Modules

1. There is one device driver module for each supported hardware controller. Since there are a large number of incompatible hardware devices, there are a large number of device drivers. The most common extension of a Linux system is the addition of a new device driver.

2. The device-independent interface module provides a consistent view of all devices.

3. There is one logical file system module for each supported file system.

4. The system independent interface presents a hardware and logical-file-system independent view of the hardware resources. This module presents all resources using either a block-oriented or character-oriented file interface.

5. Finally, the system call interface provides controlled access to the file system for user processes. The virtual file system exports only specific functionality to user processes.

2.3.3 Data Representation

All files are represented using i-nodes. Each i-node structure contains location information for specifying where on the physical device the file blocks are. In addition, the i-node stores pointers to routines in the logical file system module and device driver that will perform required read and write operations. By storing function pointers in this fashion, logical file systems and device drivers can register themselves with the kernel without having the kernel depend on any specific module.

2.3.4 Data Flow, Control Flow, And Dependencies

One specific device driver is a ramdisk; this device allocates an area of main memory and treats it as a persistent storage device. This device driver uses the memory manager to accomplish its tasks, and thus there is a dependency, control flow, and data flow between the file system device drivers and the memory manager.

One of the specific logical file systems that is supported is the network file system (as a client only). This file system accesses files on another machine as if they were part of the local machine. To accomplish this, one of the logical file system modules uses the network subsystem to complete its tasks. This introduces a dependency, control flow, and data flow between the two subsystems.

As mentioned in section 2.2, the memory manager uses the virtual file system to accomplish memory swapping and memory-mapped I/O. Also, the virtual file system uses the process scheduler to disable processes while waiting for hardware requests to complete, and resume them once the request has been completed. Finally, the system call interface allows user processes to call in to the virtual file system to store or retrieve data. Unlike the previous subsystems, there is no mechanism for users to register for implicit invocation, so there is no control flow from the virtual file system toward user processes (resuming processes is not considered control flow).

2.4   Network Interface Architecture

2.4.1   Goals

The network subsystem allows Linux systems to connect to other systems over a network. There are a number of possible hardware devices that are supported, and a number of network protocols that can be used. The network subsystem abstracts both of these implementation details so that user processes and other kernel subsystems can access the network without necessarily knowing what physical devices or protocol is being used.

2.4.2   Modules

1. Network device drivers communicate with the hardware devices. There is one device driver module for each possible hardware device.

2. The device-independent interface module provides a consistent view of all of the hardware devices so that higher levels in the subsystem don't need specific knowledge of the hardware in use.

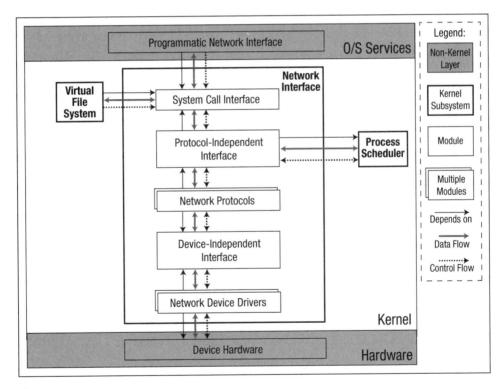

Figure 2.4
Network interface subsystem in context.

3. The network protocol modules are responsible for implementing each of the possible network transport protocols.

4. The protocol-independent interface module provides an interface that is independent of hardware devices and network protocol. This is the interface module that is used by other kernel subsystems to access the network without having a dependency on particular protocols or hardware.

Finally, the system calls interface module restricts the exported routines that user processes can access.

2.4.3   Data Representation

Each network object is represented as a socket. Sockets are associated with processes in the same way that i-nodes are associated; sockets can be share amongst processes by having both of the task data structures pointing to the same socket data structure.

2.4.4   Data Flow, Control Flow, And Dependencies

The network subsystem uses the process scheduler to suspend and resume processes while waiting for hardware requests to complete (leading to a subsystem dependency and control and data flow). In addition, the network subsystem supplies the virtual file system with the implementation of a logical file system (NFS) leading to the virtual file system depending on the network interface and having data and control flow with it.

2.5   Interprocess Communication Architecture

The architecture of the interprocess communication subsystem is omitted for brevity since it is not as interesting as the other subsystems.

Chapter 3
Conclusions

The Linux kernel is one layer in the architecture of the entire Linux system. The kernel is conceptually composed of five major subsystems: the process scheduler, the memory manager, the virtual file system, the network interface, and the interprocess communication interface. These subsystems interact with each other using function calls and shared data structures.

At the highest level, the architectural style of the Linux kernel is closes to Garlan and Shaw's data abstraction style ([Garlan 1994]); the kernel is composed of subsystems that maintain internal representation consistency by using a specific procedural interface. As each of the subsystems is elaborated, we see an architectural style that is similar to the layered style presented by Garlan and Shaw. Each of the subsystems is composed of modules that communicate only with adjacent layers.

The conceptual architecture of the Linux kernel has proved its success; essential factors for this success were the provision for the organization of developers, and the provision for system extensibility. The Linux kernel architecture was required to support a large number of independent volunteer developers. This requirement suggested that the system portions that require the most development—the hardware device drivers and the file and network protocols—be implemented in an extensible fashion. The Linux architect chose to make these systems be extensible using a data abstraction technique: Each hardware device driver is implemented as a separate module that supports a common interface. In this way, a single developer can add a new device driver, with minimal interaction required with other developers of the Linux kernel. The success of the kernel implementation by a large number of volunteer developers proves the correctness of this strategy.

Another important extension to the Linux kernel is the addition of more supported hardware platforms. The architecture of the system supports this extensibility by separating all hardware-specific code into distinct modules within each subsystem. In this way, a small group of developers can effect a port of the Linux kernel to a new hardware architecture by re-implementing only the machine-specific portions of the kernel.

Appendix A
Definition Of Terms

Device Driver
A device driver is all of the code that is required to interface with a particular hardware device. Device drivers are properly part of the kernel, but the Linux kernel has a mechanism that permits dynamic loading of device drivers.

I-Node
I-nodes, or index nodes, are used by the file system to keep track of which hardware addresses correspond to which file system data blocks. Each i-node stores a mapping of file block to physical block, plus additional information for security and accounting purposes.

Network File System (NFS)
The Network File System is a file system interface that presents files that are stored on a remote computer as a file system on the local machine.

Process
A process (also called a task) is a program in execution; it consists of executable code and dynamic data. The kernel associates enough information with each process to stop and resume it.

Ramdisk
A ramdisk is a device driver that uses an area of main memory as a file system device. This allows frequently accessed files to be placed in an area that provides reliably efficient access at all times; this can be especially useful when using Linux to support hard

real-time requirements. For usual cases, the normal file system caching will make the most efficient use of memory to provide reasonably efficient access to files.

Swapping

Linux supports processes that use memory that exceeds the amount of physical memory on the computer. This is accomplished by the memory manager swapping unused pages of memory to a persistent store; when the memory is later accessed, it is swapped back into the main memory (possibly causing other pages to be swapped out).

Task

See Process.

Appendix B
References

Garlan 1994

David Garlan and Mary Shaw, *An Introduction to Software Architecture*, *Advances in Software Engineering and Knowledge Engineering*, Volume I, World Scientific Publishing Company, 1993.

Monroe 1997

Robert T. Monroe, Andrew Kompanek, Ralph Melton, and David Garlan, *Architectural Styles, Design Patterns, and Objects*, IEEE Software, January 1997, pp 43-52.

Parker 1997

Slackware Linux Unleashed, by Timothy Parker, et al, Sams Publishing, 201 West 103rd Street, Indianapolis.

Perry 1992

Dewayne E. Perry and Alexander L. Wolf, *Foundations for the Study of Software Architecture*, ACM SIGSOFT Software Engineering Notes, 17:4, October 1992 pp. 40-52.

Raymond 1993

The New Hackers Dictionary, 2nd edition, compiled by Eric S. Raymond. The MIT Press, Cambridge Massachusetts, 1993.

Rusling 1997

The Linux Kernel, by David A. Rusling, draft, version 0.1-13(19), **ftp://sunsite.unc.edu/pub/Linux/docs/linux-doc-project/linux-kernel/** or **http://www.linuxhq.com/guides/TLK/index.html**.

Soni 1995

Soni, D.; Nord, R. L.; Hofmeister, C., *Software Architecture in Industrial Applications*, IEEE ICSE 1995, pp. 196-210.

Tanenbaum 1992

Modern Operating Systems, by Andrew S. Tanenbaum, Prentice Hall, 1992.

Wirzenius 1997

Linux System Administrators' Guide 0.6, by Lars Wirzenius, **http://www.iki.fi/liw/linux/sag/** or **http://www.linuxhq.com/LDP/LDP/sag/index.html**.

Part V

Concrete Architecture
Of The Linux Kernel

by Ivan Bowman, Saheem Siddiqi,
and Meyer C. Tanuan

Ivan Bowman
(**ibowman@sybase.com**)

Saheem Siddiqi
(**s4siddiqi@neumann**)

Meyer C. Tanuan
(**mtanuan@descartes.com**)

Department of Computer Science
University of Waterloo
Waterloo, Ontario N2L 3G1
CS 746G, Winter 1998
12-Feb-98

Available at: **http://plg.uwaterloo.ca/~itbowman/CS746G/a2**

Abstract

The objective of this report is to describe the concrete (as-built) architecture of the Linux kernel. A concrete architecture description of the Linux kernel serves as a high-level specification for developers to modify and extend the existing kernel source code.

We used a reverse engineering tool (Portable Bookshelf) to extract the detailed design information out of the Linux kernel source. The biggest challenge we had to overcome was to cluster the enormous volume of extracted information into subsystems. We clustered the extracted information based on our domain-specific knowledge about modern operating systems; the Software Landscape visualization tool was used in an iterative process to view and refine this clustering.

Although the Portable Bookshelf tool provided detailed design information and some initial clustering based on file names, we found that this was not sufficient to form a concrete architecture description. The extraction tool didn't accurately extract dependencies. It missed some dependencies, and asserted some that did not exist. The tool didn't automatically provide a structure that helped understand the system. We verified the extracted design facts and refined the clustering using our conceptual model of the Linux kernel.

We concluded that the Portable Bookshelf tool by itself cannot accurately describe the concrete architecture of the Linux kernel. We remedied this limitation by using domain-specific knowledge to describe the concrete architecture.

Chapter 1

Introduction

Purpose

The goal of this report is to describe the concrete architecture of the Linux kernel. *Concrete architecture* refers to the architecture of the system as it is built. We intend to develop the concrete architecture to provide high-level documentation of the existing Linux kernel.

Introduction To Linux

Linus B. Torvalds wrote the first Linux kernel in 1991. Linux gained in popularity because it has always been distributed as free software. Since the source code is readily available, users can freely change the kernel to suit their needs. However, it is important to understand how the Linux kernel has evolved and how it currently works before new system programs are written.

A concrete architecture based on the Linux kernel source code can provide a reliable and up-to-date reference for Linux kernel hackers and developers. Linux has been revised several times since 1991 by a group of volunteers who communicate through the Usenet newsgroups on the Internet. To date, Torvalds has acted as the as the main kernel developer. In the event that Linus Torvalds is no longer part of the Linux kernel project, we can reasonably expect that the Linux kernel can be enhanced and modified if an accurate and up-to-date concrete architecture is maintained.

Linux is a Unix-compatible system. Most of the common Unix tools and programs now run under Linux. Linux was originally developed to run on the Intel 80386 microprocessor. The original version was not readily portable to other platforms because it uses Intel's specific interrupt handling routines. When Linux was ported to other hardware platforms such as the DEC Alpha and Sun SPARC, much of the platform-dependent code was moved into platform-specific modules that support a common interface.

The Linux user base is large. In 1994, Ed Chi estimated Linux has approximately 40,000 users ([Chi 1994]). The Linux Documentation Project (LDP) is working on developing useful and reliable documentation for the Linux kernel; both for use by Linux users and by Linux developers. To our knowledge, LDP does not maintain an up-to-date concrete architecture using reverse engineering practices. There are many books and documents about the Linux kernel [CS746G Bibliography]. However, no available documentation adequately describes both the conceptual and concrete architecture of Linux. Publications (such as [Beck 1996] and [Rusling 1997]) talk about how the Linux kernel works. However, these books do not thoroughly explain the subsystems and the interdependencies of the subsystems.

Background On Software Architecture

The study of *software architecture* has gained recent popularity in both the industrial and academic community. Software architecture involves the study of large software systems. Recent studies have shown that software architecture is important because it enhances communication among stakeholders of the system. Software architecture can be used to support earlier design decisions; also, it can be used as a transferable abstraction of a system ([Bass 1998]).

Software architecture is related to the study of software maintenance. Maintaining existing, or legacy systems is often problematic. The status of these existing systems can be described in a spectrum ranging from well designed and well documented to poorly designed and undocumented. In many cases, some or all of the original architects and developers may no longer be involved with the existing system. This lack of live architecture knowledge tremendously complicates the software maintenance task. In order to change, extend, modify, or remove functionality of an existing system, the implementation of the system needs to be understood. This problem reinforces the need to develop techniques to extract architectural and design information from existing system. The process of extracting high-level models from the source code is often referred to as *reverse engineering*.

The discipline of reverse engineering has two main areas [Bass 1998]:

1. **Technical approaches:** These extraction approaches derive information about a system based on existing artifacts. In particular, source code, comments, user documentation, executable modules, and system descriptions are often extracted.

2. **Human knowledge and inference:** These approaches focus on how humans understand software. Typically, human investigators use the following strategies:

- **Top-down strategies:** start at the highest level of abstraction and recursively fill in understanding of the sub-parts.

- **Bottom-up strategies:** understand the lowest level components and how these work together to accomplish the system's goals

- **Model-based strategies**: understand the mental model of how the system works and try to deepen the understanding of selected areas

- **Opportunistic strategies**: use some combination of the above approaches.

In this report, we used both the technical and human knowledge approaches to describe the concrete architecture of the Linux kernel. The opportunistic strategy follows the same strategy as the hybrid approach of [Tzerpos 1996]. Instead of using "live" information from the developers of the Linux kernel, we used our domain-specific knowledge of modern operating systems (i.e., the conceptual architecture from Assignment 1) to repeatedly refine the concrete architecture of the Linux kernel.

Methodology/Approach

In this report, we used the opportunistic strategy to develop the concrete architecture of the Linux kernel. We used a modified version of the hybrid approach of [Tzerpos 1996] to determine the structure of the Linux kernel. The steps, which are not necessarily in sequential order, are:

- *Define conceptual architecture*. Since we have no direct access to "live" information from the developers, we used our modern operating system domain knowledge to create the Conceptual Architecture of the Linux kernel. This step was done in Assignment 1 ([Bowman 1998], [Siddiqi 1998], and [Tanuan 1998]).

- *Extract facts from source code*. We used the Portable Bookshelf's C Fact Extractor (cfx) and Fact Base Generator (fbgen) (described in [Holt 1997]) to extract dependency facts from the source code.

- *Cluster into subsystems*. We used the Fact Manipulator (i.e., grok and grok scripts) to cluster facts into subsystems. This clustering was performed partially by the tool (using file names and directories), and partially using our conceptual model of the Linux kernel.

- *Review the generated software structure*. We used the Landscape Layouter, Adjuster, Editor and Viewer ([Holt 1997]) to visualize the extracted design information. Based on these diagrams, we could visually see the dependencies between the subsystems. The landscape diagrams confirmed our understanding of the concrete architecture. In cases where the extracted architecture disagreed with the conceptual architecture, we inspected the source code and documentation manually.

- *Refine clustering using conceptual architecture*. We used the conceptual architecture of the Linux kernel to verify the clustering of the components and the dependencies of these components.

♦ *Refine layout using conceptual architecture.* In conjunction with the previous step, we drew the layout of the Linux kernel structure manually using Visio drawing tool.

There are many views of the Linux kernel, depending on the motive and viewpoint. In this report, we described the concrete architecture using a *software structure* ([Mancoridis Slides]). We used the software structure to do the following:

♦ specify the decomposition of the Linux kernel into five major subsystems

♦ describe the interfaces of the components (i.e., subsystems and modules)

♦ describe the dependencies between components.

We describe dependencies between resources, where a resources can be subsystems, modules, procedures, or variable. The dependency relation is quite broad; usually we do not distinguish between function calls, variable reference, and type usage.

The software structure says little about the run-time structure of the Linux kernel. However, we believe that the software structure together with the detailed specifications will give enough information for a potential Linux developer to modify or extend the Linux without reviewing all the source code. We are not mainly concerned with the process view [Kruchten 1995] of the Linux kernel because we treat the Linux kernel as one single executing process.

Reader Profile

We assume that the reader has a sufficient background in computer science and operating systems to thoroughly understand the discussion on the major components and interactions of the components of the Linux kernel in this report. We do not assume a detailed knowledge of the Linux operating system.

Organization Of This Report

This remainder of this report is organized as follows:

♦ Section 2 describes the overall system architecture. It describes the system architecture showing the five major subsystems and the interdependencies between them.

♦ Section 3 describes the subsystem architecture of the major subsystems: Process Scheduler, Memory Manager, Virtual File System, Interprocess Communication, Network Interface. Each subsystem description will be supported with a diagram to show the subsystem in context with lines showing dependencies. It also includes an interpretation of the system abstraction and design information extracted from the Linux kernel source code.

♦ Section 4 describes the problems that we encountered in the report, and describe the findings and conclusion that we arrived at.

Chapter 2
System Structure

Τhe Linux Kernel is useless by itself; it participates as one layer in the overall system ([Bowman 1998]).

Within the kernel layer, Linux is composed of five major subsystems: the process scheduler (sched), the memory manager (mm), the virtual file system (vfs), the network interface (net), and the interprocess communication (ipc). The as-built architecture decomposition is similar to the conceptual architecture decomposition of [Siddiqi 1998], [Tanuan 1998], and [Bowman 1998]. This correspondence is not too surprising given that the conceptual architecture was derived from the as-built architecture. Our decomposition does not exactly follow the directory structure of the source code, as we believe that this doesn't perfectly match the subsystem grouping; however, our clustering is quite close to this directory structure.

One difference that became clear after visualizing the extracted design details is that the subsystem dependencies differ quite radically from the conceptual dependencies. The conceptual architecture suggested very few intersystem dependencies, as shown by Figure 2.1.a (derived from [Bowman 1998]).

Although the conceptual architecture has few dependencies, the concrete architecture shows that the five major subsystems of the Linux kernel are highly interdependent. Figure 2.1.b shows that the connection is only missing two edges from a complete graph ([PBS:Kernel.html] gives the details of which modules interact across subsystems). This interdependency is a striking disagreement with the conceptual architecture. It seems that any reverse-engineering technique based on interconnection properties (such as the Rigi

485

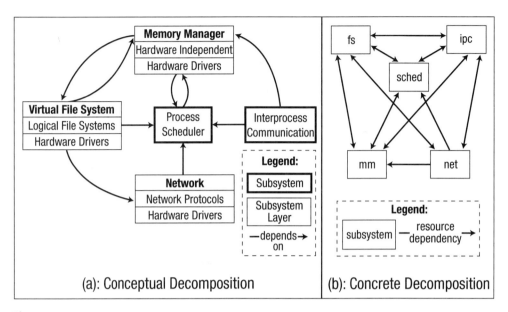

Figure 2.1
Conceptual versus concrete system decomposition.

system described in [Müller 1993]) would fail to extract any relevant structure from such a system. This validates the hybrid approach discussed by Tzerpos ([Tzerpos 1996]).

The differences at the system level are characteristic of differences at the subsystem level. The subsystem structure corresponds largely to the conceptual structure. However, we found many dependencies in the concrete architecture that weren't in the conceptual architecture (*divergences* in the sense of [Murphy 1995]). The reasons for these additional dependencies are discussed in the following section, where we examine the detailed design of each of the major subsystems.

Chapter 3
Subsystem Structure

Process Scheduler
Goals

Process scheduling is the heart of the Linux operating system. The process scheduler has the following responsibilities:

- allow processes to create new copies of themselves
- determine which process will have access to the CPU and effect the transfer between running processes
- receive interrupts and route them to the appropriate kernel subsystem
- send signals to user processes
- manage the timer hardware
- clean up process resources when a processes finishes executing

The process scheduler also provides support for dynamically loaded modules; these modules represent kernel functionality that can be loaded after the kernel has started executing. This loadable module functionality is used by the virtual file system and the network interface.

External Interface

The process scheduler provides two interfaces: first, it provides a limited system call interface that user processes may call; second, it provides a rich interface to the rest of the kernel system.

Processes can only create other processes by copying the existing process. At boot time, the Linux system has only one running process: **init.** This process then spawns others, which can also spawn off copies of themselves, through the **fork()** system call. The **fork()** call generates a new child process that is a copy of its parent. Upon termination, a user process (implicitly or explicitly) calls the **_exit()** system call.

Several routines are provided to handle loadable modules. A **create_module()** system call will allocate enough memory to load a module. The call will initialize the **module** structure, described below, with the name, size, starting address, and initial status for the allocated module. The **init_module()** system call loads the module from disk and activates it. Finally, **delete_module()** unloads a running module.

Timer management can be done through the **setitimer()** and **getitimer()** routines. The former sets a timer while the latter gets a timer's value.

Among the most important signal functions is **signal().** This routine allows a user process to associate a function handler with a particular signal.

Subsystem Description

The process scheduler subsystem is primarily responsible for the loading, execution, and proper termination of user processes. The scheduling algorithm is called at two different points during the execution of a user process. First, there are system calls that call the scheduler directly, such as **sleep()**. Second, after every system call, and after every slow system interrupt (described in a moment), the schedule algorithm is called.

Signals can be considered an IPC mechanism, thus are discussed in the interprocess communication section.

Interrupts allow hardware to communicate with the operating system. Linux distinguishes between slow and fast interrupts. A slow interrupt is a typical interrupt. Other interrupts are legal while they are being processed, and once processing has completed on a slow interrupt, Linux conducts business as usual, such as calling the scheduling algorithm. A timer interrupt is exemplary of a slow interrupt. A fast interrupt is one that is used for much less complex tasks, such as processing keyboard input. Other interrupts are disabled as they are being processed, unless explicitly enabled by the fast interrupt handler.

The Linux OS uses a timer interrupt to fire off once every 10 ms. Thus, according to our scheduler description given above, task rescheduling should occur at lease once every 10 ms.

Data Structures

The structure **task_struct** represents a Linux task. There is a field that represents the process state; this may have the following values:

♦ running

♦ returning from system call

- processing an interrupt routine
- processing a system call
- ready
- waiting

In addition, there is a field that indicates the process priority, and a field that holds the number of clock ticks (10 ms intervals) which the process can continue executing without forced rescheduling. There is also a field that holds the error number of the last faulting system call.

In order to keep track of all executing processes, a doubly linked list is maintained (through two fields that point to **task_struct**). Since every process is related to some other process, there are fields which describe a processes: original parent, parent, youngest child, younger sibling, and finally older sibling.

There is a nested structure, **mm_struct**, which contains a process's memory management information (such as start and end address of the code segment).

Process ID information is also kept within the **task_struct**. The process and group ID are stored. An array of group IDs is provided so that a process can be associated with more than one group.

File-specific process data is located in a **fs_struct** substructure. This will hold a pointer to the inode corresponding to a processor's root directory, and its current working directory.

All files opened by a process will be kept track of through a **files_struct** substructure of the **task_struct**.

Finally, there are fields that hold timing information; for example, the amount of time the process has spent in user mode.

All executing processes have an entry in the process table. The process table is implemented as an array of pointers to task structures. The first entry in the process table is the special **init** process, which is the first process executed by the Linux system.

Finally, a **module** structure is implemented to represent the loaded modules. This structure contains fields that are used to implement a list of module structure: a field which points to the modules symbol table, and another field that holds the name of the module. The module size (in pages), and a pointer to the starting memory for the module are also fields within the **module** structure.

Subsystem Structure

Figure 3.1 shows the process scheduler subsystem. It is used to represent, collectively, process scheduling and management (i.e., loading and unloading), as well as timer management and module management functionality.

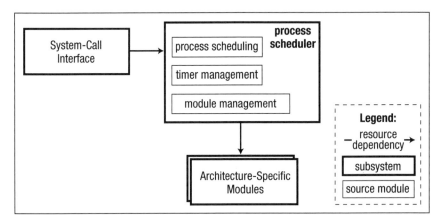

Figure 3.1
Process scheduler structure.

Subsystem Dependencies

Figure 3.2 shows how the process scheduler depends on other kernel subsystems. The process scheduler requires the memory manager to set up the memory mapping when a process is scheduled. Further, the process scheduler depends on the IPC subsystem for the wait queues that are used in bottom-half-handling (discussed in Section 3.3). Finally, the process scheduler depends on the file system to load loadable modules from the persistent device. All subsystems depend on the process scheduler, since they need to suspend user processes while hardware operations complete. For more details about the specific dependencies between subsystem modules, please see [PBS:Kernel.html].

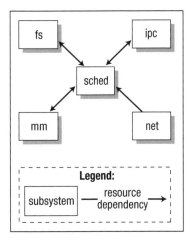

Figure 3.2
Process scheduler dependencies.

Memory Manager

Goals

As discussed in [Rusling 1997] pp. 13-30, the memory manager provides the following capabilities to its clients:

♦ *Large address space*—user programs can reference more memory than physically exists.

♦ *Protection*—the memory for a process is private and cannot be read or modified by another process; also, the memory manager prevents processes from overwriting code and read-only data.

♦ *Memory mapping*—clients can map a file into an area of virtual memory and access the file as memory

♦ *Fair access to physical memory*—the memory manager ensures that processes all have fair access to the machine's memory resources, thus ensuring reasonable system performance.

♦ *Shared memory*—the memory manager allows processes to share some portion of their memory. For example, executable code is usually shared among processes.

External Interface

The memory manager provides two interfaces to its functionality: a system-call interface that is used by user processes, and an interface that is used by other kernel subsystems to accomplish their tasks.

♦ System call interface

  ♦ **malloc() / free()**—allocate or free a region of memory for the process's use

  ♦ **mmap() / munmap() / msync() / mremap()**—map files into virtual memory regions

  ♦ **mprotect**—change the protection on a region of virtual memory

  ♦ **mlock() / mlockall() / munlock() / munlockall()**—super-user routines to prevent memory being swapped

  ♦ **swapon() / swapoff()**—super-user routines to add and remove swap files for the system

♦ Intra-kernel interface

  ♦ **kmalloc() / kfree()**—allocate and free memory for use by the kernel's data structures

  ♦ **verify_area()**—verify that a region of user memory is mapped with required permissions

  ♦ **get_free_page() / free_page()**—allocate and free physical memory pages

In addition to the above interfaces, the memory manager makes all of its data structures and most of its routines available within the kernel. Many kernel modules interface with the memory manager through access to the data structures and implementation details of the subsystem.

Subsystem Description

Since Linux supports several hardware platforms, there is a platform-specific part of the memory manager that abstracts the details of all hardware platforms into one common interface. All access to the hardware memory manager is through this abstract interface.

The memory manager uses the hardware memory manager to map virtual addresses (used by user processes) to physical memory addresses. When a user process accesses a memory location, the hardware memory manager translates this virtual memory address to a physical address, then uses the physical address to perform the access. Because of this mapping, user processes are not aware of what physical address is associated with a particular virtual memory address. This allows the memory manager subsystem to move the process's memory around in physical memory. In addition, this mapping permits two user processes to share physical memory if regions of their virtual memory address space map to the same physical address space.

In addition, the memory manager *swaps* process memory out to a paging file when it is not in use. This allows the system to execute processes that use more physical memory than is available on the system. The memory manager contains a *daemon* (kswapd). Linux uses the term daemon to refer to kernel threads; a daemon is scheduled by the process scheduler in the same way that user processes are, but daemons can directly access kernel data structures. Thus, the concept of a daemon is closer to a thread than a process.

The kswapd daemon periodically checks to see if there are any physical memory pages that haven't been referenced recently. These pages are evicted from physical memory; if necessary, they are stored on disk. The memory manager subsystem takes special care to minimize the amount of disk activity that is required. The memory manager avoids writing pages to disk if they could be retrieved another way.

The hardware memory manager detects when a user process accesses a memory address that is not currently mapped to a physical memory location. The hardware memory manager notifies the Linux kernel of this *page fault*, and it is up to the memory manager subsystem to resolve the fault. There are two possibilities: either the page is currently swapped out to disk, and must be swapped back in, or else the user process is making an invalid reference to a memory address outside of its mapped memory. The hardware memory manager also detects invalid references to memory addresses, such as writing to executable code or executing data. These references also result in page faults that are reported to the memory manager subsystem. If the memory manager detects an invalid memory access, it notifies the user process with a *signal*; if the process doesn't handle this signal, it is terminated.

Data Structures

The following data structures are architecturally relevant:

1. **vm_area**—the memory manager stores a data structure with each process that records what regions of virtual memory are mapped to which physical pages. This data structure also stores a set of function pointers that allow it to perform actions on a particular

region of the process's virtual memory. For example, the executable code region of the process does not need to be swapped to the system paging file since it can use the executable file as a backing store. When regions of a process's virtual memory are mapped (for example when an executable is loaded), a vm_area_struct is set up for each contiguous region in the virtual address space. Since speed is critical when looking up a vm_area_struct for a page fault, the structures are stored in an AVL tree.

2. **mem_map**—the memory manager maintains a data structure for each page of physical memory on a system. This data structure contains flags that indicate the status of the page (for example, whether it is currently in use). All page data structures are available in a vector (mem_map), which is initialized at kernel boot time. As page status changes, the attributes in this data structure are updated.

3. **free_area**—the free_area vector is used to store unallocated physical memory pages; pages are removed from the free_area when allocated, and returned when freed. The Buddy system [Knowlton 1965; Tanenbaum 1992] is used when allocating pages from the free_area.

Subsystem Structure

The memory manager subsystem is composed of several source code modules; these can be decomposed by areas of responsibility into the following groups (shown in Figure 3.3):

♦ **System call interface**—this group of modules is responsible for presenting the services of the memory manager to user processes through a well-defined interface (discussed earlier).

♦ **Memory-mapped files (mmap)**—this group of modules is responsible for supported memory-mapped file I/O.

♦ **Swapfile access (swap)**—this group of modules controls memory swapping. These modules initiate page-in and page-out operations.

♦ **Core memory manager (core)**—these modules are responsible for the core memory manager functionality that is used by other kernel subsystems.

♦ **Architecture-specific modules**—these modules provide a common interface to all supported hardware platforms. These modules execute commands to change the hardware MMU's virtual memory map, and provide a common means of notifying the rest of the memory-manager subsystem when a page fault occurs.

One interesting aspect of the memory manager structure is the use of kswapd, a daemon that determines which pages of memory should be swapped out. kswapd executes as a kernel thread, and periodically scans the physical pages in use to see if any are candidates to be swapped. This daemon executes concurrently with the rest of the memory manager subsystem.

Subsystem Dependencies

The memory manager is used directly (via data structures and implementation functions) by each of sched, fs, ipc, and net. This dependency is difficult to describe succinctly; please

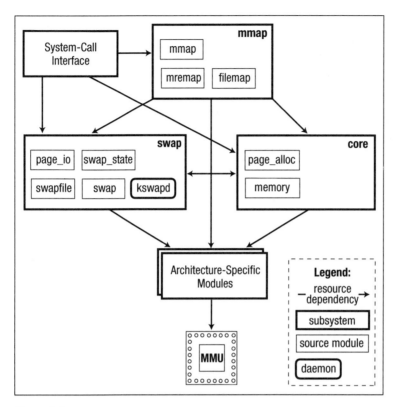

Figure 3.3
Memory manager structure.

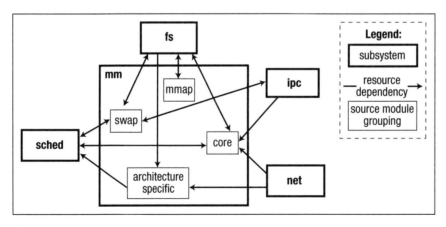

Figure 3.4
Memory manager dependencies.

refer to [PBS:mm.html] for a detailed view of the subsystem dependencies. Figure 3.4 shows the high-level dependencies between the memory manager and other subsystems. Internal dependencies are elided for clarity.

Virtual File System
Goals

Linux is designed to support many different physical devices. Even for one specific type of device, such as hard drives, there are many interface differences between different hardware vendors. In addition to the physical devices that Linux supports, Linux supports a number of logical file systems. By supporting many logical file systems, Linux can inter-operate easily with other operating systems. The Linux file system supports the following goals:

♦ *Multiple hardware devices*—provide access to many different hardware devices

♦ *Multiple logical file systems*—support many different logical file systems

♦ *Multiple executable formats*—support several different executable file formats (like a.out, ELF, java)

♦ *Homogeneity*—present a common interface to all of the logical file systems and all hardware devices

♦ *Performance*—provide high-speed access to files

♦ *Safety*—do not lose or corrupt data

♦ *Security*—restrict user access to access files; restrict user total file size with quotas

External Interface

The file system provides two levels of interface: a system-call interface that is available to user processes, and an internal interface that is used by other kernel subsystems. The system-call interface deals with files and directories. Operations on files include the usual **open/close/read/write/seek/tell** that are provided by POSIX-compliant systems; operations on directories include **readdir/creat/unlink/chmod/stat** as usual for POSIX systems.

The interface that the file subsystem supports for other kernel subsystems is much richer. The file subsystem exposes data structures and implementation function for direct manipulation by other kernel subsystems. In particular, two interfaces are exposed to the rest of the kernel—inodes and files. Other implementation details of the file subsystem are also used by other kernel subsystems, but this use is less common.

♦ Inode Interface:

  ♦ **create():** create a file in a directory

  ♦ **lookup():** find a file by name within a directory

  ♦ **link() / symlink() / unlink() / readlink() / follow_link():** manage file system links

- **mkdir() / rmdir():** create or remove subdirectories
- **mknod():** create a directory, special file, or regular file
- **readpage() / writepage():** read or write a page of physical memory to a backing store
- **truncate():** set the length of a file to zero
- **permission():** check to see if a user process has permission to execute an operation
- **smap():** map a logical file block to a physical device sector
- **bmap():** map a logical file block to a physical device block
- **rename():** rename a file or directory

In addition to the methods you can call with an inode, the namei() function is provided to allow other kernel subsystems to find the inode associated with a file or directory.

- File interface:
  - **open() / release():** open or close the file
  - **read() / write():** read or write to the file
  - **select():** wait until the file is in a particular state (readable or writeable)
  - **lseek():** if supported, move to a particular offset in the file
  - **mmap():** map a region of the file into the virtual memory of a user process
  - **fsync() / fasync():** synchronize any memory buffers with the physical device
  - **readdir:** read the files that are pointed to by a directory file
  - **ioctl:** set file attributes
  - **check_media_change:** check to see if a removable media has been removed (such as a floppy)
  - **revalidate:** verify that all cached information is valid

Subsystem Description

The file subsystem needs to support many different logical file systems and many different hardware devices. It does this by having two conceptual layers that are easily extended. The *device driver* layer represents all physical devices with a common interface. The *virtual file system* layer (VFS) represents all logical file systems with a common interface. The conceptual architecture of the Linux kernel ([Bowman 1998], [Siddiqi 1998]) shows how this decomposition is conceptually arranged.

Device Drivers

The device driver layer is responsible for presenting a common interface to all physical devices. The Linux kernel has three types of device driver: character, block, and network. The two types relevant to the file subsystem are character and block devices. Character devices must be accessed sequentially; typical examples are tape drives, modems, and mice. Block devices can be accessed in any order, but can only be read and written to in multiples of the block size.

All device drivers support the file operations interface described earlier. Therefore, each device can be accessed as though it was a file in the file system (this file is referred to as a *device special file*). Since most of the kernel deals with devices through this file interface, it is relatively easy to add a new device driver by implementing the hardware-specific code to support this abstract file interface. It is important that it is easy to write new device drivers since there is a large number of different hardware devices.

The Linux kernel uses a *buffer cache* to improve performance when accessing block devices. All access to block devices occurs through a buffer cache subsystem. The buffer cache greatly increases system performance by minimizing reads and writes to hardware devices. Each hardware device has a *request queue*; when the buffer cache cannot fulfill a request from in-memory buffers, it adds a request to the device's request queue and sleeps until this request has been satisfied. The buffer cache uses a separate kernel thread, kflushd, to write buffer pages out to the devices and remove them from the cache.

When a device driver needs to satisfy a request, it begins by initiating the operation with the hardware device manipulating the device's control and status registers (CSRs). There are three general mechanisms for moving data from the main computer to the peripheral device: polling, direct memory access (DMA), and interrupts. In the polling case, the device driver periodically checks the CSRs of the peripheral to see if the current request has been completed. If so, the driver initiates the next request and continues. Polling is appropriate for low-speed hardware devices such as floppy drives and modems. Another mechanism for transfer is DMA. In this case, the device driver initiates a DMA transfer between the computer's main memory and the peripheral. This transfer operates concurrently with the main CPU, and allows the CPU to process other tasks while the operation is continuing. When the DMA operation is complete, the CPU receives an interrupt. Interrupt handling is very common in the Linux kernel, and it is more complicated than the other two approaches.

When a hardware device wants to report a change in condition (mouse button pushed, key pressed) or to report the completion of an operation, it sends an interrupt to the CPU. If interrupts are enabled, the CPU stops executing the current instruction and begins executing the Linux kernel's interrupt handling code. The kernel finds the appropriate *interrupt handler* to invoke (each device driver registers handlers for the interrupts the device generates). While an interrupt is being handled, the CPU executes in a special context; other interrupts may be delayed until the interrupt is handled. Because of this restriction, interrupt handlers need to be quite efficient so that other interrupts won't be lost. Sometimes an interrupt handler cannot complete all required work within the time constraints; in this case, the interrupt handler schedules the remainder of the work in a *bottom-half handler*. A bottom-half handler is code that will be executed by the scheduler the next time that a system call has been completed. By deferring noncritical work to a bottom half handler, device drivers can reduce *interrupt latency* and promote concurrency.

In summary, device drivers hide the details of manipulating a peripheral's CSRs and the data transfer mechanism for each device. The buffer cache helps improve system performance by attempting to satisfy file system requests from in-memory buffers for block devices.

Logical File Systems

Although it is possible to access physical devices through their device special file, it is more common to access block devices through a logical file system. A logical file system can be *mounted* at a *mount point* in the virtual file system. This means that the associated block device contains files and structure information that allow the logical file system to access the device. At any one time, a physical device can only support one logical file system; however, the device can be reformatted to support a different logical file system. At the time of writing, Linux supports 15 logical file systems; this promotes interoperability with other operating systems.

When a file system is mounted as a subdirectory, all of the directories and files available on the device are made visible as subdirectories of the mount point. Users of the virtual file system do not need to be aware what logical file system is implementing which parts of the directory tree, nor which physical devices are containing those logical file systems. This abstraction provides a great deal of flexibility in both choice of physical devices and logical file systems, and this flexibility is one of the essential factors in the success of the Linux operating system.

To support the virtual file system, Linux uses the concept of inodes. Linux uses an inode to represent a file on a block device. The inode is virtual in the sense that it contains operations that are implemented differently depending both on the logical system and physical system where the file resides. The inode interface makes all files appear the same to other Linux subsystems. The inode is used as a storage location for all of the information related to an open file on disk. The inode stores associated buffers, the total length of the file in blocks, and the mapping between file offsets and device blocks.

Modules

Most of the functionality of the virtual file system is available in the form of dynamically loaded modules (described in section 3.1). This dynamic configuration allows Linux users to compile a kernel that is as small as possible, while still allowing it to load required device driver and file system modules if necessary during a single session. For example, a Linux system might optionally have a printer attached to its parallel port. If the printer driver were always linked in to the kernel, then memory would be wasted when the printer isn't available. By making the printer driver be a loadable module, Linux allows the user to load the driver if the hardware is available.

Data Structures

The following data structures are architecturally relevant to the file subsystem:

- **super_block:** each logical file system has an associated superblock that is used to represent it to the rest of the Linux kernel. This superblock contains information about the entire mounted file system—what blocks are in use, what the block size is, etc. The superblock is similar to inodes in that they behave as a virtual interface to the logical file system.

- **inode:** an inode is an in-memory data structure that represents all of the information that the kernel needs to know about a file on disk. A single inode might be used by several processes that all have the file open. The inode stores all of the information that the kernel needs to associate with a single file. Accounting, buffering, and memory mapping information are all stored in the inode. Some logical file systems also have an inode structure on disk that maintains this information persistently, but this is distinct from the inode data structure used within the rest of the kernel.

- **file:** the file structure represents a file that is opened by a particular process. All open files are stored in a doubly-linked list (pointed to by first_file); the file descriptor that is used in POSIX style routines (open, read, write) is the index of a particular open file in this linked list.

Subsystem Structure

Subsystem Dependencies

Figure 3.6 shows how the file system is dependent on other kernel subsystems. Again, the file system depends on all other kernel subsystems, and all other kernel subsystems depend on the file subsystem. In particular, the network subsystem depends on the file system because network sockets are presented to user processes as file descriptors. The memory manager depends on the file system to support swapping. The IPC subsystem depends on the file system for implementing pipes and FIFOs. The process scheduler depends on the file system to load loadable modules.

The file system uses the network interface to support NFS; it uses the memory manager to implement the buffer cache and for a ramdisk device; it uses the IPC subsystem to help support loadable modules, and it uses the process scheduler to put user processes to sleep while hardware requests are completed. For more details, see [PBS:fs.html].

Interprocess Communication
Goals

The Linux IPC mechanism is provided so that concurrently executing processes have a means to share resources, synchronize and exchange data with one another. Linux implements all forms of IPC between processes executing on the same system through shared resources, kernel data structures, and wait queues.

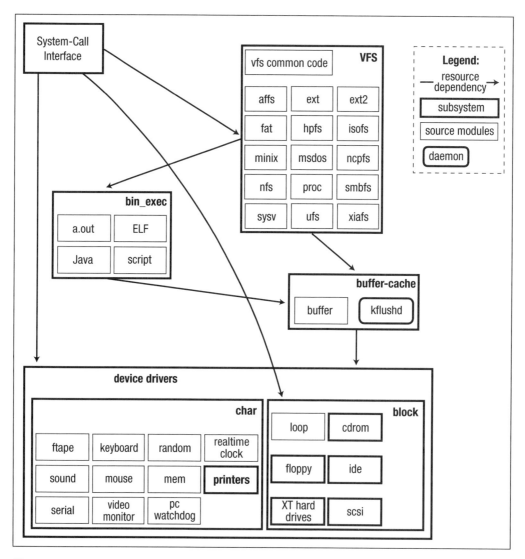

Figure 3.5
File subsystem structure.

Linux provides the following forms of IPC:

♦ *Signal*—perhaps the oldest form of Unix IPC, signals are asynchronous messages sent to a process.

♦ *Wait queues*—provides a mechanism to put processes to sleep while they are waiting for an operation to complete. This mechanism is used by the process scheduler to implement bottom-half handling as described in section 3.3.3.

♦ *File locks*—provides a mechanism to allow processes to declare either regions of a file, or the entire file itself, as read-only to all processes except the one which holds the file lock.

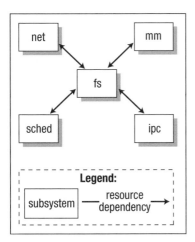

Figure 3.6
File subsystem dependencies.

- *Pipes and named pipes*—allows connection-oriented, bidirectional data transfer between two processes either by explicitly setting up the pipe connection, or communicating through a named pipe residing in the file system.

- *System V IPC*

  - *Semaphores*—an implementation of a classical semaphore model. The model also allows for the creation of arrays of semaphores.

  - *Message queues*—a connectionless data-transfer model. A message is a sequence of bytes, with an associated type. Messages are written to message queues, and messages can be obtained by reading from the message queue, possibly restricting which messages are read in by type.

  - *Shared memory*—a mechanism by which several processes have access to the same region of physical memory.

- *Unix domain sockets*—another connection-oriented data-transfer mechanism that provides the same communication model as the INET sockets, discussed in the next section.

External Interface

A signal is a notification sent to a process by the kernel or another process. Signals are sent with the **send_sig()** function. The signal number is provided as a parameter, as well as the destination process. Processes may register to handle signals by using the **signal()** function.

File locks are supported directly by the Linux file system. To lock an entire file, the **open()** system call can be used, or the **sys_fcntl()** system call can be used. Locking areas within a file is done through the **sys_fcntl()** system call.

Pipes are created by using the **pipe()** system call. The file system **read()** and **write()** calls are then used to transfer data on the pipe. Named pipes are opened using the **open()** system call.

The System V IPC mechanisms have a common interface, which is the **ipc()** system call. The various IPC operations are specified using parameters to the system call.

The Unix domain socket functionality is also encapsulated by a single system call, **socketcall()**.

Each of the system calls mentioned above are well documented, and the reader is encouraged to consult the corresponding man page.

The IPC subsystem exposes wait calls to other kernel subsystems. Since wait queues are not used by user processes, they do not have a system call interface. Wait queues are used in implementing semaphores, pipes, and bottom-half handlers (see section 3.3.3). The procedure **add_wait_queue()** inserts a task into a wait queue. The procedure **remove_wait_queue()** removes a task from the wait queue.

Subsystem Description

The following is a brief description of the low-level functioning of each IPC mechanism identified in section 3.4.1.

Signals are used to notify a process of an event. A signal has the effect of altering the state of the recipient process, depending on the semantics of the particular signal. The kernel can send signals to any executing process. A user process may only send a signal to a process or process group if it possesses the associated PID or GID. Signals are not handled immediately for dormant processes. Rather, before the scheduler sets a process running in user mode again, it checks if a signal was sent to the process. If so, then the scheduler calls the **do_signal()** function, which handles the signal appropriately.

Wait queues are simply linked lists of pointers to task structures that correspond to processes that are waiting for a kernel event, such as the conclusion of a DMA transfer. A process can enter itself on the wait queue by either calling the **sleep_on()** or **interruptable_sleep_on()** functions. Similarly, the functions **wake_up()** and **wake_up_interruptable()** remove the process from the wait queue. Interrupt routines also use wait queues to avoid race conditions.

Linux allows user process to prevent other processes from accessing a file. This exclusion can be based on a whole file, or a region of a file. File locks are used to implement this exclusion. The file system implementation contains appropriate data fields in its data structures to allow the kernel to determine if a lock has been placed on a file, or a region inside a file. In the former case, a lock attempt on a locked file will fail. In the latter case, an attempt to lock a region already locked will fail. In either case, the requesting process is not permitted to access the file since the lock has not been granted by the kernel.

Pipes and named pipes have a similar implementation, as their functionality is almost the same. The creation process is different. However, in either case a file descriptor is returned which refers to the pipe. Upon creation, one page of memory is associated with the opened pipe. This memory is treated like a circular buffer, to which write operations are done atomically. When the buffer is full, the writing processes block. If a read request is made for more data than what is available, the reading processes block. Thus, each pipe has a wait queue associated with it. Processes are added and removed from the queue during the read and writes.

Semaphores are implemented using wait queues, and follow the classical semaphore model. Each semaphore has an associated value. Two operations, **up()** and **down()**, are implemented on the semaphore. When the value of the semaphore is zero, the process performing the decrement on the semaphore is blocked on the wait queue. Semaphore arrays are simply a contiguous set of semaphores. Each process also maintains a list of semaphore operations it has performed, so that if the process exits prematurely, these operations can be undone.

The message queue is a linear linked list, to which processes read or write a sequence of bytes. Messages are received in the same order that they are written. Two wait queues are associated with the message queues, one for processes that are writing to a full message queue, and another for serializing the message writes. The actual size of the message is set when the message queue is created.

Shared memory is the fastest form of IPC. This mechanism allows processes to share a region of their memory. Creation of shared memory areas is handled by the memory management system. Shared pages are attached to the user processes virtual memory space by the system call **sys_shmat()**. A shared page can be removed from the user segment of a process by calling the **sys_shmdt()** call.

The Unix domain sockets are implemented in a similar fashion to pipes, in the sense that both are based on a circular buffer based on a page of memory. However, sockets provide a separate buffer for each communication direction.

Data Structures

In this section, the important data structures needed to implement the above IPC mechanisms are described.

Signals are implemented through the **signal** field in the **task_struct** structure. Each signal is represented by a bit in this field. Thus, the number of signals a version of Linux can support is limited to the number of bits in a word. The field **blocked** holds the signals that are being blocked by a process.

There is only one data structure associated with the wait queues, the **wait_queue** structure. These structures contain a pointer to the associated **task_struct**, and are linked into a list.

File locks have an associated **file_lock** structure. This structure contains a pointer to a **task_struct** for the owning process, the file descriptor of the locked file, a wait queue for processes which are waiting for the cancellation of the file lock, and which region of the file is locked. The **file_lock** structures are linked into a list for each open file.

Pipes, both nameless and named, are represented by a file system inode. This inode stores extra pipe-specific information in the **pipe_inode_info** structure. This structure contains a wait queue for processes which are blocking on a read or write, a pointer to the page of memory used as the circular buffer for the pipe, the amount of data in the pipe, and the number of processes which are currently reading and writing from/to the pipe.

All system V IPC objects are created in the kernel, and each have associated access permissions. These access permissions are held in the **ipc_perm** structure. Semaphores are represented with the **sem** structure, which holds the value of the semaphore and the pid of the process that performed the last operation on the semaphore. Semaphore arrays are represented by the **semid_ds** structure, which holds the access permissions, the time of the last semaphore operation, a pointer to the first semaphore in the array, and queues on which processes block when performing semaphore operations. The structure **sem_undo** is used to create a list of semaphore operations performed by a process, so that they can all be undone when the process is killed.

Message queues are based on the **msquid_ds** structure, which holds management and control information. This structure stores the following fields:

♦ access permissions

♦ link fields to implement the message queue (i.e., pointers to **msquid_ds**)

♦ times for the last send, receipt, and change

♦ queues on which processes block, as described in the previous section

♦ the current number of bytes in the queue

♦ the number of messages

♦ the size of the queue (in bytes)

♦ the process number of the last sender

♦ the process number of the last receiver

A message itself is stored in the kernel with a **msg** structure. This structure holds a link field, to implement a link list of messages, the type of message, the address of the message data, and the length of the message.

The shared memory implementation is based on the **shmid_ds** structure, which, like the **msquid_ds** structure, holds management and control information. The structure contains access control permissions, last attach, detach and change times, pids of the creator and last process to call an operation for the shared segment, number of processes to which the shared memory region is attached to, the number of pages which make up the shared memory region, and a field for page table entries.

The Unix domain sockets are based on the **socket** data structure, described in the Network Interface section (3.5).

Subsystem Structure

Figure 3.7 shows the IPC subsystem resource dependencies. Control flows from the system call layer down into each module. The System V IPC facilities are implemented in the **ipc** directory of the kernel source. The kernel IPC module refers to IPC facilities implemented within the **kernel** directory. Similar conventions hold for the File and Net IPC facilities.

The System V IPC module is dependant on the Kernel IPC mechanism. In particular, semaphores are implemented with wait queues. All other IPC facilities are implemented independently of each other.

Subsystem Dependencies

Figure 3.8 shows the resource dependencies between the IPC subsystem and other kernel subsystems.

The IPC subsystem depends on the file system for sockets. Sockets use file descriptors, and once they are opened, they are assigned to an inode. Memory management depends on IPC as the page swapping routine calls the IPC subsystem to perform swapping of shared memory. IPC depends on memory management primarily for the allocation of buffers and the implementation of shared memory.

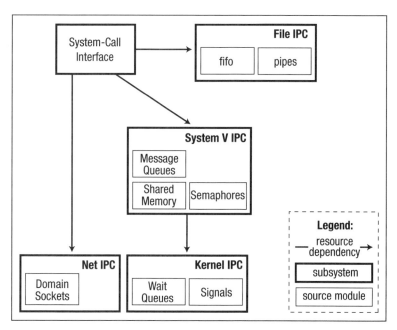

Figure 3.7
IPC subsystem structure.

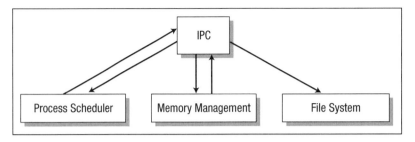

Figure 3.8
IPC subsystem dependencies.

Some IPC mechanisms use timers, which are implemented in the process scheduler subsystem. Process scheduling relies on signals. For these two reasons, the IPC and Process Scheduler modules depend on each other. For more details about the dependencies between the IPC subsystem modules and other kernel subsystems, see [PBS:ipc.html].

Network Interface
Goals
The Linux network system provides network connectivity between machines, and a socket communication model. Two types of socket implementations are provided: BSD sockets and INET sockets. BSD sockets are implemented using INET sockets.

The Linux network system provides two transport protocols with differing communication models and quality of service. These are the unreliable, message-based UDP protocol and the reliable, streamed TCP protocol. These are implemented on top of the IP networking protocol. The INET sockets are implemented on top of both transport protocols and the IP protocol.

Finally, the IP protocol sits on top of the underlying device drivers. Device drivers are provided for three different types of connections: serial line connections (SLIP), parallel line connections (PLIP), and Ethernet connections. An address resolution protocol mediates between the IP and ethernet drivers. The address resolver's role is to translate between the logical IP addresses and the physical ethernet addresses.

External Interface
The network services are used by other subsystems and the user through the socket interface. Sockets are created and manipulated through the **socketcall()** system call. Data is sent and received using **read()** and **write()** calls on the socket file descriptor.

No other network mechanism/functionality is exported from the network subsystem.

Subsystem Description

The BSD socket model is presented to the user processes. The model is that of a connection-oriented, streamed, and buffered communication service. The BSD socket is implemented on top of the INET socket model.

The BSD socket model handles tasks similar to that of the VFS, and administers a general data structure for socket connections. The purpose of the BSD socket model is to provide greater portability by abstracting communication details to a common interface. The BSD interface is widely used in modern operating systems such as Unix and Microsoft Windows. The INET socket model manages the actual communication end points for the IP-based protocols TCP and UDP.

Network I/O begins with a read or write to a socket. This invokes a read/write system call, which is handled by a component of the virtual file system (the chain of read/write calls down the network subsystem layers are symmetric, thus from this point forward, only writes are considered). From there, it is determined that the BSD socket **sock_write()** is what implements the actual file system write call; thus, it is called. This routine handles administrative details, and control is then passed to **inet_write()** function. This in turn calls a transport layer write call (such as **tcp_write()**).

The transport layer write routines are responsible for splitting the incoming data into transport packets. These routines pass control to the **ip_build_header()** routine, which builds an IP protocol header to be inserted into the packet to be sent, and then **tcp_build_header()** is called to build a TCP protocol header. Once this is done, the underlying device drivers are used to actually send the data.

The network system provides two different transport services, each with a different communication model and quality of service. UDP provides a connectionless, unreliable data transmission service. It is responsible for receiving packets from the IP layer, and finding the destination socket to which the packet data should be sent. If the destination socket is not present, an error is reported. Otherwise, if there is sufficient buffer memory, the packet data is entered into a list of packets received for a socket. Any sockets sleeping on a read operation are notified, and awoken.

The TCP transport protocol offers a much more complicated scheme. In addition to handling data transfer between sending and receiving processes, the TCP protocol also performs complicated connection management. TCP sends data up to the socket layer as a stream, rather than as a sequence of packets, and guarantees a reliable transport service.

The IP protocol provides a packet transfer service. Given a packet, and a destination of the packet, the IP communication layer is responsible for the routing of the packet to the correct host. For an outgoing data stream, the IP is responsible for the following:

♦ partitioning the stream into IP packets
♦ routing the IP packets to the destination address

♦ generating a header to be used by the hardware device drivers

♦ selecting the appropriate network device to send out on

For an incoming packet stream, the IP must do the following:

♦ check the header for validity

♦ compare the destination address with the local address and forwarding it along if the packet is not at it's correct destination

♦ defragment the IP packet

♦ send the packets up to the TCP or UDP layer to be further processed

The ARP (address resolution protocol) is responsible for converting between the IP and the real hardware address. The ARP supports a variety of hardware devices such as Ethernet, FDDI, and so on. This function is necessary as sockets deal with IP addresses, which cannot be used directly by the underlying hardware devices. Because a neutral addressing scheme is used, the same communication protocols can be implemented across a variety of hardware devices.

The network subsystem provides its own device drivers for serial connections, parallel connections, and ethernet connections. An abstract interface to the various hardware devices is provided to hide the differences between communication mediums from the upper layers of the network subsystem.

Data Structures

The BSD socket implementation is represented by the **socket** structure. It contains a field which identifies the type of socket (streamed or datagram), and the state of the socket (connected or unconnected). A field that holds flags which modify the operation of the socket, and a pointer to a structure that describes the operations that can be performed on the socket are also provided. A pointer to the associated INET socket implementation is provided, as well as a reference to an inode. Each BSD socket is associated with an inode.

The structure **sk_buff** is used to manage individual communication packets. The buffer points to the socket to which it belongs, contains the time it was last transferred, and link fields so that all packets associated with a given socket can be linked together (in a doubly linked list). The source and destination addresses, header information, and packet data are also contained within the buffer. This structure encapsulates all packets used by the networking system (i.e. TCP packet, UDP packets, IP packets, and so on).

The **sock** structure refers to the INET socket-specific information. The members of this structure include counts of the read and write memory requested by the socket, sequence numbers required by the TCP protocol, flags which can be set to alter the behavior of the socket, buffer management fields (for example, to maintain a list of all packets received for the given socket), and a wait queue for blocking reads and writes. A pointer to a structure that maintains a list of function pointers that handle protocol-specific routines, the **proto**

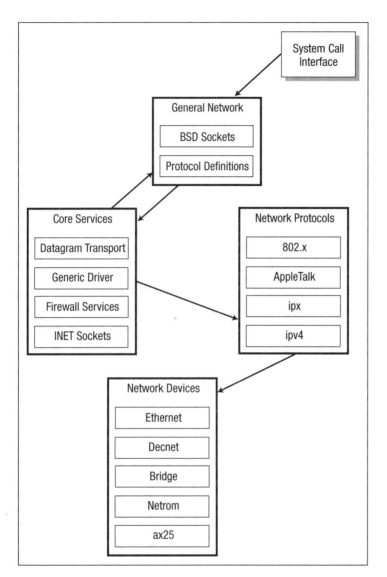

Figure 3.9
Network subsystem structure.

structure, is also provided. The **proto** structure is rather large and complex, but essentially, it provides an abstract interface to the TCP and UDP protocols. The source and destination addresses, and more TCP-specific data fields are provided. TCP uses timers extensively to handle time-outs, etc., thus the **sock** structure contains data fields pertaining to timer operations, as well as function pointers which are used as callbacks for timer alarms.

Finally, the **device** structure is used to define a network device driver. This is the same structure used to represent file system device drivers.

Subsystem Structure

The General Network contains those modules that provide the highest level interface to user processes. This is essentially the BSD Socket interface, as well as a definition of the protocols supported by the network layer. Included here are the MAC protocols of 802.x, ip, ipx, and AppleTalk.

The Core services correspond to high-level implementation facilities, such as INET sockets, support for firewalls, a common network device driver interface, and facilities for datagram and TCP transport services.

The system call interface interacts with the BSD socket interface. The BSD socket layer provides a general abstraction for socket communication, and this abstraction is implemented using the INET sockets. This is the reason for the dependency between the general network module and the core services module.

The protocol modules contain the code that takes user data and formats them as required by a particular protocol. The protocol layer finally sends the data to the proper hardware device, hence the dependency between the network protocols and network devices modules.

The network devices module contains high-level device-type specific routines. The actual device drivers reside with the regular device drivers under the directory **drivers/net**.

Subsystem Dependencies

Figure 3.10 shows the dependencies between the networking subsystem and other subsystems.

The network subsystem depends on the memory management system for buffers. The file system is used to provide an inode interface to sockets. The file system uses the network system to implement NFS. The network subsystem uses the kerneld daemon, and thus it depends on IPC. The network subsystem uses the process scheduler for timer functions and to suspend processes while network transmissions are executed. For more details about the specific dependencies between the network subsystem modules and other kernel subsystems, see [PBS:net.html].

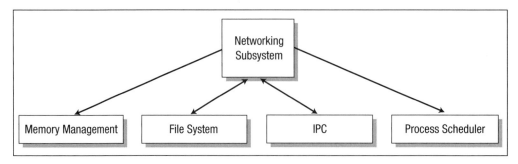

Figure 3.11
Network subsystem dependencies.

Chapter 4
Findings

In summary, we reviewed existing documentation, extracted source file facts, clustered modules into subsystems, and refined these clusters using domain knowledge about modern operating systems. We found that the concrete architecture did not match the conceptual architecture we formed earlier. The initial extracted structure showed missing dependencies due to limitations in the extraction tool. After manually verifying the dependencies, we found that all absences were caused by these tool limitations. On the other hand, the final concrete architecture exhibited several dependencies that were not accounted for in the conceptual architecture. These dependencies were due to design decisions such as having the IPC subsystem perform some of the memory manager swapping functions. These unexpected dependencies, or divergences as described in [Murphy 1995], could indicate that the conceptual architecture wasn't properly presented, or that the concrete architecture didn't use an appropriate clustering mechanism. However, we believe that these divergences are the result of the Linux developers ignoring architectural considerations.

We reviewed the documentation available for the Linux kernel. There is a large quantity of system documentation, such as [Rusling 1997]. There was even some limited documentation available with the source code. However, this documentation was at too high a level to serve as a detailed concrete architecture.

We used the cfx tool to extract detailed design information from the Linux kernel source. The cfx extractor tool produced 100,000 facts, which were combined using grok into 15,000 dependencies between 1,600 source modules. After examining the output of the fact extractor, we noticed that there were two problems with the results. First, some dependencies were not detected. This occurred in particular in the case of implicit invocation. In the implicit invocation case, a subsystem registers its capabilities with another subsystem; since the access to the registered subsystem is through function pointers, the cfx tool was not able to detect these dependencies. Secondly, the cfx tool reported dependencies that did not exist. One example of this occurred in the IPC subsystem. Three source modules in the IPC subsystem have a function (findkey) that has the same name. Since the cfx tool uses a name-equivalency assumption, it reported that all three modules depended on each other when a manual verification showed they did not.

In addition to the artifacts introduced by the cfx tool, we encountered some problems because of the assumption by the grok scripts that each source module (*.c) had an associated header file (*.h). This is generally true in the Linux kernel, but there are some header files that are implemented in many source modules. For example, **mm.h** is implemented in several source modules in the memory manager subsystem. Since all calls to functions are abstracted to calls to the header file where the function is declared, we had difficulty separating source modules into subsystems. All of the source modules were shown depending on **mm.h** rather than the specific source module that implemented the resources being used. This problem could be corrected by adjusting the grok scripts; perhaps some combination that recognized the special nature of header files such as **mm.h** would be best.

Because of these problems (missed, spurious, and misplaced dependencies), we manually verified the extracted facts where they differed from our expectations. Unfortunately, the volume of source code and our relative inexperience with Linux means that our extracted dependencies cannot be viewed as completely accurate.

Future Work

The PBS tools should be adjusted to handle the Linux source structure. The conceptual and concrete architectures we have presented should be refined through discussions with the Linux developer community. After refinement, the two models can be compared using the reflexion model [Murphy 1995].

Appendix A
Definitions

BSD
Berkeley System Distribution: A version of Unix based on the AT&T System V Unix developed by the Computer System Research Group of the University of California at Berkeley.

device special file
A file on the file system that represents a physical device. Reading or writing to this file will result in direct access to the physical device. These files are rarely used directly, with the exception of character mode devices.

fs
The file system subsystem of the Linux kernel

interrupt latency
The time between when an interrupt is reported to the CPU and the time that it is handled. If interrupt latency is too large, then high-speed peripherals will fail because their interrupts are not processed (by reading data from their CSRs) before the next interrupt is asserted. The subsequent interrupt overwrites the data in the CSRs.

IPC
Interprocess communication. Linux supports signals, pipes and the System V IPC mechanisms named after the Unix release in which they first appeared.

kernel thread (daemon)

A kernel thread is a process that runs in kernel mode. These processes are properly part of the kernel since they have access to all of the kernel's data structures and functions, but they are treated as separate processes that can be suspended and resumed. Kernel threads do not have virtual memory, but access the same physical memory that the rest of the kernel does.

logical file system

A system that present blocks of data as files and directories; these files and directories store attributes that are specific to the logical file system, but can include permissions, access and modification time, and other accounting information.

mm

The memory manager subsystem of the Linux kernel

mount point

The directory within the virtual file system where a logical file system is mounted. All files on the mounted logical file system appear as subdirectories of the mount point. The root file system is mounted at '/'.

Net

The network interface subsystem of the Linux kernel

reverse engineering

The process of extracting high-level models from the source code.

Sched

The process scheduler subsystem of the Linux kernel

software architecture

The structure(s) of the system, which comprise software components, the externally visible properties of those components, and the relationships among them.

System V

A version of Unix developed by the Bell Laboratories of AT&T.

Unix

An operating system originally designed at the Bell Laboratories of AT&T in the 1970s.

Appendix B
References

Bass 1998

Bass, Len, Clements, Paul, Kazman, Rick: *Software Architecture in Practice*, ISBN 0-201-19930-0, Addison Wesley, 1998.

Beck 1996

Beck, M. et al: *Linux Kernel Internals*, Addison Wesley, 1996.

Bowman 1998

Bowman, I.: "Conceptual Architecture of the Linux Kernel," **http://www.grad.math.uwaterloo.ca/~itbowman/CS746G/a1/**, 1998.

Chi 1994

Chi, E.: "Introduction and History of Linux," **http://lenti.med. umn.edu/~chi/technolog.html**, 1994.

CS746G Bibliography

http://plg.uwaterloo.ca/~holt/cs/746/98/linuxbib.html.

Holt 1997

Holt, R.: "Portable Bookshelf Tools," **http://www. turing.toronto. edu/homes/holt/pbs/tools.html**.

Knowlton 1965

Knowlton, K.C.: "A Fast Storage Allocator," *Communications of the ACM*, vol. 8, pp. 623-625, Oct. 1965.

Kruchten 1995
Kruchten, P.B.: *The 4+1 Views Model of Architecture*, IEEE Software, Nov 95, pp 42-50.

LDP
Linux Documentation Project: http://sunsite.unc.edu/mdw/linux.html.

Mancoridis Slides
Mancoridis, S.: MCS680 Slides, Drexel University.

Muller 1993
Muller, Hausi A., Mehmet, O.A., Tilley, S.R., and Uhl, J.S.: "A Reverse Engineering Approach to Subsystem Identification," *Software Maintenance and Practice*, Vol. 5, 181-204, 1993.

Murphy 1995
Murphy, G.C, Notkin, D., and Sullivan, K.: "Software Reflexion Models: Bridging the Gap between Source and High-Level Models," *Proceedings of the Third ACM Symposium on the Foundations of Software Engineering* (FSE '95).

PBS
Our Extracted Linux Landscapes: http://plg.uwaterloo.ca/~itbowman/pbs/.

Rusling 1997
Rusling, D.A.: *The Linux Kernel*, ftp://sunsite.unc.edu/pub/Linux/docs/linux-doc-project/linux-kernel/, 1997.

Siddiqi 1998
Siddiqi, S.: "A Conceptual Architecture for the Linux Kernel," http://se.math.uwaterloo.ca/~s4siddiq/CS746G/LA.html, 1998.

Tanenbaum 1992
Tanenbaum, A.S.: *Modern Operating Systems*, Englewood Cliffs, NJ: Prentice-Hall, 1992.

Tanuan 1998
Tanuan, M.: "An Introduction to the Linux Operating System Architecture," http://www.grad.math.uwaterloo.ca/~mctanuan/cs746g/LinuxCA.html, 1998.

Tzerpos 1996
Tzerpos, V. and Holt, R.: "A Hybrid Process for Recovering Software Architecture," http://www.turing.toronto.edu/homes/vtzer/papers/hybrid.ps, 1996.

Part VI

Appendixes

Appendix A
Linux Documentation Project Copying License

Last Modified 6 January 1997

The following copyright license applies to all works by the Linux Documentation Project.

Please read the license carefully—it is somewhat like the GNU General Public License, but there are several conditions in it that differ from what you may be used to. If you have any questions, please email the LDP coordinator at **mdw@metalab.unc.edu**.

The Linux Documentation Project manuals may be reproduced and distributed in whole or in part, subject to the following conditions.

All Linux Documentation Project manuals are copyrighted by their respective authors. *They are not in the public domain.*

- The copyright notice above and this permission notice must be preserved complete on all complete or partial copies.

- Any translation or derivative work of Linux Installation And Getting Started must be approved by the author in writing before distribution.

- If you distribute Linux Installation And Getting Started in part, instructions for obtaining the complete version of this manual must be included, and a means for obtaining a complete version provided.

- Small portions may be reproduced as illustrations for reviews or quotes in other works without this permission notice if proper citation is given.

- The GNU General Public License referenced below may be reproduced under the conditions given within it.

Exceptions to these rules may be granted for academic purposes: Write to the author and ask. These restrictions are here to protect us as authors, not to restrict you as educators and learners. All source code in Linux Installation And Getting Started is placed under the GNU General Public License, available via anonymous FTP from the GNU archive site at **ftp://prep.ai.mit.edu:/pub/gnu/COPYING**.

Publishing LDP Manuals

If you're a publishing company interested in distributing any of the LDP manuals, read on.

By the license given in the previous section, anyone is allowed to publish and distribute verbatim copies of the Linux Documentation Project manuals. You don't need our explicit permission for this. However, if you would like to distribute a translation or derivative work based on any of the LDP manuals, you must obtain permission from the author, in writing, before doing so.

All translations and derivative works of LDP manuals must be placed under the Linux Documentation License given in the previous section. That is, if you plan to release a translation of one of the manuals, it must be freely distributable by the above terms.

You may, of course, sell the LDP manuals for profit. We encourage you to do so. Keep in mind, however, that because the LDP manuals are freely distributable, anyone may photocopy or distribute printed copies free of charge, if they wish to do so.

We do not require to be paid royalties for any profit earned from selling LDP manuals. However, we would like to suggest that if you do sell LDP manuals for profit, that you either offer the author royalties, or donate a portion of your earnings to the author, the LDP as a whole, or to the Linux development community. You may also wish to send one or more free copies of the LDP manual that you are distributing to the author. Your show of support for the LDP and the Linux community will be very appreciated.

We would like to be informed of any plans to publish or distribute LDP manuals, just so we know how they're becoming available. If you are publishing or planning to publish any LDP manuals, please send email to Matt Welsh at **mdw@metalab.unc.edu**.

We encourage Linux software distributors to distribute the LDP manuals (such as the Installation And Getting Started Guide) with their software. The LDP manuals are intended to be used as the "official" Linux documentation, and we'd like to see mail-order distributors bundling the LDP manuals with the software. As the LDP manuals mature, hopefully they will fulfill this goal more adequately.

Appendix B
GNU General Public License

W*e have included the GNU General Public License (GPL) for your reference as it applies to the software this book was about. However, the GPL does not apply to the text of this book.*

Version 2, June 1991
Copyright © 1989, 1991 Free Software Foundation, Inc.
59 Temple Place, Suite 330, Boston, MA 02111-1307 USA

Preamble

The licenses for most software are designed to take away your freedom to share and change it. By contrast, the GNU General Public License is intended to guarantee your freedom to share and change free software—to make sure the software is free for all its users. This General Public License applies to most of the Free Software Foundation's software and to any other program whose authors commit to using it. (Some other Free Software Foundation software is covered by the GNU Library General Public License instead.) You can apply it to your programs, too.

When we speak of free software, we are referring to freedom, not price. Our General Public Licenses are designed to make sure that you have the freedom to distribute copies of free software (and charge for this service if you wish), that you receive source code or can get it if you want it, that you can change the software or use pieces of it in new free programs; and that you know you can do these things.

To protect your rights, we need to make restrictions that forbid anyone to deny you these rights or to ask you to surrender the rights. These restrictions translate to certain responsibilities for you if you distribute copies of the software, or if you modify it.

For example, if you distribute copies of such a program, whether gratis or for a fee, you must give the recipients all the rights that you have. You must make sure that they, too, receive or can get the source code. And you must show them these terms so they know their rights.

We protect your rights with two steps: (1) copyright the software, and (2) offer you this license which gives you legal permission to copy, distribute and/or modify the software.

Also, for each author's protection and ours, we want to make certain that everyone understands that there is no warranty for this free software. If the software is modified by someone else and passed on, we want its recipients to know that what they have is not the original, so that any problems introduced by others will not reflect on the original authors' reputations.

Finally, any free program is threatened constantly by software patents. We wish to avoid the danger that redistributors of a free program will individually obtain patent licenses, in effect making the program proprietary. To prevent this, we have made it clear that any patent must be licensed for everyone's free use or not licensed at all.

The precise terms and conditions for copying, distribution and modification follow.

Terms And Conditions For Copying, Distribution And Modification

This License applies to any program or other work which contains a notice placed by the copyright holder saying it may be distributed under the terms of this General Public License. The "Program", below, refers to any such program or work, and a "work based on the Program" means either the Program or any derivative work under copyright law: that is to say, a work containing the Program or a portion of it, either verbatim or with modifications and/or translated into another language. (Hereinafter, translation is included without limitation in the term "modification".) Each licensee is addressed as "you".

Activities other than copying, distribution and modification are not covered by this License; they are outside its scope. The act of running the Program is not restricted, and the output from the Program is covered only if its contents constitute a work based on the Program (independent of having been made by running the Program). Whether that is true depends on what the Program does.

1. You may copy and distribute verbatim copies of the Program's source code as you receive it, in any medium, provided that you conspicuously and appropriately publish on each copy an appropriate copyright notice and disclaimer of warranty; keep intact all the notices that refer to this License and to the absence of any warranty; and give any other recipients of the Program a copy of this License along with the Program.

You may charge a fee for the physical act of transferring a copy, and you may at your option offer warranty protection in exchange for a fee.

2. You may modify your copy or copies of the Program or any portion of it, thus forming a work based on the Program, and copy and distribute such modifications or work under the terms of Section 1 above, provided that you also meet all of these conditions:

  a) You must cause the modified files to carry prominent notices stating that you changed the files and the date of any change.

  b) You must cause any work that you distribute or publish, that in whole or in part contains or is derived from the Program or any part thereof, to be licensed as a whole at no charge to all third parties under the terms of this License.

  c) If the modified program normally reads commands interactively when run, you must cause it, when started running for such interactive use in the most ordinary way, to print or display an announcement including an appropriate copyright notice and a notice that there is no warranty (or else, saying that you provide a warranty) and that users may redistribute the program under these conditions, and telling the user how to view a copy of this License. (Exception: if the Program itself is interactive but does not normally print such an announcement, your work based on the Program is not required to print an announcement.)

These requirements apply to the modified work as a whole. If identifiable sections of that work are not derived from the Program, and can be reasonably considered independent and separate works in themselves, then this License, and its terms, do not apply to those sections when you distribute them as separate works. But when you distribute the same sections as part of a whole which is a work based on the Program, the distribution of the whole must be on the terms of this License, whose permissions for other licensees extend to the entire whole, and thus to each and every part regardless of who wrote it.

Thus, it is not the intent of this section to claim rights or contest your rights to work written entirely by you; rather, the intent is to exercise the right to control the distribution of derivative or collective works based on the Program.

In addition, mere aggregation of another work not based on the Program with the Program (or with a work based on the Program) on a volume of a storage or distribution medium does not bring the other work under the scope of this License.

3. You may copy and distribute the Program (or a work based on it, under Section 2) in object code or executable form under the terms of Sections 1 and 2 above provided that you also do one of the following:

  a) Accompany it with the complete corresponding machine-readable source code, which must be distributed under the terms of Sections 1 and 2 above on a medium customarily used for software interchange; or,

  b) Accompany it with a written offer, valid for at least three years, to give any third party, for a charge no more than your cost of physically performing source distribution, a complete machine-readable copy of the corresponding source code, to be distributed under the terms of Sections 1 and 2 above on a medium customarily used for software interchange; or,

c) Accompany it with the information you received as to the offer to distribute corresponding source code. (This alternative is allowed only for noncommercial distribution and only if you received the program in object code or executable form with such an offer, in accord with Subsection b above.)

The source code for a work means the preferred form of the work for making modifications to it. For an executable work, complete source code means all the source code for all modules it contains, plus any associated interface definition files, plus the scripts used to control compilation and installation of the executable. However, as a special exception, the source code distributed need not include anything that is normally distributed (in either source or binary form) with the major components (compiler, kernel, and so on) of the operating system on which the executable runs, unless that component itself accompanies the executable.

If distribution of executable or object code is made by offering access to copy from a designated place, then offering equivalent access to copy the source code from the same place counts as distribution of the source code, even though third parties are not compelled to copy the source along with the object code.

4. You may not copy, modify, sublicense, or distribute the Program except as expressly provided under this License. Any attempt otherwise to copy, modify, sublicense or distribute the Program is void, and will automatically terminate your rights under this License. However, parties who have received copies, or rights, from you under this License will not have their licenses terminated so long as such parties remain in full compliance.

5. You are not required to accept this License, since you have not signed it. However, nothing else grants you permission to modify or distribute the Program or its derivative works. These actions are prohibited by law if you do not accept this License. Therefore, by modifying or distributing the Program (or any work based on the Program), you indicate your acceptance of this License to do so, and all its terms and conditions for copying, distributing or modifying the Program or works based on it.

6. Each time you redistribute the Program (or any work based on the Program), the recipient automatically receives a license from the original licensor to copy, distribute or modify the Program subject to these terms and conditions. You may not impose any further restrictions on the recipients' exercise of the rights granted herein. You are not responsible for enforcing compliance by third parties to this License.

7. If, as a consequence of a court judgment or allegation of patent infringement or for any other reason (not limited to patent issues), conditions are imposed on you (whether by court order, agreement or otherwise) that contradict the conditions of this License, they do not excuse you from the conditions of this License. If you cannot distribute so

as to satisfy simultaneously your obligations under this License and any other pertinent obligations, then as a consequence you may not distribute the Program at all. For example, if a patent license would not permit royalty-free redistribution of the Program by all those who receive copies directly or indirectly through you, then the only way you could satisfy both it and this License would be to refrain entirely from distribution of the Program.

If any portion of this section is held invalid or unenforceable under any particular circumstance, the balance of the section is intended to apply and the section as a whole is intended to apply in other circumstances.

It is not the purpose of this section to induce you to infringe any patents or other property right claims or to contest validity of any such claims; this section has the sole purpose of protecting the integrity of the free software distribution system, which is implemented by public license practices. Many people have made generous contributions to the wide range of software distributed through that system in reliance on consistent application of that system; it is up to the author/donor to decide if he or she is willing to distribute software through any other system and a licensee cannot impose that choice.

This section is intended to make thoroughly clear what is believed to be a consequence of the rest of this License.

8. If the distribution and/or use of the Program is restricted in certain countries either by patents or by copyrighted interfaces, the original copyright holder who places the Program under this License may add an explicit geographical distribution limitation excluding those countries, so that distribution is permitted only in or among countries not thus excluded. In such case, this License incorporates the limitation as if written in the body of this License.

9. The Free Software Foundation may publish revised and/or new versions of the General Public License from time to time. Such new versions will be similar in spirit to the present version, but may differ in detail to address new problems or concerns.

   Each version is given a distinguishing version number. If the Program specifies a version number of this License which applies to it and "any later version", you have the option of following the terms and conditions either of that version or of any later version published by the Free Software Foundation. If the Program does not specify a version number of this License, you may choose any version ever published by the Free Software Foundation.

10. If you wish to incorporate parts of the Program into other free programs whose distribution conditions are different, write to the author to ask for permission. For software which is copyrighted by the Free Software Foundation, write to the Free Software Foundation; we sometimes make exceptions for this. Our decision will be guided by the two goals of preserving the free status of all derivatives of our free software and of promoting the sharing and reuse of software generally.

No Warranty

11. BECAUSE THE PROGRAM IS LICENSED FREE OF CHARGE, THERE IS NO WARRANTY FOR THE PROGRAM, TO THE EXTENT PERMITTED BY APPLICABLE LAW. EXCEPT WHEN OTHERWISE STATED IN WRITING THE COPYRIGHT HOLDERS AND/OR OTHER PARTIES PROVIDE THE PROGRAM "AS IS" WITHOUT WARRANTY OF ANY KIND, EITHER EXPRESSED OR IMPLIED, INCLUDING, BUT NOT LIMITED TO, THE IMPLIED WARRANTIES OF MERCHANTABILITY AND FITNESS FOR A PARTICULAR PURPOSE. THE ENTIRE RISK AS TO THE QUALITY AND PERFORMANCE OF THE PROGRAM IS WITH YOU. SHOULD THE PROGRAM PROVE DEFECTIVE, YOU ASSUME THE COST OF ALL NECESSARY SERVICING, REPAIR OR CORRECTION.

12. IN NO EVENT UNLESS REQUIRED BY APPLICABLE LAW OR AGREED TO IN WRITING WILL ANY COPYRIGHT HOLDER, OR ANY OTHER PARTY WHO MAY MODIFY AND/OR REDISTRIBUTE THE PROGRAM AS PERMITTED ABOVE, BE LIABLE TO YOU FOR DAMAGES, INCLUDING ANY GENERAL, SPECIAL, INCIDENTAL OR CONSEQUENTIAL DAMAGES ARISING OUT OF THE USE OR INABILITY TO USE THE PROGRAM (INCLUDING BUT NOT LIMITED TO LOSS OF DATA OR DATA BEING RENDERED INACCURATE OR LOSSES SUSTAINED BY YOU OR THIRD PARTIES OR A FAILURE OF THE PROGRAM TO OPERATE WITH ANY OTHER PROGRAMS), EVEN IF SUCH HOLDER OR OTHER PARTY HAS BEEN ADVISED OF THE POSSIBILITY OF SUCH DAMAGES.

How To Apply These Terms To Your New Programs

If you develop a new program, and you want it to be of the greatest possible use to the public, the best way to achieve this is to make it free software which everyone can redistribute and change under these terms.

To do so, attach the following notices to the program. It is safest to attach them to the start of each source file to most effectively convey the exclusion of warranty; and each file should have at least the "copyright" line and a pointer to where the full notice is found.

```
<one line to give the program's name and
 a brief idea of what it does.>
Copyright (C) 19yy <name of author>

This program is free software; you can
redistribute it and/or modify it under the
terms of the GNU General Public License as
published by the Free Software Foundation;
either version 2 of the License, or
(at your option) any later version.
```

```
This program is distributed in the hope that
it will be useful, but WITHOUT ANY WARRANTY;
without even the implied warranty of
MERCHANTABILITY or FITNESS FOR A PARTICULAR
PURPOSE. See the GNU General Public License
for more details.

You should have received a copy of the GNU
General Public License along with this
program; if not, write to the Free Software
Foundation, Inc., 59 Temple Place, Suite 330,
Boston, MA 02111-1307 USA
```

Also add information on how to contact you by electronic and paper mail.

If the program is interactive, make it output a short notice like this when it starts in an interactive mode:

```
Gnomovision version 69, Copyright (C) 19yy
name of author Gnomovision comes with
ABSOLUTELY NO WARRANTY; for details type
'show w'. This is free software, and you are
welcome to redistribute it under certain
conditions; type 'show c' for details.
```

The hypothetical commands 'show w' and 'show c' should show the appropriate parts of the General Public License. Of course, the commands you use may be called something other than 'show w' and 'show c'; they could even be mouse-clicks or menu items—whatever suits your program.

You should also get your employer (if you work as a programmer) or your school, if any, to sign a "copyright disclaimer" for the program, if necessary. Here is a sample; alter the names:

```
Yoyodyne, Inc., hereby disclaims all copyright
interest in the program 'Gnomovision'
(which makes passes at compilers) written
by James Hacker.

<signature of Ty Coon>, 1 April 1989
Ty Coon, President of Vice
```

This General Public License does not permit incorporating your program into proprietary programs. If your program is a subroutine library, you may consider it more useful to permit linking proprietary applications with the library. If this is what you want to do, use the GNU Library General Public License instead of this License.

Index